SYSTEMATIC THEOLOGY

SYSTEMATIC THEOLOGY

Perspectives from Liberation Theology

(Readings from *Mysterium Liberationis*)

Edited by
JON SOBRINO, S. J.
and
IGNACIO ELLACURÍA, S. J.

ORBIS BOOKS
Maryknoll, New York 10545

The Catholic Foreign Mission Society of America (Maryknoll) recruits and trains people for overseas missionary service. Through Orbis Books, Maryknoll aims to foster the international dialogue that is essential to mission. The books published, however, reflect the opinions of their authors and are not meant to represent the official position of the society.

Published by Orbis Books, Maryknoll, NY 10545-0308

The essays included here are drawn and in some cases abridged from *Mysterium Liberationis: Fundamental Concepts of Liberation Theology*, edited by Ignacio Ellacuría, S.J. and Jon Sobrino, S.J., copyright © 1993 by Orbis Books.

Originally published in *Mysterium Liberationis: Conceptos Fundamentales de la Teología de la Liberación* 2 vols., © 1990 by Editorial Trotta, S.A., Ferraz 55, 28008 Madrid, Spain.

These essays were translated with the assistance of the Department of Books and Libraries of the Spanish Ministry of Culture.

Manufactured in the United States of America

Library of Congress Cataloging-in-Publication Data

Mysterium liberationis. English. Selections.
Systematic theology : perspectives from liberation theology : readings from Mysterium liberationis / edited by Jon Sobrino and Ignacio Ellacuría.
p. cm.
Includes bibliographical references and index.
ISBN 1-57075-068-8 (alk. paper)
1. Theology, Doctrinal. 2. Liberation theology. 3. Catholic Church—Doctrines. I. Sobrino, Jon. II. Ellacuría, Ignacio.
BT78.M95213 1996
230′.046—dc20 95-50123
CIP

Contents

Preface *by Jon Sobrino* vii

Abbreviations xiii

1. Methodology of the Theology of Liberation 1
   by Clodovis Boff

2. Option for the Poor 22
   by Gustavo Gutiérrez

3. Central Position of the Reign of God in Liberation Theology 38
   by Jon Sobrino

4. Trinity 75
   by Leonardo Boff

5. God the Father 90
   by Ronaldo Muñoz

6. Jesus of Nazareth, Christ the Liberator 106
   by Carlos Bravo

7. Systematic Christology: Jesus Christ, the Absolute Mediator of the Reign of God 124
   by Jon Sobrino

8. The Holy Spirit 146
   by José Comblin

9. Mary 165
   by Ivone Gebara and María Clara Bingemer

10. Ecclesiology in the Theology of Liberation 178
    by Alvaro Quiroz Magaña

11. Sin 194
    by José Ignacio González Faus

12. Grace 205
by José Comblin

13. Sacraments 216
by Victor Codina

14. Spirituality and the Following of Jesus 233
by Jon Sobrino

15. The Crucified People 257
by Ignacio Ellacuría

16. Hope, Utopia, Resurrection 279
by João Batista Libânio

Bibliography 291

Contributors 297

Index 299

Preface

In 1993 Orbis Books published *Mysterium Liberationis: Fundamental Concepts of Liberation Theology.* Now the publisher has decided to make that book available to a broader audience in an abridged, paperback version. Accordingly, the editors have selected the concepts that in their judgment best express the contributions of liberation theology from a systematic viewpoint, and will have the greatest utility for the North American reader.

The editors have asked me to write a preface for this new edition. It seems to me that there could not be a better introduction to the reading of this book than a brief sketch of how it originated, along with something about the course of its successive editions. The story of its origin will indicate, in itself, what it means to do liberation theology. And the history of its various editions is appropriate because of all that has happened in recent years, both in the church and in society.

In 1987, Ignacio Ellacuría and I began to plan the structure, themes, and authorship of the book. Our purpose was to gather together and develop the fundamental concepts of liberation theology. Two years later, in 1989, we had received most of the manuscripts when, on November 16, Ignacio Ellacuría was murdered at the Central American University, along with his fellow Jesuits Segundo Montes, Joaquín López y López, Juan Ramón Moreno, Ignacio Martín Baró, Amando López, and two humble women of the people, Julia Elba and her daughter Celina. They were my community and my family.

The news reached me in Thailand, and the reader can imagine the ice that gripped my heart. My mind was empty at first. Then, as I gradually came to myself, I began to think of the things I had on my hands, and among them was the book I had been preparing along with Ignacio Ellacuría. To tell the truth, I did not know what was going to become of it.

Along with my inward devastation, I had some serious problems on the outside. Ignacio Ellacuría and Juan Ramón Moreno could no longer submit their texts. This did not disturb me, since they had written a far more real text with their very lives. But then came the word that, after having murdered my brothers and sisters, the soldiers had destroyed a number of offices, and burned part of mine, where I kept the manuscripts. I did not know whether these documents had been spared by the fire or not. Also, about a quarter of the material had not come in yet, and the manuscripts in Portuguese had not been translated into Spanish. And I was at Santa Clara, in California, without any sure knowledge of when I should be returning to El Salvador.

I have begun with this personal recollection in order to give the reader some little idea of the vicissitudes of this book. Another reason for my choice, however, is that martyrdom—here, the martyrdom of Ignacio Ellacuría, theologian, author, and co-editor—is fundamental, concrete reality, and to a certain extent irreplaceable for an understanding of the content of this book. There are, in this cruel world, idols of death and antichrists who struggle with the God of life and the Christ of that God, Jesus of Nazareth. It is only from amidst oppression, carried to its maximal expression in martyrdom, that the theology of liberation can be understood. A true theology of liberation, which would attempt to "take the crucified people down from the cross," in Ignacio Ellacuría's words, must be prepared to share the fate of that people. This is what Ignacio Ellacuría's martyrdom, better than any theological word, expresses, and that martyrdom is the best hermeneutics for understanding this book.

Despite all, the book was finished, and in 1991 it was published in Spanish both in Madrid and in San Salvador. I said in my introduction to that first edition that the finality of the book consisted in "setting forth in systematized fashion the central elements of the theology of liberation, since we believe that this theology continues to be necessary and beneficial for the liberation of the poor and the Christian practice of Latin American reality." It is our conviction that liberation theology has "put its finger on the sore point of reality"—on a wound that is spreading and becoming more inflamed, and a wound that needs to be cleansed. It is for this reason above all—along with other epistemological options—that liberation theology understands itself as "theory of a historical and ecclesial praxis," in Ellacuría's words, or in my own, "*intellectus amoris, misericordiae, justitiae, liberationis.*"

But we added—and with this we concluded our introduction to the first edition—that the reality of the Latin American continent is shot through with hope and commitment, as well, and that that reality, too, would take the floor. On the suffering, then, on the hope, and on the martyrdom of these crucified peoples, liberation theology lives. This theology seeks to give them a voice, determined as it is to struggle with injustice and the lie and to take sides with truth and familial partnership. This is what our book formulates and conceptualizes.

This was our thinking at that time with regard to the theology of liberation—and this continues to be our thinking, basically, although so many things began to change with the 1990s. New criticisms of this theology have appeared. We are speaking of new criticisms. In the seventies and eighties, the old criticisms abounded, the most belligerent ones—attacks, defamation, persecution. They were voiced by the powers of this world (capital, the armed forces, governments and parties, the media, the CIA, and so on), as well as by the church institution. The new criticisms no longer center on the identity of liberation theology—whether or not it is orthodox. Now the focus is on its relevance: whether it contributes anything to theology and to the liberation of peoples, especially since the fall of the communist regimes.

This being the situation, in the Preface to the 1993 edition I wrote a brief *Apologia pro Theologia Liberationis*, intended as a more important apologia pro pauperibus or defense of the poor. To put it briefly, it seemed to me then, as it seems to me now, that not only has this theology not become irrelevant, but it is the theology that takes most seriously, and focuses on most determinedly, the reality of oppression, and this world's need for deliverance.

I formulated the core of my *apologia* by repeating the basic element: "The most novel and most fruitful thing about the theology of liberation, more than its concrete content, continues to be its manner of conceiving the theological task as reflection on a praxis (or *intellectus amoris*), its definition of the poor of this world as a *locus theologicus*, and the goal of the theological endeavor in terms of "taking the crucified peoples down from the cross."

All of this still continues to be of supreme importance, and supremely relevant, today. Among other things, one scarcely sees that other theologies seriously concern themselves with liberation and oppression, with utopia and prophecy. And if these things do not concern theology, we may well wonder what it means to believe in God according to these theologies, at least in the God of Jesus, and how to distinguish that faith, a faith so alien from the themes that we have indicated, from a dissimulated self-centeredness, not to say sordid selfishness. Indeed, one might well ask whether a theology that ignores those themes isn't an unreal theology, in the plainest sense of the word, since, quantitatively, it fails to touch the reality of the greater part of humanity—horrible poverty and injustice—and qualitatively, it refuses to be affected by the most flagrant aspect of that reality, the death, slow or violent, of the poor and the urgency of transforming that death.

As for the notion that liberation theology is no longer relevant due to the fall of socialism, let us observe that socialism was never at the root of this theology, although obviously—as with some of the encyclicals of Pope John Paul II—it may have contributed to the critique of capitalism and the positing of certain utopian horizons. The origin, thrust, and direction of the theology of liberation is not in socialism, but in the experience of God in the poor, an experience of grace and exigency. Therefore so long as this experience exists and is conceptualized, there can be a theology of liberation. And so long as oppression exists, there must be a theology of liberation.

And now: does the theology of liberation have anything to offer in 1995? Let us begin with some self-criticism. It could perhaps be drawn up under the following headings.

1. We ought to take up and consider in depth the various kinds of oppression, not only the socioeconomic versions, but also those perpetrated in the areas of culture, ethnicity, religion, women, children, and nature.

2. We ought to analyze not only the needs of the poor, but also their particular faith, which supplies the light by which to do theology.

3. We ought to come to the aid of the poor in moments of "revolution," yes, but we ought also to assist them in their humanization in the midst of "ordinary time."

4. We ought to recognize and accept changes in the world and the consequences of these changes for the pathways and mediations of liberation without, however, falling into the trap that we have just exposed ("Socialism has fallen, ergo liberation theology is no more"), and we must continue to point to the grave evils with which this world is pervaded—as these have been acknowledged at Rio de Janeiro, Cairo, Copenhagen, and Beijing.

5. Finally, we ought to overcome the deficiencies and limitations of liberation theology in its exegetical, systematic, and historical understandings.

These critical reflections seem to me to be fruitful and on target for the theology of liberation. But in reality there is another type of critique, apparently more subtle but for that reason more dangerous. This is the claim that liberation theology represents one mode of theology which has passed its time, having given of itself all that it had to give. In the face of this argument, it is certainly important to respond in order to do justice to the theology of liberation, but also to respond adequately, as human beings and Christians, to the cruel reality of our world.

The notion that liberation theology is passé is a notion that ought to be carefully analyzed. Gustavo Gutiérrez, one of the founders, says, altogether naturally, that "the theology of liberation will pass, as all theologies pass." "Passing," then, is not the problem. But the oversimplification with which the theology of liberation is proclaimed to have "already passed" is indeed a problem, and especially the superficiality with which "passing" is analyzed. It is one thing to be a "thing of the past" in the sense of passing *from* history, and something else again to be a thing of the past in the sense of passing *into* history by leaving something perennial there, something *classic*. For this reason, it likewise seems to me to be simplistic to judge this or any other theology as an undifferentiated whole, without asking, at least in principle, whether and what there is in it of the contingent or "conjunctural," and whether and what there is in it of the quasi-perennial or "classic."

In my opinion, several things about the theology of liberation continue to be valid. Among the valid methodological elements, I would highlight such features as taking seriously the signs of the times; treating the poor as a *locus theologicus*; liberation theology's self-understanding as reflection on praxis; and other elements. Of its valid systematic content, there is the dialectic of the God of life and the idols of death, of the Reign of God and the anti-reign, of grace and sin; the emphasis on the historical Jesus, the church of the poor, martyrdom, and of course salvation as liberation from all oppression. Among the elements of spirituality: the pathos of truth and mercy, the praxis of justice, the following of Jesus, and so on. These themes continue to be current. But what is more, by reason of their rediscovered evangelical rooting, and the echo they find in the human condition, they have in some manner been transformed—more or less, according to the case—into "classic" themes of theology.

This, we hope, is what the reader will find in this book. Without a doubt, its content can be improved and complemented. But what continues to give life to this theology is the pathos of liberation that pervades it, a pathos that not only stands at the origin but also originates the theological reflection. In other words, liberation is not only the primary content of this theology, but its shaping principle. The decisive element in the theology of liberation is that it is shaped by—we shall be forgiven the redundancy—the *principle of liberation*. This is what gives the theology of liberation its evangelical Christian identity, and its historical relevance in a world of oppression.

Jon Sobrino

San Salvador
November 16, 1995
Sixth Anniversary of the Martyrs of the Central American University

—*Translated by Robert R. Barr*

Abbreviations

EN	Exhortation *Evangelii nuntiandi* (Pope Paul VI), 1975.
GS	*Gaudium et spes* (Vatican II). Pastoral Constitution on the Church in the Modern World.
LC	*Libertatis conscientia* (Congregation for the Doctrine of the Faith). Instruction on Christian Freedom and Liberation, 1986.
LE	Encyclical *Laborem exercens* (Pope John Paul II), 1981.
LG	*Lumen Gentium* (Vatican II). Dogmatic Constitution on the Church.
LN	*Libertatis nuntius* (Congregation for the Doctrine of the Faith). Instruction on Certain Aspects of the Theology of Liberation, 1984.
Medellín	Second General Conference of the Latin American Bishops' Conference, 1968.
MM	Encyclical *Mater et magistra* (Pope John XXIII), 1963.
OA	Apostolic Letter *Octogesima adveniens* (Pope Paul VI), 1971.
Puebla	Third General Conference of the Latin American Bishops' Conference, 1979.
QA	Encyclical *Quadragesimo anno* (Pope Pius XI), 1931.
RN	Encyclical *Rerum novarum* (Pope Leo XIII), 1891.

SYSTEMATIC THEOLOGY

1

Methodology of the Theology of Liberation

CLODOVIS BOFF

We shall address our subject under three heads: the theoretical status of the theology of liberation; the forms this theology takes; and its method.

I. THEORETICAL STATUS OF LIBERATION THEOLOGY

What is the epistemological identity of the theology of liberation? Here it is in order to observe two things. On the one hand, the visage of liberation theology has not yet acquired its complete physiognomy: it finds itself entirely in an (accelerating) developmental stage. At the same time, its outlines at least, while not yet definitive—liberation theology is still too new for that—have acquired a certain delineation.

Let us posit certain basic theses from the outset, with a view to determining, insofar as possible, the situation in which the epistemological profile of liberation theology is presently to be found. Thus, we shall attempt to resolve some of the (seeming) gaps of this theology, which have become targets of attack and even condemnation. Furthermore, we shall take into account the "Instruction on Certain Aspects of the Theology of Liberation" (*Libertatis Nuntius*) of 1984 and "Instruction on Christian Freedom and Liberation" (*Libertatis Conscientia*) of 1986, as well as the important "Message of John Paul II to the Episcopate of Brazil" of April 9, 1986.

Thesis 1: The theology of liberation is an integral theology, treating all of the positivity of faith from a particular perspective: that of the poor and their liberation.

It must be said that in theory as well as in practice, liberation theology comes forward as a *global* or comprehensive theology. It spans the entire spectrum of theological thematics. But it does not rest there. It is not content with a general, abstract view of the Christian faith. From the general it advances to the *particular*, that is, it develops the meaning of the gospel as historically liberative. To borrow a metaphor from the morphology of language, it "declines" *all* of theology in specific terms: those of liberation. Taking its point of departure in a comprehensive faith viewpoint, it develops a particular (special, but not exclusive) faith viewpoint. Furthermore, it includes in its theological thematics the themes of the oppression and liberation of the poor, for example, economic production, shared power, the land questions, democracy, the historical project, and so on.

So, while liberation theology is general, it is not abstract. And while it is particular, it is not "sectarian" or partial. It is *materially* general and *formally* particular.

What, indeed, is the object of the theology of liberation? Is it faith, or is it history? It is both. It is the entire deposit of faith, inasmuch as liberation theology develops the liberative meaning of that deposit; and it is the process of oppression/liberation itself, inasmuch as it interprets that process in the light of faith.

Thesis 2: The primary, basic viewpoint of the theology of liberation, as of any theology, is the givenness of faith; its secondary, particular viewpoint, as one theology among others, is the experience of the oppressed.

This means that while the larger horizon of liberation theology will always be the plane of salvation, its secondary horizon is the concrete, historical process of the liberation of the poor. In other words, at the ultimate root of liberation theology, whether thematically or operatively, is *objective* (positive) *faith*, the word of God, or revelation. This is what makes it theology. But this is not all. Next, structurally and dialectically connected to the perspective of objective faith, comes the perspective of the oppressed, that is, *subjective faith*. This is what makes our theology precisely a theology of *liberation*.

This same problem can be posed in terms of the point of departure of the theology of liberation. Will that point of departure be faith or praxis—God or the poor?

Here it is important to situate the question concretely. What is this point of departure, this starting point? If it were a *pre-theological* experience that framed the genesis of liberation theology, in terms of the "spiritual experience of the poor," then we would have to say that the point of departure is actually *living faith*, or, in other words, the *praxis of faith*, as a "synthetic experience." Here, de facto, elements come in not only of positive faith (viewpoint, interpretation, and so on), but of praxis, as well (compassion, solidarity, and so on). Hence the structural origin of liberation theology. And hence the origin of its "proper manner" of theologizing, as we shall see.

If we now move to the properly *theological* sphere, we can say that liberation theology's starting point is a distinct one. True, we are dealing with faith as well as with praxis, but each of the two retains its place. Faith is the *formal* starting point or the "determining hermeneutic principle" (*Libertatis Nuntius*, part 10, no. 2), and praxis is the *material* starting point, that is, the raw material. There is no contradiction here, but only an interrelationship of distinct "instances" standing in reciprocal relation and duly ordered. Only a dialectical logic permits a correct approach to these questions.

Although the vocabulary of liberation theology is not always fine tuned here, its actual theological practice usually operates correctly; that is, it starts with the poor, and with Christ as the first among them. To be sure, when we theologians say we start with the poor—just as when we say we start with reality—we are actually starting further away than that: with faith. It is only methodologically that we begin with "seeing," or "reality," when in fact faith is always there as the alpha and omega of the entire process. And this is even more evident in the reflection, the liberation theology, of the people themselves, who are at once oppressed and religious.

Thesis 3: The theology of liberation represents a "new stage" in the long evolution of theological reflection, and today constitutes a historically necessary theology.

This is the position of Pope John Paul II in his 1986 "Message to the Episcopate of Brazil" (no. 5). Thus, liberation theology is far from being a theology that happens to be in style—a purely conjunctural theology. Rather, it is an *epochal theology*—as the question of the liberation of the oppressed is epochal. The problems treated are authentically structural and historical.

But the theology of liberation is more than this. Inasmuch as liberation theology has discovered the "continent that is history" (always from a point of departure in the outcast), it has come to stay. Henceforth all theology will have to confront *faith* (and its power for liberation) with *history* (and its contradictions, or injustices). Were any theology not to do so, it would be suspect of alienation, it would be vulnerable to all manner of manipulation and could become "opium religion." It is becoming ever more difficult to understand how a theology could close its eyes to the real history of the oppressed. This would be true even in a society in which abject poverty had been eliminated. Even in such a society the theology of liberation would be valid, since the questions would remain: Who are the last ones here? Who are the victims? In this sense, liberation theology constitutes an intrinsic dimension, henceforward permanent, of any present or future theology.

Although the theology of liberation is not an *exclusive* theology, inasmuch as it defines itself strictly as a theology developing the social function of faith from the perspective of the poor, nevertheless it is *not merely one theology among others*. It is a theology which, from a point of departure in its fundamental project, challenges all theologians, precisely because it bears on a question having a relation to all other questions: the concrete question of the social emancipation of today's oppressed. Through its official documents on the theology of liberation, addressed to the whole church, Rome has made a decisive contribution to the acceptance of this theology as a universal (catholic) theology.

Pope John Paul II has declared the theology of liberation "necessary" for the church. He has stated this repeatedly. Both of the Roman "Instructions" speak in the same way: "It is impossible to forget for a single instant the situations of traumatic destitution from which this challenge to theologians springs" (*Libertatis Nuntius*, no. 1). And "A theology of freedom and liberation . . . constitutes a *demand* of our time" (*Libertatis Conscientia*, no. 98).

Is a theology conceivable today that would address the great truths of faith and not thematically develop their social and political content? In the abstract, it is possible. The reason is that faith cannot be exhausted by the social and political dimension. Faith has an intrinsic and supremely *human* meaning, independent of its direct political bearing. Even when theology is done in behalf of the poor, all dimensions of faith must always be addressed: personal, social, and eschatological. Christianity is not only social *transformation*, it is individual *conversion*, and it is *resurrection* of the dead, as well. Therefore metaphysical or transcendent questions may not be suppressed in favor of (or on the pretext of) physical or immanent questions—precisely because the poor are not only poor, but men and women called to eternal communion with God.

Nevertheless, this theological reflection must remain open to a potential thematic and practical broadening in terms of historical liberation. It must remain very attentive to the question of social justice; otherwise it may be manipulated as a tool for alienation and injustice.

Furthermore, we must recall that if the great question of our era is the liberation of the oppressed, then this must also be the dominant or privileged perspective of the comprehensive theological reflection of our day.

Thesis 4: The theology of liberation comprehensively integrates ethico-political liberation, which holds the primacy of urgency (and thereby also the methodological, and at times the pastoral, primacy), with soteriological liberation, which unequivocally maintains its primacy of value.

Obviously the axiological primacy (the primacy of value) belongs to evangelization and the soteriological dimension of liberation. Nevertheless, the primacy of historical *urgency* does not always coincide with the primacy of value. For a hungry people, the first concern will be bread, as Jesus showed when he saw the hungry crowd (Mark 6:30–44). Paul, too, says: "The spiritual was not first; first came the natural and after that the spiritual" (1 Cor. 15:46).

As the practice of work with the people shows, these two levels or orders can be combined very well without special problems. The confusion arises from the fact that frequently the "first" in the order of the hierarchy of values is confused with the "first" in the order of time; or again, when the "first" in the order of *intention* is not distinguished from the "first" in the order of *execution.*

As a matter of fact, *liberation* in liberation theology denotes first of all *social liberation*. This is *the* question of our time. And this was the question from which the theology of liberation sprang. This was the reason it arose in the Third World.

At first sight, or initially, *liberation* is liberation from physical wretchedness. However, this idea is open to what is above, open to faith, to communion with God—open to soteriological liberation. But our historical and methodological point of departure has always been the process of oppression-and-liberation of the excluded of history.

As for the magisterium of the church, it has adopted the thematic of the theology of liberation. But it has adopted it in its own way. First, it has transformed the notion of liberation into the great notion that embraces the whole mystery of salvation. Second, it starts with the soteriological dimension of liberation (liberation from sin and death), and from there moves to the social dimension (liberation from historical oppression). For its part, the theology of concrete liberation has begun with the latter, to move to the former. From the beginning liberation theology plunged *in medias res*; it began with the raw, naked reality of oppression.

In this wise, Rome *arrives* at ethico-social liberation, while Latin American liberation theology *arrives* at soteriological liberation. The semantic weight of liberation is distinct in either of the two discourses. But the two weights are not contrary. Indeed, far from being opposed, the two perspectives complement each other; in each case, the one opens out upon the other.

To enter by the door of material and historical liberation or by the door of spiritual and eternal liberation is a question of purely *methodological and pastoral* convenience, and not of theological truth. For example, in Europe it is faith that is surely without a safe footing, while in Latin America it is bread that is not guaranteed. Hence the distinct but not contradictory emphases.

What influence has Latin American liberation theology had on Rome's position, and through the latter, on the universal church? The principal historical merit of the theology of liberation has been to have introduced into the church the cry of the masses of the poor—and this from the starting point of the *particular viewpoint* of these masses—no longer in a perspective of natural law (that of mere human rights), but in one of *biblical theology.*

Indeed, what is actually in question in the debate over liberation theology is not God, Christ, or the church, but the *oppressed*—and how, beginning with them, one is situated anew in relation to God, Christ, and the church, even in the Roman documents.

Thesis 5: Vis-à-vis other theologies, present and past, the theology of liberation stands in a relation not of opposition or substitution, but of critical complementarity. Meanwhile, its radical novelty compared with these others is the encounter with the poor as historical subject.

In the first place, liberation theology is not distinguished from or opposed to the great theologies of the past, such as patristic theology or scholastic theology. On the contrary, it may be regarded as their successor or heir. As we have seen, the pope, in his "Message to the Episcopate of Brazil," states very clearly that the theology of liberation "must constitute a new stage—*intimately connected with those that have gone before*—of the theological reflection" developed throughout the course of history (no. 5; emphasis added). Later in the same document the pope returns to the same point, insisting that "this correct, necessary theology of liberation" must "develop . . . *in homogenous and not heterogeneous fashion* vis-à-vis the theology of all times" (no. 5).

The relationship between liberation theology and the great theologies of the past, then, is one of critical complementarity. Liberation theology *adopts on the level of liberation* of the poor the great intuitions of the theology of the past. Thus it brings these theologies up to date by applying them to the series of problems faced by the oppressed. The relationship between today's liberation theology and these theologies is that of a fruit to its seed. We are dealing with a harmonious development, like that of the history of dogma.

From the standpoint of the perspective of faith (pertinency) and doctrinal content, liberation theology can only be homogeneous with the great theologies of old. But there is an undeniable heterogeneity on the level of *themes*, *language*, and *posing of the problems* (the problematic), as well as with regard to concrete *methodology* (cultural mediations, etc.).

One must ask, for example, whether the theologies of St. Augustine, St. Thomas Aquinas, or Karl Rahner could not be regarded as forms of the theology of liberation, inasmuch as—according to the Roman documents—they treat particularly of soteriological liberation.

But it is not appropriate, in this case, to speak of theologies of soteriological liberation. The acceptance of the term *liberation* would thereby be too much, and abusively, broadened, thus entirely depriving liberation theology of its interests and specific character.

Surely there is danger of falling into generalities—but not in the direction in which the dominant semantics of liberation theology is headed, as in the Third World.

Furthermore, one must take care that liberation as the foundational concept of theology not eliminate the inescapable, traumatic question of the *material* liberation of the poor. To use the same term to designate both liberation from destitution and liberation from sin might *appear* to foster an interconnection of these distinct levels of an "integral liberation." However, such language tends to absorb material liberation into spiritual liberation (contrary to the pope's prescription in "Message to the Episcopate of Brazil," no. 6b), as well as to eliminate the discontinuities between the one and the other (faith does not immediately entail bread, nor bread faith).

In this sense, the very notion of integral liberation, in the current usage of Latin American liberation theology, has occasioned facile solutions, which, while their practical advantages are undeniable, betray a reductionistic theoretical scope.

But what would be new in current Latin American theology of liberation compared with previously existing theologies that reflect on the social and political dimension of faith, such as "political theology," the "theology of hope," and so on? Will not all of these be "liberation theologies," without distinction, regardless of whether they bear the name?

We respond as follows.

1. In current liberation theology, as done, for example, in Latin America, the *starting point is the oppressed* and not abstract topics or general ideas like "justice," "politics," "praxis," or even "liberation." Concrete liberation theology supposes a practical relation with practice, and not a merely theoretical (thematic) relation. It implies a living contact with the struggle of the poor. Today's "liberation theologian" is someone concretely committed to the cause of the oppressed. Thus it is said that the theology of liberation has always sprung from compassion with those who suffer and from a commitment to their pilgrimage of liberation.

2. From its point of departure in a concrete praxis at the side of the oppressed, liberation theology comes forward today as a new way of doing theology. It is not so much a specific method as a new theological spirit, a new manner of theologizing. This new manner is expressed in a concrete language, not an abstract one, a language charged with *pathos*, not a cold, dry one, a language that is prophetic, not doctrinaire.

3. Existing liberation theology is a theology directed upon praxis—precisely, a praxis of social transformation. Thus, it is at once critical and utopian.

For these reasons, current liberation theology must expect the opposition of all who are desirous of maintaining the status quo. Liberation theology is criticized more for political than for properly theological reasons, although the latter may justly exist.

But does liberation theology always presuppose a base or antecedent theology, such as that expressed, for example, in classical theology?

Not necessarily. What a concrete liberation theology presupposes, especially in view of its pastoral purpose, is faith. What liberation theology actually does is draw the social consequences of such and such a salvific truth, or reflect on such and such a concrete problem (hunger, popular organization, and so on) in the light of faith. It is impossible to do a theology of liberation without starting from the "deposit" of faith, whether or not theologized.

On the other hand, a liberation theology that fails to bestow a more consistent theological character upon its faith-basis runs the risk of "running out of gas" and coming to a halt. Therefore, on the level of the organic and systematic development of the theology of liberation, it is indeed essential to sink deep theological roots into the actual fundamentals of faith. Rather than speaking of a "first theology" (which would discuss the meaning *in se* of the mysteries of faith, for example, the resurrection or divinity of Jesus) and a "second theology" (which would develop the concrete impingement of the mystery in question on the social and historical field), it would be better to speak of a "first moment" and a "second moment" in a *single* theological process. Let us observe that the order of the moments here refers to the *structure* of the theological act and not to the (temporal) process of its method, which generally begins with "seeing." Between the two, an unmistakable dialectical movement obtains.

The thrust of liberation theology is toward a development of the entire deposit of faith from a point of departure in this theology's own specific sensitivity—the sensitivity that emerges from the experience of God in the poor. This is how an *integral* theology is done. Indeed, liberation theology seeks to "thematize" even the first moment of the overall theological process, the moment of the fundamental and transcendent aspect of faith: the truths concerning Christ, the Spirit, grace, and so on.

In this sense liberation theology's method incorporates the method of classical theology, but not without recasting it, in depth, from its own specific theological viewpoint: that of the oppressed. For example, a christology from Latin America utilizes all of the methodological tools of any classical christology (critical exegesis, hermeneutics of dogma, systematic reflection, and so on), but it does so in its own style.

At this point we must observe that the novelty of the theology of liberation is genuinely radical, that is, it consists in an element to be found at the very root of the theological act. This root contains something of the pre-theological: the encounter with the poor, and the shock, the rebellion, and the commitment of this encounter. The radical originality of liberation theology lies not in the topics it treats (oppression, struggle, and so on), nor in its method (the use of the social sciences or of Marxism), nor in its language (prophetic and utopian), nor in its addresses (the poor and their allies), nor even in its final cause (social transformation). The radical originality of the theology of liberation lies in the *insertion of the theologian in the real life of the poor*, understood as a collective, conflictive, and active (the poor as subject or agent) reality.

This is what is decisive in liberation theology, and what determines all else beside—its thematics, its methodology, its relationship with Marxism, its biblical reading, and so forth. All of these things are done from the starting point of the poor. As we can see, it is something in the theologian rather than in the theology. This first act of liberation theology marks the anteriority of a faith praxis over the theological theoretization of that praxis (second act).

Unquestionably, the encounter with the poor is the *indispensable* condition for doing liberation theology. But it is an *insufficient* reason. It is not enough for theologians to be committed. They must also produce the desired theology, and do so by way of a theoretical application to the theme under examination. A materially theological experience is a necessary condition for, but not a substitute for, theological *intelligence*. After all, while theology is (externally) dependent on the life of faith, yet it possesses its own (internal) autonomy where the rules of its production are concerned.

Thus, we have attempted to offer a better definition of liberation theology's epistemological profile. If that profile is not yet sufficiently clear, this is because, when all is said and done, this theology, still so new, is growing with the people on their way to liberation.

II. THREE FORMS OF LIBERATION THEOLOGY: PROFESSIONAL, PASTORAL, AND POPULAR

The term *liberation theology* calls to mind its best-known theologians, Gustavo Gutiérrez, Jon Sobrino, Pablo Richard, and so on. But the theology of liberation is far too rich and complex an ecclesial and cultural phenomenon to be limited to the output of professional theologians. It is a type of thinking that actually pervades a goodly part of the ecclesial body, especially in the Third World.

In fact, the grassroots of the church, the so-called base communities and the Bible circles, are permeated by a wholesale faith reflection that we might well describe as a theology of liberation. It is a kind of thinking that is homogeneous with a scientifically developed liberation theology. After all, this grassroots theology, too, brings Christian faith to bear on the situation of oppression; and as we shall see, it is precisely herein that the theology of liberation consists.

Finally, sandwiched in between this more elementary level and the most elevated level of liberation theology, we find an intermediate level. Here is where the reflection of our shepherds is situated: our bishops, priests, religious, and other pastoral ministers. This level is like a bridge, spanning the gap between the more elaborate theology of liberation and our Christian grassroots.

Each of these levels reflects the same thing: faith confronted with oppression. However, each of them reflects that faith in its own way, as we shall see below in more detail.

It is important to observe here that from the bases to the intermediate plane to the highest level, we find the same, continuous flow of thought in a single comprehensive theological process.

Liberation theology is like a tree. If you see only professional theologians, you are looking only at the branches. You are missing the trunk, which is the reflection of the pastors and other ministers, and you are certainly missing all the roots, which are beneath the surface of the soil and maintain the entire tree, trunk and branches alike. After all, this is how it is with the vital, concrete reflection, still underground and anonymous, of tens of thousands of Christian communities who live their faith and do their thinking in a "liberative key."

This theological current is intimately bound up with the people's very existence—with their faith and their struggle. It is part and parcel of their conception of Christian life. At the same time, it remains organically linked to the pastoral practice of the ministers; it is the theory behind these persons' action. Now, when liberation theology has arrived at this level of vital rooting and incarnation—when it has penetrated spirituality, liturgy, and ethics, when it has become social practice—then it has become practically indestructible.

This framework presents liberation theology as a broad, differentiated phenomenon. Liberation theology is any way of thinking the faith in the face of oppression. When we actually hear the term *liberation theology*, of course, it is almost always being used in its strict, technical sense, and it is primarily in this sense that we liberation theologians use it ourselves. But it is impossible to overlook those broad, dense, and fertile grassroots from which professional liberation theology draws its sustenance.

What unifies these three levels of a liberative theological reflection? Their unifying element is the singleness of their shared, single basic inspiration: a faith capable of transforming history, or, to put the same thing in different words, concrete history reflected in the light of faith. This means that the substance of Gustavo Gutiérrez's liberation theology is the same as that of a Christian tenant farmer of the Brazilian Northeast. The basic content is the same. The sap that runs through the branches of the tree is the same that runs through the trunk, rising from the roots of the tree in the secret recesses of the earth.

The distinction among these various types of theology is in their logic, and more concretely in their language. After all, theology can be explicitly articulated in a greater or lesser degree. Obviously, popular theology will be done in vernacular terms, with their spontaneity and color, while professional theology adopts a more conventional language, with its peculiar rigor and severity.

We readily understand what liberation theology is, then, by examining it first of all "from below," that is, by analyzing what the base communities do when they read the gospel and set it in confrontation with their lives of oppression and of longing for liberation. Professional liberation theology does nothing else—only, it expresses itself in a more sophisticated way. Pastoral theology, for its part, on the intermediate level, adopts a logic and language that draws from both.

The liberation theologian is not an ivory-tower intellectual. Rather he or she is an "organic intellectual," a "theological activist," a pilgrim with the people of God and a collaborator with those persons who have a pastoral charge. They have one foot in the center of reflection and the other in the life of the community. (And the latter is their right foot.)

III. METHOD OF LIBERATION THEOLOGY

What we are about to present bears on the theology of liberation as a particular theology—as the theology that deals with the concrete liberation of the oppressed. But if we conceive of liberation theology as a single and unified theology, we shall have to say that what we shall expound here is only the distinctive mark of this theology—the "second moment" in its integral theoretical process. Thus, we shall be prescinding from the method of the "first moment," which corresponds to classical theology and which is structured on its two levels: the *auditus fidei* (positive theology) and the *cogitatio fidei* (speculative theology). Let us add that the outcome of this operation can thereupon be adopted by liberation theology in its "second moment," as a series of illuminative principles in the light of faith.

The operation of the first moment is not always performed by the theology of liberation itself. Liberation theology surely presupposes faith, but not necessarily in its theologized form. When it does itself perform the first moment, liberation theology acts, if not with a method of its own, at least in a manner of its own, critically integrating theologies already built up, transcending them creatively by exploring new dimensions, and opening them to their liberative meaning. We might dub the operation one of epistemological recasting—a dialectical effect of the return of the problematic of the second moment upon the first moment.

Let us leave aside this latter, then, to limit ourselves to what is newest and most typical in the theology of liberation, framed as that theology is by the concrete problematic and by the impingement of faith upon that problematic—its second moment.

1. The Antecedent Moment

Before we do theology we have to do liberation. The first step for theology is pre-theological: We must live the faith commitment. We must share in some way in the liberative process, be committed to the oppressed.

Without this concrete antecedent condition, liberation theology remains mere literature. Here, then, it is not enough to reflect on practice. We must first establish a living nexus with living practice. Otherwise, the poor, oppression, revolution, and a new society will be reduced to mere words that may be found in any dictionary.

Let us be perfectly clear: *At the root of the method of the theology of liberation is the nexus with concrete praxis.* It is within this major dialectic of theory (of faith) and practice (of charity) that liberation theology operates.

Truly, only the actual nexus with liberative praxis can bestow on the theologian a "new spirit," a new style or new way of doing theology. To be a theologian is not to manage methods but to be imbued with the theological spirit. But before constituting a new theological method, the theology of liberation is a new way of being a theologian. Theology is always a second act, the first being "faith, which expresses itself through love" (Gal. 5:6). Theology (not the theologian) comes afterward. First comes liberative practice.

It is of the essence, then, to have a direct knowledge of the reality of oppression/liberation through a disinterested commitment of solidarity with the poor. This pre-theological moment means a concrete conversion of life and implies a class conversion in the sense of involving actual solidarity with the poor and a commitment to their liberation.

To be sure, the concrete, proper manner in which a theologian makes a commitment to the oppressed is to produce a good theology. However, what we wish to emphasize here is that this enterprise is impossible without a *minimal contact* with the world of the oppressed. Actual physical contact is necessary if a person is to acquire a new theological sensitivity. This contact can occur in various forms and degrees, depending on persons and circumstances.

In all cases, however, one thing is clear. Anyone hoping to do an adequate theology of liberation has to be willing to "take a qualifying exam" in union with the poor. Only after having been a pupil with the humble will he or she be in a position to enter the school of the doctors.

2. Basic Schema of the Method

Liberation theology develops in three fundamental moments, corresponding to the three "times" of the celebrated pastoral method: seeing, judging, and acting.

Liberation theologians speak of three principal mediations: the socioanalytic mediation, the hermeneutic mediation, and the practical mediation. We use the term *mediation* because we are speaking about means or instruments of theological construction. First, let us briefly identify these three mediations and show how they are interconnected. Then we shall examine them in greater detail.

The *socioanalytic* mediation contemplates the world of the oppressed. It seeks to understand why the oppressed are oppressed. The *hermeneutic* mediation contemplates the word of God. It attempts to see what the divine plan is with regard to the poor. Finally, the *practical* mediation contemplates the aspect of activity and seeks to discover the appropriate lines of operation for overcoming oppression in conformity with God's plan.

Now let us explain these mediations in greater detail.

1. Socioanalytic Mediation

Liberation is liberation of the oppressed. Therefore liberation theology must begin by stooping down and examining the actual conditions in which the oppressed find themselves, whatever these conditions may be.

To be sure, the primary object of all theology is God. Nevertheless, before asking what oppression means in the eyes of God, the theologian must ask what it is in itself and what its causes are. The God-event does not replace or eliminate the real-world event. "An error concerning the world," declares the great St. Thomas Aquinas, "redounds to an error concerning God."

Furthermore, if faith is to be efficacious, just as with Christian love, it must have its eyes open to the historical reality of which it seeks to be the leaven.

Thus, to know the real world of the oppressed is a material part of the overall theological process. It is a moment, or indispensable mediation (although an insufficient one), for a subsequent, more in-depth understanding of what the proper knowledge of faith is.

i) How to Understand the Phenomenon of Oppression. Confronted with the oppressed, the theologian cannot but begin by asking: Why this oppression? What are its roots?

The oppressed have many faces. Puebla lists them: the faces of children, of youth, of natives, of *campesinos*, of workers, of the underemployed and unemployed, of the marginalized, of the elderly (Puebla Final Document, nos. 32–39). Still, the characteristic visage of the third-world oppressed is that of the socioeconomically poor. It is worn by the disinherited masses of the urban and rural slums.

We must begin here—with this infrastructural oppression—if we wish correctly to understand all of the other forms of oppression and interrelate them duly and acceptably. Indeed, as we shall see more clearly below, the socioeconomic form of oppression conditions in one way or another all of the others.

Beginning with this fundamental expression of oppression—socioeconomic poverty—we ask ourselves how it is to be explained.

There are three possible alternative responses available to liberation theology: the empiricist, the functionalistic, and the dialectical. Let us briefly explain each of them.

—The *empiricist* explanation: *Poverty is a vice*. Thus poverty is "explained" in a simplistic, superficial way. Empiricism assigns the causality of poverty to indolence, ignorance, or simply human malice. It fails to see the collective or structural aspect of poverty, that the poor are entire masses, and these masses are swelling by the day. The empirical is the vulgar conception of social destitution, and the one most widespread in society.

The logical solution in this view of the question of poverty is assistance ranging from almsgiving to the most diversified campaigns of aid to the poor. The poor are regarded as "unfortunates."

—The *functionalist* explanation: *Poverty is backwardness*. This is the liberal or bourgeois interpretation of the phenomenon of social poverty. Poverty is attributed to simple economic and social lag. With time, thanks simply to the process of development fostered in the Third World by foreign loans and technology, "progress" must come and hunger disappear. So think the functionalists.

The social and political solution urged as a way out of this situation is *reform*, understood as the gradual improvement of the prevailing system. Here the poor appear as "objects" of an activity that descends from the top of the pyramid.

There is a positive element in this conception: it sees poverty as a *collective* phenomenon. But it fails to recognize its *conflictive* character. That is, it misses the fact that poverty "is not a passing phase. Instead it is the product of economic, social, and political structures," with the result that "the rich get richer at the expense of the poor, who get ever poorer" (Puebla Final Document, no. 30; citing Pope John Paul II's Opening Address at Puebla, III, 3).

—The *dialectical* explanation: *Poverty is oppression*. This explanation understands poverty as the fruit of the actual economic organization of society, which exploits some (workers), and excludes others (the underemployed, the unemployed, and the whole mass of the marginalized) from the system of production. As John Paul II indicates in his encyclical *Laborem Exercens*, the root of this situation is the primacy of capital over labor (chap. 3). In this historico-structural interpretation, poverty appears in all its reality, both as a collective phenomenon and as a conflictive one. The solution is an *alternative* social system. In other words, the way out of this situation is *revolution*, understood as the transformation of the bases of the economic and social system. Here the poor emerge as the "subject" or agent of the corrective.

ii) Historical Mediation and Struggle of the Oppressed. The socioanalytic interpretation just presented is appropriately complemented by a historical approach to the problem of poverty. The historical approach regards the present situation of the poor not only in itself, but as the terminus of an entire, broad process of exploitation and social marginalization. It attends to the struggles of the least "lowly" throughout the journey of history.

Indeed, the situation of the oppressed is defined not only by their oppressors, but also by the way in which the oppressed react, resisting oppression and struggling to be free. Thus, the poor are never considered in disjunction from their dimension as social co-agents—even in their subjection—of the historical process. Consequently, in order to analyze the world of the poor we must take account not only of their oppression, but also of their history and their liberative practices, however embryonic the latter may be.

iii) The Case of a Poorly Digested Marxism. When dealing with the poor and the oppressed, and seeking their liberation, how could anyone hope to avoid an encounter with Marxist groups (in the concrete struggle) and Marxist theory (on the level of reflection)? We have already seen this above, in our reference to the dialectical or historico-structural interpretation of the phenomenon of socioeconomic poverty.

As for the relationship between liberation theology and Marxist theory, let us limit ourselves here to some essential indications:

1. In the theology of liberation, Marxism is never dealt with in and for itself. It is always examined *with the poor as starting point, and for the sake of the poor.* Forthrightly adopting a position of solidarity with the lowly, the theologian interrogates Marx: What can you tell me about this situation of destitution and about the routes we may take to its defeat? Here the Marxist is subjected to the judgment of the poor and their cause, not the other way around.

2. Liberation theology, therefore, makes use of Marxism purely *instrumentally.* Marxism is not revered, as the holy gospels are. Nor is any obligation felt to give anyone an account of the use that may be made of Marxist words and notions (whether or not they are used correctly), except to the poor, and to their faith and hope. More concretely, let us come right out and admit that liberation theology makes use of certain Marxist "methodological indications" that have proved their usefulness for understanding the world of the oppressed. Among these are the importance of economic factors; attention to the class struggle; the mystifying power of ideologies, including religious ideologies; and so on. This is what the late Jesuit General Pedro Arrupe stated in his celebrated letter of December 8, 1980, on Marxist analysis.

3. The liberation theologian, too, maintains a decidedly critical posture vis-à-vis Marxism. Marx (like any other Marxist) can doubtless be our fellow traveler (cf. Puebla Final Document, no. 544) but can never be "the" teacher. "Only one is your teacher, the Messiah" (Matt. 23:10). This being the case, for a liberation theologian Marxist materialism and atheism are not so much as a temptation. Marxism is set against the broader horizon of faith and thus radically relativized or transcended.

iv) Toward a Broadening of the Conception of "The Poor." Liberation theology is the theology of the liberation of the oppressed—the liberation of their whole person, body and soul—and all of the oppressed—the poor, the subjugated, those who suffer discrimination, and so on. We cannot attend exclusively to the purely socioeconomic aspect of oppression—the aspect of poverty itself—however basic and determining it might be. We must also look at the other levels of social oppression: racial (*blacks*), ethnic (*Indians*), and sexual (*women*).

These various types of oppression and others besides (of youth, children, the elderly, and so forth), each possess their specific nature and call for an equally specific treatment (theoretical and practical). Accordingly, an exclusively "classist" conception of the oppressed must be broadened. The oppressed are not only the socioeconomic poor; in the ranks of the oppressed we find more persons than merely those who are poor.

Here, however, it is important to observe that the socioeconomically oppressed (the poor) do not simply exist alongside the other oppressed, like the black, the Indian, or the woman (to restrict ourselves to the most significant categories of the oppressed in the Third World). No, the oppression of a class—socioeconomic poverty—is precisely the infrastructural expression of the process of oppression. The other types represent mere superstructural expressions of oppression. As such, they are profoundly conditioned by the infrastructural. A black taxi driver and a black soccer star are not the same thing. Similarly, a female domestic servant and the first lady of the land are not the same. An Indian whose land is stolen and an Indian still in possession of it are not the same.

This enables us to understand why, in a class society, the main struggles are class struggles. They set groups whose essential interests are irreconcilably at odds with one another. By contrast, the struggles of the black, the Indian, and the woman are waged between groups nonantagonistic by nature, groups whose basic interests are reconcilable in principle. While the owner (the exploiter) and the worker (the exploited) can never be definitively reconciled, black and white can be, as can Indian and "civilized," or woman and man. These oppositions are actually nonantagonistic, and take shape in our societies with and upon the basic antagonistic contradiction—the class conflict.

Conversely, we must note that oppressions of a noneconomic type aggravate preexisting socioeconomic oppression. The poor are far more grievously oppressed when, besides being poor, they are black, Indian, women, or elderly.

Beyond any doubt, for a critical understanding of the situation of the poor, or of any group of oppressed, the socioanalytic mediation is important. However, that mediation will provide only what a scientific approach can teach about oppression. It will have its limits, which are those of positive rationality. The latter captures only (and this is a great deal, to be sure) the basic, comprehensive structure of oppression. It omits all those nuances that can be perceived only in the direct experience of daily life. To be satisfied with a merely rational, scientific understanding of oppression is to fall into rationalism and thereby to omit the greater part of the reality of an oppressed people.

After all, the oppressed are *more* than what we learn about them from the social analyst—the economist, the sociologist, the anthropologist, and so on. The oppressed themselves must be heard. The poor, in their popular wisdom, actually "know" much more about poverty than does any economist. Or rather, they know it in another way, and more concretely.

For example, what is *work* for popular wisdom and for an economist? For the latter, it is a simple category or statistical calculation, while for the people *work* connotes trauma, anxiety, dignity, security, exploitation, exhaustion, life—a whole series of complex, even contradictory, perceptions. Again, what does the *land* represent for a *campesino* and for a sociologist? For the former, *land* is far more than an economic and social reality. It has a human dimension, with a profoundly affective, even mystical signification. And this is even more true, far more true, for an Indian.

Finally, when the people say "poor," they are saying dependency, weakness, helplessness, anonymity, contempt, and humiliation. In fact, the poor do not even like to call themselves poor, out of a sense of honor and dignity. It is those who are not poor who call them that. A poor woman from the poor city of Tacaimbó, in the interior of Pernambuco, hearing that she had been referred to as poor, responded: "Poor, no. Dogs are poor. We are defenseless, but we are fighting."

Hence it follows that the liberation theologian, in contact with the people, cannot be content with social analyses but needs to seize as well the rich interpretation that the poor make of their world. Thus he or she connects the socioeconomic mediation, which is necessary, with an indispensable understanding of popular wisdom—the rationality of scientific concepts with the symbology of the ideas and images of the people.

Finally, the *Christian view* of the poor contains all this and much more. Faith sees in the poor, and in all the oppressed, precisely what the theology of liberation attempts to render explicit (and here we are already anticipating the hermeneutic mediation):

—The distorted image of God;

—A child of God become a patient, rejected servant;

—The memorial of the Nazarene, poor and persecuted;

—A sacrament of the Lord and Judge of history . . .

The concept of "the poor," without losing any of its concrete substance, is infinitely broadened by being opened to the infinite. Therefore, for the faith and mission of the church, the poor are not only persons in need and laborers; they are not only socially oppressed and historical agents. They are all of this and much more; they are vessels of an "evangelizing potential" (Puebla Final Document, no. 1147), and persons with a vocation to eternal life.

2. Hermeneutic Mediation

Once having understood the concrete situation of the oppressed, the theologian must proceed to ask: What does the word of God say about this situation? Then we find ourselves in the second moment of the process of theological construction: the specific moment by virtue of which a discourse is formally theological discourse.

It is a matter, then, of seeing the process of oppression/liberation in the light of faith. And what is the light of faith? This expression does not denote anything vague or general. The light of faith is concretely found in holy scripture. Thus, the light of faith and the light of the word of God are the same thing.

So liberation theologians go to the scriptures, carrying with them all of the problems of the suffering and hope of the oppressed. They solicit light and inspiration from the word of God. Thus they execute a new reading of the Bible: the hermeneutics of liberation.

i) The Bible of the Poor. To interrogate the totality of scripture from the viewpoint of the oppressed is to execute the hermeneutics, the specific reading, of the theology of liberation.

Let us hasten to add that this is not the only possible legitimate reading of the Bible. For us today in the Third World, however, it is the *privileged* reading. From the heart of the great biblical revelation, we extract the most enlightening and eloquent themes in the perspective of the poor: God as the Father of life and advocate of the oppressed, deliverance from the house of slavery, the prophecy of a new world, the Reign given to the poor, the church of total communion, and so on. The hermeneutics of liberation gives priority to these veins, but does not mine them exclusively. They may not be the most *important* themes (in themselves), but they are the most *appropriate* (for the poor in their situation of oppression). For the rest, it is the order of importance that determines the order of suitability.

On the other hand, the poor are more than simply poor, as we have seen. They seek life, and life "to the full" (John 10:10). Thus, the pertinent or urgent questions of the poor are interconnected with the transcendental questions: conversion, grace, resurrection.

Liberation hermeneutics actually interrogates the word of God without ideologically anticipating the divine response. As a theological hermeneutics, it is practiced in faith, or openness to the ever new and surprising revelation of God—to the unheard message that can save or condemn. The response of the word can therefore be, at any time, to call the inquiry, and even the inquirer, into question, inasmuch as it issues a call to conversion—to faith, or to a commitment of justice.

There is a hermeneutic circle, then, or "unceasing interplay" between the poor and the word of God (Paul VI, *Evangelii Nuntiandi*, no. 29). The primacy in this dialectic, however, belongs undeniably to the sovereign word of God—the primacy of value, at any rate, if not necessarily methodological priority. On the other hand, we know from the intrinsically liberative content of biblical revelation that the word of God can only sound in the ears of the poor as a message of radical comfort and liberation.

ii) Traits of the Hermeneutics of Liberation Theology. A reading of the Bible done from the starting point of the poor and their project of liberation is characterized by certain traits:

1. It is a hermeneutics that prioritizes the moment of *application* over that of explanation. On the other hand, it sees to it that the theology of liberation does nothing more than rediscover what has been the timeless call of any sound biblical reading (for example, in the Fathers of the Church), a call that for so long was neglected in favor of a rationalistic exegesis of intrinsic meaning. A liberative hermeneutics reads the Bible as a book of life, not as a book of curious stories. Surely it seeks the *textual* meaning there, but does so for the sake of its *life* meaning. Here the important thing is not so much to interpret the text of the scriptures as to interpret the book of life "according to the scriptures." In a word, the new/old

biblical reading culminates in the experience today of the sense and meaning of yesterday. And here the second trait comes in.

2. A liberative hermeneutics seeks to discover and activate the *transforming energy* of the biblical texts. The crucial thing, after all, is to reach an interpretation that will lead to a change in persons (conversion) and history (revolution). This reading is not ideologically preconceived; biblical religion is an open, dynamic religion due to its Messianic and eschatological nature. Ernst Bloch once admitted, "It is difficult to have a revolution without the Bible."

3. A reading of the Bible in terms of political theology accentuates, without reductionism, the social context of the message. It places each text in its historical context, so as to make an adequate, nonliteral translation of it in our own current historical context. For example, liberation hermeneutics emphasizes (but only emphasizes) the social context of oppression in which Jesus lived and the markedly political context of his death on the cross. It is obvious that, in this relationship, the biblical text acquires a particular importance in the context of third-world oppression, where a liberative evangelization has immediate, grave political implications, as the long list of Latin American martyrs testifies.

4. Finally, liberation hermeneutics is done *together with the poor*, incorporating on the level of the hermeneutic mediation the contribution of the popular reading of the Bible, just as it incorporates popular wisdom within the socioanalytic mediation. In this fashion the poor, or rather the church of the poor, made concrete in the base communities, appears as the privileged hermeneutical subject or agent of biblical reflection.

iii) Preferred Books of the Bible. Surely theology must take account of the entire Bible. Nevertheless, hermeneutic preferences are inevitable, and even necessary, as the liturgy itself and the homiletic art teach us. As for the theology of liberation, on any of its three levels (professional, pastoral, and mainly popular), the most appreciated books are indubitably:

—*Exodus*, which develops the politico-religious deed of liberation of a mass of slaves who become, by virtue of the divine covenant, a people of God.

—The books of the *Prophets*, for their intransigent defense of the liberator God, their vigorous denunciation of injustices, their championing of the lowly, and their proclamation of the Messianic world.

—The *Gospels*, obviously, for the central character of the divine person of Jesus with his message of the Reign, his liberative practice, and his death and resurrection, that absolute meaning of history.

—The *Acts of the Apostles*, for their portrayal of the ideal of a free and liberating Christian community.

—The *Book of Revelation*, for its collective, symbolic description of the immense struggle of the persecuted people of God against all the monsters of history.

In some locales other books are preferred, for example, those of the *wisdom literature*, for their recovery of the value of divine revelation in popular wisdom (proverbs, tales, and the like). In certain areas of Central America the books of the *Maccabees* nourished the faith of those immersed in a context of armed insurrection (legitimated, for that matter, by their pastors). Then, with the war at an end and the peaceful task of the reconstruction of their country under way, the communities have betaken themselves to a systematic reading of the books of *Ezra* and *Nehemiah*, because these texts portray the effort of restoration by God's people after the critical period of the Babylonian captivity.

It would be superfluous to observe here that any book of the Bible must be read in a "christological key," that is, from the high point of revelation as found in the gospels. Thus the perspective of the poor is placed within a grander perspective, that of the Lord of history, wherein it acquires all of its consistency and vigor.

iv) Recovery of the Great Christian Tradition. The theology of liberation is aware of being a new, contemporary theology of the current historical period, suited to the great masses of the poor of the Third World, both Christian and non-Christian.

Nonetheless, this theology seeks to maintain a bond of basic continuity with the living faith tradition of the Christian people. Therefore it interrogates the past in an effort to learn from it and to be enriched by it. The theology of liberation adopts toward theological tradition a double attitude:

1. An attitude of *criticism*, as it becomes aware of the limits and insufficiencies of the production of the past, the inevitable tribute, in part, to be paid to the particular age in which a theology took shape. For example, in scholastic theology (from the eleventh to the fourteenth centuries), granting its undeniable contributions to the precise, systematic development of Christian truth, we discover a no less undeniable tendency to theoreticism—to emptying the world of its historical or concrete nature (with a static view of things)—and thus precious little sensitivity for the social question of the poor and their historical liberation. As for classic spirituality, an effort is made to transcend its ahistorical interiorism, its elitism, and its insufficient sense of the Lord's presence in the processes of liberation.

2. An attitude of *rehabilitation*, as it reincorporates forgotten, fertile theological threads that can enrich us, and even call us to account. For example, from patristic theology (the second to the ninth centuries) we can integrate its profoundly unitary conception of salvation history, its sense of the social demands of the gospel, its perception of the prophetic dimension of the church's mission, its sensitivity to the poor, and so on.

Likewise inspiring for liberation theology are the singular evangelical experiences of so many saints and prophets, of whom not a few were condemned as heretics, but whose liberative significance we clearly perceive today. Such was the case with Francis of Assisi, Savonarola, Meister Eckhart, Catherine of Siena, Bartolomé de las Casas, and, more recently, Fathers Hidalgo and Morelos, as well as Father Cícero—not to forget the precious contribution of the medieval pauperist reform movements or the evangelical demands of the great Reformers.

v) Social Teaching of the Church. In the area of the social teaching of the church, once more liberation theology maintains an open, positive attitude. It must be said, first of all, that liberation theology does not come forward as a *competitor* to the teaching of the magisterium. It could not do so even should it so wish, inasmuch as the two discourses take place on distinct levels and with distinct competencies. But whereas the social teaching of the church offers the grand orientations for Christians' social action, liberation theology seeks, on the one hand, to *integrate* these orientations into its synthesis, and on the other, to *explicate* them in creative fashion for the concrete context of the Third World.

This operation of integration and explication is founded on the dynamic, open character of the social teaching of the church (cf. Puebla Final Document, nos. 473, 539). Furthermore, in so doing liberation theology is obeying the explicit call of the magisterium itself, which, in Paul VI's *Octogesima Adveniens* (1971), declared:

> To utter a unified message and to put forward a solution which has universal validity . . . is not our ambition, nor is it our mission. It is up to the Christian communities to analyze with objectivity the situation which is proper to their own country, to shed on it the light of the Gospel's unalterable words. . . . It is up to these Christian communities . . . to discern the options and commitments which are called for in order to bring about the social, political, and economic changes seen in many cases to be urgently needed (no. 4; cf. nos. 42, 48).

Here the pope indicates precisely the three moments of the production of the theology of liberation, through which what is less concrete in the teaching of the church becomes more concrete.

Now, as we readily see, liberation theology responds to Paul VI's challenge to the social teaching of the church. That teaching, as he asserts, "does not . . . limit itself to recalling general principles. It develops through reflection applied to the changing situations of this world" *(Octogesima Adveniens*, no. 42). Thus, liberation theology takes its position squarely along the lines of the demands of the doctrine of the church. This is how liberation theology is actually regarded when it is adopted and/or developed by pastoral ministers in the form of pastoral liberation theology.

In fact, Cardinal Ratzinger himself, in his "Instruction on Certain Aspects of the Theology of Liberation," regards the social teaching of the church as a kind of pre-theology of liberation, or as a type of "pastoral theology of liberation," inasmuch as it has sought to "respond to the challenge hurled at our epoch by oppression and by hunger" (no. 1).

The conclusion of all of this can only be that there is no incompatibility in principle between the social teaching of the church and the theology of liberation. They are complementary, to the good of the whole people of God.

vi) Creative Work of Theology. Armed with the mediations they require, and with all of the material accumulated through these mediations, liberation theologians now address the construction of genuinely new syntheses of faith and the production of new theoretical significations, with a view to meeting the great challenges of today.

Liberation theologians are never mere accumulators of theological materials. They are authentic architects of theology. Thus, they arm themselves with the necessary theoretical daring and a good dose of creative fantasy, in order to be in a position to deal with the unprecedented problems they find on the oppressed continents. Extracting and creatively developing the liberative content of the faith, they attempt to realize a new codification of the Christian mystery, in order thereby to help the church fulfill its mission of liberative evangelization in history.

3. Practical Mediation

Liberation theology is anything but an inconclusive theology. It emerges from action and leads to action, and the round trip is steeped and wrapped in the atmosphere of faith from start to finish. From an analysis of the reality of the oppressed, it moves through the word of God, finally to arrive at concrete practice. Back to Action is the motto of this theology. Thus, it seeks to be a militant, committed, and liberative theology. It is a theology that leads to the public square, because the *current form* of faith today in the underworld of the disinherited is "political love," or "macro-charity." In the Third World, among the wretched of the earth, faith is also and *especially* political.

However, faith is not reducible to action, even liberative action. It is "ever greater," and includes moments of contemplation, and profound gratitude. The theology of liberation also leads to the temple. And from the temple it leads the believer, charged now with all of the divine and divinizing energies of that Mystery of the world that is God, once more to the public square of history.

True, liberation theology leads, as well, and today principally, to action: to action for justice, to the deed of love, to conversion, to church renewal, to the transformation of society.

The logic of the Third Moment—the practical mediation—has its own internal regime. Naturally, the degree of definition of activity depends on the theological level upon which one operates: professional, pastoral, or popular.

Thus, a professional theologian can only open grand perspectives for action. A theologian who is a pastor or pastoral minister can be somewhat more determinate as to the lines of his or her activity. And popular theologians are in a position to enter upon a plane of quite precise practical and concrete action. Obviously, at the latter two levels—the pastoral and the popular—definition of the operation can only be a collective act, carried forward by all who are caught up in the question of the case, especially by the pastoral and other ministers or "agents."

The logic of action is extremely complex. It includes many steps, such as a rational, prudential assessment of all of the circumstances of the action proposed and an anticipation of the possible consequences.

In all instances, however, the practical mediation embraces certain distinct discursive levels:

1. Level of *conjunctual analysis*: an assessment of the correlation of forces at hand, such as resistance on the part of society and the church, the capacity of the people to bear the proposals made, and so forth.

2. Level of *projects and programs*: proposals of the historically viable objectives for the short and long term. Without this step, we should only have pure utopias and sheer good intentions.

3. Level of *strategy and tactics*: definition of the concrete means for reaching the proposed objectives, that is, alliances, resources, various means, all through prudential judgments that arrive at the actual concrete level in the form of tactics.

4. *Ethical and evangelical* level: assessment of the means proposed in terms of the values and criteria of morality and faith, with priority accorded to, for example, nonviolent methods such as dialogue, moral pressure, and active resistance.

5. *Performative* level. Finally, there is even a discourse of direct operation, with its appeals and attractions to action. This level of discourse performs the function of a bridge between decision and execution.

In this third moment in the method of liberation theology, we note the presence of a cognition constructed more of practice than of theory. That is, here the process is more executive than systematic. Thus, at this point, rather than formal reason, it is the wisdom of life and the prudence of action that are at work. And here the common people, those "doctors in the school of life," often have the advantage over the "wise and prudent."

—*Translated by Robert R. Barr*

2

Option for the Poor

GUSTAVO GUTIÉRREZ

The poor occupy a central position in the reflection that we call the theology of liberation. Only theological method and a concern for evangelization need be added in order to have the original—and still valid—core of this effort in understanding of the faith. From the outset, liberation theology has posited a distinction—adopted by Medellín in its "Document on Poverty"—among three notions of poverty: real poverty, as an *evil* (that is, as not desired by God); spiritual poverty, as *availability* to the will of the Lord; and *solidarity* with the poor, as well as with the situation they suffer.

The importance of this point is proclaimed by biblical revelation itself. A preferential commitment to the poor is at the very heart of Jesus' preaching of the Reign of God (and we shall take up this matter in part II). The Reign of God is a free gift, which makes demands on those who receive it in the spirit of children and in community (as we shall see in part III). Real poverty has therefore been a challenge to the church throughout history, but due to certain contemporary factors it has acquired fresh currency among us (the subject of part I).

I. A NEW PRESENCE

Our days bear the mark of a vast historical event: the *irruption of the poor*. We refer to the new presence of those who had actually been absent in our society and in the church. By *absent* we mean of little or no significance, as well as being without the opportunity to manifest their sufferings, solidarities, projects, and hopes.

As the result of a long historical process, this situation has begun to change in recent decades in Latin America. Of course the same change has been occurring in Africa, with the new nations; in Asia, with the independence of old nations; among the racial minorities of wealthy nations as well as poor ones. Another important movement, taking many forms, has also gotten under way: the new presence of women, regarded by Puebla as "doubly oppressed and marginalized" (Puebla Final Document, no. 1135, n.) among the poor of Latin America.

The poor, then, have gradually become active agents of their own destiny, initiating the solid process that is altering the condition of this world's poor and despoiled. The theology of liberation—an expression of the right of the poor to "think their faith"—is not the automatic result of this situation and its incarnations. It is an attempt to read these signs of the times—in response to the invitation issued by John XXIII and Vatican Council II—by engaging in a critical reflection in the light of the word of God. That word should lead us to make a serious effort to discern the values and limitations of this event, which read from the standpoint of faith, also represents an irruption of God into our lives.

1. The World of the Poor

Expressions like, "dominated peoples," "exploited social classes," "despised races," and "marginalized cultures"—along with the reference to that constant, coextensive phenomenon, "discrimination against women"—have become common formulations in a framework of the theology of liberation for the unjust situation of the poor. The purpose of these formulations is to call attention to the fact that the poor—who constitute a de facto social collectivity—live in a situation of "inhuman misery" (Medellín, "Document on Poverty," no. 1) and "anti-evangelical poverty" (Puebla Final Document, no. 1159).

Furthermore, a great and constantly growing commitment to the poor has afforded us a better perception of the enormous complexity of their world. We are dealing with a veritable universe, in which the socioeconomic aspect of poverty, while fundamental, is not the only aspect. Ultimately, poverty means *death.* Food shortages, housing shortages, the impossibility of attending adequately to health and educational needs, the exploitation of labor, chronic unemployment, disrespect for human worth and dignity, unjust restrictions on freedom of expression (in politics and religion alike) are the daily plight of the poor. The lot of the poor, in a word, is suffering. Theirs is a situation that destroys peoples, families, and individuals; Medellín and Puebla call it "institutionalized violence." Equally unacceptable is the terrorism and repressive violence with which they are surrounded.

At the same time—and it is important to remember this—to be poor is a way of life. It is a way of thinking, of loving, of praying, of believing and hoping, of spending free time, of struggling for a livelihood. Being poor today also means being involved in the battle for justice and peace, defending one's life and liberty, seeking a greater democratic participation in the decisions of society, "organizing to live one's faith in an integral way" (Puebla Final Document, no. 1137), and committing oneself to the liberation of every human person.

Again—by way of a convergent phenomenon—we have seen during this same period the emergence of a more acute awareness of the racial problem among us. One of our social lies is that there is no racism in Latin America. There may be no racist laws, such as prevail in other lands, but we do have racist customs—a phenomenon no less grave for being hidden away. Marginalization of and contempt for the Amerindian and black populations are things we cannot accept, neither as human beings, nor still less as Christians. Today these populations are coming to a more acute awareness of their situation and consequently are voicing an ever more powerful demand for their most elementary human rights. This raised consciousness is pregnant with implications for the future.

We must also mention the unacceptable, inhumane position of women. One of the most subtle obstacles to its perception is its almost hidden character in habitual, daily life in our cultural tradition—to the point that when we denounce it, we seem a little strange to people, as if we were simply looking for trouble.

This state of affairs among us is a challenge to pastoral work, a challenge to the commitment of the Christian churches. Consequently, it is also a challenge to theological reflection. We still have a long way to go in this area. Matters of culture, race, and gender will be (and have already begun to be) extremely important to liberation theology. Doubtless the most important part of this task will fall to persons who actually belong to these respective human groups, despite the difficulties lying in the way today. No sudden burst of resistance is in the offing, but the voice of these downtrodden has begun to be heard, and this augurs well for the future. Here we surely have one of the richest theological veins for the coming years.

The cargo of inhuman, cruel death with which all of this misery and oppression is laden is contrary to the will of the God of Christian revelation, who is a God of life. But this does not blind us to the positive elements that we have indicated. These things manifest an ever-promising human depth and strength in terms of life. All of this constitutes the complex world of the poor. But our overall judgment remains: real poverty, a lack of the necessities of life (of a life worthy of a human being); social injustice, which plunders the masses and feeds the wealth of the few; the denial of the most elementary of human rights, are evils that believers in the God of Jesus can only reject.

2. Going to the Causes

In this complicated, narrow universe of the poor, the predominant notes are, first, its insignificance in the eyes of the great powers that rule the world of today, and second, its enormous human, cultural, and religious wealth, especially in terms of a capacity for the creation of new forms of solidarity in these areas.

This is how the poor are presented to us in scripture. The various books of the Bible paint a powerful picture of the cruel situation of spoliation and abuse in which the poor abide. One of the most energetic denunciations of this state of affairs is in the shatteringly beautiful—despite the painfulness of the topic under consideration—description we find in chapter 24 of the Book of Job. But it is not a matter of a mere neutral presentation of this reality. No, the biblical writers—the prophets, especially—point the finger of blame at those responsible for the situation. The texts are many. These passages denounce the social injustice that creates poverty as contrary to the will of God and to the meaning of the liberative deed of God manifested in the exodus from Egypt.

Medellín, Puebla, and John Paul II have all adopted this outlook in recent times. Today, pointing out causes implies structural analysis. This has always been an important point in the framework of liberation theology. The approach has been a costly one. True, the privileged of this world accept with a certain amount of equanimity the fact of massive world poverty. Such a fact is scarcely to be concealed in our day. But when causes are indicated, problems arise.

Pointing out the causes inevitably means speaking of social injustice and socioeconomic structures that oppress the weak. When this happens, there is resistance—especially if the structural analysis reveals the concrete, historical responsibility of specific persons. But the strongest resistance and greatest fear are aroused by the threat of a raised consciousness and resulting organization on the part of the poor.

The tools used in an analysis of social reality vary with time and with the particular effectiveness they have demonstrated when it comes to understanding this reality and proposing approaches to the solution of problems. It is a hallmark of the scientific method to be critical of the researcher's own premises and conclusions. Thereby science constantly advances to new hypotheses of interpretation. For example, the theory of dependency, so frequently employed during the first years of our encounter with Latin American reality, has obviously turned out to be an inadequate tool. It is still an important one; but it has taken insufficient account of the internal dynamics and complexity of each country, and of the sheer magnitude of the world of the poor. Furthermore, Latin American social scientists are becoming more and more attentive to factors, not in evidence until more recent years, that express an evolution in progress in the world economy.

All of this calls for a refinement of our various means of cognition and even for the application of other, new means of the same. The social dimension is very important, but we must go deeper. There has been a great deal of insistence, in recent years, altogether correctly, on the contrast between a developed, wealthy northern world (whether capitalist or socialist), and an underdeveloped, poor, southern one (cf. John Paul II, *Sollicitudo Rei Socialis*.) This affords a different view of the world panorama, which cannot be reduced to confrontations of an ideological order or to a limited approach to confrontations between social classes. It also indicates the basic opposition implied in the confrontation between East and West. Indeed, the diversity of the factors that we have cited makes us aware of various types of social oppositions and conflicts prevailing in today's world.

The important transformation surely occurring in the field of social analysis today is needed in the theology of liberation. This circumstance has led liberation theology to incorporate into its examination of the intricate, fluid reality of poverty certain valuable new perspectives being adopted by the human sciences (psychology, ethnology, anthropology). Incorporation does not mean simply adding, without organic splicing. Attention to cultural factors makes it possible for us to penetrate basic mentalities and attitudes that explain important aspects of reality. Economic reality is no longer the same when evaluated from a cultural viewpoint. And surely the reverse is true as well.

It is not a matter of choosing among instruments. As a complex human condition, poverty can only have complex causes. We must not be simplistic. We must doggedly plunge to the root, to the underlying causes of the situation. We must be, in this sense, truly radical. Sensitivity to the new challenges will dictate changes of focus in the process of our selection of the routes to be taken to an authentic victory over the social conflicts that we have cited, and to the construction of a just world, the community of sisters and brothers for which the Christian message calls.

II. THE REASON FOR A PREFERENCE

While it is important and urgent to have a scholarly knowledge of the poverty in which the great masses of our peoples live, along with the causes that lie at the origin of this poverty, theological work properly so called begins when we undertake to read this reality in the light of Christian revelation.

The biblical meaning of poverty, then, will be one of the cornerstones of liberation theology. True, this is a classic question of Christian thinking. But the new, active presence of the poor vigorously re-posits that question. A keystone of the understanding of poverty along these theological lines is the distinction among the three notions of poverty, as we have stated. That is the context of a central theme of this theology, one broadly accepted today in the universal church: *the preferential option for the poor.* We are dealing with an outlook whose biblical roots are deep.

1. A Theocentric Option

Medellín had already encouraged giving "preference to the poorest and neediest, and to those who are segregated for any reason" ("Document on Poverty," no. 9). The very term *preference* obviously precludes any exclusivity; it simply points to who ought to be the first—not the only—objects of our solidarity. From the very first the theology of liberation has insisted on the importance of maintaining both the universality of God's love and the divine predilection for "history's last." To opt for either of these extremes to the exclusion of the other would be to mutilate the Christian message. The great challenge is to maintain a response to both demands, as Archbishop Romero used to say with reference to the church, "From among the poor, the church can be for everyone."

In the harsh, hard years of the late 1960s and early 1970s, this perspective occasioned numerous experiments in the Latin American church, along with a theological reflection bearing on these experiments. Here was a process of the refinement of expressions translating the commitment to the poor and oppressed. This became plain at Puebla, which adopted the formula "the preferential option for the poor" (cf. the chapter of the Puebla Final Document bearing that name). The expression had already begun to be used in the theological reflection of that time in Latin America. Thus, the Puebla Conference bestowed a powerful endorsement. Now the formula and the concept belong to everyone.

The word *option* has not always been well interpreted. Like any slogan, it has its limits. What it seeks to emphasize is the free commitment of a decision. This option for the poor is not optional in the sense that a Christian need not necessarily make it, any more than the love we owe every human being, without exception, is optional. It is a matter of a deep, ongoing solidarity, a voluntary daily involvement with the world of the poor. At the same time, the word *option* does not necessarily mean that those who make it do not already belong to the world of the poor. In many cases they do. But even here it is an option; the poor themselves must make this decision, as well. Some important recent documents issuing from the ecclesiastical magisterium at the universal level, echoing the outlook of the Latin American church, explicitly employ the expression *preferential option for the poor.*

Some have claimed that the magisterium would be happy to see the expression *preferential option* replaced with *preferential love* which, we are told, would change the meaning. It seems to us that the matter has been settled by the latest encyclical of John Paul II. Listing certain points and emphases enjoying priority among the considerations of the magisterium today, the pope asserts: "Among these themes, I should like to mention, here, the *preferential option or love* for the poor. This is an option or *special form* of primacy in the exercise of Christian charity" (*Sollicitudo Rei Socialis*, no. 42).

When all is said and done, the option for the poor means an option for the God of the Reign as proclaimed to us by Jesus. The whole Bible, from the story of Cain and Abel onward, is marked by God's love and predilection for the weak and abused of human history. This preference manifests precisely God's gratuitous love. This is what the evangelical Beatitudes reveal to us. The Beatitudes tell us in extremely simple fashion that a predilection for the poor, the hungry, and the suffering has its basis in the Lord's own bounty and liberality.

The ultimate reason for a commitment to the poor and oppressed does not lie in the social analysis that we employ, or in our human compassion, or in the direct experience we may have of poverty. All of these are valid reasons and surely play an important role in our commitment. But as Christians, we base that commitment fundamentally on the God of our faith. It is a theocentric, prophetic option we make, one which strikes its roots deep in the gratuity of God's love and is demanded by that love. Bartolomé de las Casas, immersed in the terrible poverty and destruction of the Indians of this continent, gave this as the reason for his option for them: "Because the least one, the most forgotten one, is altogether fresh and vivid in the memory of God." It is of this "memory" that the Bible speaks to us.

This perception was asserted in the experience of the Latin American Christian communities, and thus it came down to Puebla. Puebla maintains that for the sole reason of the love of God manifested in Christ, "the poor merit preferential attention, whatever may be the moral or personal situation in which they find themselves" (Puebla Final Document, no. 1142). In other words, the poor are preferred not because they are necessarily better than others from a moral or religious standpoint, but because God is God. No one lays conditions on God (cf. Jth. 8:11–18), for whom the last are first. This shocks our ordinary, narrow understanding of justice; it reminds us that God's ways are not our ways (cf. Isa. 55:8).

There has been no shortage of misunderstanding, then, or undue reduction on the part of self-styled champions of this preferential option as well as its overt adversaries. Still, we can safely assert that we are dealing with an indefectible part of the understanding maintained by the church as a whole today of its task in the world. We are dealing with a focus that is fraught with consequences—one which is actually only taking its first steps, and which constitutes the core of a new spirituality.

2. The Last Shall Be First

In a parable that we know from the first gospel alone, Matthew sets in relief—in the contrast between the first and the last—the gratuity of God's love by comparison with a narrow notion of justice (Matt. 20:1–16). "I intend to give this man who was hired last the same pay as you," says the Lord. Then he assails the envious with a pair of incisive questions: "I am free to do as I please with my money, am I not? Or are you envious because I am generous?" Here is the heart of the matter. The literal expression "bad eye" (for "envious") is revealing. In the Semitic mentality it denotes a fierce, jealous look—a look that petrifies reality, that leaves no room for anything new, leaves no room for generosity, and especially, here, undertakes to fix limits to the divine bounty. The parable transmits a clear lesson concerning the core of the biblical message: the gratuity of God's love. Only that gratuity can explain God's preference for the weakest and most oppressed.

"Thus the last shall be first and the first shall be last" (v. 16). Frequently we cite only the first half of the verse: "The last shall be first," forgetting that, by the same token, the first shall be last. But what we have here is an antithesis. The two statements shed light on each other, and therefore should not be separated. The antithesis is a constant in the gospels when the reference is to the addressees of the Reign of God. The gospels tell us of those who shall enter the Reign heralded by Jesus, and at the same time they tell us who shall be unable to do so. This antithetical presentation is highly instructive concerning the God of the Reign. Let us approach this matter by way of certain examples.

1. In Luke (6:20–26), the Beatitudes are followed by the Woes. The Greek word for *poor* here is *ptochoi*. Its meaning is beyond any doubt: etymologically the word means the "stooped," the "dismayed." It is actually used to speak of the needy, those who must beg in order to live—those whose existence, then, depends on others. In other words, it means the helpless. This connotation of social and economic inferiority was already present in the Hebrew words that *ptochos* translates in the version known as the Septuagint. Scholars agree that this is the basic meaning of the word *ptochos* in its thirty-four occurrences in the New Testament (twenty-four of them being in the gospels). Very different is the situation of the rich, who have already received their consolation. Here again the sense is clear: the rich (*plousioi*) are those who possess a great deal of material wealth. Luke frequently contrasts them with the poor: the parable of the rich man and the poor Lazarus, in which, it is worth mentioning, it is not the rich man, but the representative of the anonymous of history, who is designated by a name (16:19–31); the vanity of the highly placed and the oppression of the poor (20:46–47); the widow's mite, accentuating the contrast presented in the parallel text in Matthew 21:1–3, its possible source.

We also have a contrast between the hungry and the satiated. The Greek word used by Luke for the hungering, *peinontes*, like the Hebrew words it translates in the Septuagint, indicates that this is not simple hunger but a deprivation resulting from evil acts of violence perpetrated over an extended period of time. The reference is to an endemic food shortage. "Starving," then, or "famished" would be better words for *peinontes* than simply "hungry." The satiated, by contrast, are the fully satisfied. Thus, the song placed by Luke on the lips of Mary strikes a definitive contrast between the rich and the hungry (Luke 1:53). Indeed, in Luke we often find poverty and hunger associated, as we find wealth and abundance of nourishment associated.

Those who weep—now we are in the third Beatitude—are those who experience a pain so acute, a sorrow so intense, that they cannot but express it. Weeping is a manifestation of feelings to which Luke is sensitive; he uses the verb *klaiein*, "to weep," eleven times. The pain expressed by this word is not momentary. This suffering is profound and springs from permanent marginalization. Rarely, on the other hand, do the Christian scriptures mention anyone laughing (*gela-*). Laughing can be a legitimate expression of joy (Luke 6:21), but it can also be the manifestation of a merriment that is oblivious of the sufferings of others, one based on privileges (6:25).

These are real situations—even social and economic situations—of poverty and wealth, hunger and satiety, suffering and self-satisfaction. The Reign of God will belong to those who live in conditions of weakness and oppression. For the wealthy to enter the Reign will be more difficult than "for a camel to go through a needle's eye" (Luke 18:25).

2. The gospels let us know, in various ways, that it is the despised, and not persons of importance, who have access to the Reign of God and to knowledge of the word of God. When the Lord cries, "Let the children come to me. Do not hinder them. The Kingdom of God belongs to such as these" (Matt. 19:14), we immediately think of childlike docility and trust. We miss the radicality of Jesus' message. In the cultural world of Jesus' time, children were regarded as defectives. Together with the poor, the sick, and women, they were relegated to the status of the inconsequential. This shocks our modern sensitivity. But testimonials to this abound. To be "such as these," therefore, to be as children, means being insignificant, someone of no value in the eyes of society. Children are in the same category as the ignorant, on whom God our Father has willed to bestow a self-revelation (Matt. 11:25), or the "least ones," in whom we encounter Christ himself (Matt. 25:31–46).

Opposite these small, ignorant persons stand "the learned and the clever" (Matt. 11:25), who have seized control of the "key of knowledge" (Luke 11:52), and who despise the lowly, the people—*'am ha-'arets*, the people of the earth, of the land—whom they regard as ignorant and immoral. ("This lot, that knows nothing about the law" [John 7:49]). The gospel calls them the simple folk, "merest children" (Matt. 11:25)—using the Greek word *nepioi*, with its strong connotation of ignorance and simplicity.

Here again we find ourselves confronted with concrete, contrasting social situations based on unequal degrees of religious knowledge. Ignorance is not a virtue, nor is wisdom a vice. The biblical preference for simple folk springs not from a regard for their supposed moral and spiritual dispositions, but from their human frailty and from the contempt to which they are subjected.

3. We should actually do better to call the parable of those invited to the wedding banquet, as recorded in Matthew (22:2–10) and Luke (14:14–24), the parable of the *un*invited, since it is really they who constitute the core of its lesson. Exegetes are gradually abandoning the common interpretation of this text as a parable of an Israel called by God, but rejected for its faults, and thereupon a non-Israel called in place of Israel. Today the tendency is rather to understand those who were invited first as the "upper crust" of the time—persons who enjoyed both a high social rank and a knowledge of the Law; and the second group as those to whom Jesus preferentially addressed his message, the poor and the dispossessed—those regarded as sinners by the religious leaders of the people. Matthew goes so far as

to say: "The servants then went out into the byroads and rounded up everyone they met, bad as well as good. This filled the wedding hall with banqueters" (Matt. 22:10). "Bad" and "good," we read, in that order. Once more we are dealing not with a question of moral deserts, but with an objective situation of the "poor and the crippled, the blind and the lame" (Luke 14:21).

4. Jesus is emphatic. He has come not for the sake of the righteous, but for sinners; not for the sake of the healthy, but for the sick (cf. Mark 2:17). Once again we have an antithetical presentation of the addressees of Jesus' message. On this occasion the tone is ironic: Are there perhaps righteous, healthy people who have no need of Jesus' salvific love? No, the "righteous," here are the self-righteous, those who pretend to be sinless, while the "healthy" are those who think they do not need God. These, despite the tokens of respect that they receive in society, are the greatest sinners, sick with pride and self-sufficiency. Then who are the sinners and the unhealthy, for whom the Lord has come? In terms of what we have just observed concerning the righteous and the healthy, we must be dealing here with those who are not well regarded by the "upper crust" of the social and religious world.

Those afflicted with serious illnesses or physical handicaps were regarded as sinners (cf. John 9). Hence, for example, lepers were segregated from social life; Jesus returns them to society by restoring them to physical health. Similarly public sinners, like tax collectors and prostitutes, were the dregs of society. It is that condition, and not their moral or religious quality, that makes them first in the love and tenderness of Jesus. Therefore he apostrophizes the great ones of his people: "Tax collectors and prostitutes are entering the kingdom of God before you" (Matt. 21:31). The gratuity of God's love never ceases to amaze us.

III. CHURCH OF THE POOR

One month before the opening of the Council, John XXIII called into being a church of the poor. His words have become familiar ones: "As for the underdeveloped countries, the church is, and wishes to be, the church of all, and especially the church of the poor" (Discourse of September 11, 1962). This intuition had strong repercussions on Medellín, as well as on the life of the Latin American church, especially by way of the base church communities. An examination of the meaning of the notion of spiritual poverty will help us to understand why the disciple, the person who belongs to the people of God, must express an acceptance of the Reign of God in a commitment of solidarity and loving community with all, especially with the actual poor and dispossessed of this world.

1. Discipleship

The Beatitudes are recorded in two versions in the gospels, one in Luke and the other in Matthew. The contrast between the two versions is frequently attributed to an attempt on the part of Matthew to "spiritualize" the Beatitudes, that is, to convert to a recital of purely interior, disincarnate dispositions what in Luke had been a concrete, historical expression of the coming of the Messiah. We disagree with this interpretation. Among other things, it is scarcely to be denied that Matthew's gospel is particularly insistent on the importance of performing concrete, material deeds in behalf of others, especially the poor (cf. Matt. 25:31–46). What Matthew does is view the Beatitudes through the lens of the central theme of his gospel: discipleship. The spiritual poor are followers of Jesus. The Matthean Beatitudes (Matt. 5:3–17) indicate the basic attitudes of the disciple who receives the Reign of God in solidarity with others. Matthew's text can be divided into two parts.

1. The *first block* of Beatitudes closely resembles Luke's version. Luke, as we hear so frequently, speaks of materially poor persons. To whom is Matthew directing our attention, then, when he says "in spirit" in the first Beatitude? In the biblical mentality, spirit connotes dynamism. Spirit is breath, life force—something manifested through cognition, intelligence, virtue, or decision. Thus, "of spirit" transforms a reference to an economic and social situation into a disposition required in order to receive the word of God (cf. Zeph. 2:3). We are confronted with a central theme of the biblical message: the importance of *childlikeness*. We are being exhorted to live in full availability to the will of the Lord—to make that will our sustenance, as Jesus would have us do in the gospel of John. It is the attitude of those who know themselves to be the sons and daughters of God, and the sisters and brothers of the others. To be poor in spirit is to be a *disciple* of Christ.

The *second Beatitude* (the third, in some versions) is sometimes seen as implied in the first. Be this as it may, the fact is that the Hebrew words *'anaw* and *'ani* ("poor"), too, are translated by the Greek *praeis* (used later in this same block) meaning "lowly," or meek. Thus, we must be dealing with a nuance of the expression "poor in spirit." The meek, the lowly, are the unpretentious. They are open, affable, and hospitable. The quality is specifically a human one. (The Bible never ascribes "lowliness" to God. It does ascribe it to Jesus: cf. Matt. 11:28–29, where Jesus is "gentle and humble of heart"). To be meek is to be as the Teacher. To the meek is promised the earth, the land. The earth, the land, the soil is the first specification of the Reign of God in the Beatitudes, and in the Bible it carries the clear connotation of life.

In the *third Beatitude* Matthew uses a different verb from Luke's, but the meaning is similar: "sorrowing," *penthountes*. The word suggests the sorrow of mourning, catastrophe, or oppression (cf. 1 Macc. 1:25–27). Blessed, then, are those who refuse to resign themselves to injustice and oppression in the world. "They shall be consoled." The verb *parakalein*, "to console, to comfort," is an echo of Second Isaiah: "The Lord comforts his people and shows mercy to the afflicted" (Isa. 49:13). The consolation in question sounds a note of liberation. Luke presents us with a Jesus who fulfills the promise of the consolation of Israel (cf. Luke 2:25). Blessed are those who have known how to share the sorrow of others to the point of tears. For the Lord will console them: he will wipe away their tears, and "the reproach of his people he will remove from the whole earth" (Isa. 25:8; cf. Rev. 21:4).

In the *fourth Beatitude* a central theme for Matthew's gospel appears: the towering importance of *justice*. The use of the verbs "to hunger" and "to thirst" adds a note of special urgency and a religious overtone. The object of this burning desire is justice, or righteousness, as a gift of God and a human task; it determines a manner of conduct on the part of those who wish to be faithful to God. To be righteous or just means to acknowledge the rights of others, especially in the case of the defenseless; thereby it supposes a relationship with God that can appropriately be styled "holiness." The establishment of "justice and right" is the mission entrusted by the God of the Bible to the chosen people; it is the task in which God is revealed as the God of life. To hunger and thirst for justice is to hope for it from God, but it is likewise to will to put it in practice. This desire—similar to the "seeking of holiness" of Matthew 6:33—will be slaked, and its satisfaction will be an expression of the joy of the coming of the Reign of love and justice.

2. With the *fifth Beatitude*, the *second block* of Matthew's text begins. This block is constituted for the most part of Beatitudes proper to his gospel. The mercy of God is a favorite theme of Matthew. The parable he recounts in 18:23–35 is an illustration of the fifth Beatitude. The behavior required of the follower of Jesus is characterized by mercy. Matthew dovetails this outlook with that of the Hebrew scriptures when he cites Hosea 6:6: "It is love [i.e., mercy] that I desire, not sacrifice" (cf. Matt. 9:13, 12:7). These are basic attitudes, not formalities. It is practice, and not formality, upon which judgment will be rendered. The text of Matthew 25:31–46 speaks to us precisely of works of mercy. Those who refuse to practice solidarity with others will be rejected. Those who put mercy into practice are declared blessed; they shall receive God's love, which is always a gift. This grace, in turn, demands of them that they be merciful to others.

Who are the "single-hearted"? The common tendency to relegate the religious to the domain of interior attitudes and "recollection" can make the *sixth Beatitude* difficult to understand—or rather, too easy to misunderstand. Single-heartedness implies sincerity, wisdom, and determination. It is not a matter of ritual or appearances. It is a matter of profound personal attitude. This is the reason for Jesus' disputes with the Pharisees, which Matthew presents to us in such energetic terms. Every Christian runs the risk of being a hypocrite: professing one thing and doing another, separating theory from practice. The letter of James—who is like Matthew in so many ways—employs a particularly suggestive term. On two occasions, James rejects "devious" persons—literally, "double-souled" persons, *dipsychoi* (James 1:8, 4:8). The God of the Bible requires a total commitment: "No man can serve two masters. He will either hate one and love the other or be attentive to one and despise the other" (Matt. 6:24). To draw near to God means "cleansing the heart," unifying our lives, having a single soul. Being a disciple of the Lord means having the "same mind" as the Teacher. Thus, a person of pure heart, an integral person, will see God—and "face to face," as Paul says (1 Cor. 13:12). This promise is the cause of the joy of Jesus' followers.

The building of peace is a key task for the Christian. But in order to perceive the scope of this task, we must be rid of a narrow conception of peace as the absence of war or conflict. This is not the peace to which we are invited by the *seventh Beatitude*. The Hebrew word *shalom* is a familiar one and exceedingly rich in connotation. It indicates an overall, integral situation, a condition of life in harmony with God, neighbor, and nature. *Shalom* is the opposite of everything that runs contrary to the welfare and rights of persons and nations. It is not surprising, then, that there should be an intimate biblical link between justice and peace: "Justice and peace (*shalom*) shall kiss" (Ps. 85:10). The poor are denied both justice and *shalom*. This is why both are promised particularly to those deprived of life and well-being. Peace must be actively sought; the Beatitude is speaking of artisans of peace, not those who are commonly termed pacifists or peaceable individuals. Those who construct this peace, which implies harmony with God and with the divine will in history as well as an integrity of personal life (health) and social life (justice), "shall be called sons of God"—that is, will actually *be* children of God. Acceptance of the gift of filiation implies precisely the forging of community in history.

The *eighth Beatitude* joins two key terms: "reign," and "holiness," or justice. To have life and to establish justice (to hunger and to thirst for justice) is to call down upon one's head the wrath of the mighty. Of this the prophets, and Jesus' own life, are abundant testimonial. Those who have decided to be disciples cannot be above their Teacher (cf. Matt. 10:24). The fourth Lukan Beatitude had already enjoined this outlook on the disciple: "Blessed shall you be when men hate you, when they ostracize you and insult you and proscribe your name as evil because of the Son of Man" (Luke 6:22). A focus on discipleship is not directly present in the first three Lukan Beatitudes; Matthew, however, adopts it in all of his own. Furthermore, Matthew reinforces his statement concerning persecution "for holiness' sake" with a promise, in the following verse, of felicity for those who are abused "because of me." Matthew 5:11, then, comes very close to Luke 6:22, which speaks of persecution "because of the Son of Man," along with establishing an equivalency between justice and Jesus as the occasions of the hostility of which the blessed are the object. In this way, Matthew proclaims the surprising identity, which he will also maintain in chapter 25, between a deed of love in behalf of the poor and a deed done in behalf of the Son of Man come to judge the nations. To give one's life for justice is to give it for Christ himself.

To those who suffer for *justice*, or "holiness' sake," is promised the *Reign of God*. By repeating this term, "Reign of God," which he has already used in the first Beatitude, Matthew closes his text with an impact, through the use of the literary device known as inclusion. The promises of the six Beatitudes enclosed between the first and the last are but specifications of the promise with which the Beatitudes as a unit open and close: the promise of the Reign. The land, consolation, satiety, mercy, the vision of God, the divine filiation are but details of the life, love, and justice of the Reign of God.

These promises are gifts of the Lord. As the fruit of the free divine love, they call for a response in terms of a particular behavior. The Beatitudes of the third evangelist underscore the *gratuity of the love of God*, who "preferentially" loves the concrete poor. Those of Matthew flesh out this picture by indicating the *ethical requirement in order to be a follower of Jesus*, which flows from that loving initiative of God. It is a matter of accent. Both aspects are present in each of our two versions of the Beatitudes. And the focuses are complementary. The followers of Jesus are those who translate the grace received—which invests them as witnesses of the Reign of life—into works in behalf of their neighbor, especially the poor. The disciple is the one who strikes a solidarity—including "material" solidarity—with those for whom the Lord has a preferential love. Behold the sum and substance of the reason why a person is declared blessed and fit to "inherit the kingdom prepared for you from the creation of the world" (Matt. 25:34). Blessed are disciples—those who make the "preferential option for the poor." Gratuity and demand, investiture and dispatch to a mission, constitute the twin poles of the life of discipleship. Only a church in solidarity with the actual poor, a church that denounces poverty as an evil, is in any position to proclaim God's freely bestowed love—the gift that must be received in spiritual poverty (cf. Medellín "Document on Poverty," no. 4).

2. The Poor Evangelize

The "church of the poor" is a very ancient concept of church. It is as old as Paul, and Paul's description is matchless. To the church living in the splendid, wealthy city of Corinth, the Apostle writes:

> Brothers, you are among those called. Consider your situation. Not many of you are wise, as men account wisdom; not many are influential; and surely not many are well-born. God chose those whom the world considers absurd to shame the wise; he singled out the weak of this world to shame the strong. He chose the world's lowborn and despised, those who count for nothing, to reduce to nothing those who were something; so that mankind can do no boasting before God. (1 Cor. 1:26–29)

In order to perceive God's predilection for the poor, the Corinthians need only look among themselves in the Christian community. It is a question of historical experience. (2 Corinthians 8:2 will speak of the "deep poverty" of the communities of Macedonia.) But Paul's text does a theological reading of this experience and expresses a comprehension of the church from the true, most demanding focus: the viewpoint of God. The mercy of God and the divine will for life are revealed in this preference for what the world regards as foolish and weak: for the plebeian, for the condemned, for the "nonexistent." The gratuity of God's love is manifested in the confusion and humiliation of the wise, the strong, the "existing."

Thus, the church is a sign of the Reign of God. Luke gives us the content of the proclamation of the Reign in his presentation of the Messiah's program (Luke 4:18–19). The various human situations enunciated in the text (poverty, captivity, blindness, oppression) are set forth as expressions of death. With Jesus' proclamation, death will beat a retreat; Jesus injects into history a principle of life, and a principle that will lead history to its fulfillment. We find ourselves, then, before the disjunction, central to biblical revelation, between death and life. It is a disjunction that calls upon us to make a radical option.

The central fact of the Messiah's proclamation is that the proclamation itself is Good News for the poor. This Good News is then made concrete in the other actions it proclaims: liberating captives, restoring sight to the blind, and bringing freedom to the oppressed. In all of these actions freedom is the dominant notion—even in the case of sight for the blind, if we keep in mind the Hebrew text of Isaiah 61:1–2, which alludes to the deliverance of those chained in the darkness of prisons. Thus, the core of the Good News announced by the Messiah is liberation. The Reign of God, which is a Reign of life, is not only the ultimate meaning of human history. Its presence is already initiated in the attention bestowed by Jesus—and by his followers—on the poor and oppressed.

In response to the cry of the poor for liberation, Medellín proposes a church in solidarity with that aspiration for life, freedom, and grace. A beautiful, synthetic text tells us that the conference seeks to present "the face of an authentically *poor, missionary, and Paschal* church, without ties to any temporal power and boldly committed to the liberation of the whole human being and of all human beings" (Medellín, "Document on Youth," no. 15, emphasis added).

At Medellín, as in the pastoral practice and theological reflection that had preceded that conference, thereupon to be enshrined in its texts, the concept of a church of the poor has a frank christological focus. That is, there is more at stake here than a sensitivity to the vast majority of the people of our continent, the poor. The basic demand in our pastoral practice, in our theological reflection, and in the Conference of Medellín itself—the element that confers the deepest meaning on the entire matter—comes from faith in Christ. The "Document on Poverty" makes this altogether clear. There are many passages to this effect, of which we shall cite only one: "The poverty of countless people calls for justice, solidarity, witness, commitment, and extra effort to carry out fully the salvific mission entrusted to [the church] by Christ" (Medellín, "Document on Poverty," no. 7). Complete liberation in Christ, of which the church is a sacrament in history, constitutes the ultimate foundation of the church of the poor.

This christological option is inspired as well in another declaration, this time from Vatican II. In *Lumen Gentium* we read that the church "recognizes in the poor and suffering the image of its poor and patient founder . . . and seeks to serve Christ in them" (*LG*, no. 8). This identification of Christ with the poor (cf. Matt. 25:31–46) is a central theme in our reflection on the church of the poor. Puebla expresses it beautifully in one of its most important texts, speaking of the traits of Christ present in the "very concrete faces" of the poor (Puebla Final Document, nos. 31—39; here, no. 31).

In other words, in addressing the subject of the church of the poor, the Latin American church (in the magisterium, in pastoral practice, and in theology) adopts a "theo-logical" perspective. To speak of such a church is not only to accentuate the social aspects of its mission; it is to refer first and foremost to the very being of that church as a sign of the Reign of God. This is the heart and soul of John XXIII's intuition ("The church is, and wishes to be . . ."), which was developed in depth by Cardinal Lercaro in his interventions at the Council. It is important to underscore this. There is a tendency to view these matters only from the angle of "social problems" and to consider that the church has attended to the question of its poverty by setting up a secretariat for social affairs. The challenge goes deeper than that. What John XXIII had in mind was an in-depth church renewal.

The deep, demanding evangelical theme of the proclamation of the gospel to the poor was broached at Vatican II but did not become its central question, as Cardinal Lercaro had requested at the close of the first session. At Medellín, however, it did become the main question; it was the context of the preferential option for the poor that inspired the major texts of the conference. We have recalled the biblical bases of the proclamation of the gospel to the poor. What we wish to do here is emphasize that this outlook has marked the life of the Latin American church throughout all these years. A great many experiments and commitments have made of this notion—a proclamation of the gospel to the disinherited—their central intuition and have sought to make it a reality. It is by embarking on this course that the church has found its deeper inspiration in its efforts for the liberation of the poor and oppressed of our continent.

All of this has made for a very profound renewal of the activity of the church. The missionary requirement is always to break out of one's own narrow circle and enter a different world. This is what large sectors of the Latin American church have experienced as they have set out along the pathways of an evangelization of the despoiled and insignificant. They have begun to discover the world of the poor, and to encounter the difficulties and misunderstandings that their option provokes on the part of the great ones of this world.

At the same time, years of commitment to a "defense of the rights of the poor, according to the gospel mandate" (cf. Medellín, "Document on Peace," no. 22) and the creation of Christian base communities as the "prime, fundamental, basic nucleus of the church, which should make itself responsible for the wealth and expansion of the faith" (Medellín, "Document on Joint Pastoral Ministry," no. 10) have opened up new perspectives. These experiments with church "have helped the Church to discover the evangelizing potential of the poor" (Medellín, "Document on Poverty," no. 1147). This is one of Puebla's basic declarations. It has its roots in the experience of the church in Latin America. It also demonstrates Puebla's continuity with Medellín.

Not only are the poor the privileged addressees of the message of the Reign of God; they are its vessels, as well. One expression of this potential is to be seen in the base ecclesial communities, which are surely among the most promising phenomena of the church of Latin America today. These communities sail in the broad channel opened up by the Council when the latter spoke of the people of God in the world of poverty. They constitute an ecclesial presence of history's insignificant ones—or, to use the words of the Council, of a "Messianic people" (*LG*, no. 9). That is to say, here is a people who walk the roads of history in the hope of the Reign that ever realizes the Messianic paradox: "The last shall be first."

The option for the poor, with all of the pastoral and theological consequences of that option, is one of the most important contributions to the life of the church universal to have emerged from the theology of liberation and the church on our continent. As we have observed, that option has its roots in biblical revelation and the history of the church. Still, today it presents particular, novel characteristics. This is due to our better understanding of the depth and complexity of the poverty and oppression experienced by most of humanity; it is due to our perception of the economic, social, and cultural mechanisms that produce that poverty; and before all else, it is due to the new light which the word of the Lord sheds on that poverty. This outlook thereby becomes the core of the "new evangelization," which got under way in Latin America two decades ago, but which it is so important to keep fresh and up to date. The novelty we cite was acknowledged, in a certain way, by the synod held on the occasion of the twentieth anniversary of the close of Vatican II. Among the synod's conclusions: "Since the Second Vatican Council, the Church has become more aware of its mission to serve the poor, the oppressed, and the outcast."

This service is a perilous one today, in the lands we live in. The vested interests at stake are powerful, and many are the victims of imprisonment, abuse, slander, exile, and death who have met their fate as a result of a wish to enter into solidarity with the poor. This is the reality of martyrdom, a reality at once tragic and fruitful. And it is a fact of life in a church that is learning day by day that it cannot be greater than its Master.

—Translated by Robert R. Barr

3

Central Position of the Reign of God in Liberation Theology

JON SOBRINO

I. LIBERATION THEOLOGY AS A THEOLOGY OF THE REIGN OF GOD

All authentic theological renewal is the fruit of an attempt to answer the question: What is "ultimate" in Christian faith? The question implies that Christian faith is made up of divers elements that can be organized and arranged in a hierarchy. That the truths of faith are hierarchically ordered became obvious at Vatican II, but their actual organization and ordering in respect to an ultimate principle is the task of theology. It is up to theology to seek out that ultimate element that will give the best account of the totality of the faith, and the element selected will determine the character of the theology that selects it.

In our opinion, this is what has been occurring in theology for a century now, with the rediscovery that Jesus' message was eschatological. Those who made the discovery proposed a concrete content for this eschatological message: the Reign of God. But the importance of the discovery went far beyond a determination of content. For theology, it meant the end of a mere theological, dogmatic, or biblical positivism and the inauguration of the eschatological theologies—those theologies that attempted to name the ultimate element in faith and to develop from there. Unfortunately, these theologies fell into the error of identifying eschatology with the Four Last Things. Actually, to name the ultimate means to determine an *eschaton* from the specificity of the faith and the *primacy of reality*. The *eschaton* might be the proclamation or kerygma of Jesus Christ crucified and raised again (Bultmann), the communication to history of the mystery of the Holy (Rahner), the Omega Point (Teilhard de Chardin), or the universal resurrection (Pannenberg). Correlatively, then, a metaphysical and anthropological primacy would be accorded respectively to existence and decision, the future, promise and hope, evolution, unconditional openness to mystery, and so on.

1. Liberation Theology's Answer to the Question of the Eschaton

The theology of liberation is formally and organically integrated into this method and concept of theology. It names an ultimate, which then functions as an organizing and ordering principal for everything else. That to which this theology assigns the primacy is indicated in its very name: liberation, which is understood essentially as liberation of the poor. In this sense, liberation theology is also an eschatological theology, since it assigns liberation more than a mere place (however important a place) in the content of theology; it assigns it an ultimate and ordering content. Thus, it is neither a regional theology (a part of theology, or of a particular theology—the part bearing upon liberation). Still less is it a reductionistic theology (a theology whose sole object would be liberation). In assigning a primacy to the liberation of the poor, the theology of liberation is positing the liberation of the poor as that part of the content of theology around which all of theology can be organized—all questions of who God and Christ are, what grace and sin are, what the church and society are, what love and hope are, and so on. We call the theology of liberation eschatological not because by adding the adjective "integral" to the noun "liberation" we can quantitatively augment the content of liberation so that it will extend to the whole of theology, but rather because from the *viewpoint* of the liberation of the poor we deem it possible—indeed, in Latin America it is appropriate and necessary—to impose a qualitative, ordered organization on the entire content of theology.

The analyses conducted in the present chapter constitute an attempt to answer the question, What faith reality, what *eschaton*, most adequately corresponds to a theology that assigns historical primacy to the liberation of the poor? In other words, how might one formulate the ultimate in such a way as to do justice to both the revelation of God and the concrete, historical liberation of the poor? In the choice of this *eschaton* for theology—obviously there is no question of selecting it for faith—two possibilities stand out, of which much account is taken by creative theologies today and which, in principle, would also be capable of incorporating the essential liberative interest of the theology of liberation. Those two possibilities are the resurrection of Christ (understood as the initiation of the "universal" resurrection) and the Reign of God. Both realities are eschatological, in a biblical understanding as in a systematic one, and both intrinsically express liberation. Thus, they are both used in various modern theologies, although some of these incline toward the one, and some toward the other.

To recall some important examples: Bultmann inclines exclusively toward the resurrection—or more precisely, toward the preaching of the kerygma of Jesus Christ crucified and raised again, as the genuine eschatological event, with the triple connotation that, with Christ, judgment, salvation, and the presence of the ultimate have become historical. The Reign of God is not regarded, any more than anything else about the historical Jesus, as belonging to the presuppositions or the theology of the New Testament. Pannenberg places more eschatological value on the Reign of God, since the proclamation of its coming—imminent, but not realized—furnishes the possibility and the demand that one live in history in radical openness, and that thus the ultimate be realized. The definitive eschatological event, however, even for theology, is the resurrection of Jesus, since it is there that, however provisionally, the object of the openness of the human being and the revelation of God has been fulfilled. The younger Moltmann was more favorable to the resurrection and its correlative hope, but he has gradually come to formulate the *eschaton* in terms of the historical, as well, that is, in terms of the poor and their liberation, and thus, in terms of the Reign of God.

We recall these various positions on the selection of a theological *eschaton* only for the purpose of erecting a framework for a better understanding of liberation theology's solution to the same problem. For liberation theology, the ultimate is the Reign of God. This does not mean, of course, that it ignores the resurrection, or that it does not see the clearly eschatological dimension of the resurrection. It is only that, for purposes of a theology that assigns primacy to the liberation of the poor, it sees the *eschaton* better expressed in terms of the Reign of God.

This primacy of the Reign of God is deduced not from this or that explicit assertion in the Christian scriptures (although there are such assertions), but from liberation theology's concrete task—from that in which it shows more interest and which it analyzes more in detail, from that which more frequently stands in a relationship with the object of this theology's priorities: the liberation of the poor. In the very beginning, in Gustavo Gutiérrez's classic *A Theology of Liberation*, the eschatological focus of theology underwent a frank recasting, but at the service of the key problem of that book: historical liberation and salvation. The work concludes that the Reign of God is the most adequate reality for expressing liberation, although for the moment the Reign is treated not from the biblical standpoint, but from that of the ecclesiastical magisterium.[1] From the publication of *A Theology of Liberation* onward, it has been impossible to deny that the christologies[2] and ecclesiologies[3] of the theology of liberation have attributed great importance to the Reign of God and have made of it their central and ultimate element, or at least more central and ultimate an element than others. Ignacio Ellacuría has made the central character of the Reign of God in the theology of liberation explicit, stating that the latter "is the very object of Christian dogmatic, moral, and pastoral theology: the greatest possible realization of the Reign of God in history is what the authentic followers of Jesus are to pursue."[4]

2. Primacy of the Reign of God

The fact is clear, then. The theology of liberation prefers the Reign of God as the *eschaton*. But it is very important to understand why. There are various reasons. Let us attempt to summarize the most important of them.

1. In its very enterprise, liberation theology has a particular leaning that it cannot deny, whatever the advantages and disadvantages of that leaning or attitude. In this it is not altogether unlike other theologies, but it does emphasize certain dimensions of the theological undertaking that are more specific to itself than to other theologies.

Liberation theology is clearly an *historical* theology. It seeks to locate historically, to verify in history, the entire content of the faith, including strictly transcendent content. Its very name is no more than the historicization of the core of Christian faith: salvation. Liberation theology is the theology of salvation as liberation. Liberation theology is also a *prophetical* theology, which takes account of sin—and historical sin—as central to its concern, something that must be exposed and denounced. It is a *praxic* theology, which understands itself as an ideological moment of an ecclesial, historical praxis. That is, it is interested before all else in transforming reality, although it defends its *theological status* and believes itself to be a theology that can help in the transformation of history. Finally, it is a *popular* theology—although there are various understandings of this concept—a theology that sees in the people, in the twin connotation of "people" as poverty and as collectivity, the addressee, and in some theologians, however analogically, the very subject of theology.

This being the case, it is scarcely surprising that liberation theology spontaneously finds in the Reign of God a more suitable reality than others for the development of its particular tendency and the guidance of its particular endeavor. Let us see, then—since the question cannot be avoided—why liberation theology does not make of the other great symbol of the *eschaton*, the resurrection, the center and focus of its organization of the whole of theology.

Jesus' resurrection, understood as the firstfruits of the universal resurrection, would surely be an apt candidate for the function of the ultimate symbol. It is absolute fulfillment and salvation, and thereby absolute liberation—liberation from death. It is the object and pledge of a radical hope, a death-transcending, death-defeating hope; it is the ultimacy and universality of the revelation of God. The resurrection can also be interpreted—and not necessarily arbitrarily, but with a basis in the biblical texts—in such a way as to recapitulate and illuminate elements that will be of great interest for the theology of liberation. Thus, we can say that the resurrection of Christ is not only a revelation of the power of God over nothingness, but the triumph of justice; that the resurrection offers not a universal hope, but a "partial," partisan hope—although one that can thereupon be universalized—for the victims of this world, the crucified (like Jesus) of history; that the resurrection can fire an absolutely radical hope for history, since if God is shown to have the power of deliverance from death, God will have all the more power to deliver from oppression; that the resurrection is a symbol not only of personal, individual hope, but of a collective hope, as well, since Jesus' resurrection is presented in its most intimate and direct meaning as the resurrection of the firstborn One, to be followed—as demanded by the internal logic of the very concept—by the resurrection of many others; that (unlike other expressions of the hope of survival, as for example in Greek thought) the resurrection implies and communicates the due importance of the corporeal and the material, since it is the whole human being who is raised, and raised to complete fulfillment; even that the resurrection can be lived in history itself, by causing its specific power to be felt in a particular manner of living the following of Jesus in joy and freedom—two realities that reflect in limited history the fullness of the resurrection.

All of this is developed in various theologies and is valued by the theology of liberation.[5] Still, it is evident that, in order for the resurrection to function as the ultimate for a theology with the disposition and attitude that we have described, an immense effort of interpretation will be necessary. To put it another way, the resurrection can be interpreted in such a way that it will function as the ultimate for liberation theology; but this interpretation has less obvious underpinnings in a first glance at a presentation of historical reality. With all its power to express the ultimate meaning of history, with all of its radical hope, the resurrection does not have the same capacity to show how one should live in history. It has great power to show us the final utopia, but it has less to show us how we are to live here and now, to show us which pathways to walk in our journey toward that utopia.

Furthermore, like any other symbol of plenitude that might be selected, including that of the Reign of God, the resurrection—not in its concept, since that can be corrected, but for real life—comports a particular danger. These words should not dismay us, since everything we human beings touch, however good and holy it may be—prayer, the struggle for justice, or what have you—is a potential victim of our limitations and concupiscence. It cannot be denied that, as history constantly teaches us, the resurrection can and does feed an individualism without a people, a hope without a praxis, an enthusiasm without a following of Jesus—in sum, a transcendence without history. From the enthusiasm of the community at Corinth to that of Catholics, Protestants, and sectarians today, history demonstrates this abundantly. Liberation theology is especially sensitive to this danger in virtue of its attitude and inclination, as described.

All that we have said concerning the resurrection must be correctly understood. We are not denying, of course, that the resurrection of Christ, the firstfruits of the universal resurrection, is a reality, and a central reality, for faith and theology. It is not that liberation theology fails to ascribe to the resurrection its due importance; it is duly treated in our christologies and is kept in account in our formulation of the Christian utopia. We are not ignorant of the fact that in the resurrection certain aspects of our faith are better and more radically expressed than elsewhere, even better than in the Reign of God: the radical character of our utopia, the definitive manifestation of God, ultimate gratuity. We do not deny that the resurrection can function as an antidote for a purely doloristic, resigned conception of the cross, that tendency of traditional popular piety; nor, on the other hand, do we deny its utility for purposes of a criticism of utopias that fail in a consistent radicality.[6] We only wish to say that for liberation theology the resurrection is not regarded as being as suitable as the Reign of God for organizing and ordering the entire content of faith. We take great account of the resurrection, but we situate it within something more comprehensive: the Reign of God.

2. Besides corresponding better to liberation theology's posture and scope, the Reign of God evinces a greater potential for systematically organizing the whole of theology, as theology ought to be practiced in a reality like that of the Third World. Ignacio Ellacuría, who places a great deal of emphasis on the Reign of God as the object of theology, exemplifies this. While the passage we are about to cite is a lengthy one, it will spare us an extensive commentary.

> What this conception of faith from a point of departure in the Reign of God does is posit an indissoluble conjunction between God and history. . . . The Reign of God is immune to a whole series of perilous distortions. It is impervious to a dualism of (earthly) Reign and (heavenly) God, such that those who cultivate the world and history would be doing something merely positivistic, while those who devote themselves to God would be doing something transcendent, spiritual, and supernatural. It rejects an identification of the Reign of God with the church, especially with the institutional church, which would imply both an escape from the world into the church,

> and an impoverishment of the Christian message and mission that would culminate in a worldly church—a secularization of the church by way of a conformation of its institutional aspect to secularistic values of domination and wealth, and by subordinating to it something greater than it by far, the Reign of God. It rejects a manipulation of God, a taking of the name of God in vain in support of injustice, by insisting that that name and reality are properly invoked in the historical signs of justice, fraternity, freedom, a preferential option for the poor, love, mercy, and so on, and that without these it is vain to speak of a salvific presence of God in history.
>
> The Reign of God in history as a Reign of God among human beings exposes the historical wickedness of the world, and thereby the reign of sin, that negation of the Reign of God. Over and above a certain natural sin (original sin) and a personal sin (individual sin), the proclamation of the Reign and the difficulty of seeing it implanted evinces the presence of a "sin of the world," which is fundamentally historical and structural, communitarian and objective, at once the fruit and the cause of many other personal and collective sins, and its propagation and consolidation as the ongoing negation of the Reign of God. Not that structures commit sin, as liberation theologians are sometimes accused of saying; but structures manifest and actualize the power of sin, thereby causing sin, by making it exceedingly difficult for men and women to lead the life that is rightfully theirs as the daughters and sons of God.
>
> This sinful power is utterly real. It is intrinsically sin, and the fruit of sin, and here we may recall the traditional explanations of original sin; but further, it causes sin by presenting obstacles to the dynamism of the Reign of God among human beings, to the presence of the lifegiving Spirit amidst the principalities and powers of death. Thus, without being deprived of its essential immanence, the evil of the world acquires a transcendent dimension. . . . The destruction of human life, or its impoverishment, is anything but a purely moral problem: it is also, absolutely and unqualifiedly, a theological problem—the problem of sin in action, and the problem of life denied in human existence.[7]

We see very clearly, in this lengthy citation, that the primacy accorded to the Reign of God resides in the capacity of the latter to unify, without either separation or confusion, transcendence and history. It is from this point of departure that essential content such as Christ and the church can and ought to be understood, without hint of idealistic abstractions or spurious substitutions of what the Reign of God is not. Furthermore, although this terminology is not used in our citation, it is the Reign of God that enables us to rediscover the anti-Reign, the world of sin, that is—both historical and transcendent. Reality's ultimate duality, its irreconcilable duality, is properly identified not in the binomial "transcendence and history"—which can and should be reconciled—but in the irreconcilable binomial of Reign and anti-Reign, the history of grace and of sin.

Thus understood in its radical character, the Reign of God furnishes the theology of liberation with two things it cannot renounce. The first is a totality—needed if liberation theology is to be simply *theology*. The second is a particular historicization of that totality—needed in order for liberation theology to be a theology of *liberation.* The various tensions that crop up in any theology seeking to keep faith with the totality of its message are seen to have their place in the reality of the Reign of God, but in the theology of liberation these tensions are resolved in such a way as to maintain and even enhance the primary specificity of the theology of liberation. The Reign of God comports transcendence and history, salvation and liberation, hope and practice, the individual and the communitarian-and-popular. The elements appearing in the latter member of each of these tensions are more specific—in virtue of their novelty, not because they militate against a recognition of the importance of the former element in each case—to the theology of liberation. Thus, the Reign of God supplies the necessary conditions for taking the more novel aspects of liberation theology seriously and developing them within the totality of the faith. Thereby both the specificity of the theology of liberation and its Christian identity are maintained. A view of liberation in terms of the Reign of God does justice to liberation theology's original intuition and frames that theology within a totality that cannot but incline it to liberation in its plenitude—"integral liberation," as an orthodox, if not very expressive, language would have it—without which the original intuition would be deprived of its radicality.

3. One of the reasons for the primacy of the Reign of God in the theology of liberation is the thrust and intent of that theology to systematization. But there is an even more basic reason. Theology is always a second act, within and in the presence of a reality, and liberation theology lays explicit emphasis on this point. But it is the reality of Latin America and of the Third World in general that calls for a Reign of God, of whatever conceptual formulation. The major fact in Latin America is the massive, unjust poverty that threatens whole populations with death. At the same time, the most novel fact is the hope of a just life, of liberation. It is this twin reality that calls for reflection and a primary reaction—logically antecedent to any theological reflection and even any specific, determinate faith. It is reality itself that demands to be seen as a reality of life or death, that poses the question of hope or despair, that calls for an option for life or death. A grasp of the primary reality as being unjust poverty and the hope of a just life, requiring one to throw in one's lot with the alternative of life, can then be reformulated in theological reflection as the preunderstanding necessary for an adequate understanding of revelation, and theologized as a sign of the times and a manifestation of the will of God. All of this is true, and liberation theology includes all of it. But in itself this grasp is of something more primordial: it is the grasp of a reality that raises its own, autonomous cry.

After all, when theology sees Latin America's reality in this first, pre-theological moment, it finds, without falling into naiveté or anachronisms, a social situation remarkably akin to that in which the notion of the Reign of God was first formulated, biblically in so many words, or extrabiblically in other terms. It is true today, as well, that entire peoples are unjustly oppressed and that they have a hope of life. It is true today, as well, that this is the most important fact for a grasp of the totality, as well as the various ethical, praxic, and semantic dimensions that emerge from that totality. If this is the case, and if this is historically akin to the reality in which the formulation of utopia in terms of the Reign of God was originally crystallized, then it is fairly obvious why a theologization of third-world reality might be undertaken in terms of theology of the Reign of God. It is current historical reality that ultimately renders the concept of the Reign of God more useful today than other concepts for a theological elaboration of reality. It is the kinship between both realities, that of the Third World today and that of the peoples who forged the notion of the Reign of God, that makes it possible to have a better understanding of what the Reign of God meant when it was first conceived. The fusion of horizons required by hermeneutics is accomplished first and foremost in reality itself.

What has occurred then in liberation theology is that, in a pre-theological moment, reality has been grasped as an irruption of the poor with a hope of liberation. This grasp comports a prejudgment, if you will, but therein is the origin of the theology of liberation. When that theology is formally constituted a theology in terms of the primacy of the poor, or more precisely, of the liberation of the poor, then a course is set similar to that theologized so many centuries ago in the Hebrew scriptures and with Jesus: the Reign of God. It is the historical situation that ultimately forces this election. Elsewhere, where theology has been unable to discover the irruption of the poor—either because the latter has been less perceptible or because of a lack of interest in discovering it—the course taken has been in the direction not of the Reign of God, but of the resurrection. In Latin America, however, as in the Third World generally, the current, historical situation continues to force theology to strike a course toward the Reign of God. An ultimate hope in a universal resurrection can be maintained, but the more urgent cry is for the coming of the Reign of God as such. And this—above and beyond the urgency of calling attention to the theoretical and practical disregard that seems to prevail in the church—is the reason and finality of our return to this theme in this chapter. The Third World continues to stand in urgent need of liberation, and the best theological way to deal with liberation continues to be to do so in terms of the Reign of God.

II. DETERMINATION OF THE REIGN OF GOD IN THE GOSPEL

The fact that the Reign of God is central to the theology of liberation says nothing as yet about the quality and character of that Reign. Such a determination for the present time, which we shall attempt in part III, is no easy matter. But neither is an evangelical determination of the nature of the Reign of God, and this for an obvious reason: while using the expression countless times, and eager as he is to explain it in his parables, Jesus never says exactly *what* this Reign is. "Jesus nowhere tells us in so many words *what* the Reign of God is. He only says that it is near," Walter Kasper rightly says.[8]

This is not to suggest that nothing can be known of what the Reign of God meant for Jesus. What it does suggest is the need for a method, or to speak more modestly, a way of ascertaining this. To our view, the approaches used by systematic christologies are three. They might be called: (1) the notional way, (2) the way of the practice of Jesus, and (3) the way of the addressee of the Reign. These ways or paths are not mutually exclusive, but complementary. Still, depending on which is used or most emphasized, theologians' conclusions will vary. Liberation theology's contribution to a determination of the Reign of God consists not so much in exegetical discoveries, but in an insistence on the limitations and dangers of taking only the first way, and in its emphasis on the need for the second way, and especially the third. Liberation theology shows this in its own procedure when it analyzes Jesus' proclamation of the Reign of God. What we shall do in the following paragraphs is analyze each of the three ways separately, calling attention to those aspects on which the theology of liberation especially insists. The most specific contribution of our theology, then, is in its method for arriving at a determination of what the Reign of God is.

1. The Notional Way

The notional way attempts to ascertain what the Reign of God was for Jesus from a starting point in the notion Jesus himself might have had of it. This way analyzes the various notions of the Reign in the Hebrew scriptures and among Jesus' contemporaries (John the Baptist, the Zealots, the Pharisees, the apocalyptic groups, and so on). So, the researcher attempts to ferret out what Jesus thought about the Reign. The substance of these investigations—expressed in formal terms—is usually the following. Jesus proclaimed a utopia, something good and salvific, that was at hand.

All of this is true, of course, and liberation theology embraces it. Leonardo Boff, for example, has a beautiful statement: In proclaiming the coming of the Reign, "Jesus makes a radical statement about human existence, its principle of hope and its utopian dimension. He promises that it will no longer be *utopia*—the object of anxious expectancy (cf. Luke 3:14)—but *topia*, the object of happiness for all the people (cf. Luke 2:9)."[9] The problem is how this notion of the Reign of God can become rather more concrete; it is here that we note the importance, or unimportance, attributed to the other two "ways." When the latter are not actively present in the investigation—we say "actively" because they are always present in some way—the notion of the Reign tends to abide in supreme vagueness and abstraction. This does not militate against the fact that what is said of the Reign is something true, good, and holy—something, so to speak, with which Jesus himself would agree. But the vagueness and abstraction are of no help to anyone desirous of learning what, in the concrete, the Reign was for Jesus. Indeed, they can be dangerous if they relegate to a secondary level, or even simply ignore, important things that Jesus meant by the Reign of God. Let us look at a pair of examples.

In his christology[10] Kasper analyzes the Reign of God as Jesus' central message, and its eschatological and theological character. But when he wishes to tell us *what*, when all is said and done, this Reign is, he merely pauses very briefly to say a word about its addressee according to the gospels and in some of Jesus' deeds, concluding—formally—that the Reign of God is salvation. Naturally, we expect to find something concrete as to what salvation is. Kasper responds to our expectations with the following:

> We can summarize as follows: The salvation of the Reign of God means the coming to power in and through human beings of self-communicating love of God. Love reveals itself as the meaning of life. The world and the human being find fulfilment only in love. (p. 86)

Here the answer to the question of what the Reign is, is systematic, of course. But one supposes that it is intended as a conclusion from the analysis of the gospels just made. This, then, is the objective reality of the Reign: love. In that case, what the proclamation of its imminence adds is the following:

> Everyone can now know that love is the ultimate, that it is stronger than death, stronger than hatred and injustice. The news of the coming of the Reign of God is therefore a promise about everything that is done in the world out of love. It says that, against what is done for love will endure forever; that it is the only thing which lasts forever. (Ibid., p. 87)

Love, hope, and promise—these are supremely important, central realities in the gospels and throughout the Christian scriptures. They are also things that have to do with the Reign of God preached by Jesus. It is disconcerting and disappointing that they are presented—in this degree of abstraction—as the result of an investigation into the Reign of God and its proximity in the gospels. What the Reign of God is said to be here could as well have been said of Jesus' resurrection, or the First Letter of John, or the hymn to charity in 1 Corinthians 13, or the hymn of hope in Romans 8:31–39. Not that it is false in itself, but how does it explain the concrete content of the Reign of God as preached by Jesus? Instead, one has the impression that it hides something very important about this Reign. Thus, the Reign of God loses not only concreteness, but centrality; it becomes practically interchangeable with other New Testament realities.

Our second example is from Pannenberg's christology.[11] This author emphasizes the importance of the Reign of God preached by Jesus. Its imminence is salvation, as implied in the title Father, by which Jesus addresses the God who now draws near. This calls for, and makes possible, a life lived in love. But if we ask what the salvation of the Reign is and how the proximity of the Reign can be salvation, Pannenberg replies with the following solution. In itself, it seems to us, the solution is an altogether original one—indeed, a stroke of genius—but when all is said and done, not very enlightening. In Jesus' proclamation of the imminent coming of the Reign, human beings see themselves obliged to "emerge from their everyday securities," to "transcend any currently real or possible fulfillment of existence or security." Inasmuch as the God who comes is still in the future, the proclamation of God's coming calls for, and makes possible, an "openness to God's existence." In a word, faced with the imminence of the Reign of God, human beings discover themselves for what they truly are—beings essentially and radically open to God. But it is precisely this unconditional openness which makes possible, indeed demands, the proclamation of the coming of the Reign, which is the human being's salvation.

> Because salvation, the fulfilled destiny of man, consists in the fulfillment of openness for God, it is already present for those who long for the nearness of God proclaimed by Jesus. (p. 228)

Pannenberg's argument here is formal. On the basis of his own anthropology,[12] there can be salvation in the fact that the Reign, near but not realized, demands and makes possible the human being's radical openness in the form of a life rooted in trust: "Expressed in a more modern way, Jesus brings man into the radical openness that constitutes the specific fundamental element of human nature" (p. 231).

But this formal argumentation is asserted to be required and justified by Jesus' activity. "The healing he performed demonstrated concretely that where the message of God's nearness is grasped completely and in full trust, salvation itself is already effective" (pp. 228–29).

The Reign of God is salvation, then, because, in its approach, without ever arriving in fullness, it enables us to live as genuine human beings. Pannenberg concludes that once human beings have arrived at their proper essence, they come under the obligation of acting in the manner of the divinity itself, the way that God acts: in love (pp. 232–33).

Pannenberg's solution takes account of hope, love, and salvation. More than this, it is an electrifying interpretation of Cullmann's classic "already, but not yet." But once more, the notion of the Reign of God remains general; it is universalized, and ignores extremely important elements of the Reign of God.

These two examples demonstrate the use of what we have termed the notional way of approaching the question of the content ascribed by Jesus to the Reign of God—practically in isolation from the other two "ways." As we see, there are serious limitations and dangers involved in such a procedure. The theologian attempts to fit the Reign of God into a basically preconceived notion of what, in the mind of this theologian, the Reign of God ought to be. This danger is always in part inevitable and cannot be entirely overcome. But the necessary means of making the concept of the Reign of God concrete, and thereby of avoiding its precipitous universalization simply in terms of the investigator's own interest, are available in the application of the other two ways that we have listed above.

2. *The Way of the Praxis of Jesus*

The premise of the way of the praxis of Jesus is that what Jesus did will shed light on what the Reign of God is. This is Schillebeeckx's position. "The concrete content of the Kingdom arises from [Jesus'] ministry and activity considered as a whole."[13] This methodological option is clearly justified in the case of those actions which Jesus himself referred to the Reign of God, whether explicitly (as with the expulsion of demons, or preaching in parables) or implicitly (for example, in his meals). But the option is reasonable for the rest of Jesus' activity, as well—certainly for the first great part of his public life, since in that period the proclamation of the Reign was precisely the central element in his work.

In order to clarify the importance of this point, the first thing we must emphasize is the very fact of Jesus' practice, which, in strict logic, needn't have existed at all. Let us ask the following logical, hypothetical questions. If Jesus thought that the Reign of God was imminent and gratuitous, then why might he not have restricted himself to its proclamation? Why not await that coming in passivity and confidence? Why not accept the situation of his world, if it was soon to change? These purely logical questions have only a historical response. Jesus *did* many things. In pure logic, once more, one could ask whether he did them because the

Reign was already present, or in order that it might become present. Were Jesus' deeds purely sacramental, the expression of a Reign that drew near in all gratuity, or were they also service to the Reign, deeds performed in order that it might draw near? Whatever the answer to these questions, the important thing is to emphasize that Jesus did many things; he did not passively await the coming of the Reign (or ask this attitude of his hearers). Not even for the short period of hope in the imminence of the end could Jesus tolerate the situation of his world, as Cullmann says.[14]

Jesus' activity in the service of the Reign is understandable, since even in Isaiah (and in Luke's conception) the proclamation of the Good News, the content of the Reign, is essentially accompanied by activity: "This news will only be *good* to the extent that the liberation of the oppressed becomes reality."[15] But such an a priori approach is not the only way to understand Jesus' activity. Besides the programmatic summary of the proclamation of the Reign in Luke, we have other, earlier summaries of Jesus' activity: Jesus "went into their synagogues preaching the Good News and expelling demons throughout the whole of Galilee" (Mark 1:39). Jesus healed many persons, suffering from various illnesses, and drove out many demons (Mark 1:34 and par.). In the summary that we find in Acts 10:38, Jesus "went about doing good works and healing all who were in the grip of the devil."

The fact of Jesus' activity is clear. To place it in relationship with the Reign of God is often exegetically justifiable and is systematically reasonable. The important thing, then, is to see what his activity contributes to a determination of the nature of the Reign by making concrete the vagueness of the formulation of the latter. Let us briefly analyze three stages in Jesus' activity, while stating from the outset that it is only for methodological reasons that we separate this second way, the way of Jesus' praxis, from the third, the way of the addressee.

1. Jesus' Miracles

Jesus performed a series of activities that he understood as signs of the Reign. As signs, they are not the totality of the Reign. But if they render it present, then surely they must tell us something about it. Among the signs of the Reign are Jesus' miracles, his expulsion of demons, and his welcoming of sinners. His meals are signs of the celebration of the Reign. We will concentrate on the miracles.

Taken formally, the miracles are signs that the Reign of God is approaching "with power." They have been called "cries of the Kingdom." Thus, they are not the Reign in its totality, nor do they offer a comprehensive solution for the evils for which the Reign will provide the remedy. As signs of the Reign, the miracles are before all else salvation—beneficent realities, liberative realities in the presence of oppression. Hence, the miracles occasion joy by their beneficent aspect and generate hope by their liberative aspect.

How do the miracles help us understand the Reign of God if they are only signs? Basically, in affirming that the Reign of God is salvation, they make two important qualifications. The first is that salvation is concrete, and also plural. In the miracles we see that God fulfills real, immediate needs, without prejudice to what other needs the Reign will satisfy. This is important, because after the resurrection—as with other elements of the historical Jesus, his miracles are not mentioned a great deal in the Testament apart from the gospels—salvation becomes a technical, comprehensive term, and is used in the singular: Christ brings salvation. But in the Synoptics, salvation is presented in the plural. There is no such thing as salvation—only salvations, only the defeat of concrete evils. "To save, then, is to heal, to exorcize, to forgive, by way of actions that affect the body and one's life."[16] Thus it was that, precisely by reason of their concreteness, their "littleness" in comparison with the grandeur of expectations of the coming of the Reign, the miracles were not understood by all. They were not understood by the apocalyptic groups, who awaited portentous prodigies as signs of the coming of the Reign. But they were understood by those who needed salvations in their daily life. Schillebeeckx says it beautifully:

> In the miracle, we are confronted with a memory of Jesus of Nazareth as he came across more especially to the ordinary country folk of Galilee, neglected as they were by all religious movements and sectional interests.[17]

The second qualification that the miracles bring to the concept of the Reign of God as salvation is that they are not only salvation, they are liberation, and this in the strict sense. The concrete needs from which they deliver their recipients are the product of some kind of oppression. Illnesses—and this appears far more radically in the case of the demonic possessions—were understood as a product of the oppressive power of the Evil One, consistent with the demonological conceptions that permeated the mentality of the age. "An intense terror of demons reigned," says Joachim Jeremias.[18] In the case of Jesus' welcome of sinners, it was a matter not merely of benevolently accepting their company, but of receiving those whom religious society rejected, those oppressed by the prevailing piety. Jesus' miracles, and his signs generally, occur not merely in the form of the satisfaction of needs, such as could occur in a neutral context; Jesus satisfies the needs of people caught in a situation of oppression, in a situation of the anti-Reign. Therefore they are not signs of salvation alone, but of liberation, as well. They are not only salvations from concrete needs, they are concrete liberations from oppressions.

Jesus' miracles (and acceptance of sinners) also explain something very important that will become more explicit when we speak of the addressee. They explain the reason why the Reign is drawing near, and this will tell us something about what the Reign is. The basic reason for which Jesus is described as working miracles is mercy; he felt compassion for the weak and oppressed. We hear this repeatedly. "When . . . he saw the vast throng, his heart was moved with pity, and he cured their sick" (Matt. 14:14). We read that he felt compassion for a leper (Mark 1:41), for two blind persons (Matt. 20:34), for persons who had nothing to eat (Mark 8:2, Matt. 15:32), for those who were as sheep without a shepherd (Mark 6:34, Matt. 9:36), for a widow who had just lost her son (Luke 7:13). It is this mercy that also appears in the miracle accounts. On at least four occasions Jesus performs a cure upon hearing, "Have pity on me/us!" (Matt. 20:29–34 and par., 15:21–28 and par., 17:14–29; Luke 17:11–19).

It is this mercy that explains Jesus' miracles. Jesus is presented as deeply moved by the pain of others, the pain of the weak. He reacts to this pain, and more important, reacts with ultimacy. There is something ultimate in the need of the weak—

something to which one *must* react. It is important to notice that the verb with which Jesus' attitude is described in the passages cited is *splagchnizomai*, which comes from the noun *splagchnon*, meaning "belly, entrails, heart." The mercy expressed in Jesus' miracles is not a simple attitude of performing something prescribed or enjoined, then—not a reaction motivated by something apart from the pain itself. It is a reaction—therefore an action—to a reality that has been internalized, and which refuses to leave one in peace. It is a primary reaction, therefore—one which, when all is said and done, has no other explanation than the reality of the suffering of the weak, although it can be correctly denominated virtuous, or a compliance with the will of God, *afterwards*. With mercy we touch on something ultimate, something not arguable any further. So true is this that, when Jesus wishes to define the complete human being, he does so in terms of the Samaritan of the parable, who was "moved to pity" (Luke 10:33); when he defines God, in the figure of the parent of the prodigal child, he speaks again of someone who has been "deeply moved" (Luke 15:20). (Jesus himself is described in the Letter to the Hebrews as the faithful one, the person of mercy.) That the signs of the Reign are signs of mercy means that the reason—if one can speak of a reason in a free initiative of God—for the imminence of the Reign of God lies in the mercy of God, and precisely as we have explained that mercy: the gripping of God's entrails at the sight of the suffering of the weak. God will draw near for this reason, and for this reason alone.

Thus, Jesus' miracles and other signs already make somewhat concrete what the Reign of God is for Jesus, and thus we have already come a little way beyond general definitions of salvation as love, or as living in complete openness to God. Although they are only signs, the miracles express the character of the Reign of God as salvation from urgent concrete needs. This means liberation, since the needs from which one is saved are those produced by elements of oppression; the reason for the Reign is nothing other than, nothing apart from, these needs themselves.

2. Jesus' Denunciations

We have referred to the signs wrought by Jesus as actions in the service of the Reign. But we may ask whether Jesus performed some more comprehensive activity, some activity correlative to the totality of the Reign of God—something from which we might deduce what that Reign meant in its totality. Granted, Jesus formulated no theory of society as such. However, neither can it be said that Jesus has nothing to transmit to us in terms of the Reign's dimension of totality. That dimension appears in his view of the anti-Reign as a totality; from that view we can deduce something of what the Reign itself signified as a totality. After all, the anti-Reign is not only different from the Reign, it is formally its contrary. In this sense, perhaps we might denominate certain activities of Jesus as praxis, since they were intended as a denunciation of society in its totality. The purpose was to expose the causes of the anti-Reign and transform it into the Reign, although on this point Jesus offers no technical means but only calls for conversion.

That Jesus is convinced of the existence of the anti-Reign is clear. The world and the society in which he lived were not totalities in conformity with the will of his Father, God. But more than this, they were strictly the contrary. This is what we are taught by the controversies in which Jesus was caught up. These are never simple exercises in casuistry, or in the resolution of secondary *quaestiones disputatae*. They always deal with the central question of all: who God is. In the religious society of Jesus' time and place, this automatically led to the next question: what would a world according to God be like? In the controversy over the ears of grain plucked on the sabbath day in a stranger's field, for example, what is in question is the priority of life over worship (the religious dimension of the controversy) and over ownership (the social dimension). Jesus declares that, for God, life has priority over all else; he holds that, in today's language, God is a God of life, and that therefore society ought to be organized in service of life. What underlies the controversies is the exclusive alternative between the God of life and other gods, between Reign and anti-Reign. What is directly clear in the controversies is Jesus' rejection of the anti-Reign. But indirectly they also explain this minimum: in the name of God, there should exist a society organized in service of life.

Jesus' denunciations demonstrate his forthright condemnation of those responsible for the anti-Reign. Certain anathemas may be directed against individuals, but in general the addressees of the denunciations and anathemas are formulated in the plural. Not that Jesus had a theory of social classes, but he does assume the existence of social groups responsible for the anti-Reign. The wealthy, Pharisees, scribes or doctors of the Law, priests, and civil rulers are denounced and anathematized. Various things are thrown up to them: that they are hypocrites, that their existence is vain and empty, that they will have to give an accounting on the day of judgment, and so on. But in (almost) all of the denunciations there is a fundamental element: the addressees are the cause of the anti-Reign, they are oppressors, they produce victims. In the abundant denunciations of those responsible we discern a denunciation of the society that they mold as an oppressive society, rotten to the core. Here is a society in which power, at its various levels, oppresses the masses. This is the anti-Reign.

Jesus exposes the anti-Reign and its roots. He exposes the mechanisms by which the anti-Reign can masquerade as the Reign. He exposes the religious traditions human beings have created for the purpose of canceling the actual will of God and maintaining oppression in the name of God. Therefore he declares that oppression exists, why it exists, and how such and such a situation of oppression can be justified ideologically.[19]

In sum, we can say that Jesus rejects these particular social groups and the society that they shape. By way of his denunciations of the groups responsible for it, he denounces the configuration of society that they create. A society that produces this many victims is the anti-Reign; it must change in order to be in conformity with the will of God. From this it is possible to deduce only a minimum, but it is an important minimum for what the Reign of God is: it will be the contrary of the anti-Reign. There will be no oppression of some by others. In today's language, as in the language of the Hebrew scriptures, the Reign of God will be a reign of justice, a world organized in service of the life of those who had been victims, a world that will tear up death and oppression by the roots. Love as a possible formulation of the substance of the Reign will have to be made concrete in terms of justice. Otherwise Jesus' denunciations and exposés will not make much sense.

3. Jesus' Lot

Jesus' denunciations and exposés, seen as a whole, function as praxis, independently of his explicit consciousness of it; that is, they are pronounced with the purpose of transforming social reality. This is verified in Jesus' lot, which in turn will explain what the Reign of God is. Almost no one today continues to accept Bultmann's thesis that Jesus' death at the hands of the political authority as a punishment for a political misdemeanor was simply an absurd, tragic mistake. Both trials or processes, the religious more so than the political, make it abundantly clear that Jesus' adversaries knew very well what they were doing and why they were doing it. In the religious process, Jesus stands accused of blasphemy, an accusation whose formulation is religious. But alongside this indictment, which would appear to be redactional, appears the basic accusation: Jesus wants to destroy the temple. In this religious formulation, Jesus is implicitly but unambiguously accused of seeking the radical subversion of society. The temple was the symbol of the totality of society, in the religious, economic, financial, and political areas. In his political trial he is charged with acts of concrete subversion. These charges are dismissed, as they are seen to be unfounded. But he is also accused (and this is the charge of which he is found guilty and sentenced to death) of offering a distinct—and in the formulation of the gospels, exclusive—alternative to the Empire. From a historical viewpoint, the accusation leveled against him in the religious trial is far more solidly founded than his indictment in the political. But the conclusion is the same: Jesus objectively represents a menace to established society, and for that he must die. In situations very much like those in which Jesus lived and acted, Archbishop Romero used to explain, with consummate simplicity and clarity, that anyone who gets in the way is killed. The ultimate agent of Jesus' murder is not to be sought among individuals. The ultimate agent of Jesus' murder is that which Jesus disturbs: his society. In systematic language, the mediator of God is murdered by the mediators of other gods, because God's mediation, the Reign, is an objective threat to the mediations of other gods (the temple theocracy, the Empire). The attempt to do away with Jesus was a historical, structural necessity. Thus, the fact that he was killed is altogether understandable historically. The mystery lies in why God should have permitted it, which is something we cannot investigate here.[20]

But what does Jesus' murder tell us about the Reign of God? Once more, we learn something minimal, but basic. Persons who preach an exclusively transcendent Reign of God do not get themselves murdered. People who preach a Reign that is only a new relationship with God, or only "love," or only "reconciliation," or only "trust in God," are not murdered. All these things may be legitimately regarded as elements accompanying the message of the Reign of God, but they alone do not explain Jesus' death, and therefore they alone cannot be the central element of the Reign. The Reign of God must have had some bearing on the historico-social, not only on the transcendent. Jesus proclaimed it for religious reasons, surely: because the Reign of God represents the will of God, as does Jesus' proclamation of that Reign. But the content of the Reign was not religious in the sense of being nonhistorical or asocial. To bring out this point, Juan Luis Segundo asserts that the Reign of God proclaimed by Jesus was a political reality—not by contrast with the religious element, but by contrast with the purely transcendent or purely individual.[21] Segundo goes on to say that the purely religious element of the Reign of God only reinforces its political dimension, since concepts like *Reign* (and *poor*) are "all the more crucially political insofar as their underlying motivations are religious."[22] Whether the Reign of God be called a political reality or a historico-social one, the important thing to bring out is the historical, concrete dimension it had in the mind of Jesus. For Jesus, the Reign is the Reign *of God.* It is what happens in history when *God* reigns. But when God reigns, something happens *in history* that transforms that history and shapes it in a particular manner, in contrast with the anti-Reign.

It will not be superfluous to recall that, for Jesus, the Reign of God was a historical reality, which does not militate against its being an eschatological and theological reality. Rudolf Schnackenburg, in his well-known work on the subject,[23] is at pains to be altogether clear: "The salvation proclaimed and promised in the Reign of God is a purely religious dimension." Further, he draws a conclusion that will concern us below: "By reason of its purely religious character, Jesus' message concerning the Reign of God follows a universal trajectory." How can one commit such an oversimplification—or, at least, make such an undialectical assertion? In defense of his thesis, Schnackenburg rightly recalls that Jesus took his distance from exalted theocratic, apocalyptic expectancies and marvelous popular messianisms. But one may not conclude from this that the Reign of God was purely religious. It seems to us that it is possible to draw such a conclusion only by ignoring Jesus' ministry, his activity, his praxis, and his fate as things he does in the service of the Reign.

When, on the other hand, these things are taken seriously, they tell us something important about the Reign of God. The Reign is plural salvation from concrete needs (illness, hunger, demonic possession, the worthlessness and despair of the outcast sinner). It is liberation, since these needs are seen as the product of historical causes. But furthermore, in its totality the Reign stands in strict contrariety to the historical anti-Reign. As opposition, it is not an extrapolation from present possibilities; and as opposition to the historical anti-Reign, it is something occurring in history. It is a historico-social reality—a political one, if you will. None of this militates against the character of the Reign as that *of God.* On the contrary, Jesus sees it as such precisely because this is the way he understands *his* God, and he serves that God—to the point of being put to death—because he believes that the Reign is the will of God for this world.

3. The Way of the Addressee of the Reign

The third way, or approach to a determination of what the Reign of God is, is that of the addressee, which we have already sketched out to some extent in our consideration of the second way. An emphasis on the third way, it seems to us, is liberation theology's most specific contribution to theological methodology. The basic premise of this third approach is that the content and addressees of the Reign are mutually explanatory; all the more so when the addressee is considered not in a vague and undifferentiated manner, but concretely; and especially, when it becomes possible to know the reason why this is the addressee of the Reign. The effect of an analysis of the addressee is a concrete identification of the utopia and salvation of the Reign—and surely a concrete identification of the anti-Reign—such that salvation can no longer be universalized or be found in all manner of interchangeable conceptions, precisely because the addressee is concrete.

An exegetical determination of the addressee of the Reign of God had already been achieved by the time liberation theology arrived on the scene, although other theologies had not drawn the necessary consequences. Joachim Jeremias, for example, as early as 1971, had clearly identified the addressees of the Reign.[24] After an analysis of Jesus' proclamation and the imminence of the Reign, Jeremias says: "We have not yet completely described [Jesus'] preaching of the *basileia*. Indeed, we have not yet cited its essential trait." That trait consists in its addressees, who are the poor. Jeremias makes the radical assertion: "The Reign belongs *solely to the poor* . . . The first Beatitude: salvation is intended *solely* for beggars and sinners." It could scarcely be put more clearly. The same author determines the identity of these poor, who are thus proclaimed the addressees of the Reign. They are those cited in the first Beatitude (Luke 6:20), and those to whom the Good News is preached (Matt. 11:5, Luke 7:23). Jeremias tries to systematize the identity of the poor along two lines: the poor are those who are crushed under the burden of life (the absolute character of material—or, as we should say, socioeconomic—poverty), and the despised and outcast of society (the relational character of poverty: sociological marginalization).[25] While it is no easy matter to gather both lines into a univocal concept, it is obvious that poor, here, denotes a concrete, historical reality: it means those for whom life is a harsh burden for historical—economic and social—reasons. At all events, the poor are addressees of the Reign not by reason of anything in their interiority, and certainly not because they are human beings and therefore subject to limitations.

The theology of liberation takes this exegetical determination of the addressee very seriously and systematizes the reality of the poor on the basis of the data of the gospel.[26] The poor are an economic and social reality. They are those for whom to live is to bear a heavy burden, by reason of the difficulty of their lives and by reason of their marginalization. The poor are a collective reality; they are poor peoples, or poor as a people. The poor are a historical reality; they are poor not mainly for natural reasons, but historical ones—poor because of injustice. The poor are a dialectical reality; there are poor because there are rich, and vice versa. The poor are a political reality; in their very reality, they have at least a potential for conflict and the transformation of society. This systematization of the reality of the poor is not deduced, especially on the last point, immediately from evangelical data. But it does systematize fundamental traits, and we offer it in order that the reality of the poor not disappear into thin air, as so often happens. In any case, what is of interest to the theology of liberation, and what that theology proposes methodologically, is that it be taken seriously that *these* poor, the poor of the gospel, are the addressees of the Reign of God, and that it is in terms of *these* poor that the nature of the Reign of God can be made concrete. These propositions, which seem so utterly obvious and logical, are nevertheless not usually accepted, or at least not consistently. This is understandable, because they ascribe a "partiality," a partisanship, to God. God is taking sides—being partial to one group rather than to another, and this, today as in Jesus' time, is scandalous. Indeed, the preaching of the Good News to the poor, simply as such, produces scandal (cf. Matt. 11:6, Luke 7:23). After a long analysis in the work previously cited, Segundo emphasizes this partiality:

> The Reign of God is not announced to everyone. It is not "proclaimed" to all. . . . The Reign is destined for certain groups. It is theirs. It belongs to them. Only for them will it be a cause of joy. And, according to Jesus' *mind*, the dividing line between joy and woe produced by the Reign runs between *the poor* and the rich. (p. 90)

He gives the reason for this partiality, which usually causes still greater scandal:

> The Reign comes to change the *situation* of the poor, to put an end to it. As the first Beatitude tells us the poor possess the Reign of God. That is not due to any merit of theirs, much less to any value that poverty might have. On the contrary, the Reign is theirs because of the inhuman nature of their situation as poor people. . . . If the poor were still subject to (moral and religious) conditions in order to enjoy the coming Reign of God, that would mean the collapse of the original Beatitudes and their revelation of God. They could not say of the poor that the Reign is theirs, precisely *because* of what they suffer from their inhuman situation. (pp. 107, 140)

On the basis of the proposition that the poor are the addressees of the Reign of God, and that they are that simply in their quality as poor, two supremely important consequences follow. The first, an obvious one, bears on the content of the Reign. The poor define the Reign of God by what they are. They make concrete a utopia customarily formulated in the abstract—partly out of logical necessity, but for the most part because of a reluctance to make it real—in order that its addressees be not the poor alone, but others as well, and ultimately all. It is not easy to select a single term in which to formulate this reality, since, as we have said, needs—those of the poor, as we can now specify—are plural. But for the purpose of formulating the termination of the misfortunes of the poor, words like *life, justice*, and *liberation* continue to be meaningful. What the best formulation of the Reign of God would be is, at bottom, something only the poor themselves can answer, since theirs is the Reign, and it is they who know that from which the Reign delivers them. But the important thing is that, whatever the formulation, the poor make concrete the content of the Reign as the defeat of poverty. Perhaps we might simply say that the Reign of God is a world, a society, that makes life and dignity possible for the poor.

The second important thing that makes concrete the addressee of the Reign of God is precisely the element denoted by the prepositional phrase, *of God* in the name for that Reign; in other words, the transcendent dimension of the Reign. This thesis may sound strange at this point. A determination that the poor, as described, are the addressees of the Reign of God is frequently invoked in support of an indictment of liberation theology for reductionism, "economicism," "sociologism," or the like. Our proposition may sound strange for another reason, as well. In citing the transcendent, we could seem to be automatically transporting ourselves to some timeless, immaterial world. There is still the tendency, in addressing the question of transcendence and history, not only to distinguish them, but to set them in mutual opposition. Nevertheless, the transcendency of the Reign of God ought to be analyzed, at least in a first moment, in terms of the character of that Reign as being "of God," whatever the manifestation of this being "of God."

To our view, the fact that the Reign is of the poor, that it belongs to the poor, is a very effective way of expressing its being "of God," both with respect to the formality of God as mystery and with respect to the ultimate content of that mystery. As for the former, the poor are addressees of the Reign not in virtue of any moral or religious quality they may happen to possess, not because poverty makes it possible (as it in fact does make it possible) to live in greater openness to God. The reason the Reign is addressed to the poor is simply the way God is. God's being thus, and not otherwise, is neither conceptualized nor conceptualizable (in addition to being, for the adversaries of the poor, neither desired nor desirable). It is a manifestation of the divine reality, which, at least from a historical viewpoint, outstrips, transcends, the expectancies of natural reason, and certainly of sinful reason. Jesus' entire life shows the extent to which "the way God is" transcends conventional notions. The Reign's partiality to the poor occasions scandal and conflict. And having proclaimed to the poor in the Beatitudes that the Reign of God is theirs, in his parables Jesus must constantly defend this partiality of God's, in controversy with his adversaries. It is as if Jesus constantly had to say, "God is *not* the way you think God is, but just the opposite." Jesus cannot actually argue *why* God is this way; he can only assert the fact in the hope that his adversaries will accept a new God, the God who embraces the sinner, who pays the same wage to those who arrive at the eleventh hour as to those who come at the first, who is distraught and anxious over a single sheep that has gone astray.

The novelty and unthinkability that it should be the poor who are the addressees of the Reign thus becomes a historical mediation of the novelty and unthinkability of God, of the mystery of God, of the transcendency of God as regards human images. To be willing that the addressees of the Reign be the poor is tantamount to letting God be God—allowing God a self-revelation in terms of the way God actually is and in the terms in which God may elect to make that self-manifestation.

The transcendent reality of God can be analyzed from other perspectives; for example, in its suprahistorical function "in the beginning" and in the future, in creation and in final fulfillment. But the transcendence of God can also be analyzed in terms of the divine self-manifestation *thus* and not otherwise. Basically, Paul does nothing else when he proposes the cross as the wisdom of God. It is obviously insanity and scandal, but that through which God is being manifested as God. Something of the kind occurs when we assert that the Reign of God is of the poor in their quality as poor and only in that quality. It is through this that God engages in a self-manifestation *as God*, as unmanipulable mystery.

But the addressee also helps us make concrete the content of the mystery of God. The Christian scriptures make the radical statement that God is love; but the addressee of the Reign makes that love concrete in terms of love for the weak, in terms of affection for the weak, and in terms of the defense of the weak. From a point of departure in the flagrant inhumanity to which the poor are subjected, the humanity of God is manifested, in terms of tenderness, loving self-abasement, and joy when the poor and sinful accept the divine welcome. In terms of the addressees of the Reign, it is possible to know not merely that God is "this way," but that God is *this good*.

The poor as addressees of the Reign, then, have the potential to make concrete the historical content of that Reign, but they also have the potential to make the God of the Reign better known. With the poor as our starting point, we must let God show God, without attempting to determine beforehand what the divine self-revelation ought to be or what a plausible revelation would be. We must allow God the freedom to make a self-revelation as God wishes, not as desired by those who regard themselves as just and upright. We must let God be Good News as God wishes, as well as—to the consternation of many—bad news. We must let God be partial, as God showed partiality throughout the Hebrew scriptures as well as in Jesus. We must "let God be God," and let God manifest the divine love as God has decided—in a salvific approach to those who are not loved, but oppressed and despised in this world. Surely there are other ways, as well, of approaching the reality of God in fidelity to the scriptures. But it is of no small help to consider the poor as addressees of the Reign of God. At least they ensure the surprise we need to feel in order to be sure that we are actually dealing with God's revelation. And they demand a pre-understanding, which is also conversion, on the part of those who would be open and who would succeed in grasping this God whose self-manifestation proves to be thus.

In terms of Jesus' service to the Reign, as well as in terms of its addressees, then, we think it possible to say what the Reign of God was for Jesus. The Reign of God continues to be utopia, and thereby indefinable. But with what we have seen, we can safely assert that it is the utopia of the poor, the termination of their misfortunes, liberation from their slaveries, and the opportunity to live and to live with dignity. And again, from this point of departure, we can better understand the meaning of the Reign as a Reign *of God*, the God of the Reign is a God who desires life for the poor and who delivers them from the anti-Reign.

III. SYSTEMATIC CONCEPT OF THE REIGN OF GOD

An evangelical determination of the Reign of God is surely of the highest importance for our faith. But in itself it does not furnish a systematic concept of the Reign for today. Liberation theology, which unlike other theologies maintains the central character of the Reign, considers that the systematic concept of the Reign should be based on and should synthesize what is essential to the evangelical concept. But, while necessary, this is insufficient.

> The gospel invites us to creative fantasy, and to the elaboration of ideologies sprung not from some aprioristic quantity, but from an analysis of, and the challenges of, a situation, with a view to a project of liberation. This being the case, the Christian, in faith, should not be afraid to take a concrete decision—with the risks of failure that that decision will involve—a decision that can be the historically mediated com-

ing of the Reign. Therefore he or she can ask, ardently, day after day: "Thy kingdom come to us." Neither faith nor the church knows in advance what the concrete shape of such a decision will be.[27]

This citation from Leonardo Boff forbids an absolute formulation of the Reign. It emphasizes the need (and the risks) of its historicization today. But it demands some notion of what the Reign may mean today—some horizon against which a response to present challenges can be understood as a realization, however provisional, of the Reign.

1. Current Reassertion of the Reign of God

Before all else, it must be observed that the theology of liberation, with all its risks and all its provisional character, reaffirms the need to maintain the Reign of God as a central concept today. We have already seen the specific reasons for this assertion. What remains to be explained is in what sense liberation theology continues to maintain this when other theologies abandon it as their central concept. To make it more understandable, we may recall the celebrated question of *when* the Reign is to come. That answer depends basically on what we mean by the Reign. As we know, the exegetical solutions to the question of the moment of the coming of the Reign are varied. In terms of a consequent eschatology, the Reign will be reality only at the end of time (Albert Schweitzer); in terms of a realized eschatology, the Reign has already become reality, in the person and activity of Jesus (C. H. Dodd). According to Cullmann's familiar thesis, the coming of Jesus signals the commencement of the end of the ages, since the Evil One and sin have now been defeated in principle, although only at the close will the fullness of Christ be revealed; thus we have the thesis of the "already, but not yet." In systematic theology, it is said that the coming of the Reign can be regarded as "something provisionally fulfilled with the resurrection of Jesus itself," since "the universal resurrection of the dead" must be understood as "entry into the Reign of God" (Pannenberg).[28] Bultmann abandons all reference to the Reign and asserts that the ultimate occurs in history whenever the kerygma is received.[29]

The question of the *when* is ultimately answered in terms of what one understands the Reign to be, and it is this comprehension of the Reign that determines whether it will be maintained or abandoned as the central element in theology. In order to understand in what sense liberation theology continues to assign the Reign central position, let us make two antecedent clarifications.

The first clarification consists in distinguishing between a *mediator* and a *mediation* of the will of God. In the concrete economy of salvation, God always operates through a mediator, an envoy, someone who announces, and initiates by way of signs, what the will of God is for this world, and what direction the world should take in order to arrive at a condition in conformity with the divine will. In this sense, it must be said that the eschatological mediator has *already* appeared, that the mediator already is reality. And in this sense again, but only in this sense, Origen's beautiful profession is true: Christ is the *autobasileia* of God, the Reign of God in person. Of course, this is nothing but a reformulation, in the language of the Reign of God, of the nucleus of christologic faith: Christ is the definitive mediator. But at the same time, the will of God is not simply that a mediator appear in history, but also that the divine will for the world be realized in history. We call the realization of that will *mediation*—or in the language of the gospels, the Reign of God. Mediator and mediation are therefore intrinsically related but are not the same.

The second clarification will be in the form of a distinction between the *signs* and the *reality* of the Reign. The presence of signs is of the first importance for the symbolical explicitation of the reality of the Reign and for generating a hope that that reality is possible, that it is near at hand. But once more, such signs are not adequately the reality of the Reign. Acts of healing do not eradicate disease, nor the multiplication of loaves hunger, nor the expulsion of demons the omnipresent power of the Evil One, nor a welcoming of sinners marginalization and social contempt.

In what sense, then, can we say that the Reign of God is or is not reality? On what antecedent criteria will the reality of the Reign be verified and measured? The theology of liberation asserts that the Reign of God is reality in the sense of already having its mediator, no other eschatological mediator need be awaited. It asserts that the Reign is reality as far as signs are concerned, whenever they do occur in history. But it insists that the Reign is not a reality on the level of mediation, as St. Paul, using other words, insists: God is not yet "all in all" (1 Cor. 15:28). Cullmann's "already, but not yet" can be a valid response, provided it is correctly understood. The "already" is definitive as far as the *mediator* (the definitive, eschatological mediator) is concerned—although temporal mediators can and must continue to arise, now measured by the stature of Jesus himself. The Reign is "already" in history as long as signs of the Reign occur. But that Reign is "not yet"—in the reality of the Third World we should have to say "certainly not yet"—as far as *mediation* is concerned, the realization of the will of God for this world.

What the theology of liberation states, then, is the following. In the first place, this theology insists that the Reign of God has not come at the level of mediation, and that, nevertheless, the will of God continues to come to this world. From the non-arrival of the Reign, liberation theology does not adopt the conclusion leapt to by other ideologies, which, being ignorant of mediation, concentrate exclusively on the mediator, who indeed has come. That the mediation has not come raises an intrinsic difficulty for its determination, this is true; but liberation theology asserts that that determination must continue to be sought today. In the second place, liberation theology insists that there is at once a continuity and a discontinuity between the systematic and evangelical concepts of the Reign of God. The discontinuity is obvious, since it is unclear what the will of God is today for the current real world. From this liberation theologians come to their well-known demand for analytical mediations in order to arrive at a determination of the content of the Reign. The continuity is obvious, too—*for faith*. Liberation theology completely agrees that the mediator has indeed come, and that, accordingly, in its view of the Reign, in its activity in behalf of the Reign, there is something essential and permanent. This essential and permanent factor stands in need of becoming concrete but will never have to be canceled. It will always be needed in order to guide any future determination of the Reign of God. Simple as it may appear to say it, liberation theology accepts the fact that, throughout the historical life of Jesus, not only in the Jesus of the resurrection, the will of God for this world has appeared, with ultimacy, and that this has never been revoked in subsequent history.

2. Premises for a Determination of the Reign of God

What we have said up to this point shows that the theology of liberation makes a theological option for the Reign of God. It is a justified, or at least justifiable option, and therefore reasonable in terms of revelation. In terms of the situation of the Third World, it is also necessary and urgent. And it is an option that can appeal to many current church documents. But at bottom it is an option—a concrete, ultimate manner of grasping and formulating Christian faith.

In the background of this option in the formulation of the faith, however, are concrete, historical, existential premises, which are necessary for an understanding of why a basic theological option for the Reign of God is meaningful, and why this option is made concrete in the way that we are about to see. First, then, let us suggest what these premises might be.

The Basic Premise

The basic premise is the primacy of the reality of the poor. In modern language, we should say that the basic premise is the option for the poor. From this primacy flows the expectation—a logical enough premise even in itself, but reinforced by its actual realization, that the very reality and revelation of God will become more attainable and transparent.

This premise in itself is an option. When all is said and done, one cannot argue for or against it. Juan Luis Segundo has expressed this altogether radically in order to explain his own theology on the concrete point of the necessary premise for the reading of the gospel. The option for the poor, he states, "is not a theme of liberation theology, but the epistemological premise for interpreting the word of God."[30] This author insists that this premise must actually be posited before a reading of the biblical text is undertaken, that not even the text forces this presupposition on the reader (although it does require some presupposition, some pre-understanding). Thus, when all is said and done, the premise is a wager.

It will be open to discussion, as Segundo concedes,[31] whether, in the concrete case of an approach to the text of the gospels, the option for the poor is really only a pure option—a simple premise—or whether the text itself inclines in its favor and calls for it. But regardless of the answer to this question, it remains clear that, in liberation theology and in all its varieties, the option for the poor—however one comes to it—is necessary for a reading of the gospel, and furthermore, for an adequate reading of reality. Let us remember that the option for the poor is the heritage, not of Christians and believers alone, but of many other human beings as well.

The important thing is that the option for the poor is not pure evangelical or sociohistorical content, is not merely an ethical demand, and is not, of course, something that must be carried out because church documents say that it must, so that, if these documents had not said so, Christians would be under no obligation to make such an option. The option for the poor is something more primordial than this. It is an ultimate way of regarding the reality of the poor and of seeing in the liberation of the poor the necessary mode of correspondence to reality.

The internal structure of this option is open to theoretical discussion. The position of liberation theology is that it has the structure of conversion, since it is made in distinction from, and historically in opposition to, other options. This option may therefore have an ethical component. But the level on which it is taken is more primary. As St. Paul asserts, human beings tend to—indeed, according to the universalizing language of Paul, they not only tend to, but inescapably do—imprison the truth. Primary conversion, then, means letting truth be truth, seeing the world as it is, without oppressing it beforehand by dictating how it is to appear. In this sense, the option for the poor in Pauline language is necessary for a release from prison of the truth of the world, the world of the oppressed and the world of oppressors.

It is open to discussion, once more, how one manages existentially to make the option for the poor. Liberation theology insists that that option is made possible (or is strengthened) *from a point of departure* in the poor. How one manages to make an option from a point of departure in the poor is open to theoretical discussion. But in any case one must allow oneself to be affected radically by the reality of the poor—allow the poor to penetrate oneself with ultimacy and without conditions. Thus, the option for the poor is an option that one believes necessary for historical reality and the gospel, for responding and corresponding better to both, for entering into harmony and kinship with what they both say and with what they both demand. Once the option has been taken, one can grow in the conviction that all this is the case, and on the basis of this conviction come to a better and more adequate grasp of history and the gospel. Thereupon, the option can be theorized as the necessary hermeneutic premise for an understanding both of reality and of the gospel. Then the poor can be theologized, posited as a *locus theologicus*, recognized as constituting a world in which the signs of the times occur. Now one can even accept Isaiah's scandalous thesis: in the poor, in the crucified Servant, there is salvation and there is light. There is a mutual historical and theological reinforcement between an option for the poor that sheds light on reality, and the reality of the poor that convinces one that this option is right on target. But when all is said and done, what liberation theology emphasizes is simply the making of the option with (logical) anteriority to the development of a theology of liberation.

This means, concretely, that it is the poor who will guide the fleshing out of what the Reign of God is today. Theoretically and historically, the concept of the Reign of God can be worked out in terms of other primacies than the poor. It can be developed from universal human needs, from the longing for freedom, from the desire for survival after death, from the utopia of continuous progress. This has actually been the point of departure for other theologies, and the differences among them in terms of their systematic concepts of the Reign of God are ultimately to be explained by the premises on which they read the gospel text and current historical reality. In terms of the option for the poor, the systematic concept of the Reign of God plies a precise course: the Reign of God is the Reign of the poor.

Hermeneutic Premises

From the premise of the option for the poor, two important hermeneutic propositions flow. These propositions are necessary for an understanding of the Reign of God, and the option for the poor bestows on them novel formulations. The first is the question of hope. Modern theology has the great merit of having rediscovered the dimension of the future on the metaphysical level, hope on the anthropological level, and promise on the level of revelation. But it has also declared that the Reign is a reality that of its very nature demands hope in order for its meaning to be grasped. To put it another way, the reality of the Reign of God is such that, if, *by an impossiblity*, human beings had no hope, its content would be a logical contradiction. Hope, then, is essentially necessary for an understanding of what the Reign of God is. But once more, we must ask ourselves what manner of hope is in question here. Liberation theology insists that we are dealing with the hope of the poor. It does not deny, of course, that the human being is the being of hope and can therefore succeed in forging utopian concepts. However, it insists that hope as an anthropological dimension is only a necessary condition, not a sufficient one, for an understanding of the Reign of God.

By analogy with what we say of faith, we may say that there is *an object of hope* and *an act of hoping*—and that both must be made concrete in service of the poor in order to provide access to an understanding of the Reign. The object of hope is the object of the hope of the poor of this world—an end to their misfortunes, an opportunity for life, a just configuration of this world that oppresses them. The signs the poor hope for are those that already offer them a little life and enable them to hope that life is possible.

As for the act of hoping, the poor exercise their hope within a dialectic of realized signs, the foundation of hope, and a massive, cruel, structural reality that actively militates against their hope. The dimension of counter-hope is inherent in hope itself, and this has always been recognized, from Paul to modern theology: radical hope in resurrection is maintained in the face of death. But again, the poor make concrete the inherent opposite of hope: the current situation of oppression, the anti-Reign. The hope of the Reign is actively realized as hope in spite of, and in opposition to, the anti-Reign. Hope always has the structure of victorious action against what opposes it. Therefore it is important to see what it is that opposes it. For those who have no reason to see life as an object of hope because they already have life—although they may question its meaning—the obstacle to hope will be final death. But for those for whom living is still an object of hope, the obstacle to hope will be the anti-Reign. Not that the poor (at least in Latin America) have no transcendent hope in a resurrection; they surely do. But for them, to live right now would be as much of a miracle as to live after death. They see the opposite of hope not only in death, but in the impossibility of life here and now. This is why their hope, when they have it, is so radical.

The theology of liberation, then, asserts that in order to grasp what the Reign of God is, not just any hope will suffice. Only the hope of the poor will do. The hope of the poor must, in some manner, be adopted as one's own. But once this has been accomplished, one also has a better systematic understanding of what the Reign of God ought to be: a promise of life in the face of the anti-Reign.

Praxis

The second question is that of praxis. Modern theology is at one with the whole of the New Testament in insisting on the need for a praxis. The problem, then, lies not in the need for a praxis in the Christian life, but in relating this praxis to the Reign of God. The latter, we are reminded, is a gift of God and cannot be forced by human activity. As for hermeneutics, it is claimed, the Reign of God is a reality that requires hope in order to be understood, but no praxis in order to be realized.

Far from denying the gratuity of the Reign, liberation theology emphasizes it. But the same theology demands a practice, as well, even in terms of the Reign. The evangelical reason for this lies in the fact that Jesus himself did a great many things in the service of the Reign of God; he made some kind of demand on his hearers as a matter of principle. In terms of the primacy of the poor, the need for a praxis in behalf of the Reign is evident. A need for praxis, then, is not under discussion in the theology of liberation. What must be analyzed is the hermeneutic value of praxis—praxis as a means of grasping the nature of the Reign of God, in such wise that, conversely, without praxis an understanding of the Reign of God would be crippled and diminished. Indeed, praxis assists in an understanding of the very gratutity of the Reign.

A practice in the service of the Reign leads to a better concretization of the object of hope. In Ignacio Ellacuría's language,[32] taking up and adopting a reality (the praxis dimension of the intelligence) enhances one's grasp of the reality to be taken up and adopted. Let us begin with a negative consideration. In the doing of justice appears all the depth of injustice. The positing of signs of denunciation arouses a mighty reaction in those who experience the coming of the Reign as bad news. In other words, it is in praxis, and not in the pure concept, that the existence and reality of the anti-Reign appears with greater radicality. It comes to light not only that our present reality is not the Reign, not only that the Reign has not yet come, but that the anti-Reign is actively militating against the Reign. The numberless persecutions, murders, and martyrdoms of the poor who seek liberation, and of those who accompany them, demonstrate this clearly. Practice, then, helps us comprehend, with a radicality not otherwise attainable, that the anti-Reign really exists—as well as what it is in the concrete, since the anti-Reign reveals itself in its opposition to, not just any activity, but specific activities. Once again, by looking at its contrary, we find what the Reign of God is today.

Positively, it is in practice that we learn what generates hope in the poor. Many good deeds can be done in behalf of the poor. These good deeds alleviate their needs. But not all good deeds, however welcome, generate hope. It is in practice that one decides which signs, which proclamation of the Good News, which denunciation, which seedlings of a new society generate hope and therefore point in the direction of the Reign. It is in practice that one decides which things the poor celebrate as signs of the Reign. And it is also in practice, therefore, that one decides which paths lead to the Reign, paths that walk the tightrope between feasibility and the utopian "reserve" that moves one to search out new paths.

Practice, then, is not only an obvious ethical demand, but also a hermeneutic principle of comprehension. Before doing something in behalf of the Reign of God, less is known about that Reign than after doing something for it. In terms of practice, the signs of today are made concrete and thereby grasped. New signs are discovered. The roads to be traversed are identified. This sort of argumentation admittedly corresponds to a specific theory of knowledge. But it is based especially on liberation theology's reflection upon what occurs in reality when one toils for the Reign. Practice reveals what the Reign is. One might even ask whether Jesus himself may not have shaped his initial proclamation in service of his concrete activities and practices, and of reaction to them on the part of various social groups.

But further, for liberation theology, practice is not opposed to the gratuity of the Reign. Rather it presupposes it; it even helps to explain it. Liberation theology accepts and values the gratuity of the Reign, and this from two standpoints. In the first place, it confesses that the consummation of the Reign of God is the transcendent deed of God, as is its creation. Hope in the ultimate consummation is placed in God. The same gratuity that appears in the radical coming of God appears as well in the definitive attainment of God. In no way does the theology of liberation seek to place at risk the gratuity of the definitive Reign of God, and only the most backward interests would accuse it of uttering such nonsense. No, human beings will never build the perfect utopia! In the second place, liberation theology accepts and validates the notion that the reason God wishes to draw near in the Reign is in the divine initiative alone, which neither can nor need be forced by any human action. This occurs simply (as we have stated so emphatically) because this is the way *God is*.

These reminders ought to be unnecessary. They ought to be obvious, since liberation theology is authentically Christian and orthodox. But they are not obvious, since they are questioned. What may perhaps be behind these obtuse questions and accusations is an interest in ignoring or softening something on which the theology of liberation *does* insist: that gratuity is in no way opposed to practice; that, from a Christian viewpoint, it rather calls for it. What stands in need of analysis is not the need for both gratuity and practice, but a Christian understanding of their mutual relationship. From a historical viewpoint, we need only recall that Jesus proclaimed the gratuity of the Reign, and at the same time he himself exercised a practice and required one of others. From a systematic viewpoint, in scriptural language, let us remember that God has loved us "first," and draw the ineluctable conclusion in terms of the practice of a historical, concrete love, a love among brothers and sisters. Gratuity in no way exempts from practice. What Christian faith does is proclaim where the initiative is, and what it means for practice that the initiative should be with God. It means that practice must be performed not with *hubris* but with gratitude; that God's first practice, the antecedent unconditional divine love, shows how historical practice is to be carried out and how one is enabled to perform it. The mystery of God is that God "has created us creators" (Bergson). In the most gratuitous of all the divine acts, God has stamped us with this analogy with the divinity, that we may be with others what God has been with us, that we may do for others what God has done for us, and that we may deal with others as God has dealt with us.

We must hear, and proclaim, that the coming of the Reign of God is ultimately a gracious gift of God. But from this should flow not passivity, but the urgency of historical proclamations, an obsession with positing signs of its advent, with proposing ways in which human beings may live in conformity with that ultimate gift that will be reality only at the last. That the Reign is proclaimed to us and given to us ought to move us to carry out our practice with a particular attitude—that of response to gratuity. We are "free to love," as Gutiérrez says, and "liberated to liberate."[33] That the Reign is ultimately the Reign of God ought to move us to a practice without *hubris*—indeed, to a practice in a consciousness of our limitation and even sin ("to wage revolution as one forgiven," as José Ignacio Gonzalez Faus recommends). But an attitude of thankfulness and humility shapes practice; it does not suppress it.

In practice itself, furthermore, one can have the experience of gratuity. This can only be observed when it happens, but it happens. There is no reason why gratuity—the overarching fact that everything has its origin in God—should have to be expressed only with new eyes to see what without God could not be seen or with new ears to hear what without God could not be heard. It can also be expressed with new hands to do what without God could not be done. Many involved in the building of the Reign formulate gratuity in the following way. Something has been given us, and what has been given us is precisely that we can build the Reign of God, can posit signs that have not been posited before, can proclaim what has not been proclaimed before, can run risks that have not been run before, can accept a persecution that has previously been fled. *Before*, here, means what is normal, what is consonant with human potential. Now what appeared impossible has become possible; that is, to work with wholehearted determination and decision for the Reign. And this is experienced as a gift.

The theology of liberation, then, proposes the practice of the Reign not only as an obvious ethical exigency, but as a hermeneutic principle for a knowledge of the Reign of God and even for the knowledge of it as a gift. That practice, and the adoption of the hope of the poor, are concrete manifestations of the option for the poor that today bestow the ability to understand the Reign of God.

3. Systematic Concept of the Reign of God

After these reflections we can answer the question of what liberation theology understands systematically by the Reign of God. Formally speaking, by the Reign of God the theology of liberation understands a historical reality that has in itself the potential of openness to and indication of a "more." Materially speaking, it ascribes to the concept of the Reign of God the basic element of the evangelical concept as that concept is historicized in terms of the hermeneutic principles set forth above. Thus, the Reign of God is a reign of life; it is a historical reality (a just life for the poor) and a reality with an intrinsic tendency to be "more" (ultimately, utopia).

It should be clear, in this definition, by virtue of the primacy accorded them in the gospel and in the option, that the poor are the primary addressees of the Reign. A definition of the content of the Reign as *life* must be explained. What is at stake, of course, is not the term in itself; other, equivalent expressions could be found. *Life* is selected, we believe, because it is a better expression of both the historical and the utopian elements of the Reign. *Just* is added to indicate both the route to the attainment of life in the presence of the anti-Reign and to express the condition in which life subsists.

The theology of liberation insists on life as the historical content of the Reign because, in the Third World, poverty means proximity to death. The poor are those "who die before their time" (Gustavo Gutiérrez). *Life* means that, with the advent of the Reign, the poor cease to be poor. Liberation theology insists on the primary sense of life, without being over-hasty to analyze the element of the "more" that is inherent in all life. Paradoxically, it focuses more on (an idealized) protology than on eschatology: more on creation than on fulfillment. Life is not simply a leaven which, kneaded into the dough of reality, gives rise to the truly human, so that at last the Reign of God is here. In the Third World, life is not the premise; it is always the proposition itself. It is a finality in itself. In negative terms, the primary sin of the anti-Reign is not against eschatology, but against creation.

Today it is the concept of a just life that bridges the gap between the systematic and the evangelical concept of the Reign. The words, "a just life," ring as Good News in the ears of millions of human beings. It is they that move people to posit signs whose inner thrust is an overwhelming sense of mercy at the sight of the faces of the poor; and it is they that move people to denounce the pervasive presence of the anti-Reign. Efforts in behalf of life today also constitute a continuing occasion of scandal, conflict, persecution, and death. The upshot of all of this is that the Good News of the Reign can have a meaningful Christian formulation today as the life of the poor.

But life is also a reality which, of its very nature, is always open to the "more." Its concept is dynamic and directional; it points to an unfolding of itself in multilevel realization, a realization charged in turn with new opportunities and exigencies. Life points to the perpetual element of the "more" in the concept of the Reign of God.

In the Reign of God there must be bread—the prime symbol of the Good News today. But this same reality, bread, raises the question of how to obtain it, thereby demanding some kind of activity and toil. Then once there is bread, the question arises how to share it (the ethical element and the communitarian element), the temptation arises not to share it (sin), and the need arises to celebrate it, for the gladness that the bread produces. Bread obtained by some is intrinsically a question of bread for other groups, other communities, for an entire people—and the question of liberation arises. But then the attainment of bread by a whole people means practice, reflection, functional ideologies, risks, perils. And the need can arise to risk one's very life in order that bread be transformed into a symbol not of selfishness but of love.

And now bread is more than bread. It has something of the sacramental about it, and so the festival of maize is celebrated, and those who come together not only eat bread, but sing and recite poems, and bread opens out upon art and culture. And none of this happens mechanically. At each stage of the reality of bread, the need for spirit appears—a spirit of community for sharing and celebrating, a spirit of valor to fight for bread, a spirit of strength to persevere in the struggle, a spirit of love to accept the fact that to toil for the bread of others is the greatest thing a human being can do.

The Good News of bread can lead to an expression of gratitude to God for what God has done, or the question of why God does not see to it that there is plenty of bread for all. It can lead to the question of who that one is who multiplied loaves to satisfy hunger and then was killed for it. It can lead to the question of whether the church takes bread seriously as Good News, and how it relates it to its mission. It can lead to the question of whether there is anything more than bread, whether there is a bread of word, needed and Good News, even when there is no material bread; whether, if it is true that at the close of history there will be bread for all, it is worth the trouble to seek and toil in this history for the same thing, though at times darkness is everywhere; whether the hope of bread for all is really wiser than resignation; and so much more. Life is always more, and in bread there is always more than bread. But it must be emphasized that the reality of bread develops in this direction when the bread in question is not just any bread—the bread of luxury, or the bread that produces wealth—but the bread of the poor.

This brief phenomenology of the "more" that is in bread—whatever a description of that "more" may happen to be—is only intended to show how life itself always unfolds into "more." Thus, the theology of liberation emphasizes the historical character of the Reign—life—which intrinsically leads toward the "more." As it places no limits on this "more," the life of the Reign leads to the utopian. This is the ultimate reason why liberation theology has to speak of an "integral" liberation—not in order to add something that will balance "material" liberation with other, more spiritual, liberations, but because in that primary material that we call the life of the poor is always the germ of a "more" of life. It is in this sense that we can say that the Reign of God is life, abundant life, and a plenitude of life.

Thus, liberation theology emphasizes the historical and utopian aspect of the Reign. This is nothing especially new; what is new is the relationship it posits between the two, by contrast with what other theologies do in this regard.

In the first place, liberation theology insists on and defends the historical element inherent in the Reign of God, both by reason of obvious ethical exigencies, and because it believes that this is the way to come to a better grasp of the utopian element of the Reign without the usual risks of alienation. Its purpose is to prevent the final fulfillment of the Reign from becoming a pretext for ignoring or relegating to a secondary level the realization of the will of God for the poor. As Archbishop Romero said repeatedly: "One must defend the minimum, which is the maximum gift of God: life."

In the second place, the utopian element of the Reign is understood in the theology of liberation as a guide along the pathways to be traversed in history, and not merely as a relativization of the paths already traversed. Unlike other theologies, liberation theology does not emphasize, although of course it accepts, the relativizing character of the utopian Reign where anything historical is concerned. It knows the "eschatological reserve." It would be very surprising if it did not; the reality of the poor makes it abundantly clear that current history is not the Reign of God! A warning of the danger of equating history with the utopia of the Reign would, in Latin America, sound like sarcasm. The theology of liberation does not reject the function of the eschatological reserve, but it interprets it in another way. Eschatology not only posits "reservations" with regard to the historical, but it condemns the historical. In positive terms, eschatology does not relativize historical configurations on an equal basis; it ranks them. A fallacy lurks in an insistence simply that "nothing is the Reign of God"—as if the distance between that Reign and any historical configuration whatsoever is equal to any other because it is infinite. The theology of liberation knows very well that utopia is that which by definition is never realized in history (*ou topos*). But it also knows that there are *topoi* in history, and that the will of God is better realized in some than in others.

Finally, liberation theology understands the utopian element of the Reign of God not only as an element of the final event of history, but as a force of attraction that becomes present in history by way of a real anticipation of the end. This force does not reside, as Pannenberg would have it, in the unreality of the utopia, which enables us and requires us to live in a particular way and thus to live as persons saved. With all respect for the provisional nature of all historical achievements, there are formulations of the utopia that draw history onward, that make history to be more than itself: justice, a communion of sisters and brothers, liberation, or, in the great words of Rutilio Grande: "A common board, with a broad tablecloth, and set for everyone, as at this Eucharist. No one left out. Napkins and place settings for everyone." The utopia is like a powerful magnet. It mobilizes. It moves human beings time and again to give their best to make the Reign come true. The theology of liberation believes that the final utopia, while beyond history, moves history here and now.

4. Comprehensive Nature of the Reign of God

Thus understood, the Reign of God is central for liberation theology. The last question we must ask is whether and how the Reign of God, as central theological object, has the capacity to organize the whole content of theology. Let us suggest, in hasty summary, how the Reign of God can be integrated with the most important themes of theology in such a way as to organize and enrich them, with the observation that, although this organization is effected conceptually, we believe that it is based on the experience of many who believe, toil, and suffer for the Reign of God.

In the area of *theo-logia*, the concept of the Reign of God includes, by definition, God, and does so with the ultimacy proper to God. The concept of the Reign of God evinces the ultimacy of the will of God, the design of God, the transcendence of God—as well as the content of the concept of God as the supreme good: love and tenderness. Liberation theology calls this God the God of life. By virtue of the very nature of the Reign, God does not appear as a God jealous of the good of human beings; on the contrary, the glory of God consists in the life of the poor. But God is jealous of other idols—the idols with which God is in strict contrariety. Therefore the love of God can be denominated justice—love in opposition to the death procured by other gods. God becomes the God of the victims of this world, and this divine solidarity goes as far as the very cross, and so authentically that it becomes meaningful to speak of a crucified God. But that God continues to be asserted as the one who—gratuitously and definitively—is capable of extracting life where there is none, is capable of causing a definitive Reign to arise amid the anti-Reign of history.

We may wonder about the relationship between the God of the Reign and that other great symbol of the reality of God, *Abba*, Father. This title, this sacred appellation bestowed by Jesus, is also an essential of faith, and so we must ask ourselves how it can be related to the concept of the God of the Reign. The fact that God is Father for Jesus, as for today's believer, is shown in the trust Jesus placed in God, on the strength of his conviction that this Father is good. Hence the aspect of faith that is trust in and reliance on God. But this goodness of God, which enables Jesus and us to call God our Father, is what Jesus describes in his parables precisely when he speaks of a love of God not in general terms, but as a love for the addressees of the Reign. Systematically, this can be expressed as follows. The goodness of God by which God is named *Abba*, Father, is expressed precisely in the fact that God is the God of the weak, and thereby unequivocally the God who is good. Conversely, the reason, the logical reason, why Jesus can proclaim the coming of the Reign to the poor is his conviction that God indeed is, once again, a God who is good, a Father. Accordingly, the Reign of God does not militate against, but precisely endorses, the reality of God as cited by Jesus—that of Father.

In *christo-logia*, the assertion that Jesus is the proclaimer and eschatological mediator of the Reign of God is itself an affirmation of christological faith, and in the strict sense. Faith in the divinity of Jesus comes into existence only after the resurrection; nevertheless, Jesus' essential relationship with the Reign of God can shed a certain light on the logic by which this profession of his divinity is reached. One should not neglect the sheer fact that Jesus, in the midst of history, dared proclaim the ultimate secret of history and its close. The ultimate element of history is salvation, and furthermore, this salvation is at hand. Jesus' resurrection can also be interpreted as God's confirmation of the truth of this Jesus as the eschatological herald of the Reign. A believer's argumentation in favor of the divinity of Christ—as the profound reflections of the Fathers of the Church reveal—to the effect that if Christ were not God there would be no definitive salvation, can be reformulated in the language of the Reign: If Christ is not God, vain is the hope of salvation promised by the Reign.

As for the true humanity of Jesus, the relevancy of Jesus' relationship with the Reign is evident. The element of historical practice and historicity in the subjectivity of Jesus, in this constitutive relationality, shows him to be a true human being, subject to whatever is universal in the human, but also demonstrating what true humanity is. His sharing in humanity's current of hopefulness, which expects a Reign, his pro-existence or existence for others and their cause, his mercy, his love to the very end, his strength and perseverance in trials external and internal (temptations, the Galilean crisis, ignorance), his hope against hope, show him as a human being, and—according to the christological profession—as the true human being.

The Reign of God, therefore, is also a reality from which the logic of the christological profession can be explained—once it is accepted in faith—with the advantage over other formulas that it emphasizes the reality of this particular person who reveals God, and the reality of that God who is shown in the human. The dangers of a degeneration of the christological faith into abstractions lessens, and the invitation and exigency of following in the historical footsteps of Jesus as a way of coming to know him and professing him as the Christ is more obvious from a point of departure in the Reign of God.

In *ecclesio-logia*, the Reign of God furnishes the ultimate horizon of understanding of the identity and mission of the church. It reminds the church that it is not the Reign of God but of its very essence the servant of that Reign—and that its internal realizations ought to be a sign of the Reign in history. The Reign of God requires of the church that its mission, like that of Jesus, be Good News to the poor, evangelization and denunciation, proclamation of the word and historical realization of liberation. In this manner the church today can be a "sacrament of salvation."

The primary addressees of the Reign of God, the poor, require of the church a real incarnation in the history of the passion of the world, with which incarnation the church solves in principle the difficult problem of being in the world without becoming worldly, without being ruled by the worldly values with which the poor are oppressed. The poor make concrete the internal reality of the church as people of God in terms of the fundamental equality of the human, but also in terms of the partiality of that human element for which God entertains a predilection, and which of its very nature can produce a more evangelical faith and hope. The church must adopt an internal organization having its center in the materiality of the poverty of this world, with the spirit that can arise more spontaneously from that poverty. In the language of Puebla, this means in terms of the evangelization practiced by the poor themselves; and in systematic language, in terms of "the poor with spirit," as Ellacuría indicates.[34]

It is this church of the poor that is in real history and that grows in history—the church that rejoices when the signs of the Reign appear, the church that begs forgiveness when it effaces those signs itself, the church that celebrates the sacraments and the word.

Let us conclude with a few words on the *spirituality*[35] of the Reign of God, since this is something that liberation theology develops explicitly, and something that should be mentioned in view of certain accusations to the effect that this theology neglects spirituality. The spirituality of the Reign of God is before all else objectively theological, since it must come in confrontation with the ultimate. It demands that we make the inescapable choice between serving God and serving the idols. It is a spirituality that calls us to traverse the pathways of life that give life, rather than the pathways of death that deal death. It takes very seriously, then, the election between grace and sin in the concrete. In terms of the Reign of God, we gain a powerful understanding of what sin is, and its prime analogate—putting a person to death—as well as of what grace is—giving someone life. We understand the historical, social, and structural dimension of both, but we grasp their personal dimension as well. This is so because, whether by action or omission, all of one's humanity, all of one's power of decision, is engaged in the choice of one of these alternatives.

A spirituality of the Reign of God is a christologic spirituality, since it sees in the following of Jesus the paradigm of all spirituality—a following that is practice, mission, and a building of the Reign. This following, however, this discipleship, must be practiced not mechanically but "with spirit"—with the very spirit that became present in Jesus' life and Jesus' exigencies, precisely when he served the Reign and when he spoke of the Reign: a spirit of mercy, of single-heartedness, of courage, of impoverishment, and all the rest.

The spirituality of the Reign of God is a spirituality, finally, that believes in the activity of the Spirit of God in history today. This is the Spirit who animates every search for and discovery of new historical pathways to the building of the Reign, the Spirit who animates the hope that the Reign really is at hand despite appearances, the Spirit who animates the maintenance, actualization, and deepening of faith in God. The possibility and necessity today of prayer, of placing ourselves before God, of allowing God to speak to us and ourselves to speak to God, is no routine affair; it is something which of its very nature confronts one who labors for the Reign, and something that is made possible by the Spirit of God.

Liberation theology insists on the need for spirituality. Liberation, the practice of justice, the construction of the Reign is not optional. It is a basic decision in behalf of the life of the poor. But this basic decision must be filled with spirit. Both—practice and spirit—are necessary and mutually reinforcing. The epistemological primacy of liberation practice calls for spirit, but it renders possible a particular spirit, one that is not drawn from other wellsprings. The spirit with which the practice of liberation is to be filled does not incline the "spiritual" person to renounce that liberation, but it does heal the inevitable dangers and one-sidedness of liberation—and even endows it with greater force. This mutual relationship has been expressed in the concept of a "contemplative in liberation" (Leonardo Boff), or a "contemplative in action for justice" (Ignacio Ellacuría). One can speak of "political health and wholeness"—of a unification of faith and justice, of knowing God by doing justice, and the like. The formulas are varied, but they all imply the same basic element; that is, that the building of the Reign of God requires a particular spirit, but that it makes that spirit possible, as well. And this is why the theology of liberation has a spirituality.

This sole purpose of this rapid overview has been to illustrate what liberation theology does as a whole. But it may be sufficient to show not only that the Reign of God is the central material object of theology, but that it can be the formal object, as well: the organizing principle—in the Third World better than elsewhere—of the whole of theology. In selecting the Reign of God as its material object, liberation theology intends neither to diminish nor reduce the totality of theology, nor has it actually done so. Indeed, the contrary is the case. In the concrete reality of the Third World it thinks it has found the best way to enhance the power of the whole of theology.[36]

In the last analysis, what liberation theology says is that the Reign of God is to be built in history—together with other human beings, hence the radical ecumenism of the concept of the Reign of God—and that, in the light of faith, we see ourselves to be on the road, as we accomplish this partial construction, to the definitive Reign of God. Like the prophet Micah, the theology of liberation knows very well what is to be done: "To do right and to love goodness" (Micah 6:8), to foster the life of the poor in history. And like that prophet, the theology of liberation has faith in what in the last analysis this practice means: "To walk humbly with your God" (ibid.) in history. The former calls for a constant positing of signs that shape the

Reign, denouncing the anti-Reign, and proposing forms of more abundant life for the poor. The latter calls for faith in the ultimate meaning of history, faith in the fulfilling design of God—simply faith in God as God has been manifested in Jesus. This faith is the hope that history will be saved by God. Thereupon—but not before—the Reign of God becomes theologically interchangeable with the resurrection of the dead or with the Pauline "God . . . all in all."

—Translated by Robert R. Barr

NOTES

1. Gustavo Gutiérrez, *A Theology of Liberation: History, Politics and Salvation*, trans. Caridad Inda and John Eagleson (Maryknoll, N.Y.: Orbis Books, 1973), pp. 153–68.

2. Leonardo Boff, *Jesucristo y la liberación del hombre* (Madrid, 1981); Juan Luis Segundo, *Jesus of Nazareth*, trans. John Drury (Maryknoll, N.Y.: Orbis Books, 1984–88); Hugo Echegaray, *The Practice of Jesus*, trans. Matthew J. O'Connell (Maryknoll, N.Y.: Orbis Books, 1984); Jon Sobrino, *Christology at the Crossroads: A Latin American Approach*, trans. John Drury (Maryknoll, N.Y.: Orbis Books, 1978); idem, *Jesus in Latin America* (Maryknoll, N.Y.: Orbis Books, 1987); idem, "Jesús de Nazaret," in *Conceptos fundamentales de pastoral*, ed. C. Floristán and J. J. Tamayo (Madrid, 1983), pp. 480–513.

3. Leonardo Boff, *Ecclesiogenesis: The Base Communities Reinvent the Church*, trans. Robert R. Barr (Maryknoll, N.Y.: Orbis Books, 1986); idem, *Church: Charism and Power* (New York: Crossroad, 1985); Ignacio Ellacuría, *Conversión de la Iglesia al reino de Dios* (Santander, Spain, 1984); R. Munöz, *La Iglesia en el pueblo* (Lima, 1983); A. Quiroz, *Eclesiología en la teologia de la liberación* (Salamanca, 1983); Sobrino, *The True Church and the Poor*, trans. Matthew J. O'Connell (Maryknoll, N.Y.: Orbis Books, 1984).

4. Ignacio Ellacuría, "Aporte de la teologia de la liberación a las religiones abrahámicas en la superación del individualismo y del positivismo," manuscript of an address to the Congress of Abrahamic Religions held at Córdoba, Spain, in February 1987.

5. We have developed various aspects of this interpretation of the resurrection in *Jesus in Latin America.*

6. José Porfirio Miranda goes so far to say that Marx lacked the dialectic to arrive at a conception of a transformation of the world that would include the "resurrection of the dead" (José Porfirio Miranda, *Marx and the Bible: A Critique of the Philosophy of Oppression*, trans. John Eagleson [Maryknoll, N.Y.: Orbis Books, 1974], p. 277).

7. Ellacuría, "Aporte de la teología de la liberación," pp. 10–12.

8. Walter Kasper, *Jesus the Christ* (London: Burns and Oates, 1976), p. 72.

9. Leonardo Boff, "Salvation in Jesus Christ and the Process of Liberation," *Concilium* 96 (1974), p. 81. A consideration of the other two "ways" also plays a very important role in Boff's reflection.

10. Kasper, *Jesus the Christ*, pp. 72–88.

11. Cf. Wolfhart Pannenberg, *Jesus—God and Man* (Philadelphia: Westminster Press, 1968). In a later book, *Theology and the Kingdom of God* (Philadelphia: Westminster Press, 1969), Pannenberg approaches the subject of the Reign of God with a bit more attention to its social and historical repercussions.

12. Wolfhart Pannenberg, *Was ist der Mensch*? (Göttingen, 1962).

13. Edward Schillebeeckx, *Jesus: An Experiment in Christology* (New York: Seabury Press, 1979), p. 143.

14. Oscar Cullmann, *Jesus and the Revolutionaries* (New York: Harper & Row, 1970).

15. C. Escudero Freire, *Devolver el evangelio a los pobres* (Salamanca, 1978), p. 270.

16. G. Baena, "El sacerdocio de Cristo," *Diakonia* (1983), p. 26.

17. Edward Schillebeeckx, *Jesus*, p. 184.

18. Joachim Jeremias, *New Testament Theology* (New York: Scribner, 1971), p. 115.

19. See Segundo's suggestive interpretation (*Jesus of Nazareth*, vol. II, pp. 119–30) of Jesus' parables as exposing and shattering ideologies.

20. Cf. Sobrino, "Jesús de Nazaret"; Ignacio Ellacuría, "Por qué muere Jesús y por qué to matan," *Diakonia* (1978), pp. 65–75.

21. Cf. Segundo, *Jesus of Nazareth*, pp. 87–103.

22. Ibid., p. 88.

23. Rudolf Schnackenburg, *God's Rule and Kingdom* (New York: Herder and Herder, 1963).

24. Jeremias, *New Testament Theology*.

25. In his interpretation of Luke 6:20 Jeremias refers to the material poverty of Jesus' followers, which he distinguishes from that of Matthew 5:3. But he enlarges the concept of real poverty in a systematization consistent with the line of the prophets.

26. Cf. Ignacio Ellacuría, "Pobres," in Floristán and Tamayo, *Conceptos fundamentales de pastoral*, pp. 786–802.

27. Boff, *Jesucristo y la liberación del hombre*, p. 388.

28. Pannenberg, *Jesus—God and Man*.

29. According to "the New Testament, *Jesus Christ is the eschatological event*—the action of God by which God has set an end to the old world. In the preaching of the Christian Church the eschatological event will ever again become present and does become present ever and again in faith. The old world has reached its end for the believer, he is a 'new creature in Christ.' For the old world has reached its end with the fact that he himself as the 'old man' has reached his end and is now 'a new man,' a free man." Rudolf Bultmann, *The Presence of Eternity* (New York: Harper & Bros., 1957), p. 151.

30. Juan Luis Segundo, "La opción por los pobres, clave hermenéutica para leer el evangelio," *Sal Terrae* (June 1986), p. 476.

31. "I am not very sure where this circle has begun. I do not know to what extent, by the very reading of the Bible, I have come to realize that the gospel says something. . . . Once we have entered into the hermeneutic circle with the pre-understanding of which we have spoken, of course we convince ourselves that the gospel says this" (ibid., p. 482).

32. Ignacio Ellacuría, "Hacia una fundamentación filosófica del método teológico latinoamericano," *ECA* 322–23 (1975), pp. 418ff.

33. Cf. his basic work on spirituality, *We Drink from Our Own Wells*, trans. Matthew J. O'Connell (Maryknoll. N.Y.: Orbis Books, 1984).

34. Ellacuría, *Conversión de la Iglesia*, pp. 129–51.

35. See the work mentioned above by Gutiérrez as well as Jon Sobrino, *Spirituality of Liberation: Toward Political Holiness*, trans. Robert R. Barr (Maryknoll, N.Y.: Orbis Books, 1988).

36. This does not mean that liberation theology has developed all of the topics of theology with the same creativity. The ones we have mentioned are the ones that seem to be the most important. But as liberation theology itself is well aware, many tasks remain to be completed, among others, the problem of inculturation, the theology of women, the personal and family aspects of daily life, and so on.

4

Trinity

LEONARDO BOFF

John Paul II, in his opening address to the Latin American bishops assembled at Puebla, made a statement of fundamental importance for our trinitarian understanding of God:

> Our God, in his most intimate mystery, is not a solitude, but a family. For he intrinsically contains paternity, filiation, and the essence of the family that is love: this love in the divine family is the Holy Spirit. (Puebla, January 28, 1979)

Christianity's most transcendent assertion may well be this: In the beginning is not the solitude of One, but the communion of Three eternal Persons: Father, Son, and Holy Spirit. In the remotest beginning, communion prevails. This communion constitutes both the essence of God and at the same time the concrete dynamic of every being of the whole creation. Nothing exists only in itself and for itself. Everything is situated in an interplay of relationships through which all beings live in a coexistence with one another, by one another, and in one another. The Trinity, which is the coexistence and co-life of the Father with the Son and the Holy Spirit, constitutes the root and prototype of this universal communion. Unfortunately, this trinitarian truth and this reality of communion have largely fallen into oblivion. It is of the first importance to carry out a critique of the causes that produce this amnesia so deleterious to society and to our local and regional churches.

I. POLITICO-RELIGIOUS DIFFICULTIES FOR THE LIVING EXPERIENCE OF A TRINITARIAN FAITH

The difficulties besetting an authentic, profound experience of our trinitarian faith are many. We should like to emphasize two of these—one of a political and the other of a religious nature.

In the area of the *political*, we are heir to an age-old political authoritarianism, a concrete historical concentration of power. In the family, the father holds sway; a centuries-old patriarchy has forged relations of inequality in family and parental bonds. In civil government, monarchs have created a monopoly of power in their own hands. The chiefs of tribes or nations have almost always exercised power autocratically. The ideology created by these political phenomena has taught that, just as there is but one God, so there is but one king and one law. Genghis Khan's dictum, which could have come from the lips of any Christian ruler, has become paradigmatic: "In heaven is one God alone, and on earth but one lord: Genghis Khan, the son of God." A similar mentality prevails in religious discourse. Just as there is one God, so also there is but one Christ, one church, and one representative of Christ; for the whole world the pope, for the diocese the bishop, and for the local community the pastor. The organization of social coexistence on the basis of the concentration of power in the hands of one or few persons does not create favorable conditions for the experience of God as communion.

In the *religious* sphere, we witness a phenomenon similar to that of the political. We know of the centralized exercise of sacred power in the figure of the High Priest or *Pontifex Maximus*. Indeed, it is not rare to see the accumulation of royal and priestly power in one and the same figure. The hierarchical conception of the Roman Catholic Church has favored a unitarian view of God. A certain understanding of theological monotheism, inasmuch as it conceives God as the vertex of a pyramid of all beings, is the upshot of political and religious experiences characterized by authoritarianism and despotism. A twin phenomenon is the result. Socioreligious reality serves as a basis for the construction of a non-trinitarian, pre-trinitarian monotheism; and monotheism serves as the sacred legitimation for centralized forms of the exercise of political and religious power. It is the merit of Erik Peterson (*Monoteismo como problema politico*, 1931) to have demonstrated that, behind a certain rigid monotheism, a political problem lurks, in antiquity as in our own time. A trinitarian amnesia in the Christian experience of God is in large part owing to these phenomena. The faithful have few concrete experiences of communion, participation, and inclusive relationships that furnish them with any concrete, created reflections of a God who, in their faith, is a Trinity of persons. Dogma may teach that the true God is a communion of three divine persons until it is blue in the face; our common experience, expressed in language, is that of an exclusively monotheistic conception of God. This is not to deny, of course, the legitimacy of emphasizing the true sense of monotheism within a trinitarian understanding of God; after all, the union among the three divine persons is due to the oneness of the essence or nature of God, which is life, love, and communion.

This ascendency of monotheism occasions in many Christians a disintegrated experience of the Trinitarian mystery. Each divine person is adored as a kind of separate God, to the exclusion of the other two persons. Thus, we have a kind of modern tritheism (the doctrine that there are three gods).

Thus, there is a religion of God the Father, found in social groups of an agrarian cultural mentality. In patriarchal societies God is represented primordially as the almighty, all-knowing Father, the Judge who is Lord of life and death. There is no room beside him for a Son; created persons, instead of being God's daughters and sons, are only servants who must conform to the sovereign will of the Father in heaven. The Son and the Holy Spirit are regarded as somehow dependent on the Father (subordinationism).

There is also a religion of God the Son in certain modern circles where horizontal relations predominate and leaders and committed activists rise up in the interests of a great cause, with charismatic figures leading groups and moving the masses. In this context the figure of Christ emerges and is honored as our Teacher, our Brother, our Chief and Leader. But this "christocentrism" becomes a christomonism, in which Christ seems all, as if he had not been sent by his Father or did not have a Spirit who would see to it that his message and person would be relevant for each successive stage in history.

Finally, there is a religion of God the Holy Spirit, found particularly among charismatic groups, whether in popular milieus or among the social elite. Its hallmarks are enthusiasm, spiritual creativity, and respect for the intimate meaning found by each individual in an inner quest. In this experience, valid as it is in itself, interiority prevails to the detriment of the historical dimension and to the neglect of a crucial concern for the impoverished and their concrete, integral liberation.

The disintegration of the trinitarian experience is due to a neglect of the principal, essential perspective of the mystery of the triune God, which is communion among the divine persons. Actually, God is a coexistence of upward (the Father), lateral (the Son), and depth (the Holy Spirit) dimensions, all of which ought to be integrally present in the living experience of the believer. In trinitarian language, the Father is ever with the Son in the Spirit. The Son is interiorized in the Father by the Spirit. The Spirit joins the Father to the Son and is itself united in them. Finally, the Trinity permeates creation in its proper divine reality. Communion is the first and last word of the mystery of God and the mystery of the world.

II. LATIN AMERICAN PERSPECTIVE ON THE TRINITARIAN MYSTERY

Any theology must evince its evangelical dimension. It must be a piece of good news for persons in the situation in which they live. In Latin America the crucial challenge comes from the side of the poor, who constitute the vast majority of our population. What does it mean for the poor to believe in the Trinity? It is more than a matter of professing a dogmatic truth and managing to understand its terms. It is also a matter of an existential actualization of the mystery of communion, so that people may be concretely helped to live their humanity in a fuller and freer way.

For the believing Christian, then, two lines of reflection are available. The first begins with the trinitarian faith and meditates the insights that derive from that faith for personal and social life. The second begins with personal and social reality and asks to what extent this reality is an image and likeness of the Trinity; to what extent it contradicts, in its concrete organization, a communion among differences; and finally, whether concrete reality permits an experience of the essence of the Trinitarian mystery: the egalitarian interrelationship among the three divine persons in a communion of life and love. In the case of Latin America, we perceive how great a change in individual and social reality will be required if that reality is to become a sacrament of the holy Trinity. Here are the trinitarian roots of a Christian commitment to the transformation of society; we seek to change society because we see, in faith, that the supreme reality is the prototype of all other things, and that this supreme reality is the absolute communion of three distinct Realities, each of equal dignity, with equal love and full reciprocal communion of love and life. Furthermore, we wish our society, our visible reality, to be able to speak to us of the Trinity through our egalitarian and communitarian organization, and thus to afford us an experience of the three divine persons. Ours is the motto of the late nineteenth-century Orthodox socialist reformers of Russia: "The holy Trinity is our social program."

Having concluded our introduction, let us now address the normative data of the trinitarian faith.

III. THE FATHER'S TWO HANDS: SON AND HOLY SPIRIT

How has the holy Trinity been revealed? The holy Trinity has been revealed along two routes, and both routes must be kept in mind: the route of history, and the route of the word. Both are expressions of revelation. First, the Trinity was revealed in the lives of persons, in religions, and in the common history of human beings. Subsequently, it has been revealed in the life, passion, death, and resurrection of Jesus Christ. And finally, it has been revealed in the manifestation of the Spirit in the Christian communities. Despite the fact that men and women knew nothing of the Trinity, nevertheless the Father, the Son, and the Holy Spirit have always dwelt in the lives of all of these persons and were present in all historical processes. St. Irenaeus proclaimed, in phraseology pregnant with theological meaning: "The Son and the Holy Spirit are the two hands of the Father, by which he touches us, embraces us, and molds us to his image and likeness." These two divine persons have been sent to humanity that humanity may be inserted into the trinitarian communion. An explicit revelation of this mystery occurred only with Jesus and with manifestations of the Spirit, particularly in the primitive church. Until then, the presence of the Trinity had been conveyed only through indirect intimations. The phenomenon of Jesus made it possible for us to have a clear awareness that God is a Father who sends a Son in order to bring about, in and through the Spirit, an integral liberation of human history. We find, therefore, that the Trinity was revealed not as a doctrine but as a practice—in the attitudes and words of Christ, and in the action of the Spirit in history and in people's lives.

The most important text commonly cited to establish the revelation of the trinitarian mystery is that of Matthew 28:19: "Go, therefore, and make disciples of all the nations. Baptize them in the name of the Father, and of the Son, and of the Holy Spirit." Exegetes are of the opinion that the formula reported in this verse came into being considerably later than other sayings attributed to Jesus, alluding as it does to the baptismal experience of the primitive community at the time when the Gospel of Matthew was written, around the year 85. By then, the community had meditated a great deal on the life and words of Jesus. They understood that Jesus had actually revealed who God is: the three divine persons, in whose name all who had come to believe were to be baptized. In this sense, Jesus is indeed the source of this ecclesial formula.

It is in Jesus that we find the revelation of the trinitarian mystery.

Let us begin with the revelation of the *Father*. We know from the gospels that Jesus expressed his experience of God by constantly referring to God as a Father. He uses an expression taken from baby talk—*Abba*—especially in his personal prayer (cf. Luke 3:21–22, 5:16, 6:12, 11:1–5; Mark 14:32–42). This Father is of an infinite goodness and mercy, one who "is good to the ungrateful and the wicked" (Luke 6:35). This experience is more than a doctrine. It is at the origin of a practice of liberation in favor of the poor and outcast, the straying and the sinful. Jesus' relationship with his Father reveals a certain distance and distinction, along with a deep intimacy. Distinction is revealed in the fact that Jesus prays and prostrates himself in God's presence. Intimacy is evinced in his name for God: Papa. Someone who calls God "Father" does so because of a sense of actually being God's child (cf. Matt. 11:25–27; Mark 12:1–9, 13:32).

In Jesus is also revealed the *Son*—not so much because he referred to himself in this way (cf. Matt. 11:25–27; Mark 12:1–9, 13:32), but because he acted as the Son of God. His actual, living practice bespeaks an authority that can only be situated in the sphere of the divine. He represents the Father in the world, and he makes that Father visible in his goodness and mercy. As his fellow Jews said so well, Jesus "made himself God's equal" (cf. John 5:18). Peter grasps the mystery of Jesus and professes, "You are the Messiah, the Son of the living God!" (Matt. 16:16). The text that most directly speaks of the Trinity is that reported by Matthew (11:25–27), especially in its Lucan version:

> At that moment Jesus rejoiced in the Holy Spirit and said: "I offer you praise, O Father, Lord of heaven and earth, because what you have hidden from the learned and the clever you have revealed to the merest children.
>
> "Yes, Father, you have graciously willed it so. Everything has been given over to me by my Father. No one knows the Son except the Father and no one knows the Father except the Son—and anyone to whom the Son wishes to reveal him." (Luke 10:21–22)

Here we have an explicit reference to the three persons, and in their reciprocal relationship.

As for the revelation of the *Son*, the testimony from heaven on the occasion of Jesus' baptism is also important. We do not know whether the account refers to an actual event, or whether it is simply an attempt to express Jesus' intimate experience in a literary form. In any case, in his baptism, just as in his transfiguration on Tabor, the divine testimony is explicit: "This is my beloved Son. My favor rests on him" (Matt. 3:17; cf. 17:5).

Another text of basic importance is the one formulated by the theology of John: "The Father and I are one" (John 10:30); "That all may be one as you, Father, are in me, and I in you; I pray that they may be [one] in us, that the world may believe that you sent me" (John 17:21). The text does not say that Jesus and the Father are "one" in the sense of being one *person* (for which the Greek would have used the masculine gender, *heis*, "one [person]"); it says that they are one *thing* (using the neuter *hen*, "one [thing]")—that is, a reality of participation or sharing, and of reciprocal communion. Finally, the moment of the great revelation of the Son is surely the moment of the Paschal mystery, in which we have the essence of the Trinity as communion, with the Son delivering himself up out of love and in loyalty to the Father, and the Father, once more out of love, responding to the Son by raising him from the dead. The fullness of Jesus' new life shows the presence of the Spirit, an expression of the new life of communion prevailing among the divine persons.

Theological reflection has sought to express this mutual implication by developing the doctrine of the Trinity, from the first centuries of Christianity until our very day.

Finally, we have the revelation of the *Holy Spirit*. This occurs in Jesus' own life. He is the permanent vehicle of the Spirit. The Spirit is that power (*dynamis*) and that authority (*exousia*) by which he performs wonders and deeds of liberation (Mark 3:20–30). Jesus says explicitly: "If it is by the Spirit of God that I expel demons, then the reign of God has overtaken you" (Matt. 12:28). The Spirit is the power dwelling in Jesus and taking everyone by surprise, as in the case of the woman with a hemorrhage: "Jesus was conscious at once that healing power had gone out from him" (Mark 5:30). This power is in Jesus, and at the same time it is distinct from Jesus. A trinitarian understanding will later say: the Spirit and the Son have the same nature of life, communion, and love, but are distinct divine persons.

There are other texts in the Christian scriptures that speak of God in trinitarian fashion. They present not a developed doctrine, but an awareness that Jesus Christ, the Holy Spirit, and the Father are equally God. For example, the text from Second Corinthians that we use in our eucharistic celebrations reads, "The grace of the Lord Jesus Christ, and the love of God, and the fellowship of the Holy Spirit be with you all!" (2 Cor. 13:13). Another very meaningful text is that of Second Thessalonians: "We are bound to thank God for you always, beloved brothers in the Lord, because you are the first fruits of those whom God has chosen for salvation, in holiness of spirit and fidelity to truth. He called you through our preaching of the good news so that you might achieve the glory of our Lord Jesus Christ" (2 Thess. 2:13). Here a thought is formulated that is organized in trinitarian style; it will culminate later in the theological reflection of the second to the fifth centuries. See also this other text, from Galatians: "The proof that you are sons is the fact that God has sent forth into our hearts the spirit of his Son which cries out 'Abba!' ('Father!')" (Gal. 4:6). Many other texts reveal the conviction of the first Christians that, with the Jesus event, there had been communicated to them the true understanding of God as a communion of persons (see 1 Cor. 12:4–5; 2 Cor. 1:21–22, 3:3; Rom. 15:16, 15:4; Phil. 3:3; Gal. 3:11–14; Eph. 2:18,20–22, 3:14–16; Rev. 1:4–5; among others). The sense of all of these texts is that, in God's approach to us for our salvation, there was revealed the communion of the divine three who always act together and who insert persons into their life and their love.

We Christians take a trinitarian point of departure in reading the Hebrew scriptures, as well. There we discover signs of the trinitarian mystery in the personification of the word of God (Pss. 119:89, 147:15ff.; Wisd. 16:12) and wisdom (cf. Prov. 1:20–23, 8, 9:1–6; Job 28; Sir. 24; Wisd. 16:12), and the hypostatization of the Holy Spirit. Basically, the Spirit is God in the divine strength. The Spirit is the divine presence in creation and history. This strength and presence gradually come to be seen as autonomous, while always "relational," realities, such that they appear as the Spirit of the Son, the Spirit that has us say *Abba*, Father, the Spirit who dwells in us as in its own temple.

IV. HUMAN REASON AND TRINITARIAN MYSTERY

Reflexive thought never has the first word. First comes life, celebration of life, and work. Only then do reflection and doctrines appear. This is what occurred with the trinitarian faith of the first Christians. They began by expressing their trinitarian faith in doxologies (prayers of praise), sacraments (baptism and the eucharist), and the first professions of faith. Afterward, they began to reflect on what they celebrated and believed. It was then that the trinitarian doctrine came into being.

The first question to arise was: How is faith in one God, to which the whole of the Hebrew scriptures attest, to be reconciled with faith in the Trinity, as professed in the Christian scriptures? In an attempt to answer this question, the first heresies arose—erroneous ways of understanding the mystery. What generally occurs in theology is what happens in the other sciences: it is in combating errors that we arrive at truth. The Christian community rejected three forms of representation of the trinitarian mystery: modalism, subordinationism, and tritheism.

Modalism declares that there can only be one God, who dwells in inaccessible light. But, the modalists teach, when that God undertakes a self-revelation to human beings, God appears under three distinct "modes," which are a kind of mask with which one and the same God is presented now as Father, now as Son, now as Holy Spirit. This interpretation, which was never accepted by the church, rejects Christianity's original understanding of the communion of three really distinct divine persons. Modalism leaves us with an unqualified monotheism.

Subordinationism says that only the Father is fully God. The Son and Holy Spirit are subordinate to the Father. Surely they are the most exalted of creatures, nearest to the Father, but they do not have the same nature as the Father. Some subordinationists went so far as to say that the Son is adopted by the Father (adoptionism) and therefore is elevated above the station of any other creature, but is not God as the Father is God. This formulation rejects the equality of the divine persons, who are all equally God by virtue of the same nature of life and love. The Council of Nicea (325) condemned this doctrine in particular.

Tritheism asserts that the three divine persons are indeed distinct, in fact, completely autonomous and independent of one another. Thus, there are three Gods. But how can there be three infinite things, three absolutes? This doctrine, too, was rejected by the church, because it neglects the communion obtaining among the three divine persons, an interrelationship so profound and so absolute that the three persons are but one God.

After a hundred and fifty years of reflection, discussion, and ecumenical councils (the principal ones, bearing directly on our subject, are Nicea in 325, Constantinople in 381, Chalcedon in 451, as well as the Fourth Lateran in 1215, and Florence in 1431–47), a technical language was created, a language of theological reflection that could obviate mistaken understandings of the trinitarian faith. But the language coined paid a high price in terms of faith experience in exchange for its great theoretical rigor. It is formalistic. Let us consider its key words.

1. *Nature* or *essence* or *substance*. These words each denote the unitive factor in God, which is absolutely identical in each of the divine persons. The divine nature (essence, substance) is numerically one, and unique.

2. *Person* or *hypostasis* is the distinguishing element in God. It denotes each of the respective persons of Father, Son, and Holy Spirit. By *person* we mean concrete, intellectual individuality, existing in itself, but always in openness to other persons. Thus, the Father is distinct from the Son (each person exists *in* itself), but the entire existence of the First Person consists in its "facing" the Son and the Holy Spirit (each exists *for* the others). The same is true in turn for the Son and the Holy Spirit.

3. The term *procession* designates the manner and order in which one person "proceeds" from another. The word *procession* is not to be understood in a causal sense, as if the Son and Holy Spirit were less eternal, infinite, or almighty than the Father. It is a technical expression denoting communion in a certain logical, but real, order of understanding. There are two processions in the Trinity: the generation of the Son and the "spiration" of the Holy Spirit. The explanation that has prevailed is that the Father knows himself so perfectly that he generates an absolute image of himself, which is the Son. The Father and the Son contemplate each other and love each other so radically that the expression of this relation emerges concretely: the Holy Spirit, as bond between Father and Son, as their love for each other.

4. *Relations*: These are the connections among the divine persons. The Father, in relation to the Son, has parenthood; the Son, in relation to the Father, has filiation; Father and Son, in relation to the Holy Spirit, have active spiration; the Holy Spirit, in relation to the Father and the Son, has passive spiration. The relations distinguish the persons from one another.

5. *Perichoresis* or *circuminsession*: As the etymology of the words suggests, these expressions denote the radical coexistence, cohabitation, and interpenetration of the three divine persons with one another in virtue of the relations among them. It is a total circulation of life and love, in perfect coequality, without any anteriority or superiority. This is the model on which we Christians develop our social utopia, which is also a community of equality in respect for differences: a full, living communion of the most diverse relationships.

6. A *mission* is the presence of one or more of the divine persons in the concrete history of creation. It denotes the self-communication of a divine person to someone distinct from it. We know of two missions: that of the Son, who became incarnate in order to divinize us, and that of the Holy Spirit, who dwells in us in order to unify all things and to lead all creation to the Reign of the Trinity.

With these theoretical instruments, we can construct an orthodox reading of our faith in the Trinity of persons and unity of the single nature consisting of one communion and love. The history of trinitarian reflection is the history of three great tendencies to systematization. These tendencies do not materialize in a vacuum. We find them in social and ideological conditions that explain precisely why one of them surfaced in a given case rather than either of the others.

The Christians of the Roman Empire lived in an atmosphere of social dissolution, in which the prevailing religion was polytheistic. It was natural, then, for them to underscore the oneness of God, and to de-emphasize the distinction among the divine persons. To preach the Trinity was to run the risk of misinterpretation on the part of their pagan audiences; the Christian discourse could sound to them like a confirmation of their own polytheism. Thus, the social and ideological context of the time and place encouraged Christians to focus their reflection first and foremost on the oneness of God, and only then, on this basis, on the distinction of persons in God.

In another atmosphere, that of the Greeks, an insistence on monotheism and the absolute monarchy of God might have made it impossible to profess a faith in Jesus Christ as the divine Son. Here, reflection shifted from the distinction among the divine persons to their unity.

In a situation in which individualism and a lack of communion predominate, as in the modern world, especially in Latin America, reflection will appropriately direct its examination not so much to monotheism or trinitarianism, but to the manner of relationship that prevails among the divine persons. Consequently, insistence is on communion as the essence of the Trinity and the foundation of all human solidarity.

Throughout, we discern the presence of the history that permits an appropriation of the mystery conformed to prevailing human questions. Detailing the various kinds of systematization, we have:

1. The *Greeks* begin with the person of the Father. Here is the source and origin of all divinity. The Creed suggests this: "We believe in one God, the Father, the Almighty." In the act of self-expression, the person of the almighty Father generates the Son as its Word, at the same time as it spirates the Spirit as its Breath. To both it communicates its nature. Thus, the persons are "consubstantial"; they possess the same nature as the Father. Therefore there is no multiplicity in God; that is, the persons are but one God. The principal significance of this systematization resides in its constant personalization of God. God is thought of as Father, and not merely as an infinite, eternal substance that is God. There is still the risk of subordinationism. All is concentrated in the Father. The Son and the Spirit are expressions of the single principle contained in the Father.

2. The *Latins* begin with the single divine nature. In the Creed, they underscore the first part of the initial verse: "We believe in one God." This God is an absolute, and absolutely perfect, Spirit. But it is the property of spirit to be *reflexivus sui*: to think and to will. Now, in thinking itself absolutely, the person of the Father generates an absolute expression of itself: the Word, or Son. In generating the Son, God is revealed as Father. Father and Son love one another so completely that they spirate the Holy Spirit as the expression of their reciprocal love, thus consummating the trinitarian circle. This approach safeguards the trinitarian oneness from the outset. But it runs the risk of modalism—the doctrine that the persons are only distinct presentations of the one divine substance, rather than being really distinct persons.

3. Many *modern theologians* begin with the relations among the divine persons. The primary datum of the revelation in the Christian scriptures is that God is Father, Son, and Holy Spirit. But that revelation also insists upon a perichoresis among the persons: an "intimate, perfect indwelling of each person in the others," such that among the persons prevails the unity of one God. The persons are three infinite subjects of a single communion, or three lovers in the same love. It is this third approach that we adopt, as it responds to the deepest needs of the poor, who seek

participation, communion, and a more egalitarian coexistence, maintained in respect for differences. The poor find inspiration in the holy Trinity.

V. A LIBERATIVE CONCEPTION OF THE TRINITY

As we have already indicated, the harsh contradictions of Latin American reality invite us to experience and reflect on the trinitarian mystery as a mystery of communion among distinct persons. This perspective offers Christians the ultimate foundation of their commitment to the liberation of the oppressed—a liberation undertaken with a view to social justice, equity, and the construction of a society of sisters and brothers that will be viable in our conditions.

We shall have to begin with the major theo-logical datum of the Christian scriptures: that God is the Father, the Son, and the Holy Spirit, in communion. The only God who exists is the Trinity of persons. The divine oneness is communitarian; each person subsists in total, absolute communion with the other two.

What does it mean to say that God is communion, and therefore is Trinity? Let us observe that only persons can be in communion. To be in communion implies that one person is present to another in radical reciprocity. It implies that one person "opens" to the other in a self-bestowal without reserve. To say that God is communion means that the Father, the Son, and the Holy Spirit are ever together, emerging together and constantly face to face. The scriptures proclaim this reciprocal communication among the divine persons in these terms: God is one God of life and of all life. Jesus himself, the eternal Son incarnate, presented himself as a vessel of life, and of life in abundance (John 10:10). Let us briefly analyze what *life* implies, with a view to a better grasp of the communion obtaining among the three divine persons. Life is a mystery of spontaneity, in an inexhaustible process of giving and receiving, of assimilating and of surrendering one's own life for the life of another. All life has presence. To be present is not simply to be "here." Presence is an intensification of existence. A living being "speaks for itself"; it has no need of words in order to communicate itself. It is already communication—so much so that its very being forces others to take a position in its regard, a position either of acceptance or of rejection. All life expands and enters into communion with its surroundings, establishing relations with those surroundings. Every living being is "for" another living being, and this relation guarantees its own life. Something of the kind occurs in the case of the holy Trinity. Each of the divine persons is for the others, with the others, and in the others. Accordingly, we understand that the only category capable of expressing this reality is *communion*, and that this concrete communion will generate the divine community. There will be no simple Father-Son duality here—an independent relationship of two and only two distinct persons face to face. This is a Trinity, and thus it will include a third member, the Holy Spirit, thus establishing a richer manner of living coexistence than that of the mutual contemplation of two divine persons alone.

Life is the essence of God. And life is communion given and received. This kind of communion is love. Communion and love are the essence of God the Trinity.

In order to express this interpenetration of the divine persons, theology has coined a special word. The term achieved its currency with St. John Damascene:

perichoresis. *Perichoresis* denotes, first of all, the action of involvement of each person with the other two. Each of the divine persons penetrates each of the others and allows itself to be penetrated by it. This phenomenon is the property of love, and it is natural in the process of communion. Thus, the divine three are locked from all eternity in an infinite encounter of love and life, each in the direction of each of the others. The second meaning of the divine perichoresis is that, as an effect of this interpenetration, each person lives and dwells in each of the others. As the Council of Florence (1441) taught: "The Father is wholly in the Son and wholly in the Holy Spirit. The Son is wholly in the Father and in the Holy Spirit. The Holy Spirit is wholly in the Father and in the Son. None precedes another in eternity, exceeds it in greatness, or surpasses it in power." The holy Trinity, then, is a mystery of inclusion. The Son and the Spirit have been sent to us that all creation may "participate" or share in them.

By reason of the perichoresis obtaining among the divine persons, the relations among them are always triple. Thus, the Father is revealed by the Son in the Holy Spirit. The Son, in turn, reveals the Father in the power of the Spirit. Finally, the Holy Spirit "proceeds" from the Father and rests upon the Son. In this wise, the Spirit is from the Father through the Son ("*ex Patre Filioque*"), as the person of the Son recognizes itself in the Father by the love of the Spirit ("*a Patre Spirituque*," we might say). The divine perichoresis precludes any superimposition upon or subordination of one person to another. All are equally eternal and infinite. The perichoresis permits us to say: There are not first the three persons, and thereupon their relation; the three are intertwined, and live their relation of eternal communion from the outset. Therefore there is one God: God-Trinity.

The trinitarian dynamic enables us to construct a social and ecclesial critique and to discover in the perichoresis of the divine persons inspiration for our human relationships. Undeniably, human beings have a basic aspiration for participation, equality, respect for differences, and communion with God. In our peripheral societies these values are by and large denied. Hence the longings for liberation there, and the age-old struggles of the oppressed for their life and freedom.

In the capitalist system, under which we all suffer, everything is centered upon the individual and individual development. There is no essential regard for others or for society. Goods are privately appropriated, to the exclusion of ownership on the part of the vast majority of persons. Individual differences are valued to the detriment of communion. The socialist system, for its part, emphasizes universal participation, which, as far as the ideal is concerned, more nearly resembles the trinitarian dynamic. But personal differences mean little here. Socialist society tends to constitute a mass rather than a people, because a people is the fruit of a whole network of communities and associations in which persons count. The trinitarian mystery invites us to adopt social forms that value *all* relations among persons and institutions and foster an egalitarian, familial community in which differences will be positively welcomed. As the Christians of the base church communities have formulated it: The holy Trinity is the best community.

A contemplation of the mystery of the Trinity helps local and regional churches improve their internal organization. The Roman Catholic Church, especially, tends to live a societal model rather than a communitarian one. Power is centralized in the clerical corps, and the faithful are guided in a manner that tends to be authoritarian, with very little differentiated participation on the part of all. A monarchical conception of power was imposed on the church historically. Here it was not a trinitarian reflection, a mindset governed by the notion of communion, that prevailed; instead, the dominant view was pre-trinitarian, even a-trinitarian. If we accept, in faith, that the holy Trinity is the best community, and that it is by communion that the divine persons are joined together in one God, we can then postulate a model of church more adequate to its source, from which its life and oneness spring (cf. *Lumen Gentium*, no. 4). The church, theologically, is the *communitas fidelium*—the community of believers. Each member has his or her gifts, and these gifts ought to be experienced in such a way that they are turned to the benefit of all. What builds community is precisely the living experience of communion, which involves everyone's acceptance of and respect for everyone else.

To the extent that anyone creates communion, that person becomes a sacrament of the holy Trinity. In the church community a consideration of the trinitarian communion ought to prevent the concentration of power and open the way for a broad, egalitarian participation on the part of all. Not everyone can do everything. Each person performs his or her own task, but in communion with everyone else. In this fashion the whole church is transformed into a sign of the Trinity; after all, now it lives the essence of the holy Trinity itself, which is communion.

VI. DISTINCT PERSONS

Having set forth the principal considerations of the trinitarian mystery, let us now consider—still in the perichoretic dialectic—the distinct persons.

1. The Father: Unfathomable Mystery

The person of the Father is bottomless mystery, and therefore invisible. "No one has ever seen God. It is God the only Son, ever at the Father's side, who has revealed him" (John 1:18; cf. 6:46; 1 Tim. 6:16; 1 John 4:12). The Son has revealed the Father precisely as a Father who has a Son and who lives in an eternal coexistence with the Holy Spirit. Jesus' intimacy with his Father is such that he was able to say: "Whoever has seen me has seen the Father" (John 14:9). The Father is the one who eternally is, even if no creature had ever existed. This person is the Father, not because the Father has created anything, but because the Father has "generated" the Son in the Holy Spirit. In the Son, the Father has projected all created or creatable daughters and sons. Thus the Father is the root of all parenthood, as well as of all brotherhood and sisterhood.

When we refer to the Father, we indicate the ultimate horizon of all, the One at the origin of all and containing all. Only from a point of departure in the Father is it possible to understand anything of the Son or of the Holy Spirit. True, the three divine persons are ever "simultaneous," eternally together. But in order to grasp anything of the mystery of God, we must begin with the Father. Here is the person who is "first" among the simultaneous three, if we wish to set down a certain order among the divine persons. But this is our manner of speaking, in our human faith.

It is always important to remember that in the trinitarian communion no person is before, after, higher, or lower than either of the others. The divine three are coequal, coeternal, and co-loving. But it is in the person of the Father that the entire divine mystery demonstrates its bottomlessness.

2. The Son: Mystery of Communication and Integral Liberation

God's self-revelation is the revelation of God as God actually is: as a Trinity of persons. In revealing themselves in the world, the divine persons reveal their essential condition as members of a Trinity. The Son is the absolute expression of the Father. All that is communicable of the mystery achieves concrete form in the person of the Son. The Son is the visible image of the unfathomable Father (cf. Col. 1:15). Thus, this person is supreme communication. Now, this eternal Son has been sent by the Father and has become incarnate by the power of the Holy Spirit. His life, his liberative practice, his struggles with those who hold power, his tenderness with the abandoned, his passion, death, and resurrection have revealed God in a definitive way. Not only has he communicated to us the truth of God as Father of all and advocate of the poor, but he has acted as the Son sent by that Father. He adopts the same attitudes of mercy as his Father. He builds the Reign of the Father: "My Father is at work until now, and I am at work as well" (John 5:17). But the Son's grandest communication has been that of making us, as well, sons and daughters of God. The meaning of his incarnation is not exhausted in the process of redemption, although the latter is a necessary step for a fallen creation. The most radical element in his incarnation consists in giving all creatures a share in his filiation. By its incarnation, the word [*Verbo*] has "verbified" the entire universe, and thus has led it into the very heart of the trinitarian mystery.

3. The Holy Spirit: Mover of Creation Toward the Reign of the Trinity

The Holy Spirit transcends the face-to-face relation of the Father and the Son to introduce a new element: the "we" of the divine persons. Thus, the Holy Spirit is, par excellence, the unity of the divine persons. All of the persons face one another, but it is in the person of the Holy Spirit that we best see this characteristic of the whole divine perichoresis. What the Spirit is in the "immanent" Trinity, thereupon appears in the "economic" Trinity—the Trinity in the history of creation. The Holy Spirit is the power of union within all beings. By the power of the Spirit, radical novelty bursts into history and thus anticipates the substance of the Reign of the Holy Trinity. In particular, it is the Holy Spirit who bestirs our memory of Jesus. The Spirit does not allow the words of Christ to remain a dead letter, but brings it about that they ever be reread, gain new meanings, and inspire liberative practices. The Spirit is also the principle of liberation from all that diminishes existence "in the flesh," to use the scriptural term. Where the Spirit is, there is freedom (cf. 1 Cor. 3:17). And where there is freedom, differences emerge, along with the most varied gifts. It is the Spirit who prevents differences from degenerating into inequalities and discrimination, maintaining all things in communion.

The Spirit, too, has been sent to the world, along with the Son. Luke suggests that it was the Virgin Mary who first received the Holy Spirit substantially: "The angel answered her: 'The Holy Spirit will come upon you and the power of the Most High will overshadow you; hence, the holy offspring to be born will be called Son of God' " (Luke 1:35). *Overshadow* is the expression the Bible uses when God enters a tent to dwell there (cf. Exod. 40:34–35). Thus, in our text from Luke, the Holy Spirit is said to be not only about to enter Mary, but to dwell within her permanently. Well does tradition call Mary the "sacrarium of the Holy Spirit" (cf. *Lumen Gentium*, no. 53). A unique relationship obtains between Mary and the Spirit, inasmuch as it is through the presence of the Spirit within her that the Son takes flesh and human form. The humanity of the eternal Word is the humanity of Mary, who, by the action of the Holy Spirit, brings it about that her offspring is a being both divine and human.

Finally, it is the deed of the Spirit to "lead back" to its eschatological plenitude the whole of creation. The new creation, redeemed and spiritualized, will finally be introduced into the Reign of the Holy Trinity. Only then will God-Trinity be "all in all"—everything in everything.

VII. SACRAMENTS OF THE TRINITY IN HISTORY

Faith is not expressed only by the intellect that delves into mysteries, nor indeed only by the heart that loves and trustingly surrenders itself to the divine persons. We think that it is expressed by the imagination, as well—that measureless capacity of the human being ever to add something to reality, ever to identify the potentialities concealed in every being. Imagination sees connections to which reason is often blind. And so, for the sake of a nearer approach to the trinitarian mystery, many analogies have been used. Let us briefly refer to three of them.

First, the human person is seen as a great parable of the trinitarian mystery. Every person is an unfathomable mystery. But this mystery is communicated through the light of the intelligence and opens to others in love and commitment through the will. Now, these three dimensions are not merely juxtaposed realities; they interpenetrate to constitute the single dynamics of the person in his or her existential oneness. The Father appears in the dimension of the human person that is mystery, the Son in the intelligence that communicates this mystery, and the Spirit in the love that unites it with all other beings.

Another symbol of the Trinity is the human family. The psychological unity of the person is structured as a triad. Man opens to woman and vice versa. This relation does not turn in upon itself but bears fruit in the generation of a child. If this openness is missing, the human relationship falls short of its fullness. In the family we have all three relational terms: father, mother, and child. Each of the three is distinct from each of the others, but all are intertwined by bonds of love. They are three, but they are one communion of life. The case is somewhat the same with the divine family: here too are three distinct persons, bound together in a single dynamic of life, love, and complete communion.

Finally, human society itself can be seen as a symbolic reference to the mystery of the holy Trinity. Any society will be constructed on the basis of an articulation of three forces, which always operate in simultaneity: the economic, the political, and the cultural. Through the economic force we ensure the production and reproduction of life. This is the most fundamental force, as it is the necessary condition for each of the others. By the political force we organize socially, distributing power and common responsibilities. Politics, or the political force, is a function of the human relationships through which we build the kind of society that is possible in a given segment of history. By culture, we project values—existential meanings, including transcendent meanings, through which we express the nature of the human being as that being that can view its existence as a problem and endow its task with a meaning.

Every society is constructed, consolidated, and developed by the coexistence and interpenetration of these three forces. They always act together in such wise that the economic is in the political and the cultural, and so on in turn. There is a certain similarity here with the holy Trinity; the three divine persons, while distinct, are everlastingly together, and they act together within and without the trinitarian circle.

In conclusion, we acknowledge the insufficiency of our human concepts and expressions to signify the mystery of the Father, the Son, and the Holy Spirit in their reciprocal communion. Our words conceal more than they reveal. The end of our quest, then, must be not in the intelligence that examines, but in the heart that praises—the heart that opens itself to an acceptance of the divine mystery within the human mystery. All of the great theologians—St. Augustine, St. Bonaventure, St. Thomas Aquinas, and the rest—concluded their treatises on the holy Trinity with hymns of adoration to such an august mystery. We honor the Trinity with our silence, in the awareness that all that we can say is no more than stammering concerning a mystery ever to be lauded and praised: Glory to the Father, and to the Son, and to the Holy Spirit. Amen.

—Translated by Robert R. Barr

5

God the Father

RONALDO MUÑOZ

I. CURRENCY OF THE TOPIC OF GOD

A renewed *experience* of God has been the core of the new Christian consciousness in Latin America ever since this reawakening began.[1] Reflection on the *topic* of God, however, has acquired its importance in Latin American theology only more gradually. Indeed, only recently have our theologians begun to address that topic in systematic fashion.[2]

From the earliest years of this renewal, the biblical image of a God of liberation and justice for the oppressed of the earth has been an ongoing, joyful discovery for us. Precisely this God is the heart and soul of our movement. The God of our discovery contrasts sharply with the God of punishment and passive resignation—whom we now begin to recognize as having been imposed by dominant groups and by agents of the church having ties to the same.[3]

In a first stage (the late 1960s and early 1970s), the experience to which we refer was primarily that of small groups of educated persons concerned with "becoming more political." In those years the principal biblical referents were the God of the Exodus and of the prophets, together with certain psalms, and the historical Jesus seen as the inspiration for an urgent social and cultural revolution.

Further down the road (in the late 1970s and in the 1980s) our experience broadened to include the people of the poor themselves, in and through the base communities and with the support of a considerable number of priests and pastoral ministers of the various local churches. Here the effort was not only to inspire social struggles, but to rescue popular life in all its facets. Now the central biblical referent for the renewed experience of God was Jesus Christ himself, the Messiah of the poor and the preacher of the Reign,[4] the one crucified by the mighty and raised again by the God of life, the Son of the Father.

This shift, this process of Christian maturation, has not meant a blurring of the profile of our new experience of the biblical God, or any tempering of the conflict that experience implies with received religious forms and the beliefs of the dominant groups. On the contrary, while we had originally spoken of a diversity of *images* of God, now our tendency was to adopt the realism of the radical confrontation posited by the Bible itself between the one God, living and true (revealed to the poor, and standing in solidarity with their cause) and the *idols* of death and the lie (revealed in the discourse and practices of the dominant groups and in the "structures of sin" imposed by these latter).[5]

II. THE GOD OF JESUS AMONG US

The Latin American recovery of the experience of a God of liberation, who has always acted in the history of the poor, is profoundly marked by a rediscovery of the *human Jesus*, who lived and made commitments in a public ministry and concrete history.[6] The question here is not that of any possible distinction between a "Jesus of history" and a "Christ of faith." The latter is a question posed by the academic theology of Europe. On the contrary, what is important to us on our continent, what gives us rebirth and liberation, is precisely the rediscovery of the full humanity of Jesus Christ, the Lord who was raised and the Son of the Father—that very one who walks with us now, the one in communion with whom we live by faith. We make this rediscovery in those two, inseparable loci of our Christian faith: the people of the poor, with the beliefs and practices of their popular Christianity and with their liberative solidarity; and the church community among these same poor, with its concrete brotherhood and sisterhood, its proclamation and celebration of the word, and its ministries and services. Here is the twin font of our engagement in an ongoing reencounter with the Jesus of the gospels—our rediscovery of the one who has shown us the love, presence, and project of his divine Father in a historical situation that offers so many profound analogies with our own, and who has done so through human attitudes and deeds, through concrete social options and liberative practices that are our norm and our hope precisely because they are the testimony and call of the living God in our midst.

In this sense the rediscovery of the historical Jesus is becoming more and more a characteristic of our very experience of God. Little by little, along this route, we are transcending the schema of the customary Catholic catechesis, which has only been a simplified summary of the scholastic theology taught in seminaries. That theology had started with God *in se*, whom it attempted to "explain" in a speculative philosophical language; it then went on with the Trinity, approaching the latter as a kind of divine secret revealed to Christians, and then showed that Jesus Christ is one of this Trinity, the Son, who became incarnate, founded the church, and then returned to the Father. In this schema it seemed taken for granted that God as such was a more or less evident reality for us, and the Trinity a kind of enigmatic code for the divine transcendence.

But we cannot actually be sure of knowing the true God, nor can the Trinity have any meaning for us before we meet that singular human being called Jesus of Nazareth. Failing this encounter with the historical Jesus, then, frequently the God conjured up for us resembled more the supreme principle and changeless perfection of the philosophy of an intellectual elite than the merciful Father who is revealed to the simple. God seemed more the almighty one invoked by the ideology of the dominant classes than the liberator of the oppressed and avenger of the lowly. We even projected this celestial personage upon our image of Christ, whom we therefore frequently confounded with the figure of this almighty, impassible "God."

Today we apply something of a reverse schema. More and more in the foreground is Jesus of Nazareth, in his Messianic history as narrated in the gospels. Then this Jesus the Christ shows us the Reign of God as a dynamism of liberation and life, a dynamism among the poor. Next, here is a Jesus who personally experiences, and restores to us, a communion with our divine Father, a communion we share with all his brothers and sisters, who thus become *our* brothers and sisters. But Jesus is rejected by those who feel secure and who hold power; indeed, he is executed by the authorities on the gallows of the cross. This same Jesus—raised from the dead—now walks with us, calls to us, and encourages us.

"God as such," then, appears before us only in an indirect manner. God *in se* is not the central "theme" of Jesus' preaching, nor therefore is it the direct "object" of Christian experience. What we properly experience and practice, what we suffer and build, is our human history. But in this history of liberative solidarity and shared joy—the history of Jesus, and our own history "in his name"—the living God becomes present in God's liberating love and God's joy. This God of the Reign, the Father of Jesus Christ, is the one who raises the Crucified One from the dead, and who bestows on us the gift of the Spirit of the one raised, that we too may embrace his cause and follow his way, and thus "ver-ify" and "know" the one true God.[7]

This is why the first Christian preaching, like the whole of Christian scriptures, calls upon its hearers with such urgency to "follow Jesus Christ," to "believe in the Son," to "accept the word" and to respond to that word with their whole lives, insisting that Jesus alone "has the words of eternal life," and is "the way, the truth, and the life." Hence the decisive importance ascribed by ancient Christian theology and by the church's Creed to the assertion of the full divinity of Christ and his equality with the Father. For it is this Jesus, and he alone—Mary's son, crucified under Pontius Pilate, as human and historical a person as ourselves—who is "the only Son of God, eternally begotten of the Father, God [proceeding] from God, Light from Light, true God from true God, . . . one in Being [consubstantial] with the Father."[8]

Indeed, that Jesus, in exercising his public ministry and in sending forth his disciples, as recounted in the Christian scriptures, comes not to purify the concepts of the dominant religions, or to salvage the intuitions of a "natural knowledge of God," or merely to restore the religious traditions of his chosen people. That same Jesus—as God's witness—in the conflict-ridden, religiously ambiguous world of his time, made very precise options, and took very clear, concrete positions, battling upstream against so many oppressive religious and social practices. He struggled to reverse the deformations in the conception of God that these practices betrayed, and—when it was all over—he was sentenced and executed for acting in consistency with his testimony to a God in contradiction with the "God" of the established sociopolitical and religious order.

Accordingly, in the testimony of this Jesus concerning God, a testimony which God has personally confirmed by raising him from the dead, we have been given the definitive key to the recognition—at any time, in any social or ecclesiastical situation—of the true image of the living God, which we can now distinguish from its caricatures and falsifications.

III. GOD IN THE LIBERATION OF THE OPPRESSED

We have "known" the God of the Bible—we have had the experience of the living reality of this God, we have been caught up and involved in communion with this God—because God has personally sought to intervene *in collective history.* That is, God has executed "judgments" upon this history, in order to liberate oppressed, exploited, and disintegrated human groups and make of them a people of free human beings living in solidarity. These groups have lived their condition of oppression and servitude as a condition "sacralized" in the cult of the false gods of the despotic power and the privatized wealth of the dominators: of Pharaoh and the magnates of Egypt, of the haughty monarchs and monopolistic groups of Israel itself, of the heads and privileged groups of the great empires. Their new condition as an organized, free people, a people of brothers and sisters, is the product of their encounter with the true God, a product of the covenant that this God bestows upon us. Here is a covenant of humble service, and of the sharing of goods among the poor of the earth. Liberation and access to the Reign of God mean abandoning the idols of domination and massacre, and converting and belonging to the living and true God, the God of solidarity and a fully human life for all. In our reading of the Bible today—Old and New Testaments—in the faith-filled pilgrimage of our people, we do not "confuse" our Christian faith with the tasks of collective liberation that we may share with nonbelievers, we do not "reduce" that faith to these tasks. But neither do we separate, in our Christian faith and practice, the spiritual, religious dimension from the more temporal, social one. We do not sever our experience of the living God, and fidelity to that God, from our commitment to the liberation of the oppressed and our struggle for a just society of brothers and sisters.[9]

Thus the one true God personally reveals an active presence and call not in the great ones of the earth, not in the "sacred power" of human hierarchies, not in an elitist culture and the prestige of the "governing classes," but *in our neighbor in need*, recognized and served as our brother or sister, and *in the multitude of poor and outcast*, with their privations, their misery, and their hope. God's dynamic presence and summons is not in the simulated order and cliquish security of a classist, repressive society, but in a longing and an effort for a more just and more human life and coexistence, along the path of love, solidarity, and the surrender of our very life. The God of liberation is not in competitive, monopolistic economic success, not in the technological progress and finicky welfare of a privileged minority, but in the experience of solidarity we behold in a lowly people, in communities of brothers and sisters, in which we acknowledge ourselves to be responsible for one another, and where we learn to share goods and services. The God of our deliverance comes to us in the inspiring utopia of a universal relationship of love, a utopia that mobilizes us for action.

As we read the Bible and discover its living tradition from the outlook of the poor, we find that if there is a "sacred" dimension and "religious" experience when it comes to the power of the great, repressive order, and the individualistic accumulation of wealth, it is the experience of the negative or perverse sacred: an idolatry of wealth and "structures of sin," the gods of oppression, the "Prince of this world." These are lying, lethal gods. They are this for the outcast, oppressed multitudes, of course; this goes without saying. But they are deadly, mendacious gods for the dominating minorities as well (cf. Matt. 6:19–24; Luke 4:5–8, 12:13–34, 16:1–15, 20:20–26, 22:39–53; John 12:31–32, 14:30; Rev. 13:1–18). The true God is the God of the Beatitudes and the Magnificat, the God of the Reign bestowed on the poor and those who hunger and thirst for justice, the God who raises him who has been crucified by the powers and sacred hierarchies of this world, the "all in all" God of universal reconciliation and kinship; in brief, the God of life, the God of a full life, shared by all.

From the locus of the impoverished and repressed of the earth, that true God communicates the wisdom and power of the divine Spirit, distributes gifts and talents, *with an appeal to human responsibility* to reverse the social dynamics of greed and domination and build a coexistence of justice, solidarity, and love. This God appeals to the generous, intelligent responsibility of individuals, groups, and organizations, and a whole people. This God is determined to have a response on the part of the individual or the people to a divine, summoning, and challenging word—to the divine initiative of the first deliverance and founding covenant, and then of radical deliverance and a new covenant of Jesus Christ. This God will have a response that will mean *conversion*—a turning away from idols to the service of the one God living and true, a renunciation of endless apostasies of sin in favor of perseverance in fidelity to the God of the covenant. Or conversely, this God will have radical liberation from sin—a conversion and fidelity to the living God verified in a love marked by solidarity with the needy and a commitment to justice in behalf of the oppressed.

The revelation of God in the history of the oppressed—a revelation bestowed in behalf of their liberation, committing the responsibility of human beings—has been documented, as we have suggested, all through the Bible.[10] This revelation stretches from the founding event of the Exodus from Egypt and the covenant of Sinai, to the gospel of the Reign and the Paschal event of Jesus Christ, to the sure hope of new heavens and a new earth where justice shall dwell and God will actually be "all in all." This is the content of the historical traditions of Israel, and of the laws intended to guarantee the people's coexistence in the land of promise. This is the burden of the preaching of the prophets, the prayer of the psalms, and the hope of the apocalypses. This is the proclamation, when all is said and done, of the gospel of Jesus, the message of the apostles, and the practice of the primitive Christian communities. The God of the Bible is always—and ever more clearly and more radically—the God who liberates the oppressed, the God who is revealed to us and challenges us from the midst of the poor of the earth, the God who expects of us, as the substance of authentic religious worship, that we show mercy to the needy and make a commitment to justice and peace in our world.

IV. GOD IN UNJUST SUFFERING AND VIOLENT DEATH

We notice, however, in the step-by-step faith pilgrimage of which we speak, and in the theology that accompanies it, a certain shift of focus, roughly corresponding to the two periods referred to above. No mere academic research is at stake here. What is at stake is a response to the historical process experienced by our peoples, whose poverty, cruel repression, and frustrations have generally worsened. In the first period, then, the crucial task was the arousal of a social awareness and of practices of political liberation. Currently, in wide regions of Latin America, fortitude in suffering and the hope of future liberation are more evident. In the former circumstances, the focus of reflection was on the "oppression/liberation" antithesis; now it appears to be rather on "death/life."

This shift of focus is reflected in the very titles of the more important theological works published in these respective periods. For the first period, we might cite *A Theology of Liberation*[11] and *The Power of the Poor in History*[12] by Gustavo Gutiérrez, as well as *Theology for a Nomad Church* by Hugo Assmann.[13] Here, God as such appears especially as the *God who delivers* from oppression. For the second period, we may mention *La misión del pueblo que sufre* (Carlos Mesters),[14] *Desde el lugar del pobre* (Leonardo Boff),[15] "Dios de vida, urgencia de solidaridad" (Jon Sobrino),[16] and *On Job: God-Talk and the Suffering of the Innocent* (Gutiérrez).[17] And here God appears especially as the *God of life* amid so many forces of death.

In the first period—as we have indicated—the principal biblical referents are the Exodus, the pre-Exilic prophets, and Jesus' ministry in Galilee. In the second, they are rather the prophets of the Exile, the psalms and the apocalypses, and Jesus' final journey to Jerusalem. In the former circumstances Jesus appears as the new Moses, the Messiah "Son of David," and God as the *God of the Reign*, who takes the side of the poor and marginalized to lead them to the new land of justice. In the latter circumstances Jesus appears also as the "servant of Yahweh" and the new Job, and God more emphatically as the *Father of Jesus*, who allows his dearly beloved Son to die in the extreme impotence of the cross, and who then raises the Crucified One from the dead.

But what we find reflected in this shift is not only an objective process in the history of our peoples. We also find the subjective change experienced by personnel of the church, who have shifted the focus of their activity from the dominant sociocultural centers or small, more politicized minorities to the "peripheral" majorities of the poor and marginalized. Here they not only proclaim anew the Paschal message and summon the people to read the gospel in community, but also learn things from the age-old suffering and traditional Christianity of the poor themselves.[18]

Jesus Christ, the Messiah of God who reveals to us God's true face and committed love for us, is the one who was persecuted and crucified, who continues his passion in the oppressed of our land and in all of the crucified of history. At the same time he is the one who was raised—the conqueror of unjust suffering and violent death, the liberator of human beings from the root of all their oppressions. He is the "Author of life" (Acts 3:15; cf. Heb. 2:10, 12:2), authentically human life and community, the "firstborn of many brothers" and sisters (Rom. 8:29; cf. Col. 1:18) in the full joy of the Father and the Reign of God.

The first dimension of Jesus, that of the *Crucified One*, has always had deep roots in the religious faith of our humble people, ever since the first evangelization of the continent and the first prophetic testimonials of the "scourged Christs of the

Indies" (Las Casas). This dimension is the identification the oppressed themselves recognize in the images—so abundant and expressive throughout Latin America—of Christ humiliated and covered with wounds. The crucifix and Good Friday are the core of the traditional piety of the people. It is always accompanied by the Christian recollection, so important and expressive among the poor, of the beloved departed, especially when they have been victims of a violent death.

The second dimension, that of the one who was *raised*, has become more and more salient with the new evangelization of the religious faith and life expressions of our people, in and around the base communities. In fact, this new evangelical awareness has entailed a new outlook on the other dimension, that of Jesus Crucified, the more historical perspective of the conflict that prevails in society. Jesus suffers persecution and dies on the gibbet of the cross not only because "thus it had been written," and surely not by the direct "will of God." He suffers all of this because he is faithful to his mission to the end, in a society dominated by the power of sin. In a society ruled by an idolatry of money, by the arrogance of the great, and by a formalistic, corrupt "piety" and "religious observance," it is logical to expect that Jesus' proclamation of the Reign to the poor, his program of the Beatitudes, and his practice of the liberation of the oppressed, should enter into a conflict to the death with the dominant "values" and power groups. It is these groups who slander and persecute, sentence and execute, Jesus the Christ of God.

In contrast with the religious ideology of sacrifice, or the theological theory of penal expiation for sin, the Crucified One is not seen as having taken on sin, supposedly replacing sinners and making reparation "for" them.[19] On the contrary—in a theological perspective that we see to be more Johannine than Pauline—sin, with all of its lying, murderous might, is seen in the crucifiers. These persons—far from being instruments of God!—are instruments of sin, oppression of the humble, and deicide.

In this explanation, God—the God of the Reign, the Father of Jesus—is regarded as present and active not so much in the passion and cross as in the resurrection. On the cross, God is seen as absent—rejected, routed. God as mighty God is absent, present as a suffering God, suffering with the Crucified One God is held to be revealed, paradoxically, as a God marginalized, outcast, repressed, tortured to death. Where God is seen acting with grandeur and power, on the other hand, is in the God who raises Jesus, the Christ and the dearly beloved Son. As in the first apostolic preaching,[20] God appears as the one who wondrously vindicates the one unjustly condemned—the God who raises and bestows glorious, astonishingly fecund life on the one the oppressors have executed so cruelly in their attempt to erase his countenance from the face of the earth.

Thus, our sisters and brothers, this oppressed people, can say: God is with us always, especially at the most difficult times. It is then that we experience the God who inspires and encourages, who unites us in service and commitment. Thus, the church communities more directly affected by the repression of the church have been empowered, through the Spirit of the one who was raised, to live, in our own day, the rich Christian tradition of persecution and martyrdom.[21] Here is an authentic evangelical tradition, and one that has been of enormous enlightenment and support to us in these years. Shepherds like Romero and Angelelli have known how to interpret it with prophetic lucidity—and deepen it with the witness of their martyrdom.

And so it comes about that, *beyond the death* of those persecuted and murdered "for the sake of the justice" of the Reign of God, words like these keep echoing in our ears: "If they kill me, I shall rise again in the Salvadoran people." "May my blood be the seed of freedom." "You shall rise again in the struggle of the people." Today, men and women like these are our confessors and our martyrs. It is they who, along the course of the pilgrimage of our oppressed people, are the great witnesses of Jesus raised, and of the God of life.

V. MERCIFUL FATHER

The invocation of the divinity as Father is not exclusive with biblical religion. On the contrary, the occurrence of this invocation in the Hebrew scriptures is rather discreet by comparison with its frequency among the peoples who precede or surround Israel in the ancient East.[22] For the Bible, in contrast with the other religions, God is the creator of human beings, their maker, on the basis of a free divine initiative. They are different from God. It is not as if God had generated them by some natural process; nor have they emanated from the divine being itself in the form of a more or less deficient expression of the same. Rather, the God of Israel is the God *of* the poor, *of* the patriarch Abraham. In no wise does God appear as the actual patriarch or mythic ancestor of the people. In this sense, Yahweh, for Israel, is first of all a God of gratuitous encounter and concrete pilgrimage, rather than of origins and of universal, necessary destiny. Yahweh is the God of history and historical hope, rather than the God of cosmic nature and an absolute future. Therefore when God is called Father in the Bible, and human beings (or the people) are called God's children, the reference is to an option, or "ad-option," on the part of God, and not to an intrinsic property of the human condition.

In the Bible expressions like "merciful Father" or "rich in mercy" do not refer to a necessary essence of God from which the nature of human beings would derive. Instead, they speak—symbolically—of an attitude freely adopted by a transcendent, intensely personal God. This attitude is understood as that of a father who is attentive to the call of his children, a parent ever disposed to pardon from the heart those who have withdrawn but who turn back once more, ever ready to lift the fallen, ever desirous of giving them good things and leading his children along the road of liberty and life. Indeed, more than an attitude of the "heart" of a father, this attitude is rather that of the "bowels" of a mother, which wrench at the sight of the suffering of her innocent creatures, or thrill with inexpressible delight at the return of a lost child. Nothing could be further from the philosophic conception of impassible perfection and immutable principle, essentially beyond the reach of human contingency.[23] The living God of the Bible, whom our people are rediscovering today, and continuing to seek along their route, is the holy, transcendent God, the fullness of life and power. But the people discover this God because this God has wished to become involved in our history in order to enter into communion with us. This God has done so from the free and gratuitous movement of a visceral love for us—for a suffering, sinful people.[24]

It is against this background that we must understand the God of Jesus' gospel message, the God of the Beatitudes.

The material of the Sermon on the Mount, which Matthew presents as Jesus' inaugural discourse (Matt. 5–7), is not the transcendent world of God as such, nor even—directly—the "supernatural" activity of God in our own world. The material of the Sermon on the Mount is precisely this world of ours itself, the most ordinary elements of human existence: wailing and rejoicing, work performed for food and clothing, poverty and wealth, domestic relations, injustice toward or solidarity with neighbors and companions, condemnation or pardon of enemies, and everything of the sort. The proclamation of the Sermon on the Mount focuses on all of these things in order to announce to us the unbelievable novelty that what is at stake in these affairs of ours is actually God, who seeks to intervene in them as our solicitous, infinitely able Parent.

But Jesus knows that this same God can allow us to be hungry, to suffer hatred and persecution, and to die. In fact, Jesus proclaims blessed those who suffer, the persecuted, and so on. How can this be reconciled with his call to concrete, unlimited filial trust?

The answer is simple. Jesus is telling us that the hour has come for rejoicing, because the Father has become attentive to the misery and exploitation that weigh upon the children of God. He summons us to make an effort to eradicate poverty and oppression from our midst. After all, God wishes to do away with them!

Thus, in his discourse, as in his entire messianic practice ("Go back and report to John what you hear and see" [Matt. 11:4; cf. Luke 4:16–22, 7:18–23]), Jesus reveals to us the tender, efficacious attention of God to the life of each of us, and especially to the multitude of the poor and forsaken. But Jesus' "revealing" this to us does not mean drawing back the curtain hiding "another world." He is only affording us the intuition that, at the center of our own lives, at the heart of this world, and among the poor and outcast of the earth, is the mysterious, salvific presence of God—of a God who takes our life and world just as they are—with their noblest expressions and aspirations, as well as all their weight of selfishness, cruelty and death—and has determined to set his creation free.

This message of a merciful Father appears with the greatest force in Jesus' confrontation with the God of the temple and the priests, and especially of the scribes and Pharisees (cf. Mark 2:1–3, 12, 12:38–40; Matt. 5:23–24, 7:21–23, 21:28–31, 23:1–36; Luke 8:1–3, 13:22–30, 15:1–32; John 7:11–11:54). In the power and authority of this particular elite—which was closest to the daily life of the simple people and possibly their worst oppressor—the gospels find the antagonist of Jesus' most frequently recurring, and most profound, confrontations. The scribes and Pharisees were the educated, and they were the teachers. Here were the fraternities of the pious—"clergy" and "religious"—who were closest to the people and who taught them. In their practice, and even more in the moral and religious discipline that they sought to impose on the people, Jesus discovers a formalistic degradation of biblical faith. The God of the covenant, who chooses persons out of pure love, gathers them together, and delivers them, has become a "god of law," the enjoiner of myriad "observances," and the appointer of stern retribution. Jesus' God has become the marginalizer and oppressor of the lowly, the people. Here is a harsh god, obsessed with a long series of prohibitions and commandments, taboos or religious practices, missteps to be avoided or good works to be multiplied, all of which he draws up on his balance sheet, his "book," and all of which deserve the reward or punishment sure to come, in just measure, in this life or the next. Along this route, a relationship with the living God, freely loving and acting in human history, forgiving and radically liberating, and awaiting from men and women a response from the heart, is degraded into a cold moralism of intrinsic justice, a prideful pretension to an accumulation of merit before God and in competition with one's fellows, in a ritualism of religious practices motivated by fear or niggardly interests. Here Jesus' criticism of temple ritualism converges with a criticism that had already seen a long history in the prophetic tradition of Israel: "It is love that I desire, not sacrifice, and knowledge of God rather than holocausts" (Hos. 6:6; cf. Matt. 9:13, 12:7). Here is Jesus' criticism of a sacral god, the god of a "religious world" apart, a god cut off from daily life, with his castes of consecrated holiness specialists. Here is Jesus' criticism of a hierarchic god, one accessible to the people only through the mediation precisely of these castes with their supposed monopoly on religious knowledge and sacred power.

In this sociocultural and religious context—so strongly marked by Pharisaism and the formalistic worship to which we have just referred—Jesus is born and lives. He is a member of the laity. He is interested in the lives and concerns of the common folk, and in those lives and concerns reveals to the people directly—and not by way of "religious" words or symbols—the Father's love and human beings' responsibility for the coming Reign. The signs wrought by Jesus are not liturgical rites, but human deeds calculated to heal and save men and women suffering from misery, marginalization, and demonic possession. Jesus "relativizes" any practice or religious "performance" with a concrete appeal to the well-being and worthy life of concrete persons. He teaches his disciples to recognize his risen presence and the Father's love, not in the temple and its rites, not in solitary contemplation, but in their neighbor suffering or sharing, and in the living experience of a community of sisters and brothers.

Jesus' God, then, appears, most strikingly, as the God of the lowly and simple, not of the learned and prudent (Matt. 11:25–27). Here is the God who is most radically revealed as a God of grace and pardon, as the Father who is gladdest when forgiving and giving life and who awaits our wholehearted response, in the divine presence, in behalf of our neighbors. In the condensed and mighty formulas of John's gospel, Jesus' God is a God of life and truth, a God in stark contrast with the god of the religious and cultural establishment, which shows by its practice that its god has been a murderer and a liar "from the beginning" (John 8:44; cf. 1 John 3:8–15). Here is the God of daily, "profane" life, with all of its so material joys and miseries, the God of the common folk, of the simple, of "this lot, that knows nothing about the law," the God of these sinners (John 7:49).

VI. FATHER OF JESUS AND OUR FATHER

The content of the entire biblical tradition reaches its plenitude and is synthesized in the gospel proclaimed by Jesus of Nazareth to the poor and outcast of his people, the message that the witnesses of the one who was raised began to spread throughout the underworld of the Roman Empire. The Good News is that God is at hand, preparing to exercise a royal and divine authority in a Reign that has already begun with the humble practice of Jesus as he tore sin up by its very roots, and just as radically subverted the dominations of this world. Behold, that God has raised up the Servant of God Jesus, whom the tribunals of his nation had condemned, vindicating his divine sonship and universal Messianism, and our own universal kinship. Now God has vindicated the Holy Spirit, with its signs of interior activity, as the witness and invisible agent of this profound transformation of human life and coexistence, making all human beings children of God and setting them free, establishing them as co-heirs of the divine Reign and collaborators, in a communion of sisters and brothers, in the arrival of the fullness of this same Reign of justice and knowledge of the Father.

The actual power of the message of Jesus of Nazareth concerning the merciful Father lies neither in its internal logic or appearance of likelihood, nor in its consoling effect as religious discourse, but in the fact that it transmits Jesus' own experience—an authentically human experience of our life and our world, and at the heart of that human experience, an intimate experience of God as his Parent.

The Sermon on the Mount—like all of Jesus' preaching, dialogues, and polemical confrontations—transmits to us the words of a person who practices what he preaches and preaches what he practices. Jesus himself experiences the hard indifference of the rich. He knows the hatred and persecution of enemies. He meets the hungry and the weeping every day along his life journey, and he has made them his companions. He sees through hypocrites and superficial people at a glance. He knows the loving gaze of his divine Parent upon all of this misery and reacts to it just as that Parent does.

Jesus lives in the sight of women and men the life he describes in his parables and offers to his followers: a life staked entirely on the grand cause of the human being, which is God's cause; a poor life, threatened and assaulted, in the unwavering, serene certitude of being in the Father's hands. Jesus' entire life—all the way to his "*Abba*, . . . take this cup away from me" (Mark 14:36)—shows us his intimate secure conviction that nothing would be able to separate him from the love of his Parent. And he invites us to share this bedrock security by trusting in his personal experience as dearly beloved Son of God.

Indeed, for the gospel tradition, Jesus' life is governed by his awareness of living it in a unique relationship with God—with God his *Abba*. According to Luke, for example, the first and last words of his earthly life refer to his Father (Luke 2:49, 23:46). According to Matthew and Luke, "No one knows the Son but the Father, and no one knows the Father but the Son—and anyone to whom the Son wishes to reveal him" (Matt. 11:27, Luke 10:22; cf. Matt. 21:37, 24:36; John 1:18, 10:15, 17:1–8, 20–26). The knowledge here is one of intimate transparency, unlimited trust, and total commitment, a knowledge revealed precisely to "the merest children," to those "who are weary and find life burdensome" (Matt. 11:25–28). And Jesus' prayer, usually reported by the gospels in some particularly difficult or tragic situation in his life, expresses his limitless trust in his Father's love for him, and his own unreserved determination, in all things, with no ifs, ands, or buts, to try to see to it that that Father's "will be done."[25] Thus, on the eve of his passion,

Mark tells us, Jesus addresses God with the Aramaic term *Abba* (Mark 14:36), the word children used in addressing their fathers in the intimacy of the family. It was unheard of, in Jesus' time and culture, that God would be addressed with this word.[26] Christians took the liberty of employing this same word—in the Spirit of Jesus—when they called "Our Father" (cf. Rom. 8:15, Gal. 4:6; cf. also Matt. 6:9, Luke 11:2, John 20:17). They were expressing this same shared experience that "neither death nor life, . . . neither the present nor the future, nor powers, neither height nor depth nor any other creature, will be able to separate us from the love of God that comes to us in Christ Jesus, our Lord" (Rom. 8:38–39).

It is the very bones and blood of the gospel, then, that the *God of the Reign* is identical with the *Father of Jesus Christ*, his *Abba*. *Reign* is a political term; *Abba* connotes family intimacy.[27] In concrete terms, the Reign Jesus shows us in his practice as Messiah of the poor and the filial experience he reveals to his "least brothers" and sisters do not bring to the world a new hierarchy, a new religious dependency that would leave a people in the status of religious minors. Quite the contrary! This Reign and filial experience bring to the world a profound dynamism of equality, communion, and service among equals. Jesus the servant, the Messiah as persecuted prophet, who brings the world this kind of Reign of God, is God's only Son, now seated at the right hand of the Father. Jesus calls his disciples, whom he sends forth, not as servants, but as friends, his sisters and brothers. For them, the fact of having one Father and one Teacher does not authorize them to force themselves on one another as parents or teachers, but just the opposite; this fact is the strength of their companionship, deep friendship, and humble service among equals (cf. Mark 12:38–40, Matt. 20:20–28, 23:1–12; Luke 22:24–30; John 13:1–17).

After all, in the last analysis the root content of the message of Jesus Christ—and of the mystery of God—is love. And the love that is truly worthy of the name, the love in which God consists and which has been revealed to us in Jesus Christ, is not, in its profoundest mystery, a cascade of benefits in a relationship of monarchy and subordination, but rather communion among equals: the Father, the Son, and the Holy Spirit. The Spirit is in us and with us in the Son, facing the Father.[28]

Granted—and this, too, is part of the mystery of love and life—this communion among equals does not suppress difference in origin, or gratitude for the gift that founds that communion. The Father is still the Father, even, and especially, of the only Son. The Lord is still the Lord, even, and most of all, for his disciples and friends, among whom he is as one who serves. God is still God, even, and especially, of creatures whom God has personally chosen and sanctified and whom God loves "in the Son." But the very difference is assumed and transformed in the dynamism of communion among equals—to their inexhaustible surprise and greater joy in love.

On the limited level of our experience we may experience this when it falls to us to be teachers, with a certain degree of commitment. The youth of our popular world may experience this when they themselves come to be parents. In either case our concern will not be to assert our own authority, to maintain distance or possession, but quite the contrary; now our urgent desire will be to give the best we have to offer, in order that our child or disciple may grow, may become open to receive from others rather than merely disposed to bestow, may be free. Now our impatient longing and hope will be that this "minor" of ours may come to be equal to ourselves as soon as possible, and be—if he or she so desires, freely—our friend and companion.

In this perspective there appears in our cultural situation, even for the youth of our people with their so frequently traumatic family history, a new access route to the understanding that God is our Father.[29] We can understand God as Parent from a point of departure in our experience of *having* earthly parents, of course; but we can understand the same thing (and this is often the only way for our youth, as far as having a father is concerned) from our experience of *being* a parent. This seems to be the route Jesus himself suggests in the gospel: "Would one of you hand his son a stone when he asks for a loaf . . .? If you, with all your sins, know how to give your children what is good, how much more will your heavenly Father!" (Matt. 7:9–11). In the same Sermon on the Mount we are taught to ask the Father to give us "our daily bread," and to "forgive us the wrong we have done as we forgive those [our children?] who wrong us" (Matt. 6:11–12). God our Father is like the parent in the parable in Luke (15:11–32), who so tenderly welcomes and forgives, who will not even think of leaving his prodigal child in this servile condition, but forgives and forgets and spreads a feast—and hopes that his other child ("You are with me always, and everything I have is yours")—will act in the same way with his returning brother.

VII. FIRST PERSON OF THE TRINITY

In conclusion, I should like to observe that (except in the passage in which we speak expressly of the divine mystery of the communion of Father, Son, and Spirit) whenever we speak of God here we are referring concretely to the God of Abraham, Isaac, and Jacob—the intensely personal God of a self-revelation to our ancestors as liberator and God of life, the very God whom Jesus of Nazareth acknowledged as his own God and with whom, as his *Abba*, he maintained a unique relationship, the very God who raised the Crucified One and whom we, moved by the Spirit, can invoke in truth as our Father. We are not referring to a "God" of the universe and of life in the sense of the religions of the earth, or to a supreme Being or absolute Future discerned by philosophy. Neither are we referring, in terms of Christian theology beginning in the fourth century, to that "one God who is the Most Holy Trinity" (St. Augustine).[30] We are not calling these perspectives into question, but here we have preferred to follow the obvious usage of the Christian scriptures itself, as we have rediscovered how to read it today in our communities among the poor.

In the Christian scriptures the terms *one God*, or simply *God* (*ho Theos*), does not mean—as it does for later theology—the unity (of substance) of the three divine Persons. In the Christian scriptures, these terms are more direct and concrete. They designate the "God of our fathers," who has been revealed to believers today as the "God and Father of Jesus Christ."[31] This is always the case, first of all, when we find these expressions on the lips of Jesus. But it is also the case, for example, in the trinitarian formulas of Christian faith that we find so frequently in the Pauline letters: "Lord Jesus . . . Spirit . . . God" (Rom. 15:30; cf. 1 Cor. 12:4–6, 2 Cor. 1:21–22, 13:13; Eph. 4:4–6; 1 Pet. 1:2). In other words, these terms denote (in later theological language) the person of God the Father. This is the denotation these terms still have in the ancient Christian "symbols" (which we still use today as the "creed" of our common faith). Through these "symbols," with their tripartite structure, we profess the trinitarian faith of the church. But when, in the first article of the Creed, we state our faith in "one God," we are speaking not of the "one God in three persons," but of the person of the Father. This is concretely "the God" (*ho theos*), one and personal, of whom the "one Lord" Jesus Christ is the "only Son," and who (with that Son) pours forth in our hearts "the Holy Spirit."

—*Translated by Robert R. Barr*

NOTES

1. Cf. Juan Luis Segundo, *Our Idea of God*, trans. John Drury (Maryknoll, N.Y.: Orbis Books, 1973); Ronaldo Muñoz, *Nueva conciencia de la Iglesia en América latina* (Santiago de Chile, 1973); CLAR, *La vida según el Espiritu en las comunidades religiosas de América latina* (Bogota, 1973); Frei Betto, et al., *Experimentar Deus hoje* (Petrópolis, Brazil, 1974).

2. Cf. Victorio Araya, *God of the Poor: The Mystery of God in Latin American Liberation Theology*, trans. Robert R. Barr (Maryknoll, N.Y.: Orbis Books, 1987), with its extensive bibliography.

3. Cf. Rubem Alves, *Religión: ¿opio o instrumento de liberación?* (Montevideo, 1970); Gustavo Gutiérrez, *A Theology of Liberation: History, Politics and Salvation*, trans. Caridad Inda and John Eagleson (Maryknoll, N.Y.: Orbis Books, 1973); Hugo Assmann, *Opresión-liberación: desafio a los cristianos* (Montevideo, 1971).

4. Cf. Jon Sobrino, "La centralidad del 'reino de Dios' en la teología de la liberación," *RLT* (San Salvador) 9 (1986), pp. 247–81; reprinted as chapter 3 in this volume.

5. Cf. J. L. Sicre, *Los dioses olvidados: poder y riqueza en los profetas preexilicos* (Madrid, 1979); Pablo Richard, et al., *The Idols of Death and the God of Life: A Theology*, trans. Barbara E. Campbell and Bonnie Shepard (Maryknoll, N.Y.: Orbis Books, 1983); Sobrino, "Reflexiones sobre el significado del ateísmo y la idolatría para la teología," *RLT* (San Salvador) 7 (1986), pp. 45–81.

6. Cf. Leonardo Boff, *Jesus Christ Liberator: A Critical Christology for Our Time*, trans. Patrick Hughes (Maryknoll, N.Y.: Orbis Books, 1978); Jon Sobrino, *Christology at the Crossroads: A Latin American Approach*, trans. John Drury (Maryknoll, N.Y.: Orbis Books, 1978); José Comblin, *Jesus of Nazareth*, trans. Carl Kabat (Maryknoll, N.Y.: Orbis Books, 1976); Hugo Echegaray, *The Practice of Jesus*, trans. Matthew J. O'Connell (Maryknoll, N.Y.: Orbis Books, 1984).

7. Cf. K. Schäfer, "The Testimony of Jesus about God," *Concilium* vol. 6, no. 8 (1972); Edward Schillebeeckx, "The 'God of Jesus' and the 'Jesus of God,' " *Concilium* vol. 3, no. 10 (1974). Sobrino, *Christology at the Crossroads*.

8. These are the words of the *Symbolum* of the First Council of Constantinople, A.D. 381 (Denziger, no. 150).

9. Cf. Vatican Council II, *Gaudium et Spes*, nos. 34, 38–39.

10. Cf. J. Severino Croatto, *Liberación y libertad: pautas hermenéuticas* (Buenos Aires, 1973); Carlos Mesters, *El misterioso mundo de la Biblia* (Buenos Aires, 1977); idem, *Defenseless Flower: A New Reading of the Bible*, trans. Francis McDonagh (Maryknoll,

N.Y.: Orbis Books, 1989), pp. 55–155; Elsa Tamez, *Bible of the Oppressed*, trans. Matthew J. O'Connell (Maryknoll, N.Y.: Orbis Books, 1982); Carlos Mesters et al., "A Biblia como memoria dos pobres," *Revista Eclesiástica Brasileira* (Petrópolis, Brazil) 173 (1984); Ana Flora Anderson, et al., "Caminho da libertaçaõ," *Revista Eclesiástica Brasileira* (Petrópolis, Brazil) (1984).

11. As cited in note 3.

12. *The Power of the Poor in History: Selected Writings*, trans. Robert R. Barr (Maryknoll, N.Y.: Orbis Books, 1983), a collection of earlier writings.

13. Hugo Assmann, *Theology for a Nomad Church*, trans. Paul Burns (Maryknoll, N.Y.: Orbis Books, 1975; originally published in Spanish in 1973).

14. Carlos Mesters, *La misíon del pueblo que sufre* (Madrid, 1983).

15. Leonardo Boff, *Desde el lugar del pobre* (Bogota, 1984). Cf. idem, *Faith on the Edge: Religion and Marginalized Existence*, trans. Robert R. Barr (New York: Harper & Row, 1989).

16. *Diakonía* (Managua), no. 35 (1985). Cf. idem, *The True Church and the Poor*, trans. Matthew J. O'Connell (Maryknoll, N.Y.: Orbis Books, 1984), pp. 125–59.

17. Gustavo Gutiérrez, *On Job: God-Talk and the Suffering of the Innocent*, trans. Matthew J. O'Connell (Maryknoll, N.Y.: Orbis Books, 1987).

18. Cf. Ronaldo Muñoz, *The God of Christians*, trans. Paul Burns (Maryknoll, N.Y.: Orbis Books, 1990), chap. 2: "God on Our Journey in Faith."

19. We are not questioning the biblical theology of expiatory sacrifice, applied to the death of Christ by the New Testament with reference—especially—to the Servant of Yahweh in Isaiah 53. Our communities' faith perception does contrast with the "theological theory" (of medieval origin) and the "ideology" that we have mentioned and that are so used and abused in the pulpit today. See Boff, *Teología del cautiverio y de la liberación*, 3d ed. (Madrid, 1985), pp. 179–204; idem, "How to Preach the Cross of Jesus Christ Today?" in *Passion of Christ—Passion of the World* (Maryknoll, N.Y.: Orbis Books, 1987), pp. 129–133.

20. Cf. J. Schmitt, *Jésus ressuscité dans la prédicatión apostolique* (Paris, 1949).

21. Cf. Ivo Lesbaupin, *Blessed are the Persecuted: Christian Life in the Roman Empire, A.D. 64–313*, trans. Robert R. Barr (Maryknoll, N.Y.: Orbis Books, 1987); Boff, *Passion of Christ—Passion of the World*; idem, "Systematic Reflection on Martyrdom," *Concilium* 163 (1983). J. Hernández, "Martyrdom Today in Latin America," *Concilium* 163 (1983); "Espiritualidad del martirio," *Diakonía* (Managua) 27 (1983).

22. Cf. W. Marchel, *Abba, Vater*! (Düsseldorf, 1963); C. Orrieux, "La paternité de Dieu dans l'Ancien Testament," *Lumière et Vie* (Lyon) 104 (1971):59–74.

23. Cf. Abraham Heschel, *The Prophets* vol. 2 (New York: Harper & Row, 1962), chap. 6; Wolfhart Pannenberg, "La asimilación del concepto filosófico de Dios como problema dogmático de la antigua teología cristiana," in Pannenberg et al., *Cuestiones fundamentales de la teología sistemática* (Salamanca, 1976), pp. 93–149; Jürgen Moltmann, *The Trinity and the Kingdom: The Doctrine of God*, trans. Margaret Kohl (San Francisco: Harper & Row, 1981).

24. Cf. Albert Gélin, *The Key Concepts of the Old Testament*, trans. George Lamb (New York: Sheed and Ward, 1955); T. C. Vriezen, *An Outline of Old Testament Theology* (Oxford, 1958); Yves Congar, "Mercy, Sovereign Attribute of God," in Congar, *The Revelation of God*, trans. A. Manson and L.C. Sheppard (New York: Herder and Herder, 1968); W. Eichrodt, *Theology of the Old Testament* vol. 1 (Philadelphia: Westminster, 1961); G. Von Rad, *Old Testament Theology*, vols. 1–2 (New York: Harper, 1962–65); Heschel, *The Prophets* vol. 2; A. Deissler, "La revelación personal de Dios en el Antiguo Testamento," in *Mysterium*

Salutis, ed. vol. 2/1 (Madrid, 1969), pp. 262–311; H. Cazelles, "Le Dieu du Yahviste et de l'Elohiste . . .," in *La notion biblique de Dieu* (Gembloux, 1976), pp. 77–89; B. Andrade, *Encuentro con Dios en la historia: estudio de la concepción de Dios en el Pentateuco* (Salamanca, 1985).

25. Cf. José Comblin, *La oración de Jesús* (Santiago de Chile, n.d.); Sobrino, *Christology at the Crossroads*, pp. 146–78.

26. Cf. T. W. Manson, *The Teaching of Jesus* (Cambridge, 1959), pp. 89–115.

27. Cf. Moltmann, *The Trinity and the Kingdom*; Leonardo Boff, *Trinity and Society*, trans. Paul Burns (Maryknoll, N.Y.: Orbis Books, 1988), pp. 28–30.

28. S. Vergés, *Dios es amor: el amor de Dios revelado en Cristo según Juan* (Salamanca, 1982); Boff, *Trinity and Society*.

29. Cf. A. Vergote, *The Religious Man*, trans. Marie-Bernard Said (Dayton, Ohio: Pflaum Press, 1969); Paul Ricoeur, et al., *The Conflict of Interpretations*, ed. Don Ihde (Evanston: Northwestern University Press, 1974); A. Manaranche, *Creo en Jesucristo hoy* (Salamanca, 1973), pp. 149–57: "La simbólica del Padre."

30. Augustine, *De Trinitate*, Book I, chap. 6, no. 9.

31. See Karl Rahner, "*Theos* in the New Testament," in Rahner, *Theological Investigations*, vol. 1 (Baltimore: Helicon Press, 1961); Bernard Lonergan, *De Verbo Incarnato*: "Thesis Prima (ad Usum Auditorum Editio Altera)" (Rome, 1961); J.N.D. Kelly, *Early Christian Creeds* (London: Longmans, 1950; New York: Green, 1950).

6

Jesus of Nazareth, Christ the Liberator

CARLOS BRAVO

I. STARTING POINT

1. The Faith of an Oppressed and Believing People

Christian faith refers to three histories: (1) present history; (2) its founding history, of Jesus; (3) which is mediated by the history of the church community, and is an experience of life rather than a reflection on life.

In Latin America this is the faith of an oppressed and believing people, in whose five-hundred-year history faith has been interrelated with both oppression and liberation. When we speak of oppression we are speaking about a conquest that manipulated God's name in favor of its economic and political interests, institutionalized violence, infant deaths, violation of human rights, illiteracy, hunger, unpayable foreign debt. And when we speak of living faith we are talking about love in practice, solidarity, the search for justice, organization, a sense of festival, and the experience of freely receiving in the presence of God, while struggling for life and freedom.

In an unjust and unequal society the person of the risen Jesus acquires a new dimension as the inspirer of liberating utopias. We who have been found by him see oppression and injustice in a different manner, not just as a social phenomenon, but as that which makes the Kingdom impossible and betrays the Father's name. Once this encounter has taken place we cannot behave as if it had not happened.

So faith begins to develop new formulations to speak about him. Our experience of Jesus as Messiah is mediated by the experience of life-threatening evils. This requires us to make a political and social commitment—to stand against the situation that prevents the Father's reign. In Jesus' life we do not find the explanation for why history is as it is. But we do find the impulse driving it to cease being a history of death and become a history of life. This is very important both to overcome the christology of resignation (of a suffering Christ with no resurrection) and the christology of domination (the imperial or conquering Christ who manipulates the memory of Jesus in favor of imperialist projects).

So we start by assuming that in Latin America we believe in Jesus as the Son of God, Lord of history, liberating Messiah. But we have to explain the content of these titles. They mean different things from the viewpoint of the conqueror's world and the world in which Indians die, from the viewpoint of the White House and that of Nicaragua.

2. The Truth of Confessions of Faith

This does not mean that the titles given to Jesus are neutral. They are formulas which in their time faithfully expressed in symbols of their own culture Jesus' saving significance for believers. Their validity comes from their continuity with the founding reality of Jesus as their *norm*, and the cultural reality of believers as their *cultural conditioning*.

Every expression of faith has to pass the double truth test: truth to Jesus in whom Emmanuel (the Son of God with us) was given and revealed to us, and truth to the particular people whose faith it expresses and bears. Hence the need for many different formulations of the inexhaustible mystery of Jesus. The Christian scriptures model this with many functional christologies, corresponding to different communities.[1]

First and foremost the Christian community must submit its formulations and practices to the critique made of them by Jesus' own practice. Otherwise they are subject to fashion and their language merely trendy (academic, neo-liberal, guerrilla, even extraterrestrial). This fails to convey the fundamental novelty of the fact of Jesus; that is, that God, while remaining transcendent and unattainable ("no one has ever seen God" [1 John 4:12]), entered history, moved within our reach in Jesus.

This raises a series of questions: why did Jesus come? To confirm history as it is, leaving it untouched? To condemn it? To save it? But how? By spiritualizing it? Ritualizing it? Telling it about God? Or by subverting it? In the unequal and oppressive society in which Jesus lived, which side was he on and what kind of life did he lead? The answers to these questions cannot be deduced from an idea of God prior to what was revealed about God in the new and unrepeatable life of Jesus of Nazareth. This is what gives meaning to the titles we give him, not the other way around with the titles showing the meaning of his life and behavior.

Second, in order to be faithful to Jesus the formulations reached by the Christian community must be mediated by a knowledge of the actual oppression from which history needs to be liberated in order to be faithful to Jesus. A Christian cannot just stand contemplating Jesus, or gasp in moral indignation against injustice. We must move on to make the connection, that is, to "the effective pity" which liberates (cf. Exod. 3:7 ff.).

This leads to further questions: Is the christology elaborated faithful to this Jesus and to what continues to be his cause: liberation? To whom is it committed: the oppressors or the oppressed? Is it in solidarity with the actual project for which Jesus gave his life? Does it realize that all theology, in fact, regardless of its intentions, takes sides and is involved, even when it claims to be neutral?

We realize that discipleship is the indispensable way to reach the mystery of Jesus, and that without it no theology enables us to "see" Jesus. In this chapter we shall try to express what we believe about Jesus from the standpoint of the poor.

The two aspects of theology, the narrative and the systematic, intermingle. The gospel narrative justifies us in not doing our theological thinking from above, but from below, not deductively but inductively. Finally, by way of conclusion, we shall briefly sum up the fundamental statements of faith in Jesus.

II. CHRISTOLOGICAL NARRATIVE

1. Methodological Base: The Jesus Who Makes History

A fundamental task of biblical studies has been to determine the minimal structure of Jesus' practice. This is very important to ensure we do not end up with a fundamentalist reading, out of context, which manipulates Jesus' work to suit us. (We might turn him into a moral teacher or an ahistorical figure whose death would have nothing to do with his choices and his practice.) But this minimal structure is not enough for discipleship. In Latin America the search for the historical minimum regarding Jesus does not *formally* require the objective determination of what Jesus *did*, but rather what he *would do today*, if he were driven by the Spirit in this different situation. This task also requires a knowledge of the present situation. Both faith in Jesus and commitment to the situation today are fundamental for discipleship.[2]

In "Jesus who makes history" there are three dialectical terms which make up the fact of Jesus: (1) Jesus of Nazareth as the originating fact; (2) the Risen Jesus confirmed by the Father; (3) the movement of his followers in which his Spirit continues to inspire the promotion of his cause. This is what appears in Mark's final narrative (16:6ff.)

The first term, the thesis, is the life of Jesus of Nazareth, which is denied in the antithesis, the crucifixion. This in turn is overcome (but not ignored) by the resurrection, which is the synthesis, a "negation of the negation." It is not a return to life but a leap forward, which assumes the life denied by death and the death itself, whose marks are kept by the Risen Christ on his hands and side. But in its turn this resurrection becomes a thesis, which is denied as "verifiable here" in the tomb (antithesis). His new presence is in Galilee, by way of "going before them." He only precedes those who follow him. So following is the final synthesis; it is the epistemological condition for the experience of Jesus. Galilee, the place where Jesus worked, now becomes the place to follow him to, the only place where he can be "seen."

So, to "see" Jesus it is not enough to have access to the historical Jesus, who could become entombed. This would be like the women who sought him in the memory of one who died, to find and leave embalmed and inactive for the rest of history. We have to have the Paschal experience and to bear witness, which is what gives him permanent presence in history.

In this task of following it is important to take seriously the humanity of Jesus' consciousness. Not out of psychological curiosity. The important thing is his human reality and the very possibility of our being able to follow him. If Jesus was just an ordinary man, if he had not been confirmed by the Father as his Son in the resurrection, we *would not have* the Christian duty to follow him. If he was just God and not man (that is, if he were a kind of superman) we *could not* follow him. Neither could we follow him unless a chain of witnesses to his life had come down to us through the church, a chain which continues.

Therefore, it is important not only to know *what he did* but also *how and why* he did it; to respect God's decision to become human; and to assume the responsibility of following Jesus in promoting his cause.

2. Jesus' Roots

We know about the situation in the time of Jesus through research. We know about the principal groups that existed and their practices and ideologies. There is a correlation of forces between them which determines the people's situation. This people's history was not written down because no one writes about the fate of the conquered. Nevertheless, we can read it between the lines of the conqueror's history. Thus we can place Jesus' practice as a response to this situation.

From the *economic* point of view Jesus' people are deprived of their land, exploited by an unjust system. They must pay tribute and are impoverished; they lack living space and security. And this has a religious dimension, because it empties of content the promise of the land and goes against God's plan for the people. Jesus responds by helping the people in their basic living requirements: health and food. He breaks the exclusive circle of property and prophetically criticizes the rich. He turns human values upside down—the central thing is not to accumulate and to have, but to share. Therefore it will be the poor who possess the Kingdom and also the land. From this conviction he outlines the egalitarian utopia of the Kingdom: abundance for all based on the free gift of the Father to all God's children.

Politically this is a subject people, sometimes with bloody repression. No one responds to their just aspirations; they have no power to decide their own destiny. The people resist and agitate with Messianic hopes of liberation. But they are caught up in passivity and fatalism born of historical frustrations and the present foreign rule. This also has a religious dimension, because it is an affront to the reality of God's dominion over the people. In the face of this, Jesus announces the Father's sovereignty in favor of the poor. He prophetically denounces the ruling power through a lucid critical analysis and breaks the vicious circle of power and violence by denouncing its inability to build a new world. He subverts the idea of authority by saying it can only be exercised in service. He outlines the egalitarian utopia of the Kingdom: peace born of justice, in which all God's children share.

In the *religious* sphere they are an expectant people but disorientated in their expectations. Excluded by their religious leaders as impure and as "the accursed people" without rights before God, they are marginalised from the promise of the Kingdom. This is where Jesus points to the principal contradiction: the establishment has deprived the people of hope. Jesus responds by offering them an alternative in God's preference for the poor and the marginalised. Thus he generates new hope. He corrects the Messianic idea of God's vengeance against sinners. He breaks the exclusive circle of the law of purity. He reincorporates the marginalised into the people of God. He strips the Jewish establishment of its authority and its interpretation of the law, by teaching with authority. He changes the center of value for the law, which becomes a matter of loving—mercy and justice—rather than a matter of knowing or being pure. He prophetically criticizes the cult and its ritual observances. Thus he outlines the egalitarian utopia of the Kingdom. It is brotherhood and sisterhood deriving from a common Father and requires truth and freedom in this relationship.

3. Becoming Incarnate: Being a People

As he was a Jew, Jesus' image of God would be on the following lines: Yahweh is the God of the promise made to a people who do not possess the land; Yahweh is the God of the covenant, the people's only Lord, who has been supplanted by a foreign idolatrous power. Yahweh is the God of resistance to injustice, who hears the cry of the people and acts upon it. And now the time has come for Yahweh God to intervene.

Like the lay people to whom he belongs, and to whom he never ceases to belong, Jesus is offered many religious options: Apocalyptic thinking speaks of a world governed by evil, in which God has decided to intervene finally to inaugurate the kingdom. The Sadducees reject this, secure in their own well-being, because the prophetic proclamations seem to them to be "liberationist novelties." The Pharisees commandeer the Kingdom, excluding the "accursed people who do not know the law" (John 7:39); they believe they can hasten its coming by strict observance of the law of purity and exclusion of the impure. There is an incipient armed resistance movement. John the Baptist speaks of another way of saving oneself from the "wrath to come," through baptism and conversion.

4. A Different God

This movement of John's is a challenge to the Jewish leaders: forgiveness is being offered in an outsider context, not just in Jerusalem. It is offered through conversion and baptism, and not through sacrifices and ritual purifications. Further, the mediator is a lay prophet, not a priest. News of the hopes being raised by John reach Jesus in Nazareth. The decision to leave home and go to find John is a vital one, which changes the direction of Jesus' life forever.

Jesus has an experience of a different God. This God is the people's *Abba* (Daddy). Poor people's lives matter to *Abba* (Matt. 6:9–13). They manifest the reality of God's fatherhood in history. God has decided to reign *now*, changing the situation of those who are outcast, not by magic, not through a power like that of the powerful, but through *kenosis* and hiddenness, because what is being offered is love.

Jesus experiences himself as absolutely and unconditionally committed to the task of announcing this Reign and making it accepted. It is in this that "being the Son of God in history" consists—being responsible for his life-project in a world of death, answering in the Father's name, doing it justice. We can speak of a conversion in Jesus: a change of life that leads him inward and drives him to communicate this new experience of God, to regenerate hope.

But how to go about it? What he has experienced clashes with the ideas of those in authority, even with what John is preaching. Jesus is tempted about the means.

Should he continue along the same lines as John? Should he throw himself into a spectacular campaign of public Messianism? Should he ally himself with any of the already existing groups? What should he do about the foreseeable antagonistic reactions of the Jewish establishment? What is at stake is his faith in God—a God concerned with life, the *Father*, who cannot be subjected to a magic test doing violence to history, because God is offering *a free gift*, one which does not enter into alliance with other powers or do deals with any system. God's gift is free and not negotiable.

Mark and Matthew refer to the event that offered Jesus the occasion to avoid this situation of temptation: the arrest of John (Mark 1:14ff.; Matt. 4:12 ff.). Jesus will not continue John's work; he leaves the Jordan and decides to go off to Galilee to preach the Good News of the *Abba, who is coming to reign.*

5. The Reign of Life in a World of Death

Henceforth this will be his only cause. The life of the poor is where the Father's name is proved holy. The Kingdom cannot come until the lot of the poor has changed; it will not come while there is still injustice and inequality. Jesus' project is the reordering of two relationships (1) between human beings and God; whom they must treat as a Father; and (2) among human beings themselves, who should treat one another as brothers and sisters, God's family. The earth is the common heritage given by God for the life of all. Thus human beings can live together in the right way, dependent upon God and upon each other. Jesus says he has been sent to announce this Good News to the poor; it is the year of grace for the blind, the oppressed, the prisoners (Luke 4:18 ff.). His experience of the Father does not remain in heaven, because he knows his Reign is also an earthly and historical matter. It has to do with food for all people, forgiveness of sins, the overcoming of the actual evil that threatens us, the recognition of God's fatherhood, which makes us all equally children of God. For this to be possible Jesus makes three things clear: there is an irreducible opposition between the Kingdom and money, the Kingdom and prestige, and the Kingdom and power.

The Kingdom and Money

The Kingdom belongs to the poor (Luke 6:20), and the rich as such have no part in it (Luke 6:24ff.; 16:19–31; Mark 10:23–25). Because money is an idol that seeks to be an absolute, it is not possible to serve God and money (Matt. 6:24). Jesus does not idealize poverty; it is the result of sin, of exclusive possession. His ideal is abundance for all (expressed in the symbol of the banquet of the Kingdom). But for this to become possible he teaches detachment and giving up the goods of this world (Matt. 6:25–33). He invites people to share in the life of the poor (Luke 14:13ff.), so that we can have a common family life on earth, neither rich nor poor. Meanwhile he stands firmly on the side of the poor, through effective pity for them and at the same time through love for the rich, whose complicity with the kingdom of Satan places them in danger. Money creates a divided society of haves and have-nots. It makes God's fatherhood in history impossible.

The Kingdom and Prestige

In a society which gave enormous importance to social status, Jesus stands on the wrong side, with those no one wants to be with; he realizes that prestige is also a divisive principle, opposed to equality. He declares that God is on the side of the little people, those who have no value for society (cf. Matt. 18:10). He says that welcoming them is welcoming him and the Father (Mark 9:37). He attacks the scribes and pharisees (Matt. 6:2, 5, 16; 23:5–7; Luke 11:45–52), and he is glad that the Father's self-revelation has been to the simple, not the wise (Matt. 11:25 ff.). This is why Jesus makes himself the last of all and the servant of all, when in an act of "madness" to the world he kneels down before his disciples (John 13:2–5). In the end he will die disgraced before all (Mark 15:29–32), outside the walls of the city, between two rebels (Mark 15:27ff.).[3]

The Kingdom and Power

The final divisive principle is what decides who has power over whom. This power tends to be murderous because it stays on top only by suppressing the rights of those it dominates. Against this power Jesus places service as the constructive force in the new society. He unmasks political power when he says "those who claim to govern nations behave despotically and the powerful oppress the people" (Mark 10:42). Speaking in code language—because of the danger he runs—he denies that Caesar has any right to collect an idolatrous tax. He demands that what belongs to God should be given back to God; that is, the government of the people, which Caesar unjustly holds (Luke 11:39–52; Matt. 23:1–36; Mark 7:1–23; 11:15–17; 12:1–12, 35–40). Because he stands on the side of the oppressed, Jesus will die "under the power of Pontius Pilate" as an accursed criminal (Gal 3:13) in total powerlessness and abandon.

6. The Galilean Spring

There was a real blooming of life around Jesus. Many hopes found an echo in his message and his behavior. To enlarge his sphere of action Jesus gathered a group of disciples, as new shepherds for the forsaken and ill-treated people (Matt. 9:36). At one point this call seems to have had an eschatological character; they will be the twelve foundations of the people of the promise. This is provocative to the establishment. The real Israel is being set up now in Galilee by common people. In this initial heterogeneous group some probably secretly hoped that Jesus was the Messiah, one who would put an end to Roman rule, by military means, of course.[4]

Jesus' popularity becomes a temptation to Peter and other comrades, who see the opportunity for a popular triumph for their imagined Messiah. Jesus overcomes this temptation to regionalize the Kingdom in the illusion of a facile territorial triumph and decides to enlarge his field of action (Mark 1:35–38).

By his cures Jesus is not claiming to prove anything about himself, but to give signs of the liberating presence of the Father who reigns. Their importance does not lie in being anything exceptional, but rather in pointing people to God: "If by the finger of God I cast out demons, this is a sign that the Kingdom of God has come upon you" (Luke 11:20). Identifying in a "scandalous" way with sinners, he also restores them to the promise, rescuing their dignity and freeing them from shame and guilt. By his solidarity he shows people that God accepts them.

The effects do not take long to show. The change taking place in the world of the poor through Jesus' actions makes people compare teaching with teaching, practice with practice, that of Jesus and that of the scribes, and to conclude that Jesus indeed teaches with authority. He speaks and changes the situation for the outcast. With the scribes it is the opposite; they talk and talk and nothing new ever happens. But this comparison is a warning to Jesus. The establishment will not easily tolerate such parallel authority (Mark 3:6), which is moreover beginning to make the people criticize their leaders (Mark 1:22, 23).

The connection between the miracles and the Kingdom was not plain. Jesus did not respond to the apocalyptic type of expectations and those aroused by John. He does not present himself as the bringer of God's judgment. To the question whether he is the one or should they wait for another, Jesus replies by quoting Isaiah. The culminating point of this text is not the miracles but the final phrase: "The poor have the good news preached to them" (Luke 7:22). The miracles are the sign that what the alternative God is offering is true. They do not put an end to all misfortune and evil, but they clearly signal the direction faith in him should follow; his most important task is the struggle against all human misery, disease, hunger, ignorance, slavery, all kinds of inhumanity. And blessed are they who are not scandalized that this is what the Kingdom of God is like (Luke 7:23).

The first cloud appears when Jesus begins to increase activities that transgress the law of purity: he heals on the sabbath (Mark 1:21–23; 3:1–6; Luke 13:14ff.; Matt. 12:9–13); he becomes impure by touching the impure (Mark 1:3–31; 5:27,41; 6:5; Luke 13:12ff.), especially a leper (Mark 1:41–45), to make them feel God's nearness, which the establishment has deprived them of, declaring them to be accursed by God (John 7:39); he calls a tax-collector to follow him and eats with him and his friends (Matt. 9:9 ff.); he is not afraid of dealing with prostitutes (Luke 7:36–50), to whom he also opens a door of hope in the Kingdom (Matt. 21:31). A number of women work with him. They too have been barred from any activity for the Kingdom by the Jewish laws of purity (Luke 8:1–3; Mark 15:40 ff.).

Arguments with the scribes and pharisees seem to have been frequent (Mark 2:1–3,6; 7:1–23; 11:15–12:48; Luke 11:37–53; Matt. 23; John 2:13–22; 5:16–47; 7:14–39; 8:12–59; 10:22–39). What is in question is not something peripheral to his faith but the very core of the reality of the God in whom he believes. The consequence is that very early on we hear of plans to bring about Jesus' death (Mark 3:6; Luke 4:22ff.; Matt. 12:14; John 5:16; 7:30, 44; 8:20, 59; 10:31; 11:8, 49–53, 56).

Jesus tries to protect himself against these threats. He never acts with foolish imprudence (cf. John 6:1, 15; 7:1–10; 8:1, 59b; 10:39ff.; 11:54; Luke 4:30; Matt. 12:15; Mark 3:7). In Mark, one of the objects of the parables appears to be to give the message in cryptic form to protect Jesus, who was accused of blasphemy (punishable by death 2:7), breaking the sabbath (also punishable by death, 3:2,6), being possessed by the devil (3:22) and mad (3:20). Perhaps he is expressing his own experience in his advice to his disciples to be "cunning as serpents and simple as doves" (Matt. 10:16b).

7. The Beginning of the Crisis

But what happens to the Kingdom? In the beginning Jesus expected the triumph of his religious mission, but later he began to realize that his mission would lead to a fatal conflict with his politicoreligious society. His disciples have false hopes and cannot understand (Mark 4:13, 35–41). He himself realizes he is at risk from his own work and the people (Mark 3:9ff.; 5:30–32). His compatriots are shocked by the works he does, seeing he is one of them (Mark 6:2 ff.). Jesus understands the mortal logic of all this: no prophet is accepted by his own people (Matt. 13:57); prophets are murdered. But why does his work not arouse faith? (Mark 6:6a).

It is painful not to be able to make himself understood by his people. They did not understand John, and they do not understand him (Matt. 11:18 ff.). They do not realize that now the final era has arrived, that Elijah has already come. The cities in which he has done the most miracles are the ones most closed against him. His people have stubborn hearts; they do not want to think of anything beyond their own health and food for the day.

In this context Jesus intensifies his activity in the service of life and sends out the Twelve to widen his sphere of action. There was one event which must have had particular resonance among the oppressed people: what Mark enigmatically calls "that of the loaves" (6:52). A large crowd, which had been following Jesus for several days, was hungry. The people's situation does not bother their shepherds at all. So Jesus takes care of them (Mark 6:34). He not only gives them the word of God but also gives them food in abundance. In this way he shows that God feeds his people and that physical needs, hunger, and sickness are a matter for the Kingdom.

The people go in another direction. They want him to lead them as their king (John 6:15). Jesus sends his disciples away, so that they do not encourage this kind of uprising (Mark 6:45); he takes leave of the people and goes into hiding (John 6:15). He faces this moment of temptation in prayer to his Father (Mark 6:46). Why do the people not see the signs of the Kingdom? Why are they only concerned with the material side of his activities?

The growing conflict with the establishment reaches its height, according to Mark's narrative, because his disciples eat without bothering about purification rites (7:1 ff.). The Pharisees' criticism becomes the occasion for Jesus to unmask the deep unfaithfulness they hide beneath their apparent piety. They fuss about trivialities but violate the fundamental tenets of the law—mercy and justice—which are truly a matter of life and death for the people, whereas fulfilling ritual prescriptions is not.

Now Jesus is a danger to the Jewish establishment. So he has to get out of their reach. He does not go into Syrian territory on a missionary journey but to take refuge (Mark 7:24). And there the Galilee crisis brews.

8. Crisis and Confirmation

Rahner speaks of "extreme crises of self-identification"[5] in Jesus. There are sufficient indications of the people's dismay as their interest in Jesus declines. They are disappointed by this Kingdom he proclaims. John the Baptist himself expresses this disappointment: "Are you the one who was to come or should we look for another?" (Matt. 11:2–6). Some of his disciples desert (John 6:67). Jesus stakes everything. "Who do people say that I am . . . And you, who do you say that I am?" This is not an educational question laying the ground for teaching. The disciples' reply stays at a merely human level: "You are the Messiah" (Mark 8:29), with whose triumph they hope to be associated (Mark 9:34; 10:35–45). They misinterpret his Messiahship.

Such a proclamation does not fit the truth about Jesus, and under Roman rule it places him in obvious danger. This is why he corrects the reply and enjoins silence (Mark 8:30), but he takes on the struggle to the end: "I am going to die at the hands of men" (cf. Luke 9:44). It is quite clear what is important to Jesus and for what he has risked his life. Now he has to accept the consequences of having adopted the Father's cause and the cause of the poor. He does this convinced that the Kingdom is greater than the failure of his strategy. Violent death, perhaps by stoning (cf. John 8:59; 10:31–33), is now a real threat to him.

There must have been a serious problem with Peter in this matter; the community would not have just invented this confrontation between them. We are told that Peter rebuked Jesus (Mark 8:33). Orthodox in its formulation, his confession remained at the purely human level, and there was no room in it for such a radical commitment to the death. Jesus remonstrates with him in the harshest words he ever uses against anyone: "Get behind me, Satan." Peter's proposal is a temptation for him.

Jesus risks remaining alone (John 6:68). But he has to state honestly the change that has taken place in his mission. Because of it, anyone who goes on following him has to be ready for death (Mark 8:34–38). He proposes a new radical mode of discipleship. During the first stage the Kingdom was mediated by the preaching of conversion and by miracles. Now it is not just a matter of words and deeds. What is required is total commitment (Luke 12:49f.) to unmask the power that makes the Kingdom impossible: the religious power which has kidnapped the freely-giving God of the covenant and put in God's place a deity of laws, merits and purifications. Only with a total commitment can a free space for the Kingdom be created; the only way of saving one's life is to risk it with Jesus for the Kingdom (Luke 9:24–26).

In his prayer Jesus has a deep experience of confirmation by the Father (Luke 9:28). He has not preached himself or focused the people on his person; in everything he has behaved as the Son. Disaster strikes him because of the inevitable confrontation between his declaration for the Father and the poor, the outcast, in a world which speaks of a "God" who favors the select few. "This is my beloved Son in whom I am well pleased. Listen to him" (Matt. 17:5). The voice confirms Jesus as the only way for the disciples. Now there will be neither Moses (Law) nor Elijah (Prophets) (Matt. 17:8); Jesus alone is enough, the Son who has done what pleases the Father and who is the one to follow.

9. Training of the Disciples

Unmasking the religious power is a challenge to the Jewish establishment, which will very probably end in death. But the disciples are not yet well enough trained to take on the cause of the Kingdom. In view of the certainty of approaching death, Jesus leaves off working with the people and decides to train his disciples (Mark 9:30–31a), in order to consolidate more organically the community which will make his mission possible. One by one he starts correcting their judgments and values. They have to understand that these are new times now; the coming of Elijah (John the Baptist, cf. Matt. 17:13) is the signal. In these times the conditions for fighting against evil are faith and prayer (Mark 9:14–29). They must welcome the little ones (Mark 9:36ff.) because they are the ones God prefers (Mark 10:13–16); they have to understand that riches are a fundamental obstacle to the Kingdom (Mark 10:17–27), and as the ideal of the Kingdom is abundance for all, the way to it is poverty in order to share with those who have nothing (Mark 10:28–31); in the Kingdom the original equality between man and woman is fundamental (Mark 10:2–12). But above all, their hearts must be preparing for the style of the Kingdom. Instead of the disciples' ambitions for power, Jesus offers them service as the norm (Mark 9:33–35; 10:35–45); then they will be able to discern what alliances to make and which to reject (Mark 9:38 ff.).

10. The Final Confrontation with the Jewish Establishment

Jesus' death only has meaning when it is seen from *after* the resurrection. But it is not enough to look at it from a Paschal perspective. We must also look at it as it was *before* the resurrection. And to do this first we must ask these questions: Why did Jesus go to Jerusalem and for what? Let us reply to these questions from the gospel texts themselves.

We will not go into the controversy about the number of times Jesus went up to Jerusalem and when. We start, rather, from the obvious fact that there was a *last* journey to Jerusalem, in which the whole history of Jesus' difficult relationship with the establishment culminated. Jesus made this journey aware that "every prophet dies in Jerusalem."

Rather than formulating hypotheses on his intentions, let us look at what he in fact *does*. Three large blocks appear. In the first two Jesus is the principal character, and his actions unmask and condemn the establishment. In the third, Jesus hardly acts at all, he is the passive object of the whole drama and is condemned and assassinated by the establishment.

Jesus Unmasks the Establishment at Its Center

John and the Synoptics show the confrontation over the temple differently. We shall follow the Synoptic account because, whatever happened, this fact was decisive in Jesus' last confrontation with the Jewish establishment: the fundamental accusation is that he intends to destroy it.

The moment comes when Jesus decides to confront the establishment at its center. What he said in outlying Galilee is not enough. He chooses the moment of the passover celebration, the festival of Jewish liberation. It is a careful, thought-out decision, and he knows his life is at stake. He is aware of the Messianic hopes that have arisen around him. The corrections he has made to these expectations have not been enough. Therefore his first action is symbolic; he enters Jerusalem on a donkey. This means hopes of his leadership cannot be maintained.

The scope of the temple episode has been much discussed. We think it should be interpreted not as a purification, after which it could go on being the symbolic center of the people of the promise. We see it as a taking over of the temple, whose sterility it unmasks. Jesus preaches its destruction and the need to abandon it, because God's presence is no longer to be found there (cf. Matt. 27:51 ff.).

But why does Jesus go against the religious establishment and not against the Roman political establishment? We must seek for what light we can find on this question. It is evident that Jesus rejects Roman rule, which goes against the exclusive Reign of Yahweh. The burden of the tribute is not only unjust, but it is also intolerable because it appertains to the cult of the emperor. Because of the danger of the situation he says in coded language: "Render to Caesar this idolatrous coin which is a blot upon Israel and give to God what belongs to him, which is the government of the people, unjustly held in Caesar's power." He analyzes Rome's political domination and judges it unjust (cf. Mark 5:9,13; 10:42; 12:16,17; 13:14; Luke 13:32ff.)[6] But the travesty the religious leaders make of God and his project is the principal obstacle to the people's hope.

So two elements are fundamental to Jesus' condemnation: the way in which he unmasks the temple, revealing its sterility and injustice ("not one stone will be left upon another"), and the opposition to the payment of tribute, for this is how his enemies interpret his words. The people, or at least some of them, support him and acclaim him. We may suppose these are the ones who have come with him from Galilee, not the people of Jerusalem, who are keener to maintain their status than to support change. But this only sharpens the conflict with the authorities, who cannot find a way to kill him. The opportunity is offered by the treachery of one of the Twelve, Judas.

The Meaning of Meaninglessness

The circle closes round Jesus. What is he to do? In the context of the memorial of the passover, a liberation frustrated by the domination under which they are living in their own country, and facing betrayal, Jesus understands that this is not the moment to flee or to resist violence.

Now the word *denounce* is not enough. The moment has come to *renounce*, so that his death will openly show the murderous nature of that power which is so seductive, especially when it is exercised in God's name, but which continues to cause the death of every prophet, because it continues to cause the death of the poor, God's children.

In a prophetic action with deep symbolic meaning, and with the eschatological certainty that the Kingdom will triumph, Jesus expresses the meaning of his life.

He gathers together with his friends for the last time and sums up in a gesture what he has always done: he is departing and he shares himself for the life of the people, so that they may have a part in him; he pours out his life so that the crowd can become an organized *people*, the people *of God*. This is how he wants us always to remember him—in the shared bread and his blood poured out for the life of the people. He orders us to do likewise, to break apart and share the bread, and to depart, to set out and share ourselves so that his subversive memory may go on generating this same way of being-in-the-world. This will be his new form of presence in history: giving himself for the life of the people. This subversive memory of Jesus is betrayed again every time it is ritualized and held up for worship so that it need not be disturbing and transforming.

This taking on of renunciation is not done openly in broad daylight. He experiences the deepest threat that a human life and work can suffer—the meaninglessness of an unjust and violent death. A natural death would not threaten the future of his work in the same way, even though it would also be a final point. But to die (perhaps by stoning) as a false prophet? Who will believe in his proclamation of the Kingdom? Won't his death mean the death of his Father's cause?

This is the next to last moment of temptation. How is Jesus to react to the unjust violence of the Jewish establishment? To flee would leave the field open to the lie that the establishment operated with regard to God. It would be equivalent to saying that the cause he had lived for was not important enough to risk his life for. Neither can he defend himself by violence. But there is no reply to his questions. The Son has to trust in his *Abba*, even in his silence. God is different from how he imagined. "Everything is possible," God says, but Jesus discovers that God cannot go against human decisions. God does not leap into history and spare him any of the human condition. As it says in Romans, "He did not spare his own Son" anything (8:32); he did not spare himself the pain of giving up thus unconditionally his Son. Jesus discovers that God's way of being in history is not in power but in *kenosis*, in hiddenness, respecting human freedom even when it is used against God's plan.

Jesus goes down into an abyss of loneliness. The disciples do not seem to understand what is about to happen. Jesus decides not to assume his own defense but to leave himself in his *Abba's* hands, with a faith greater even than the catastrophe. The Son's trust is answered by the Father's faithfulness. The Father "cannot" reassure his Son that God is near and give him the certainty that his cry is heard (cf. Heb. 5:7–10). The Father also shows trust in Jesus; the Father keeps quiet and does not intervene. This tells us that it is not God we need to call to account for silence in the face of human violence. We have to question the murderers themselves. God did not manipulate history either in the face of the Son's death or in answer to his cries.

The Establishment Against Jesus

Jesus is not so much judged as condemned. However, the accusations sound truthful. From the religious point of view the leaders understood very well what this was about: the Yahweh of their cult against Jesus' *Abba*. Jesus' behavior was an attack on the Temple. He himself understood it to be so: "I give you my word that anyone who says *to that mountain*: 'Move and throw yourself into the sea' will get what he asks for" (Mark 11:23). He is confident that his faith will obtain the overthrow of the religious establishment of Israel.

From the political point of view, an effective love, which confronts an unjust situation, can be misinterpreted as an ambition for power. Jesus ran this risk rather than run the greater risk of letting it be thought that his love was neutral—a matter of feelings and wishes but inactive.

What finally brings Jesus to judgment is his fight for the outcast masses, so that they are not banished from the Kingdom. Jesus is condemned for the God in whom he believes, the *Abba* whose fatherhood is a public matter. And he is condemned for the way he says this Father can be reached: through grace and his preference for the poor rather than through sacrifices; by the practice of love, not in the Temple but in suffering human beings.

Whether there are two religious trials or just one, whether the Jewish authorities could really pass sentence of death, whether Pilate tried to save Jesus or not, are all things which do not qualitatively change the reality: we human beings killed the Son whom God sent to save us. We cannot minimize this great injustice by calling it a superhuman drama in which God "settles accounts" with humanity at the price of the Son's blood. We killed him, and we go on killing God's children whenever they disturb the plans of the powerful. We condemned God's own Son as a blasphemer; he sought total and complete liberation for humanity, and we condemned him as subversive of the established order.

This explanation of the historical background to Jesus' death (reasons of state and national security, orthodoxy) does not give an adequate account of the total meaning of this event, which from faith's point of view is the chief milestone in history. God integrated this injustice into the plan of salvation. God did not annihilate the murderers, but showed the final salvation of Jesus and his cause through his resurrection and followers. Without the resurrection our faith in him cannot be justified; without followers faith in him would be impossible.

In the search for this explanation many formulations of faith developed: "he died for our sins;" "it was necessary for Christ to suffer and thus enter into his glory;" thus the Father's love is shown (Rom. 8:31; John 3:16).

There are three basic soteriological schemes that try to explain the meaning of Jesus' death: it is a sacrifice offered to God for sinners; it is a worthy satisfaction to God for human offenses; it is the redemption (release) payment to free us from the power of the devil. These were formulated in cultural contexts very different from our own and need to be reformulated to determine what they contain of normative revelation and what is cultural accretion, which today covers up rather than *dis*-covers the meaning.

Does speaking of salvation mean we are talking about overcoming a previous situation of perdition? What does *perdition* mean today in Latin America? Is it something that refers only to another life? Does it only concern our relations with God, or has it got anything to do with interhuman relations? And what is salvation? Is it a change in the situation regarding a broken relationship in the past? Does this future have anything to do with present history, or does it merely have an eschatological dimension? Is it only of an intimately subjective order, or has it got anything to do with transforming the external world?

Both the sacrificial schema and the satisfaction schema see sin as an offense directly against God. The redemption schema sees it also as slavery in the power of the devil. The first of these schemes sees the passion as placating God and purifying humanity. The satisfaction schema sees it as the way to restore God's blemished honor; the redemption formula sees it as the price to be paid to release a slave. There are three principal objections to these schemes: they are fundamentally sin-centered; they reduce the work of salvation to the suffering of the passion; and they are not talking about the God revealed by Jesus, the Father who appears in the gospels. Moreover, they turn human salvation into a suprahistorical drama in which humanity has no part; everything is arranged between Jesus and God. Further, reducing the saving dimension merely to the cross runs the risk of canonizing suffering, inducing passivity, and hiding the saving dimension of Jesus' life, including his resurrection, and therefore also that of discipleship.

Nevertheless, we cannot ignore the fact that these schemes speak in the language used by revelation. This is because they contain a fundamental nucleus which must not be lost.

1. The sacrificial schema contains the popular insight that we have to sacrifice our life for others. *Sacrifice* means "make sacred, dedicate, consecrate." This was Jesus' life, a life consecrated to others; he offers us an alternative to the inhuman. In this life consecrated to the Kingdom we see revealed what it means to be children of God and how we should live as brothers and sisters.

2. The schema of substitute satisfaction contains the Hebrew insight of human solidarity. Properly speaking, nobody substitutes or stands in for anybody; rather, we are all involved with one another. It is not a matter of Jesus taking our place "before" God, but that he takes his proper place, which is to head (be the head) of this "great I" of salvation, in which each one of us has our own place and responsibility. He heads us, but not instead of us. He lives as the Son so that those of us who believe in him can also live as God's children and as brothers and sisters with our fellow human beings (cf. John 1:10–13). The letter to the Hebrews speaks of Jesus as the "first in line," the first of those who believe (6:20; 12:1ff). Brought to life with him, we will be his body in history so that "by his stripes we are healed" (Isa. 53:5). Through his wounds we learn the damage done by power to God's children and by money, lies, exploitation, injustice, and the law. On the other hand, we have to be clear that it is not precisely God whom we have to "satisfy" or make up to, because God lacks nothing. It is the Creator's project for humanity and history that we have to "satisfy" (= fulfill sufficiently), because this is what is not "satisfied" in history.

3. Finally, the fundamental core of the redemption-release schema coincides with the Latin American intuition that one has to pay a price for freedom and for life; and this price can be life itself. This is what Jesus offered to release us, in pure blood, from slavery to the anti-values in which we were caught and the fear that engulfed us. The Letter to the Hebrews formulates this dimension in an interpretative synthesis which embraces both the theological and the historical: "That through death he might destroy him who has the power of death, that is, the devil,

and deliver all those who through fear of death were subject to lifelong bondage" (Heb. 2:14f).

11. Resurrection and God's Protest

God was absolutely dissatisfied with the death of his Son. In the last resort death resolves nothing, only life does. Hence God's absolute and radical protest, which did not involve the death of the murderer but confirming and bringing to life his murdered Son. True protest consists in confirming life. Only this response does justice to God's fatherhood.

The Father confirms Jesus by exalting him and placing him at the Father's right hand; thus God confirms Jesus' whole life (as a road to go along) and his doings (as a cause to pursue). The faith of the disciples is confirmed through the Paschal experience. Thanks to this we have witnesses, a reconstructed community, and the possibility of following Jesus. The essence of the resurrection is for it to be proclaimed. Both things require one another dialectically, and one cannot exist without the other. Without its proclamation the resurrection would only be the suprahistorical denouncement of the drama, but history with its injustice and death would remain untouched and have no exit. Without a real resurrection, its proclamation would be mere ideology.

So it is not death (suffering) that brings salvation, but the loving whole of the mystery of the Lord's passage through our history: his life, whose consequence is death, and the resurrection, which is its fulfillment. Once again we can express this in a dialectical schema.

Life (thesis, God's gift to humanity) is denied by death (antithesis, humanity's response). Life is not ignored or annulled by death, but death is the consequence of a life lived *in this way*. This resurrection (new synthesis, God's gift to Jesus and humanity) is the "negation of the negation." But again this negation does not delete life and death; it confirms both. Once again we have Mark's synthesis: Jesus of Nazareth (life), who was crucified (death), has risen (new life) to make possible his return to "Galilee" and new experience (there they will see him). The resurrection does not save Jesus from death and life; he passes through them and is saved with them. That is why the risen Christ still bears the marks of this life-and-death: the wounds of his hands and side.

But the truth about all this will only be known by those who return to Galilee to follow him.

III. FUNDAMENTAL STATEMENTS ABOUT JESUS

Beneath narrative christology, which puts us formally in touch with what Jesus *did*, there are underlying statements that tell us formally who Jesus of Nazareth, the Liberator, is. By way of conclusion, we list them in the form of theses, or if you like, a creed.

• The final and absolute reality, which conditions all Jesus' practice, the ultimate criterion of discernment, what is not negotiable for him, is the Kingdom of

God, the Father. This absolute reference to the Father's reign is the fount of his freedom in the face of every human mediation and proposal.

• Jesus is the Son of God in human history. It is his life and work that gives historical density to the title; he lives unconditionally referred to the Father and the Father's project. He who is "from the beginning" in eternity, the Son, had to learn how to be this in a human manner in history (cf. Heb. 5:7 ff.). What makes him the Son in history is that he makes himself responsible for the Father's name, the Father's cause.

• Jesus is truly man; he is not man in the generic sense, but rather this particular man. This is the pole of the mystery of the incarnation that is immediately accessible to us. Precisely *in this* particular human life he is truly God. He is not a superman (like the mythological heroes), but "tempted in every respect as we are, yet without sinning" (Heb. 4:15). In this way he fully becomes the new man, the new human being.

• The titles we give him gain their reality from his life and practice. They do not say any *more* than this. Formulated in particular cultural circumstances, they contain a normative nucleus and a conceptual apparatus, which is in dialectical relationship with the cultural changes taking place during the course of history. Therefore these titles must be reformulated so that they go on faithfully expressing the deep reality of what Jesus *continues to be for us today.*

• Jesus' whole life is a work of salvation. This characteristic is sealed definitively by his death and resurrection. It is the totality of the mystery of his passage through our history which makes total liberation possible for us, both historically and eschatologically, as a task and a gift, for "now and not yet." We are saved not because he reveals to us a new, more demanding law than the first, but because he gives us a new capacity, a Spirit to enable us to live as children of the Father, as brothers and sisters of our fellow human beings. This is how we pursue Jesus' cause. And this is how Jesus is fully the Liberator.

• Through his resurrection Jesus becomes "a vivifying Spirit" (1 Cor. 15:45). We are integrated into him and form his body in history. The horizon of our understanding of the resurrection and incorporation into him is the hope we have for history. Only those who hope for better possibilities in history realize the definitive reality of Jesus. And the final horizon of our experience of the risen Jesus is following him by promoting his cause.

—Translated by Dinah Livingstone

NOTES

1. "The New Testament feels free to speak of the experience of salvation with Jesus in a variety of ways, though in fact these differing interpretations simply articulate what has really come into being with Jesus. This also gives us the freedom to express in a new form the experience of salvation in Jesus that we may have described in terms taken from our modern culture with its own particular problems, expectations and needs, though these in turn must also be subjected to the criticism of Israel's expectation and to what has found fulfillment in Jesus. Moreover, we should do this *in order* to remain faithful to what the New

Testament Christians felt to be an experience of salvation in Jesus" (E. Schillebeeckx, *Interim Report on the Books Jesus and Christ* (New York: Crossroad, 1982), p. 16.

2. This is how Jon Sobrino formulates it: "By historical we formally mean here the practice of Jesus as that place of greater metaphysical density of his person. This practice is all activity, in deeds and words, by which it transforms the surrounding reality towards the kingdom of God and through which he creates and expresses his own person. This practice of Jesus is what gives us the best access to his person. But it has also unleashed a history which has reached *us* in order to be continued. Thus our present-day practice is a requirement of Jesus, but it is also the hermeneutic place for understanding Jesus" (Jon Sobrino, "Jesus de Nazaret," in C. Floristán and J. J. Tamayo, eds., *Conceptos fundamentales de pastoral* [Madrid, 1983], pp. 483 ff.).

3. The word *lestes* in Greek does not mean an ordinary thief, but a rioter, a rebel, a violent person. Cf. Fl. Jos., *Bell. Jud.* 2.254–7.

4. It is not clear whether we can speak of any of them belonging to the Zealot movement, which came later (66 C.E.). But it is very probable that some of them were sympathetic to armed resistance against the Romans and the temptation was increased at this period of apocalyptic expectations.

5. See Karl Rahner and W. Thüsing, *A New Christology*, trans. David Smith and Verdant Green (New York: Seabury Press, 1980).

6. Only by regarding Jesus as the guardian of Caesar's interests (then and henceforth) can we interpret his response to the trap about paying tribute to Caesar (Mark 12:13–18) as representing approval.

7

Systematic Christology: Jesus Christ, the Absolute Mediator of the Reign of God

JON SOBRINO

The preceding article has presented a christological account of Jesus of Nazareth as Liberator. The present chapter will develop, in the form of a sketch, the core of a systematic christology that presupposes the content of the foregoing account, as well as the specific premises of liberation theology,[1] that is: (1) that the central object of the theology of liberation is the *Reign of God*,[2] (2) that the goal of this theology is *liberation*, and therefore that it understands itself as the theory of a praxis,[3] and (3) that liberation theology is developed from a determinate locus, that of *the poor of this world*.[4]

I. THEORETICAL CHRISTOLOGY: JESUS AS THE MEDIATOR OF THE REIGN OF GOD

All christology must assert the ultimacy and transcendence of Christ, and the christology of liberation must do so from what it regards as actually ultimate: the Reign of God. To this end, methodologically, liberation christology begins its reflection with the person of Jesus of Nazareth himself, since it is here that the relationship between Jesus and the Reign of God appears with all clarity.

Let us state from the outset that our attention to Jesus is not a reduction of christology to a pure "Jesuology," but only the selection of a determinate methodology. Whether our approach will be a fruitful one will be seen after the execution of our analysis. But let us observe that it is at least possible for it to be fruitful, as other systematic christologies today have established. Karl Rahner, for example, concludes that a christology could be developed from something central to the historical Jesus and wonders "whether a human being who is the vessel of an absolute, pure love, free of any kind of selfishness, must not be something more than merely human."[5] For our purposes, the important thing in this citation does not reside so much in its specific understanding of Jesus ("an absolute, pure love"), but in the proposition of the possibility of constructing christology on the historical Jesus. For our part, we shall attempt to do so in terms of the relationship of the historical Jesus with the Reign of God.

1. Ultimacy of Jesus in Terms of the Reign of God

In the Synoptics, Jesus' relationship with the Reign of God, which we here define formally as the ultimate will of God for this world, is central. That Reign and its proximity are presented by Jesus as the *actual ultimate*. This shapes his person, in the exteriority of his mission (with respect to "making history") and in the interiority of his subjectivity (his own historicity). It is also this that precipitates his historical destiny, that of the cross. His very resurrection is God's response to one who, for serving the Reign, has been put to death by the anti-Reign. In other words, in order to come to know the specifically Christian element of the Reign of God, one must turn to Jesus. But just so, conversely, in order to know Jesus one must turn to the Reign of God.

Jesus himself asserts this relationship between the Reign of God and his person. At times his assertion is explicit: "If it is by the Spirit of God that I expel demons, then the reign of God has overtaken you" (Matt. 12:28 and par.). At other times he posits this relationship in an implicit but real way: in various of the actions of his praxis which can and should be interpreted as signs of the coming of the Reign in behalf of the poor (his miracles, his exorcisms, the welcome he extends to the weak and oppressed); in his struggle with the anti-Reign (controversies, denunciations, exposé of oppressors); or in his celebration of the presence of the Reign (meals).

Thus, Jesus appears in an essential and constitutive relationship with the Reign of God, with the ultimate will of God—with that which we call systematically the *mediation* of God. And systematically we call this Jesus, in his relationship with the mediation, the *mediator* of the will of God; that is, the person who proclaims the Reign, who posits signs of its reality and points to its totality.

For systematic christology, the question is how to move from the reality of Jesus as mediator to his reality as *definitive mediator* of the Reign of God. All christologies must face this question, since all of them must take the step—the leap, really—from Jesus' historical reality to a profession of his ultimacy. (We could make an exception for those obsolete christologies in which certain of Jesus' deeds—his miracles, or his prophecies—or his resurrection automatically provide the step, the leap, to the ultimacy of Christ. But almost no one today accepts the miracles and prophecies as automatically forcing this transition, and the leap justified by the resurrection ultimately requires faith in the resurrection.)

In an analysis of the qualitative bound from Jesus as mediator to Jesus as the definitive mediator of the Reign, it must be taken into account whether and where there is some kind of *discontinuity* that would make that transition reasonable—although to accept it as radical discontinuity will in the last analysis always be a matter of faith. Along these lines we might recall Jesus' daring proclamation of the imminence of this Reign and the indefectible victory of God, his daring in declaring the symmetry broken forever in which God could possibly come as a savior or possibly as a condemning judge—to all of which would correspond the discontinuity in his hearers: "At last salvation has come for the poor." This daring on Jesus' part in announcing the coming of God in the Reign, and in proclaiming the gratuitous, salvific, and liberative reality of God that draws near with the proximity of God, would offer some kind of discontinuity regarding the historical viewpoint, in terms of which theology could now reflect upon the special relationship of Jesus with the transcendent.

At the same time, Jesus appears in *continuity* with other, earlier mediators—Moses, the prophets, the Servant, and so on. In other words, Jesus appears as a human being immersed in this same current of a historical course traversed with honesty before the truth, mercy before the suffering of another, justice before the oppression of the masses, a loving dedication to his mission, total fidelity to God, indestructible hope, the sacrifice of his life. (This last element—although disdained by christologies that seek only the specific, peculiar element in Jesus—offers a very considerable systematic advantage when it comes to establishing the later dogmatic tenet of the true humanity of Jesus as a participation in the best that the human being has ever been or done.)

The assertion of Jesus' absolute discontinuity is a matter of faith, as we have said. We cannot, therefore, propose a reality of Jesus that would mechanically force the qualitative leap to his status as *the* mediator (as Rahner cannot move mechanically from Jesus' love presented historically to a total love in total discontinuity). What we can propose is a reality of Jesus in terms of which we can also gain a meaningful formulation—in our opinion, a more meaningful formulation than we gain from a point of departure in other realities—of this leap to *the* mediator. What we have called Jesus' daring can function as an index, a pointer, an indicator, of the transcendent ultimacy of his person. And a grasp of what is human in Jesus—which is in no way novel in its formal characterization—can point to his human ultimacy, not as differentiation, but as fullness of the human.

Christians actually made this qualitative leap after the resurrection. From our perspective we add that the resurrection can also be presented as confirmation of the truth of Jesus as the mediator of the Reign, and not only as an arbitrary act posited by God for the purpose of revealing the reality of that God—which could have just as well occurred in the resuscitation of any other corpse. If this had been the only "reason" for the resurrection, the resurrection would be something extrinsic to Jesus' life and would say nothing of his being as mediator. But if the one to whom "life has been restored" is one who proclaimed the commencement of life for the poor and therefore was deprived of life himself, if the one who has been raised is one who ended as a victim of the anti-Reign, then the resurrection can very well be understood systematically as the confirmation of the mediator, the confirmation of his (objectively) theological daring, and the confirmation of the fullness of the human occurring in his person. Then the qualitative leap of faith can be made, and the christological concept formulated of Jesus of Nazareth as *the* mediator of the Reign of God.

In terms of the Reign of God, then, the reality of Jesus can be formulated, and in terms of the ultimacy of the Reign the ultimacy of Jesus can be formulated. What must be analyzed—due to the fact that it has been consecrated in the dogmatic formulations—is whether this formulation, in terms of the Reign of God, is compatible with the more usual focus on the divine ultimacy of Jesus in relation to the person of God the Father, as well as with a focus on his human ultimacy (the former, surely, usually being held much more in account in a theological analysis of the historical Jesus than the latter).

Jesus' Divinity

With respect to establishing the divinity of Jesus, it is clear that the gospels place Jesus in a relationship with the person of God in which he calls God his Father. However, the content of this concept of God as Father is not incompatible with that of the God of the Reign—although each of these expressions of ultimacy has its own specificity. They are not interchangeable as concepts, nor can either be adequately deduced from the other by way of pure conceptual reflection. But at least it must be admitted that they are related, and that to a large extent they converge. To this same extent, Jesus' relationship with the divine ultimate—on which his own divine ultimacy will be based—can be developed in terms of the God of the Reign and in terms of God as Father. And then, also in terms of the ultimacy of the Reign of God, the divine element in Jesus can be approached. Let us briefly examine the convergence of the God of the Reign with the Father of Jesus.

In both perspectives Jesus appears in a relationship with a God who has a specific content—a positive one for human beings, with the qualities of mercy, justice, partiality toward the poor, the weak, and the little ones, and a God who generates, and elicits, honesty, trust, hope, freedom, joy, and the like. This fundamental convergence can be observed in the texts in which Jesus appears in his personal relationship with God the Father, as well as in the many parables of the Reign that show this kind of God, a God who makes possible and who demands such a relationship.

At the same time, once more in both perspectives, Jesus appears in a relationship with a God who is mystery—who must be allowed to be God, and with whom one must strike a relationship of absolute openness and availability. Thus, in darkness before this Father, Jesus asks that the divine will be done; and in the darkness of the coming of the Reign, he exclaims that only the Father knows the hour of that coming.

Jesus' personal relationship with the divinity, then, can be analyzed in terms of his relationship with his Father, surely; but it can also be analyzed in terms of his relationship with the God of the Reign. In this sense the *mediator* of the Reign of God can also be understood as the *Son* of God without doing violence to either term.

Jesus' Humanity

When it comes to establishing the humanity of Jesus, Jesus' relationship with the Reign of God offers greater advantages than any other biblical or dogmatic focus (such as a general profession of his human nature, an analysis of his attitudes, or the like). The fundamental reason for this is that, in confrontation with the Reign of God, the totality of the person of Jesus in action comes into view. Guided by Kant's three questions—to which we shall add a fourth—in the answer to which is expressed the totality of the human, we readily observe that Jesus' relationship with the Reign of God evinces (1) the *knowledge* Jesus has and communicates concerning the Reign of God and the anti-Reign, (2) the *hope* that he stirs in others and that supports him as well (hope in the coming of the Reign),

(3) the *praxis* he performs in the service of that Reign, and his historical *celebration* of the fact that the Reign has "already" come.

Should someone wish to argue that this comprehensive actualization of the human element of Jesus can also be deduced from his relationship with the Father, we answer that, quantitatively, there are far fewer texts bearing on Jesus' relationship with the Father than with the Reign of God; systematically, Jesus' human interiority is better known from the exteriority of his relationship with the Reign. It is this exteriority that shows us concretely a Jesus who is honest with the truth, merciful and just, a denouncer and exposer, available and faithful. It is this exteriority, required by the building of the Reign of God, that shapes his personal interiority with reference to God.

Finally, his relationship with the Reign sets in deeper relief the specific characteristics of the authentically human: honesty with reality, mercy as a primary reaction, justice demanded in the face of the oppression of the masses, fidelity in trial and persecution, and the "greatest love" of the laying down of one's life.

In synthesis, Jesus' human element, when seen in relationship with the Reign of God and in its service, appears with certain particular characteristics. Furthermore—something that is not usually emphasized in systematic christologies—this human element appears as *partiality*, in Jesus' placement and incarnation, in the addressees of his mission, and in his very fate. It appears as a human element in *solidarity*—as a specific realization of the human in regard to other persons, as their brother, as a human being who is for others and who wills to be with others.

2. Comparison of the Christology of "the Mediator of the Reign of God" with Other Theoretical Christologies of the New Testament

The ultimacy of Jesus can be established from a point of departure in the Reign of God, then. Now let us compare this way of proceeding with the christologies of the New Testament. We make this comparison for the sake of a better understanding of the specificity, and novelty, of the focus that we have presented, as well as in order to discover a possible biblical justification for our focus.[6]

The Titles

Generally speaking, as the New Testament proceeds, the Reign of God tends to disappear as an expression of the ultimate, and more specifically, as an explanation of the ultimacy of Jesus. Not that there is no longer an expectation of the arrival of the ultimate—now joined to the parousia of Christ—or that the notion of the Reign has no theological equivalent, such as the "new creation," or "new covenant," which are also set in an essential relationship with Jesus. But while there are surely these analogies with the Reign of God, the latter—as Jesus proclaimed it—gradually dwindles away, along with an attempt to identify Jesus' ultimacy in terms of his relationship with that Reign.

Indeed, the christologies of Jesus' titles and destiny show that some titles by their nature bear more directly on the Reign of God (the Prophet who announces it, the Son of Man who proclaims it at the end of the ages, the High Priest who strikes a new covenant, the Servant who burdens himself with the anti-Reign), but these titles never become central in the New Testament discourse itself and have practically disappeared in later history. The title of Messiah (the Anointed One, the Christ) constitutes a case apart: it does bespeak a primordial relation to a people's hopes of liberation (in various ways, as we know). It is akin, then, to our systematic title Mediator, but in coming to be transformed into the proper name Jesus *Christ*, paradoxically it lost its essential reference to the Reign of God.

In its place, New Testament christology explicitly developed the ultimacy of Christ in titles that express his direct relation to the person of God: Son of God, Lord, Word, Son. At the same time, although there are titles that express the concrete manifestation of Jesus' humanity, these never attain the importance enjoyed by the others. Expressions like Revelation's "lamb that was slain" or Hebrews' "brother," for example, do not come to be regarded as titles of Jesus' humanity.

The reason why theoretical reflection took this direction could seem to be that Jesus' humanity was too obvious to need this sort of penetration. But the fact is that we have a concentration on the titles that point to Jesus' relationship with the divinity, and the divinity understood rather as the person of God the Father of Jesus than as the God of the Reign.

The Gospel Narratives

Surprisingly, along with these theoretical "title" christologies, and after certain of them have been developed, the Christian scriptures show us another way of doing theoretical christology: that of the gospel narratives. The latter have, on the other hand, assimilated Jesus' special relationship with the Father and so profess Jesus as Son of God (in John, simply as Son). But the Synoptics react to this previously established christology by showing Jesus' ultimacy in his relationship with the Reign of God, and showing the reality of his humanity as history. They do not doubt that Christ is the Son of God; but they emphasize, and from the very outset, that—in our terminology—the mediator of the Reign of God has a concrete, specific history.

In the first place, the gospels turn to Jesus of Nazareth in a very precise manner: by narrating his history. True, the gospels find themselves unable to historicize Jesus without theologizing him. The gospels are theological narratives, then. But the converse is also true: they are unable to theologize Jesus without historicizing him. This is supremely important for systematic christology, at least as a possibility, and it is this possibility that the narrative christology of the preceding chapter reduces to reality.

In the second place—and more decisively for our topic—in the gospel narratives what for Jesus is the ultimate is presented, it is true, in two expressions: Reign of God and *Abba*. But quantitatively, the former appears more than the latter, and the latter can well—indeed, better, to our view—be understood in terms of the former rather than vice versa. Thus we have an undeniable attempt on the part of the gospels to express the ultimacy of Jesus in terms of the Reign of God.

In the third place, the gospel narratives present the ultimacy of the Reign in the presence of what we may call an anti-Reign. The Reign, then, is a dialectical reality, subsisting in conflict with its antithesis. This point—which is not frequently made in the systematic christologies—is essential for an understanding of the mediator, as well. The mediator's mission in behalf of the ultimacy of the Reign is carried out in the presence of and in opposition to other ultimacies. Thus, the mediator proclaims and serves the Reign, but he does so precisely by denouncing and exposing the anti-Reign. He is presented in a relationship of ultimacy with a God who is his Father, but he maintains this relationship by renouncing and combating the idols (all manner of oppressive power) that hold themselves out as God. He strikes a solidarity with everything human, but he does so by taking upon himself that which is dehumanizing: sin.

To be sure, this dialectical, conflictive dimension of reality is present in other New Testament writings; but the concrete form in which it appears in the gospel is more adequate—by reason of being historical and narrative—to the purpose of making it understood. We might say that Jesus does not appear as mediator, as Son and as human being, on a *tabula rasa*, but amid a reality with which he struggles. He must *come to be* mediator, Son, and human.

Finally, the gospel narratives show forth the partiality of God, the mediation, and the mediator. This celebrated central point of the Hebrew scriptures—the partiality or partisanship of God's revelation in favor of the poor, the weak, and the oppressed—could understandably have lost its central place in the New Testament. After the resurrection, undeniably, the universality of salvation is proclaimed. That is, in order to belong to the new people of God one need no longer belong to any particular people or religion. It is enough simply to be a human being. In this sense Jesus' vision of a primary mission to the sheep of Israel is transcended. But this real universalism—in which the very existence and self-understanding of the church is at stake—implies no reason why the partiality of the mediation and the mediator for the poor should be eliminated. This is the meaning of the gospel narratives: the Reign of God is of the poor. The resurrection of Christ cancels one kind of partiality, that based on religion or ethnic origin. But there is no reason why it should cancel the partiality of the Reign and its mediator based on poverty and oppression. On the contrary, the gospels emphasize this partiality.

Choosing an Approach

We have entertained this brief reflection on two distinct theoretical ways of doing christology in the New Testament, not in order to deny the validity of one of them, that of the titles, which is the more consecrated approach in the history of christology, but in order to come to a realization that, throughout history, christology has de facto developed more along the lines of only one of these possibilities, and that it happens to have been that of an expression of the ultimacy of Jesus in terms of his relation to the person of God. The gospel narratives show that there is another possibility. Theoretical christology can also be done in terms of historico-theological narratives. As Albert Schweitzer remarked, the most important thing about the gospel of Mark is that it should have been written at all. When we proceed in this manner, the ultimacy of Jesus can be expressed in terms of his relationship with the Reign of God.

These two ways of doing christology are not mutually exclusive; indeed, they actually require one another. In this brief systematic sketch, we have expressed Jesus' ultimacy precisely with a theoretical title, that of the mediator of the Reign of God; but we have done so after, and on the basis of, the previous chapter, which concerns itself with a narrative christology. We have no intention, then, of excluding a christology of titles. However, we do wish to analyze where systematic reflection ought to assign logical priority: whether to narrative or to conceptual titles. Narrative offers the obvious advantage of history itself: Jesus' real life preceded his theorization at the hands of faith. Furthermore, a narrative approach in christology enables us to avoid the grave dangers that beset a christology of titles divorced from christological narrative. Thus, the gospel narratives not only function as expositive christology, but they also perform a critical and corrective operation vis-à-vis a christology of titles alone.

The most serious danger, in terms of the perspective adopted in this chapter, has already been cited: the titles can incline us to prescind from the central thing about Jesus, the Reign of God, and ignore a christology consistently based on the Reign. Furthermore, the titles, in their concrete, historical development, can lead us to ignore the human element in Jesus (a problem of content for christology), and to the serious error of imagining that we know the content of his titles—his being lord, being Son, being high priest, and so on—before knowing Jesus himself (a methodological problem).

In summary, we may say that Latin American systematic christology sees within the Christian scriptures the theoretical possibility of beginning christology with the evangelical narratives, and of finding in them the ultimacy from which the ultimacy of Jesus will be better understood. Thus, it sees a "New Testament justification" of its particular approach. Finally, it finds in those same scriptures the importance of assigning priority to the narrative concerning Jesus over his pure titles, inasmuch as the dangers to which the former responds in the Christian scriptures continue to be present in current history: ignoring the Reign of God, and the poor as its correlate; neglecting Jesus' humanity; and manipulating the concrete reality of Christ.

II. PRAXIC CHRISTOLOGY: THE FOLLOWING OF JESUS

The believer's faith does not create its object (*fides quae*). It is of the essence of the Christian comprehension of the faith that God has made a self-bestowal on us by grace. At the same time, however, no object would have come to be recognized as an object of faith had it not occasioned an act of faith (*fides qua*). Now if, as Rahner explains, nothing created can be an object of faith, then, if there is such a thing as faith, it must be a faith in something actually transcendent. A *fides qua*, accordingly, testifies to a reality believed in and is an existential help to understanding what the concrete content of this reality is. For christology, this means that, besides being theoretical and analyzing a *fides quae*, it must also analyze the corresponding *fides qua*—for existential and pastoral reasons, as well as because to do so will help in an understanding of the object of faith, in this case, Jesus Christ.

1. The Following of Jesus as an Existential Expression of Faith in Christ

The *fides qua* can become real in the act of accepting the transcendence of Christ, which can be proclaimed liturgically and doxologically. But this *fides qua* can be expressed in another way, and it seems to us a more radical way, by explicitly confronting the historical Jesus. To cite Rahner once more:

> If the moral personality of Jesus in word and life, really makes such a compelling impression on a person that they find the courage to commit themselves unconditionally to this Jesus in life and death and therefore to believe in the God of Jesus, that person has gone far beyond a merely horizontal humanistic Jesuolatry, and is living (perhaps not completely spontaneously, but really) an orthodox Christology.[7]

An Existential, Praxic Expression of Faith

This, we think, is what has actually occurred in the Christian scriptures. Faith in Jesus was originally expressed in an existential, praxic form, before Christians ever undertook to supply themselves with a theoretical formulation of Jesus' reality. Thus, they professed Jesus, liturgically and doxologically, as the One raised, the One exalted, the Lord. But while this is an expression of the *fides qua*, it is not its maximal expression. Jesus' ultimacy is expressed before all else—and in very principle—in the ultimacy of one's own life. This means a kind of life that, generally speaking, is nothing other than a reproduction of the life of Jesus. One must have the same sentiments as Christ (Paul), one must keep one's eyes fixed on Jesus and, as Jesus did, remain steadfast in suffering (Hebrews), and so on. Comprehensively, one must follow Jesus. Thus, the Christian scriptures testify that existential faith has priority over formulations of faith, and that the former is expressed more radically as praxis of faith, as following or discipleship.

A following of Jesus is the maximal expression of faith in Christ, since the formal reason for it (although it may be accompanied by ancillary motivations, such as the hope of a reward) is the sheer fact of the call of Jesus; its content flows simply from the fact that this is the way Jesus was. We see this relationship in the Christian scriptures between the act of faith and following; it is all the more significant when we take account of the opinion of some exegetes to the effect that the historical Jesus did not call everyone to his discipleship, but only those who wished to be his active followers. After the resurrection, however, when genuine faith in Christ begins, "following and discipleship began to be the absolute expression of Christian existence."[8]

We must conclude that, whatever the explicit consciousness that the first Christians were acquiring of Jesus, as indicated in their ascribing titles to him, they were expressing in their very lives and deaths the ultimacy they attributed to him. It is this existential ultimacy that is consecrated in the word "following" of Jesus. This is how the historical Jesus is recovered in faith. When one attempts to reproduce the following of Jesus, then the Reign of God reappears once more in a central place. Let us recall that, in the first stage of Jesus' public life, discipleship or following meant proclaiming and positing signs of the Reign, while in the second stage it meant steadfastness in the face of the mighty reaction of the anti-Reign. Without the Reign of God, the following of Jesus would have neither its central motivation nor its central content.

Historicization of the Following of Jesus

The following of Jesus throughout history must be historicized and transformed into the continuation of his deed and his intent (as actually occurred in the Christian scriptures), but the most important thing for systematic christology is that there actually be this following in history. This is what is happening in Latin America; the magnitude and quality of the phenomenon are such that christology must take it seriously into account. It cannot be doubted that the act of faith in Christ exists in Latin America, and that this is shown in the following of Jesus and martyrdom. Nor can it be doubted that the continuation of Jesus' deed and intent in Latin America recovers the fundamental structure of the historical Jesus. Therefore, following stands in an essential relationship with the building of the Reign of God and the destruction of the anti-Reign. This is occurring—in historical factuality, without passing a judgment upon subjectivities—in a clearer fashion, and in a more similar fashion to that of Jesus, than in other forms of following throughout history. Nor can it be doubted that the actual martyrdoms are historically very similar to that of Jesus and inflicted for the same reasons as that of Jesus: the proclamation to the poor of the Reign of God and the defense of the poor in combat with the anti-Reign.

2. Meaning of Following for Theoretical Christology

If this is the case, then we may say that the act of faith in Jesus, the *fides qua*, still exists today in its maximal expression, following. What we must ask ourselves is whether that following has a meaning for christology, and if so, what meaning.

Witnesses of Faith Shed Light on the Fides Quae

The follower is a witness, someone who reproduces—in historicized fashion—the life of Jesus. To what extent, and in what degree, this occurs is open to discussion, of course, and should be analyzed; but it ought to occur in principle, since otherwise the design of God that human beings be sons and daughters in the Son would be in vain. And if *per impossibile* there were no such thing as following, we should have the utter failure of God, and Christ would not be the Son. Then, of course, there would be no christology.

But if there actually is following, there can be christology, and account will have to be taken of its content. Human beings may be faulty or defective ways of being Christ, as Rahner says, but this implies positively that there is something of Christ in them. To formulate the same thing in traditional theological terms, and once more positively: if we are by grace what Christ is by nature, then something of the reality of Christ must be knowable even by looking at us, graced ones that we are.

Within this circularity, obviously the criterion of an analysis and verification of the extent to which current witnesses express what is Christian will be Jesus. But it is also clear that these current witnesses can say something about Jesus. This is the familiar hermeneutic problem, only here its circularity is demanded by the very essence of revelation. If Jesus is true God and true human being, then anyone transparent to the divine and the human will say something of Christ.

Our theoretical assertion seems to us to be an undeniable reality in Latin America. Although the argument has to stand on its own, since one can only point to the fact, it happens that many who saw Archbishop Romero—to cite a single example of a faith witness—assert that he made Jesus better known to them. It is also a fact that the Latin American witnesses have at least opened the eyes of us who are exegetes, supplying us with new hermeneutic horizons. It is a fact that peasants who hear the reading of the passion of Jesus state very simply: "Exactly what happened to Archbishop Romero." Conversely, in terms of their knowledge of Archbishop Romero they better understand the passion of Jesus. It is also a fact that the witnesses have led persons to a more in-depth understanding of how the authentically human becomes a sacrament of the authentically divine. In the words of Ignacio Ellacuría, "With Archbishop Romero, God has visited El Salvador."

Theoretical christology can and should incorporate this argumentation. It should argue in part from the reality of current witnesses. That this argumentation ought to be cautious is supremely evident; but it would be even more incomprehensible if no argumentation were ever based on witnesses in order to know the antonomastic Witness, the witness *par excellence*. It would be vain to ask the witnesses to keep their eyes fixed on the Witness, if thereupon no reflection of him could ever be found in them.

Following Makes Possible the Limit Assertion of the Reality of Christ

Besides supplying content, the following of Jesus expresses the fact that the object of faith is regarded as something ultimate. But like any ultimate reality—which will be a mystery in the strict sense—this object not only is unapproachable, it cannot be directly intuited. It can be meaningfully conceptualized and verbalized after a "journey"—a transition from what is already in some manner subject to experience and verifiable, to the limit assertion in question.

The need to make this journey in order to be able to formulate limit assertions has already been acknowledged by various christologies. For example, it has been emphasized that the limit assertions of Chalcedon can have meaning only after the completion of the theoretical pilgrimage of the New Testament and the tradition of the first centuries. That is, knowing who Jesus was and how he was theorized in the scriptures and church tradition has logical and chronological priority if the limit assertions of Chalcedon are to have any meaning.[9] Without this journey, this pilgrimage, the Chalcedonian formula would be not only mysterious and incomprehensible, in the sense of being ultimately unfathomable, but simply unintelligible, which is not the same thing.

What we wish to emphasize here is that this journey must also—and more radically—be praxic. That is, one must traverse the route of real following in order for the formulation of ultimacy to have any meaning. This need abides throughout history, and it would be naive of theoretical christology to think that the task of traversing the route of actual following, in order to be able to make limit formulations, could be delegated to the first Christians alone, while afterward it would suffice to analyze these formulations, as formulations, and to rest content with a theoretical development of their virtualities throughout the rest of history.

This ultimate task is necessary and good, but—if it is a matter of asserting the ultimacy of Christ—one cannot prescind from the *fides qua*. Thus, one cannot prescind from realized following. Only in the following of Jesus do we become like unto the reality of Jesus, and only on the basis of this realized affinity does the internal knowledge of Christ become possible. That Jesus is thereupon professed as the ultimate is the fruit of the leap of faith, but it is supremely important to determine with the greatest possible precision the locus of this leap. According to what we have said, that locus is following, since apart from following one could not actually know what is being spoken of when Christ is mentioned. After all, following means doing, in terms of the present, what Jesus did, and doing it in the way that he did it. It means the mission of building the Reign with the attitude and spirit of Jesus. In this praxis a kinship is acquired—greater or lesser, obviously—with Jesus, and this praxis (like all praxis) explains one's antecedent concept of Jesus, his mission, and his spirit.

On the other hand, our praxis, like that of Jesus, is also subject to the vagaries of history. That is, although its horizon is the ultimate, its concretions are not, and depending on how these come to be, the same praxis can be verification of or temptation for faith itself. As a logical consequence, even following could be the locus of not making the leap of faith, since it could happen that, in following Jesus, one would come to the conclusion that this route does not offer ultimacy.

Within following, then, one can make the act of faith and the limit assertion concerning Christ (just as one can omit it). But then this act of faith is transformed into victory, as well, as John's theology teaches. We can only conclude that a following realized in terms of the present is the reality in which limit assertions concerning Christ can have meaning, or cease to have it.[10]

In summary, christology must take serious account of a realized following, for two important reasons of christological epistemology. A contemplation of the witnesses of the faith can help us know the Witness better; and in actual following, a conviction of the ultimacy of Christ can be deepened (or abandoned).

III. CHRISTOPRAXIS OF LIBERATION

The ultimate finality of theology, as of all Christian activity, is—according to the theology of liberation—the maximal building of the Reign of God. But in our current situation of oppression, this building must be liberation. Therefore liberation theology understands itself as a theory of a praxis, as an *intellectus amoris*, which must be historicized as *intellectus justitiae*. This being the case, christology in the concrete must develop and supply a knowledge concerning Christ that by its nature will further the building of the Reign of God. Because that Reign is effected in opposition to the oppression of the anti-Reign, this knowledge of Christ must be a knowledge of liberation, *intellectus liberationis*.

1. Specific Christological Moment of Praxis

Christology must propose a knowledge concerning Christ such that, of his very nature, this Christ will move a person—the person who knows him, in order that this person may know him—to a salvific activity. This means introducing into the very reality of Christ the dynamism of the dispatch to that salvific activity. It is not, then, a matter of first knowing who Christ is and then adding the knowledge that one of the elements of his reality is to be someone who confers a mission. To be sure, a hermeneutic circularity obtains between an understanding of the being of Christ and a grasp of his conferral of a mission. But at least the moment of dispatch as essential to the being of Christ must be maintained as central.

In the Christian scriptures, it is a matter of conjecture whether the dispatch to a salvific activity is essential to the very being of Christ, in such wise that—systematically speaking—without the availability to be so dispatched one would be unable to know Christ adequately. That at least there is in Jesus this unified duality of being and sending appears in programmatic terms in the evangelical "being with Jesus and being sent by Jesus." In certain gospel scenes the dispatch even seems to have priority over knowledge of Jesus. And in the scenes of the apparitions, Jesus appears not to "seers," but to "witnesses"; that is, he is at the same time one appearing and one sending, and correlatively, availability for an activity—bearing witness—is essential, according to the interpretation of certain exegetes, in order to grasp the being of Jesus in the apparitions.

No unequivocal thesis can be deduced from these fragmentary reflections, but at least we have an indication of what interests us here. Both in life and after his resurrection, Christ appears not simply as a someone-in-himself who can simply be known, or even a someone-for-us of whom salvation can be hoped, but also as a someone-who-sends, whose mission must be prosecuted. Thus, the praxis inspired by Christ is essential to Christ himself (and to christology). Here we have the context in which we must speak of the christopraxis of liberation.

In this understanding of Christ as one who sends we confront a theoretical novelty. It is not a novelty that Christ is presented salvifically—and let us remember that a salvific concern is what moved the development of christology in the scriptures, in patristics, and in the conciliar dogmas. This is accepted by liberation christology, which formally prosecutes this line and radically transcends the dissociation that began to appear in the Middle Ages between christology and soteriology. The novel element is in (1) the determination of salvation as liberation, and (2) the manner in which a concern for liberation has an influence on theoretical christology, that is, not only for having to *think* the reality of Christ in such a fashion that he can be savior (the interest of the New Testament and of patristic speculation), but in thinking him in such a fashion that he may already *produce* historical salvation.

In the context of this chapter, this means that it is not enough to assert that Jesus is the mediator of the Reign of God; it must also be asserted that he is the one who of his very nature dispatches to the building of the Reign. He is a mediator by essence *sent* (the dimension of gratuity with respect to us); and he is a mediator by essence *sending* (his fundamental demand on us). Besides the sheer fact of the essential dispatch to praxis, a starting point in Christ can determine the content and utopian horizon of that praxis (the Reign of God), the spirit with which to perform it (that of the mediator), and the hope to be maintained amid the praxis (the possibility of defeating the anti-Reign).

2. Christopraxis

Inasmuch as this Reign to be constructed comes into being in the presence of and in opposition to the anti-Reign, the Reign is a good entity, of course. Specifically, it is a liberative entity. This explains why it is called Good News; it is the apparition of the good that is hoped for in the presence of evil, oppressive realities. Consequently, the praxis of building the Reign will be good, but it will also be liberative. In order to show what it is that is good and liberative in the praxis to which Christ sends, let us analyze the various levels of the reality of Jesus in which he appears as Liberator.

Liberative Aspect of Jesus' Mission

The most specific mission of the historical Jesus is the proclamation and inauguration of the Reign of God in behalf of the poor and outcast. This is how the Markan-Matthean gospel begins, and even more explicitly, in the language of the Good News, that of Luke. This does not militate against the need for salvation from sin or transcendent salvation. Indeed, part of the responsibility of current christology will be to show how all of the plural salvations converge in the Reign of God. But it is with Jesus' proclamation and inauguration of the Reign for the poor and outcast that one must begin if one would understand liberation. In other words, liberation is the coming of the Reign of God for the poor. In terms of the reality of the poor, the content of liberation will have certain basic minimal content: a just life worthy of a human being. We might call it an economic and sociological opportunity, since what is at stake is an *oikos*, house and home, the basic element of life; and a *socius*, or social relationships of authentic kinship. This Reign is formally liberation, and not simply the good that is hoped for, since it will come in contravention of the anti-Reign.

This is what is directly meant—although it is not the only thing meant—when Jesus is called Liberator, and this is why we have called him the mediator of the Reign of God. Without a central inclusion of this meaning of liberation, there can be no christology of liberation. And let us note in passing that it is in this manner, after twenty centuries, that Latin American christology recovers the nucleus of Jesus' most primitive title, that of Messiah (*christos*), which had become his proper name, but had been deprived of any reference to a popular hope of liberation.

Someone might object that this conception of liberation neglects a key element of the later New Testament: liberation from sin. Here it must be granted that one of the essentials of the historical Jesus' liberative mission in behalf of the Reign of God is his salvific attitude toward sinners. But this assertion must be understood precisely and correctly. Those we might call sinful out of weakness, or more precisely, those regarded as sinful by their oppressors, Jesus cordially and affectionately welcomes, with an attitude that includes, but goes further than, simple forgiveness of sins. To the sinners in the sense of oppressors, Jesus announces the Good News, it is true, but in the form of a demand for radical conversion, as in the case of Zacchaeus.

Liberation from sin, even the universality of such liberation, is present in Jesus' mission, then, although it is present there in historicized fashion and without the elements introduced by later speculation based on explanatory theoretical models (sacrifice, expiation, and so forth, in the New Testament; assumption of the totality of the human, in patristics; satisfaction *de congruo*, in the Middle Ages). The historical Jesus surely appears as the liberator from sin, but what we must emphasize is that sin, sinner, and forgiveness are all understood in reference to the Reign of God.

Liberative Aspect of Jesus' Person

Another assertion implied in the denomination of Jesus as Liberator is that the very person of the mediator is liberative. It is liberative because Jesus was as he was. In pure theory, the liberation of the Reign of God could have been proclaimed and furthered by another kind of mediator (acting with power, at a distance from the poor but acting in their behalf, with more rigidity and less tenderness, with more calculation and fewer risks, and so on), who thus could have delivered the victims of oppressive structures, but whose spirit or interior attitude would have been different from that of Jesus.

The liberative element in the person of the mediator is the spirit with which he executes the proclamation and inauguration of the Reign of God. His personal fidelity to God and his mercy to human beings—to summarize systematically, as Hebrews does—his way of being before God and human beings as related in the gospels, the spirit of the Beatitudes as expressed in himself, a life lived in gratuity, his empowerment by truth—all of this is something good, as well as human, and humanizing for others.

We call this spirit of Jesus liberative, not only good, because Jesus came to be thus in the presence of the temptation to be otherwise, as appears in the scene of the temptations. The mediator is shown to be liberated himself, then. This is also liberative for others; yes, one can live this way, delivered from self, delivered from selfishness and dehumanization (a problem that also occurs in historical liberation processes), one can walk humbly with God in history, at once in absolute confidence in a God who is Parent and in total availability to a Parent who is still God.

In Latin America christology has focused from the very beginning on the Jesus who is Liberator of the poor and marginalized, but it is coming to emphasize more and more as well the Jesus who is himself liberated, and who thereby delivers us from ourselves if we keep our eyes fixed on him. But Latin American christology insists on relating the two elements; without this interrelationship, the historical liberation of the poor goes one way and the personal spirit of Jesus another. It observes—not only by virtue of its acceptance in principle of the gospel narratives, but through actual historical experience—that the practice of historical liberation with the spirit of Jesus is efficacious for liberation itself, as Archbishop Romero exemplifies so very well.

To put it simply, many rejoice that Jesus proclaimed and initiated the liberation of the poor of this world (the Reign of God), and rejoice as well that the mediator (Jesus of Nazareth) was as he was. The mediation, and the mediator, are Good News.

Liberative Aspect of Jesus' Resurrection

In the Christian scriptures it is evident that the Reign of God is not the only symbol of utopia—a new earth and a new heaven. Jesus' resurrection, as well, is a symbol of this utopia. It is likewise evident that the specific element in the latter symbol is liberation from death. Liberation christology accepts all of this. Nevertheless, the theology of liberation also regards it as essential to determine what elements of historical liberation are generated here and now by Jesus' resurrection.

In the first place, Jesus' resurrection generates a specific *hope*—indirectly, perhaps, for all, but directly for this world's victims, the addressees of the Reign of God. Indeed, Jesus' resurrection is presented in Peter's first discourses as God's reaction to the injustice that human beings have committed against the just, innocent Jesus. In this sense the resurrection is hope especially for this world's victims, and it is a liberative hope, because it occurs in the presence of the despairing fear that, in history, the executioners may triumph over their victims. It occurs in the presence of the temptation to resignation or cynicism.

A further liberative aspect of Jesus' resurrection is that it indicates the present sovereignty of Christ over history by generating human beings who are not history's slaves but its sovereigns. But sovereignty over history does not consist in living immune and detached from history; still less does it mean attempting—intentionally and idealistically—to "imitate" the immaterial conditions of the state of resurrection (as ancient theologies of the religious life recommended). It consists in triumphing over the slaveries to which human beings are subjected by reason of the fact that they live in history.

The fulfilling element in Jesus' resurrection is shown forth here and now, in history, in the *freedom* with which the following of Jesus is lived. Liberty is not license here; nor is it some mere type of esthetic or existential freedom. On the contrary, the freedom of the following of Jesus is a freedom to become *more* incarnate in historical reality, to dedicate oneself *more* to the liberation of others, to practice the love that can become the *greatest* love. Here is a freedom, then, realized not in fleeing the historical and material, but in incarnating oneself in it *more*, for love. Here, when all is said and done, is Jesus' own freedom, the freedom to lay down his life without anyone's taking it from him; the freedom of a Paul, voluntarily enslaved to all to save all.

The fulfilling dimension of the resurrection is also shown forth in the ability to live with *joy* in the midst of history. It appears in finding in the following of Jesus the pearl of great price, the hidden treasure for which one will sell everything one owns, for the sake of the joy it produces. It is living for others and receiving from others (grace). It is being able to be with others, being able to celebrate life "right now," being able to call God Parent, and to call that God, in relationship with all others, *our* Parent.

This fulfilling dimension of the resurrection is also liberative because it is a victory. The freedom made flesh in history, which does not flee that history, is destined to conquer the slaveries generated by history: fears, failures, persecutions, the cross. Joy transpires in the midst of suffering, and especially in the face of the understandable temptation to sadness, the temptation of meaninglessness. Thus, Jesus' resurrection is recognized as a liberative element introduced into history itself.

In synthesis, Jesus' resurrection is liberative because it enables and inspires people to live in history itself as risen ones, as persons raised; because it enables and inspires people to live the following of Jesus, too, as a reflection of the fulfilling, triumphal note of the resurrection with indestructible hope, freedom, and joy. Let us remark in passing that, when this occurs, then the One who has been raised is shown to be Sovereign of history. In this sense, it could be said—and it comes as a shock—that he has left it in our hands to make him the true Sovereign of history.

Liberative Aspect of the (Metaphysical) Reality of Christ

Let us observe, finally, that liberation christology must show that the element of Good News, of liberation, also resides in dogmatic truth concerning Christ, a truth that liberation christology unequivocally accepts.

The assertion that dogma is not only truth but Good News is an assertion of faith, and of an intrinsically gladsome faith. Thus, it is not available to further analysis; although the *vere Deus* and *vere homo* can surely be interpreted and received not only as truth, but as the Good News of the bounty, indeed the tenderness, of a God who has deigned to descend to that which is human and the Good News that the human can be a sacrament of God.

Nevertheless, christological dogma can be specifically one of liberation if we reformulate it in the following words: Jesus Christ is *verus Deus et verus homo*. Then Jesus Christ is strict revelation of that which is supremely basic for the human being—what it is to be God and what it is to be a human being—and is victorious revelation over the innate tendency of human beings to decide beforehand, on their own authority and in their own interest, the truth of both basic realities. Christological dogma appears as liberative if it is accepted not only as an unveiling of what until now has not been known, but as the victorious revelation of repressed truth. That is, it is seen to be liberative if one accepts that the proposition that Christ is *vere Deus* and *vere homo* is true not because it fulfills the conditions that we human beings impose on the truth of both realities, but because this truth has the power to transcend—and radically—our self-interested comprehension of the divine and the human.

To say it in simple words, it is great Good News of liberation that at last, despite the innate propensity of human beings to evade and oppress the truth, the truth has appeared of what God is and of what we human beings are. What it is to be God and what it is to be a human being have been seen in Jesus, have been revealed in Jesus, triumphing over the concupiscent inclination of human reason to decide both realities in terms of its own interests.

The fact that the dogma presents the subsistence in Christ of both realities, divine and human, without division yet without confusion, is Good News, liberative news. The manner by which the divine and the human subsist in Christ is a strict mystery and hence not subject to analysis. But if we observe the reverberation of this mystery in historical reality, we can assert that it is indeed Good News.

It is good that the divine and the human be "without division," especially if their unity be understood as transcendence in history, such that history renders God present historically, and God, being transcendent, causes history to transcend itself and give more of itself. Also good is the "without confusion," the nonmixing of the two realities, let alone their mutual reduction to each other. History shows that a reduction of the divine to the human necessarily deprives the divine of its mystery, while an elevation of the human to the divine absolutizes the human and transforms it into a troop of monsters: those idolatries that go by the name of despotism and triumphalism. We might say simply that it is good to let God be God and human be human.

History shows how deleterious it is for human beings to violate, on the religious level, this elementary truth of christological dogma. But the violation is just as pernicious in its historical, secular equivalents. For example, utopia (corresponding to the divine) is sometimes divorced from concrete realities in such a way as to be relegated to the trans-historical exclusively, and thus deprived of any influence on the attempt to render it real in concrete realities; thus these realities lose their value as signs of utopia. This is the temptation of the right. Or again, all of the concrete (corresponding to the human) can be subordinated to utopia, as if the concrete had no entity of its own. This is the temptation of the left, even in liberation processes, which can be tempted to replace the whole of the concrete (personal, family, social, artistic) with what is deemed to be the correct route to take to utopia—the political or the military route, depending on the case.

These attempts either to separate the two constitutive elements of dogmatic christology or to reduce one to the other have dehumanizing effects. Hence, the dogmatic formulation of the reality of Jesus Christ is both good and liberative. Despite the dehumanization occasioned by both the separation and the reduction, we human beings undertake to commit these errors because we think that we already know the ultimate structure of reality. The dogma reminds us that the structure of reality is that of transcendence in history, and this is good and liberating news.

Integral, Transcendent Liberation

On the strength of what Jesus does, of the fate that overtakes him, and of what he is, both in his historical reality and in his ultimate transcendent reality, he can and must be called the Liberator. Each of these liberative aspects enjoys its own entity and autonomy, so that none of the three can be deduced from another by pure conceptualization. But if they all be taken together and seen as a whole, then we have the christological basis for the possibility and necessity of the *integral liberation* so earnestly recalled and demanded by the magisterium.

From a point of departure in Christ, that integral liberation is possible and necessary. But in view of what has been said, we think that there are three things to be insisted upon. First, liberation is transformed into integral liberation not by the mere accumulation of disconnected liberative moments, but by the complementarity of all liberative moments in the dynamics of the following of Jesus. Second, in dealing with the christologic liberative dimension, it is necessary (or, in our view, at least very useful) to invoke a logical reproduction of the route that we have proposed chronologically: to begin with and center on the liberation of the poor, thereupon, in virtue of the very dynamics of that liberation, to integrate the other liberative aspects of Christ. Third, an analysis of the integral liberation of which Christ is the vehicle is carried out ultimately in order to foster a liberative christopraxis.

Finally, let us say that, in terms of the adoption of all of the liberative moments cited, objectively theological, transcendent liberation can be formulated. Those who implement Christ's mandate to liberate are thereby realizing the demand voiced by God in the Book of Micah: to act with justice and to love with tenderness. In so doing, these persons can walk humbly with God in history. Now they can really interpret theoretically, and live existentially, their own lives as a life with God. And they can, theoretically and existentially, interpret that life as a journeying toward the definitive encounter with God, when God will be in all—the Pauline formulation of the transcendent fullness of the Reign of God.

IV. THE POOR AS LOCUS THEOLOGICUS OF CHRISTOLOGY

Let us say a brief concluding word on the locus of christology, as we have developed it in these pages. As we know, liberation theology has developed the topic of the *locus theologicus* in a new manner, and this by way of its own existential experience. In doing theology from a determinate place or locus, with the poor as the point of departure, it has rediscovered content of extreme importance, content central for the faith. This content has not been rediscovered from a starting point in other loci; hence the extreme importance of an analysis of the theological locus. Theology knows that it must respect a methodological distinction between theological locus and font of theological cognition. "The distinction," however, as Ellacuría says, "is not a strict one, let alone an exclusive one. The locus itself, in a sense, is a font, in that it is the locus that determines whether the font yields this or that. The upshot is that, thanks to the locus, and in virtue of the same, a certain determinate content is actually rendered present."[11]

The sketch that we have attempted to present here has been constructed from the theological locus that in Latin American theology, admittedly, is constituted by the poor. We should only wish to add that, in the case of christology, there is an additional, specific reason why theology must be done from the locus of the poor. The poor are not only a reality from which one can reread the whole of theology. They are a reality with which christology must eventually come into confrontation as its object. Thus, with christology, the reason why theology must be done from a theological locus among the poor is more than one of methodological exigency or convenience. It proceeds from revelation itself: the Son of Man is present in the poor of this world.

This presence of Christ in the history of today can be accepted or rejected. But if it is accepted, it would be supremely irresponsible on the part of christology not to take it into central account. This is what is transpiring in Latin America. In simple, nontechnical words Medellín asserts that, where sin is committed against the poor, "there we have a rejection of the Lord's gift of peace and of the Lord himself" (Medellín, "Document on Peace," no. 14, citing Matt. 25). Puebla makes the very carefully considered statement that "with particular tenderness [Jesus Christ] chose to identify himself with those who are poorest and weakest" (Puebla Final Document, no. 196, citing Matt. 25). Archbishop Romero said, in his homilies to a persecuted community, "You are the image of the divine, transfixed with pain," and he compared the Salvadoran people to the Servant of Yahweh. Ellacuría, in a strictly theological reflection, declared that the great sign of the times—the current presence of God among us—is always the crucified people, the historical continuation of the Servant of Yahweh, of Christ crucified.

These statements are not casual ones, nor do their authors intend them as merely pious reflections. They are to be taken seriously. The poor function as the locus of christology in virtue of the concrete content with which they supply that discipline. They tell it something important about Christ. They tell it of his self-abasement, his *kenosis*, his concealment, his cross. And especially, they function as the locus of christology (and of course of faith and following) because, as locus of the current presence of Christ, they are a light illumining all things, and specifically illumining the truth of Christ.

This argumentation is helpless in the face of questions that can be lodged from other theological loci (and these loci always exist, acknowledged or not). Therefore, it can only invite other christologies to place themselves, as well, in the locus of the poor. But as a counterargument, Latin American christology points to the undeniable fact that, from among the poor as its *locus theologicus*, it has rediscovered basic christological realities—realities central to the gospel message, as the Vatican Instruction on the theology of liberation observes—which, lo, these many centuries, have slept the sleep of the just.

From the locus of the poor, christology has made the theoretical rediscovery of Christ as Messiah, as Liberator, and as definitive mediator of the Reign of God. But the situation of the poor and the crucified peoples is intolerable. Therefore these poor and these peoples have set christology its fundamental task. It is a praiseworthy endeavor to demythologize Christ in order to present a reasonable Christ, so that the "name" of Christ may be acceptable by the modern, enlightened human being. But it is a more urgent endeavor to "depacify" Christ, lest reality continue to be abandoned to its misery "in his name"—and in extreme cases, to replace an idolatry of Christ, that the poor may come to see in Christ someone for them rather than against them, and no longer think they have to resign themselves to being oppressed "in his name."

Understood as a substantial *quid* rather than as an accidental *ubi*, the theological locus has always been decisive for christology. It has given it its profoundly pastoral character. If Luther developed a christology of the "Christ for me," Bonhoeffer a christology of the "person for others," Teilhard de Chardin a christology of the "Omega Point of evolution," and Karl Rahner a christology of the "absolute vehicle of salvation," it is because reality demanded it, albeit in various ways. Reality itself had posed the questions: How may one encounter a benevolent God, how may one present an authentic Christ, in a world come of age, a world in evolution, a secularized, antidogmatist world? This pre-christological (but pastorally determinative for christology) reality has always been present in creative christologies. It is present today once more in the theology of liberation: the reality of a dehumanizing poverty and of the hope of its eradication.

Gustavo Gutiérrez declares that the decisive question for Latin American theology is "how to tell the poor that God loves them." Christology responds with Jesus Christ the Liberator, the absolute mediator of the Reign of God to the poor. The reality of poverty both motivates this "theorization of Christ" and renders it possible. The agreeable surprise is that, thus theorized, Christ is a bit more like—it seems to us—Jesus of Nazareth.

—*Translated by Robert R. Barr*

NOTES

1. Many of the methodological presuppositions of the theology of liberation are analyzed in this volume and in *Mysterium Liberationis*. For christology specifically, see Chapter 8 in *Mysterium*, "Christology in the Theology of Liberation."

2. See, in this volume, Chapter 3, "Central Position of the Reign of God in Liberation Theology."

3. See Ignacio Ellacuría, "La teología como momento ideológico de la praxis eclesial," *Estudios Eclesiásticos* 53 (1978):457–76; Sobrino, "Teología en un mundo sufriente: La teología de la liberación como *intellectus amoris*," *Revista Latinoamericana de Teología* 15 (1988):243–66.

4. See Ignacio Ellacuría, "Los pobres, 'lugar teológico' en América latina," in Ignacio Ellacuría, *Conversión de la Iglesia al reino de Dios* (San Salvador, 1985), pp. 153–78.

5. Karl Rahner and K. H. Weger, *Our Christian Faith* (London: Burns & Oates, 1980), p. 93.

6. An analogous comparison ought to be made with patristic theology, especially in regard to the destiny of the Reign of God, although we cannot address this here.

7. Rahner and Weger, *Our Christian Faith*, p. 93.

8. M. Hengel, *Seguimiento y carisma* (Santander, Spain, 1981), p. 105.

9. See D. Wiederkehr, in *Mysterium Salutis*, vol. 3/1 (Madrid, 1969), p. 558.

10. An analysis of the systematic concept of following or discipleship must invoke an analogy of discipleship precisely in view of the reality of the poor. In his own age—and with his expectancy of the imminence of the Reign—Jesus made different basic demands on, respectively, his disciples and the poor. Of the poor he seems to demand not discipleship, but an active hope in the coming of the Reign. Today a theological treatment of the discipleship of the poor must take into consideration the non-imminence of the Reign. Meanwhile, the material condition of the poverty of our times seems to render the following of disciples impossible, which would lead to the paradox that the poor, to whom the Good News is directly addressed, and whom Christ seeks to liberate, could not acquire a similarity to Christ precisely as disciples. Therefore one must speak of an analogy of discipleship or following. That is, while the poor participate more radically (generally speaking) in the destiny of the cross, and at times, in the hope of resurrection, than disciples do—still, the active aspect of mission can be more absent in the case of the poor, by reason of their material conditions. Thus, Ignacio Ellacuría proposes an analogy of the systematic theo-

logical concept of the poor. The poor are: (1) the material, impoverished poor, (2) the poor who have become aware of the causes of their poverty, (3) the poor organized in a struggle to be liberated, and (4) the poor who wage this struggle *with* the spirit of the Beatitudes. See Ellacuría, "Los pobres, 'lugar teológico,' " pp. 81–163.

11. Ibid., p. 168.

8

The Holy Spirit

JOSÉ COMBLIN

Latin American theology, we must acknowledge, has not developed a specific theology of the Holy Spirit. Until now, theology on our continent has been in the debt of the theology of the Latin church, which, instead of developing a theology of the Holy Spirit, has only repeated what it has received from the patristic era. So far, Latin American theology—like all Latin-tradition theology, both Protestant and Catholic—operates under the sign of a "christomonism."

Instead, a theology of the Holy Spirit is something we can discern in outline, but do not yet have in hand. From a point of departure in the basics of Latin American theology, we can project where such a theology would go.

I. EXPERIENCE OF THE HOLY SPIRIT

Very frequently the experience of the Holy Spirit is anonymous. In theology, just as among the Christian people, we hear simply of the experience of a *Dios liberador*—a God who delivers. Admittedly, the impact of the Hebrew scriptures, especially the texts of the Exodus, have been very powerful. The language of our experience takes its inspiration there. While the content of the experience has been enriched by the Christian scriptures, the formulation often remains faithful to its Hebrew sources.

Theology, like the popular Christian religious experience itself, knows very well that the *Dios liberador* will not deliver the people of God by means of physical miracles, as in Egypt or the wilderness. God will not deliver from without by sheer blows of the divine will. God delivers the people by means of the forces and energies that God places within the people, by means of the enlightenment and prophetic charisma of mighty leaders, by means of the union and solidarity of living communities, and by means of the enthusiasm of the multitudes that these communities and prophets succeed in arousing. Latin American Christians recognize the God of liberation and feel the presence of such a God in their very midst, acting in their own actions and commitments. This *Dios liberador* is the Holy Spirit—whether known by name or not.

In the heat of political action, Christians may feel that they are operating in terms only of social or political forces and factors. They may not recall the sources of their action. However, when the poor rise up to a collective action in this world, sheer social forces are surely not at work. After all, what we have here is a resurrection of the human being, a new birth of whole peoples, an utter transformation of persons.

Whence do such movements proceed? From the presence of the Holy Spirit. At the level of this divine presence, the (objectively) theological life and the political life constitute a single action. Faith, hope, charity, and political action are one reality in the human person who is really and concretely born to a new life. It is not a matter of mere pragmatic options. It is a matter of the very existence of the people: the Holy Spirit is involved here. At the heart of these experiences of historical actions, the liberative power of the Spirit is present.

1. Experience of Action

Ever since the Iberian invasion and importation of African slaves, the Latin American multitudes have been subjected to an absolute passivity. The majority of the population, until the past century, was made up of slaves. Few peoples have been reduced to such passivity for so many centuries by such a small number of dominators. Even today a great proportion of the Latin American people live in inaction—a passive object struggling to survive amid societies manipulated by the mighty. Latin Americans are but masses of isolated individuals. The native or African peoples to which they belong have been destroyed. Systematically, all efforts to reestablish community ties have been prevented. These peoples are permitted neither continuity nor solidarity. On the one hand, they have been deprived of their memory of the past; on the other, they are forbidden to imagine a future.

When communities are formed, a genuine resurrection occurs. The passive masses learn to act. The miracle accounts of the gospel that have had the strongest attraction for Latin American ears are those in which the lame walk, the deaf hear, the blind see, and the dead rise; in other words, the accounts in which those who have not acted begin to act. In the beginning the kinds of action undertaken are the most humble: simple cooperation among neighbors, meeting for particular actions like petitioning the authorities, or simpler still, celebrations of the events of the community. The mere fact of taking the initiative and assuming collective responsibility constitutes a new life. When favorable circumstances appear, these same communities, formed in such humble activities, show themselves capable of assuming concrete responsibilities decisive for the future of the peoples. This is what has occurred recently in Central America, especially in Guatemala, Nicaragua, and El Salvador. Christian communities no longer act as objects manipulated by more powerful forces. Now they act on the basis of their own initiative, their renewed consciousness, the energies that they themselves have mobilized.

The Christian communities interpret the birth of this new action of theirs in the light of the Bible. Beginning in the Hebrew scriptures, the Spirit inaugurated its liberative action by raising up the judges (Judg. 13:25, 14:6) and kings (1 Sam. 10:10, 11:6, 16:13; 2 Sam. 23:2). Later this Spirit acts by way of the prophets in the promise of a more plenteous coming of the same Spirit upon the future Messiah, that he may act with greater strength (Isa. 42:6–7, 61:1–2). This last text has been applied to Jesus by Luke in one of the most frequently cited pericopes in the theology of liberation:

> "The spirit of the Lord is upon me;
> therefore, he has anointed me.
> He has sent me to bring glad tidings to the poor,
> to proclaim liberty to captives,
> Recovery of sight to the blind
> and release to prisoners,
> To announce a year of favor from the Lord." (Luke 4:18–19)

Paul had to deal with the enthusiasm of a community that had received the gift of tongues. That gift produces no outward fruit, but only affords inward satisfaction. So Paul calls his addressees' attention to the gifts that "build" community (see 1 Cor. 14:4, 14:12). This tireless activity on the part of the Apostle Paul is itself an extraordinary manifestation of the Holy Spirit (1 Cor. 2:4–5, 10–16).

Latin American communities are beginning to experience the fulfillment of Jesus' promise to his disciples: The one "who has faith in me will do the works I do, and greater far than these" (John 14:12).

The activities of the Spirit are different from the actions produced without the Spirit. Latin America has always been famous for its pharaonic works—mighty human deeds built on the dead bodies and superhuman sufferings of millions of slaves or quasi-slaves. Such were the conquest itself, the gold and silver mines, the plantations. Today we see similar works throughout Latin America, especially in Brazil. These works have always been celebrations of the pride of their promoters, and they have revealed the utter contempt of the latter for the dignity of the millions of persons sacrificed to the glory of a few. They stand as testimony to the implacable will of a few, and to their total domination of the multitudes.

2. Experience of Freedom

From the outset the experience of the Latin American peoples has been an experience of the frustration of freedom. Promises of freedom have never been wanting, yet slavery always came. The economic, cultural, and political distance between the great and the small is such that freedom is the exclusive perquisite of the powerful. The mighty have always made the slavery of the multitudes the condition of their own freedom. Freedom is the privilege of the mighty. The Latin American peoples have expressed their longings for liberty by flight. They have fled to the rain forests: natives expelled from their lands or pursued by the slave-traders, blacks who rebelled on the plantations, rural poor whose lands were seized by the large landholders. In Latin America freedom has always meant flight and exile. And this is what it means today. It does not mean participation and responsibility.

The experience of freedom is something the poor have when they begin to gather together in order to think together to form associations, leagues, unions, and communities. They have the experience of freedom when they begin to elect representatives, seek common objectives, and struggle for their autonomy, rights, and dignity. They experience their freedom precisely in the battle for liberation. Theirs is never a complete, established freedom. It is always the freedom to fight for freedom. There is freedom when horizontal relationships appear among equals—when large numbers acknowledge one another as brothers and sisters and cooperate with one another, without any of them arrogating to themselves special privileges over the others. This freedom is the opportunity to be and to exist for oneself, to grow for oneself, not to be robbed of all one's progress by a superior power that monopolizes all production. In Latin America freedom is inchoate. It has always been the perquisite of the elite; not even national independence has ever been anything but the independence of the great.

Today, the small are beginning to learn what freedom means. They understand this freedom in the light of the Bible. True, it is the reading of the Book of Exodus that has especially fed the experience of Christian freedom. But this reading is more than a simple absorption of that scriptural text. Most meaningful of all for us has been the rereading of this book as done by Jesus and the gospels.

It is true that there has not been a great deal of insistence on the relationship between freedom and the Holy Spirit. But the teaching of Paul and John on the Spirit is first and foremost a message of freedom. This message is one of liberation for Latin America, since it sets one free from any religion of slavery. In Latin America official religion has insisted on obedience. It has erected obedience into the very foundation and core of Christianity. Official religion has been a reflection of the spirituality developed in Europe under the sign of Trent. But it has also been a reflection of a society based on the total subordination of the masses.

Paul delivers religion from any spirit of slavery, even where he must make practical concessions to the customs of Judaism or the social structures of his time. The proclamation of the Holy Spirit is the inauguration, the radical inauguration, of a new time, the time of freedom: "Where the Spirit of the Lord is, there is freedom" (2 Cor. 3:17). "Remember that you have been called to live in freedom" (Gal. 5:13). "It was for liberty that Christ freed us" (Gal. 5:1).

The message of John, as well, is the freedom of the Spirit:

> Flesh begets flesh. Spirit begets spirit. The wind blows where it will. You hear the sound it makes but you do not know where it comes from or where it goes. So it is with everyone begotten of the Spirit. (John 3:6–8)

> An hour is coming, and is already here, when authentic worshipers will worship the Father in Spirit and truth. Indeed, it is just such worshipers the Father seeks. God is Spirit, and those who worship him must worship in Spirit and truth. (John 4:23–24)

Thus Christian religion begins with the liberation of human beings from religious slavery, or slavery for religious "reasons." This is the foundation of all other kinds of emancipation.

The Second Vatican Council launched a process of emancipation of Christians in its *Declaration on Religious Freedom*, although it does not cite the dependence of this freedom on the proclamation of the Holy Spirit. The teaching of Vatican II is over twenty-five years old, and weak. Yet it has always been either attacked or ignored in practice. Vatican II had no doctrine of the Holy Spirit, and therefore was unable to develop a message of freedom that would be clearly Christian. The same shortcoming crops up in the 1984 and 1986 Instructions of the Congregation of the Faith on freedom and liberation. Nor does Cardinal Ratzinger have a theology of the Holy Spirit. Such a theology can emerge only from a genuinely and concretely free Christian people. That people can only be the people of the poor. A church that is not a church of the poor will always be afraid of freedom. A theology of the Holy Spirit can emerge only from the praxis of a free Christian people.

3. Experience of the Word

Only oppressed peoples know the value of the word. Dominators talk, and talk a great deal, but they talk mainly in order not to say anything—to prevent certain words from being pronounced. Dominators know that freedom begins with the word, and this is why they censor words. They all know that society is based on injustice, but no one says this, because with them, fear is stronger than truth. Latin America has become accustomed to the silence of the masses. In the presence of their white landlords, the natives seem mute. They make themselves seem as stupid as possible. They know that, if they happen to be right, they will be more severely punished for speaking the truth than for a lie. They lie because those who have disposition over them expect them to lie and will punish them unless they do. Thus it is with black workers, whether on the countryside or in the city. Thus it is with all of the poor; they are constrained to be ignorant and to confess their ignorance. They must confess that only the "boss" knows, and that only the "boss" has the right to know and to speak.

Hence the extraordinary impression of liberation had by the poor when they begin to speak, when they begin to tell the truth, to say what is really happening, to recount actual, factual history. The word is the first expression of rebellion against domination. The word has no magical powers, but it has the virtue of expressing personhood, and it helps personhood to exist. The word is self-assertion. What matters is not so much the content of the word as the very fact of speaking.

The word of the poor in Latin America is not a scientific word. It is not pure explanation. It is not science offering solutions by mighty means. It is not philosophy, system, or developed reflection. It may seek words or expressions in various philosophies, but it is not philosophy. It may use Marxist words or schemas, but the word itself is not identical with the Marxist system. The word of the poor communities is the self-assertion of those communities, their will to exist, an expression of their dignity.

A word of this kind denounces the silence in which the peoples have been kept under the thumb of the oppressor. It denounces the structures of domination. It announces a new life, a different society. It calls together and unites the poor. It stimulates, it animates, it strengthens the communities, it enunciates projects, it points to horizons and goals. The word of the poor is far simpler than an ideology would be. It is the arrival in society of those who have managed to exist, incapable though they may have been of forging ideologies. Subsequently, intellectuals may add ideologies, if in this way they can reinforce the word of the poor. But that word is antecedent to all ideologies, and of more worth than all of them. It would stand on its own even if all ideologies were mere illusions. It stands because it is the manifestation of actual persons who have been unable to exist and who wish to exist.

This is the word in the biblical sense. It is a basic concept in the message of the Bible. The word—at least the word in its strong, specific sense—is inspired by the Spirit.

As inspired by the Spirit, the most basic word is the outcry of the oppressed. The cry of the oppressed arises in Egypt and resounds all through the history of Israel. It is the cry of the oppressed people in Egypt, the cry of the oppressed of Israel in the land of Canaan, the cry of the people in exile, the cry that belongs to the poor by right. Jesus, too, cried out on the cross, recapitulating all the cries of the oppressed of all centuries.

The Christian people, a people poor and oppressed from birth, also have the right to cry out to the Father, and to rely on that Parent's attention and response. The Holy Spirit is at the root of the cry of the Christian people groaning in the hope of resurrection (Rom. 8:14–27):

> All who are led by the Spirit of God are sons of God. You did not receive a spirit of slavery leading you back into fear, but a spirit of adoption through which we cry out, "Abba!" (that is, "Father"). (Rom. 8:14–15)

> The proof that you are sons is the fact that God has sent forth into our hearts the spirit of his Son which cries out "Abba!" ("Father!"). (Gal. 4:6)

The cry does not die out with the resurrection. The struggles and the anguish abide. But the light of the resurrection endows the cry with a greater sureness. In the light of the resurrection, the cry wins a gospel, a proclamation of liberation. The Spirit gives strength to the gospel of the poor. It was the Spirit who inspired the prophets, as the Nicaeo-Constantinopolitan Creed declares. Since Pentecost, the number of the prophets has been multiplied many times over, for the Spirit is sent to all men and women who serve that Spirit. The elders and leaders of the people are dumbfounded, for they are ignorant of the fact that the Spirit is present: "Observing the self-assurance of Peter and John, and realizing that the speakers were uneducated men of no standing, the questioners were amazed" (Acts 4:13).

The Holy Spirit produces words. The Book of Acts is a clear exposition of this production of words by the Spirit. According to Luke's gospel, the same Spirit had already made Jesus a herald of the Reign of God. According to Paul's theology, it is the same Spirit, once more, who now makes the apostles persons of the word. Paul himself is obvious proof of the strength of the Spirit: "My message and my preaching had none of the persuasive force of 'wise' argumentation, but the convincing power of the Spirit" (1 Cor. 2:4).

In Johannine circles, as well, the Spirit is bound up with the word: "This is how you can recognize God's Spirit: every spirit that acknowledges Jesus Christ come in the flesh belongs to God" (1 John 4:2).

4. Experience of Community

Inasmuch as Christian communities acknowledge that they are word (both in the words of the Bible and in the ministries of the word that have been instituted by the Bible), they also acknowledge that they are Christian communities precisely in the light of the Bible. Here, as well, the Bible sheds light on Christian practice.

The popular Christian communities are not the simple upshot of spontaneous social factors. They are not the natural product of misery—a means the popular cultures invent in order to survive.

We shall not deny the sociological factors. Without them the phenomenon of the communities would be very difficult. True, the Latin American masses have been reduced to the state of masses by the successive conquests. Colonial and neocolonial domination have provoked immense migrations, and local solidarity, on the part of destroyed peoples and families. It crams into the mines, the plantations, the outskirts of the teeming cities, the slum ghettos and rural slums, whole populations—millions of separated, isolated, rootless persons. In a situation like this, the poor survive because they help one another. They make an effort to form new ties and new solidarities. However, the very society that has dissolved the old ties is opposed to the formation of new ones. The triumph of community over the forces of dissociation that prevail in society requires something more than purely natural forces. It is perfectly possible for a population to become simply asocial, anarchical. There are human masses that live under the permanent threat of a world without law or order.

Of themselves alone, then, sociological factors do not explain everything. There is something new in the Christian communities, and it comes on the scene as a miracle of God. There is a force at work within them that arouses generosity, dedication, and sacrifice—something akin to Christianity in its first origins. Within the spaces described by sociology—spaces open to new kinds of association—extraordinary forces are appearing in persons willing and able to devote their lives to the birth of a genuine community life. This community never arises of itself. It springs into being only by virtue of the help, inspiration, and prophetic word of persons devoted to it.

The Christian community is comprehensible only in the light of biblical revelation. In it is something of the Reign of God. It proceeds from the power of the Spirit of Jesus Christ. Christians understand what is happening among them as a renewal of what occurred in the first age of the church, when the activity of the Spirit became overt and perceptible. In a certain way, this renewal is also a sensible sign of the Spirit in the world. Furthermore, the small community does not close in upon itself; it opens up to become the seed of a new people founded on relationships of kinship rather than domination.

The community sees itself in the light of the first community of Jerusalem, and of the Pauline communities in which the Spirit was manifested in such a visible way. The communities of the primitive church clearly exhibited the model of a community church, whose life comes from the Spirit through the mediation of the apostles, but comes as the life of an autonomous, locally present entity. Today, as well, the communities are the church alive in a small number of laity. It is served by ministers, but it has its own self-consistency, and does not depend upon the clergy. The Spirit enables the poor to maintain their community by themselves, and yet to create bonds of communion with other communities.

The community is communion, and communion proceeds from charity (in Greek agape, for which "solidarity" is a better translation). Charity is the firstfruit of the Spirit, the most excellent charism of all (1 Cor. 12:30–13:13, Gal. 5:22–25). From the union of the communities springs the greater church—the communion engendered of all nations by the Spirit (Eph. 2:11–22, 4:2–4).

The Spirit creates not only a communitarian church, but a humanity-in-communion. Latin American communities seek to renew not only the shape of the church, but rather, first of all, the structure of society. Community life as lived on the basis of groups of families of the people constitutes the fabric of a new social life—a promise of renewal for all of society. Such renewal cannot be created by political decrees alone. It must emerge from the will of living, breathing persons.

5. Experience of Life

Latin America has the experience of the God of life in a world that is so often the reign of death. When existence is experienced in a situation of dangers, threats, and ongoing fear, the great miracle is life. Life is seen as victory over the forces of death.

The daily struggle is often a pure struggle for survival, for daily bread. The majority of people do not even have the opportunity to think of great liberation projects. Liberation is experienced as the gaining of their daily nourishment—a triumph that must be renewed each day, since insecurity is all-pervasive and absolute.

The life of the poor is a diminished life: stunted, emaciated bodies, prematurely shriveled up, diseased, deprived of effective remedies, without adequate means of subsistence, undernourished, undereducated, culturally deficient. The longing of the poor is that their children may know a better life than theirs. Many times, however, they wonder whether their children's life will be even worse.

Hence such a strong will to live. There are no suicides among the poor. The poor want to live. With all its limitations, they appreciate life. For the poor, life is neither wealth, nor power, nor glory, nor grandeur. Life has an intrinsic value, simply as life, even without the ingredients the rich regard as indispensable. But life is also shared; life worth living is life lived with others, in community.

The God of the Bible is the God of life. And the God of life is the Holy Spirit. In their quest for life, Latin Americans thirst for the Holy Spirit.

From Old Testament times (see Ezek. 37), the Spirit has always been the power of life. The Spirit can actually raise the dead. The gift of the Spirit bestowed by the Risen Christ is a promise of resurrection and eternal life, to follow this earthly existence (see Rom. 8:11). But Christians believe that the resurrection of Christ produces its firstfruits on this very earth:

> "If anyone thirsts, let him come to me; let him drink who believes in me. Scripture has it: 'From within him rivers of living water shall flow.'" (Here [Jesus] was referring to the Spirit, whom those that came to believe in him were to receive. . . .) (John 7:37–39)

Faith does not instantly transform enfeebled bodies, but it does confer new life on them. The frail frames of the poor become vessels of the energies of the Spirit, and their fecundity is astounding. The Spirit produces new vitality in this people shattered by so many physical and moral miseries. The Spirit is seen to be present. In the activity of the Spirit is hope of liberation for the oppressed. Thus, we profess in the Nicaeo-Constantinopolitan Creed: "We believe in the Holy Spirit . . . the giver of life."

II. THE HOLY SPIRIT IN WORLD HISTORY

In the old christendom, Christians aspired to no marvelous transformations. Official theologies were content with saying what Thomas Aquinas had said; that is, in the church God had already bestowed every divine gift that human beings would ever receive in this world. There is nothing to hope for outside the church as such. Today's Christians refuse to resign themselves to this reductionistic hope. For believers today, the biblical themes suggest something more. Christians hope for a transformation of the world. They understand that the biblical themes proclaim a new age of creation—a genuine renewal of all creation, and not only of the individual life of some saints by way of the practice of heroic virtue. Among the oppressed poor a hope is alive which the established churches seem to wish to stifle. Clergy invoke the disillusioned wisdom of Ecclesiastes: "nothing new under the sun." In Latin America the poor want more. Nor can their hope be interpreted in purely political terms. They want more than a political revolution. They want a complete conversion of the world. And this, only the Spirit of God can accomplish.

1. The Spirit and the Renewal of the World

The Holy Spirit is the source and principle of the resurrection of the body (Rom. 1:4, 8:11; 1 Cor. 14:44). If the very Spirit that will raise up our bodies is already present, will that Spirit not be able to produce effects of initial resurrection even now, right in this world?

The Holy Spirit is the presence, in our own time, of the Reign of God. The Spirit is the first stage of that Reign—the beginning of the Reign of God on this earth (2 Cor. 1:22, Gal. 5:5, Eph. 1:13–14). The substitution of the Holy Spirit for the Reign of God in the successive writings of the Christian scriptures is frequently interpreted to mean that the utopian Reign of God had now come to be replaced with a more "realistic" concept, that of the Holy Spirit. The Holy Spirit becomes the sign of a purely interior transformation of the human being. Thus, anything the expression Reign of God might suggest in terms of a social meaning, a concrete, palpable meaning, is eliminated. Little by little, we are told, Christianity had lost the utopian sense of the oldest gospel tradition. Will this interpretation be correct? Will the Holy Spirit produce only "interior" fruits, and nothing in the world, nothing in concrete history?

A mighty protest wells up among an oppressed people of the poor. The oppressed reject such interpretation. Nor is this the first time in history that they have done so. To reduce the Holy Spirit to the sphere of interiority is to project upon the Christian scriptures a restriction of meaning that will later appear in the established church. But let us observe that there has always been an element in the church that has refused to resign itself to this elimination of the Spirit from the world and from history. To be sure, in the era of christendom these believers were under a cloud of suspicion and were usually rebuffed and rejected. They were driven into "heresy" (a concept currently under thorough-going historical reexamination).

The Holy Spirit is the principle of creation and of the new creation. Christian tradition has understood that the "wind" that "swept over the waters" (Gen. 1:2) at the beginning of creation was the Holy Spirit. The medieval hymn "Veni, Sancte Spiritus" ("Come, Holy Ghost") is still sung today. The Canticle of Judith celebrates the creative Spirit: "Let every creature serve you; for you spoke, and they were made, you sent forth your spirit, and they were created" (Jth. 16:14). The Psalms, too, have it: "When you send forth your spirit, they are created, and you renew the face of the earth" (Ps. 104:30). If there is a new creation—a renewal of the face of the earth—how could it be limited to a purely interior renewal? Will there be nothing in this renewal for the present life of the world and human society?

The Spirit actually generates a new human being. It creates a new birth (John 3:5, 6, 8). Vatican II interprets the biblical texts that bear on the new creation as meaning that we are "redeemed by Christ and made a new creature in the Holy Spirit" (Gaudium et Spes, no. 37).

Similar texts, relating the Holy Spirit to creation and the new creation, occur throughout the Council documents. Here are some further examples.

> The People of God believes that it is led by the Spirit of the Lord, who fills the earth. Motivated by this faith, it labors to decipher authentic signs of God's presence and purpose in the happenings, needs, and desires in which this people has a part. (Gaudium et Spes, no. 11)

> The Lord's Spirit . . . who fills the whole earth . . . (Presbyterorum Ordinis, no. 22).

> Christ is now at work in the hearts of men through the energy of His Spirit. He arouses not only a desire for the age to come, but, by that very fact, He animates, purifies, and strengthens those noble longings too by which the human family strives to make its life more human and to render the whole earth submissive to this goal. (Gaudium et Spes, no. 38)

These texts show the Spirit at work in the renewal of the entire earth, and not only of the interior life.

In today's liberation movements among the peoples, the Spirit of God is at work. There is something of the Spirit in these movements that Christians have the task of discerning and claiming. Christians will have to follow the signs, the "tracks" left by the Spirit in these liberation movements. In other times movements for social change were rejected as inspired by the rebellion of the devil. There are Christians of this same mind in Latin America today. But these persons are no longer the whole voice of the church. Another awareness has sprung into being—a consciousness endowed with the capacity to discover the Holy Spirit active in the movements of the world itself, and not just in ecclesiastical space.

2. The Holy Spirit and the Poor

The Holy Spirit acts in the world by means of the poor. This principle has been unambiguously established by Paul (1 Cor. 1:26–2:16). Nor is it a particular, isolated statement in the Bible; on the contrary, it is the core of the biblical view of history. From the outset Israel was chosen to be the vehicle of the divine designs because it was the weakest and poorest of the peoples. Then, within Israel itself, God once more selects the very weakest to represent the authentic remnant of the people of that election. The Messiah foretold by Isaiah, Zechariah, and all the prophets was to be a king who is poor, and a king of the poor. Jesus is the fulfillment of the Messianic prophecy contained in the Isaian Servant of God, whom the great ones of the earth humiliated and despised. In his prophetic mission in the land of Israel, Jesus acts in the midst of the poor, addresses his message to the poor of Israel, selects his disciples from their number. His church begins amid the poor.

It is not to be wondered at, then, that reforms throughout church history commence with movements that set poverty as a priority. From Anthony the desert monk, to the medieval reformers, to the champions of twentieth-century renewal, the power of the Spirit has impelled the reformers to a life of poverty in an encounter with the poor and oppressed masses of the earth. Spirituality is something having to do with poverty.

Thus, the Spirit acts on the underside of history. It does not reject the mediation of concrete, historical forces—neither scientific and technological development, nor economic development, nor political power, nor even, in extreme cases, military mediations. But it subordinates them all to the power of the poor. The Spirit acts by means of patience, perseverance, protest, petition. Only as a last resort do the poor have recourse to violence. While it may be true that violence has been the womb of history, it is not the way of the poor. The poor have ever been the victims of violence, not its protagonists. The action of the Spirit runs counter to violence and the exploitation of labor. The weapons of the Spirit are the weapons wielded by the poor. The tension between the violent means of the mighty and the peaceful means of the poor is a constant in the history of the Spirit.

As a result, the Holy Spirit is the source of a radical conflict in history, an ongoing conflict fueled by that Spirit's active presence, the conflict between the forces of domination, which use the resources placed at their disposal by history itself, and the prophetic forces of resistance, which are unarmed, deprived of means of action. The poor build their means of action with their own toil.

The peace of the Spirit is built up only on the foundation of restitution to the poor of the fruits of their labor and the stripping away of the privileges unjustly accumulated by the powerful.

3. The Holy Spirit and a Temporal Messianism

The Messianic prophecies of the Hebrew scriptures proclaim the coming of an age characterized by an abundance of temporal goods. Jesus endorses these prophecies, for example in Luke 4:18–19. He focuses his own activity on the material condition of his people: he heals the sick, feeds the hungry, and alleviates bodily suffering. For centuries, especially during the christendom centuries, a dominant interpretation had it that these Messianic boons were mere images, literary figures, of the spiritual goods now at hand and available in the church: interior conversion, faith, the virtues. Christians, however, especially the poor, have tended to remain unconvinced. They have been unwilling to accept the proposition that everything Jesus promised was only a literary figure of purely interior blessings.

In medieval times these tendencies came to their most powerful literary expression in the works of a thirteenth-century monk known as Joachim of Fiore, whose writings had a great influence on the so-called spiritual Franciscans. According to Joachim, Jesus proclaimed the coming of an age of the Holy Spirit. Under the christendom of Constantine, Christianity had realized only a transitory, imperfect phase of the message of Jesus. Some kind of domination survived. But an age of the Holy Spirit was in the offing—the age of the poor and of nonviolence.

The ideal proclaimed by Joachim of Fiore coincides almost perfectly with the modern revolutionary utopias. The official church condemned Joachim's predictions, insisting that the Holy Spirit had already been completely bestowed in the church. Beyond the church was nothing. In the world, nothing could be expected from the Holy Spirit. From that moment on, Messianic and spiritualistic aspirations were constrained to keep their distance from the official church. In the fourteenth century revolutionary movements appeared, and they continued in succeeding centuries. At first the revolutionaries believed themselves to be inspired by the Holy Spirit. But as time went on they gradually shifted to a purely secular interpretation of the content and dynamism of their revolutions, as if these movements had sprung from the human being alone—from matter without the intervention of a Holy Spirit. Finally they evolved into the altogether atheistic, antireligious revolutions of the twentieth century.

The theological meaning of the revolutionary movements, like the meaning of the Christian poor, is currently under reexamination. Can the forces at work in the transformation of the world be purely natural ones? Can the Holy Spirit be aloof from such movements? The theology of liberation insists on the opposite. It seeks neither purely secular revolutions, nor a purely interior, "privatized" Christianity. It believes that there is some truth in the Messianic prophecies of the prophets and Jesus, as well as in the Messianic interpretations of Christians of all times. A transformation is possible in this world, even though it will never be definitively achieved or perfectly realized.

Above all, liberation theology now holds that modern revolutions have not been useless or devoid of human and spiritual content. It recognizes signs of the Spirit in them, in spite of all the suffering and all the violence they have occasioned. The anti-colonial revolutions, with the American Revolution of 1776 in the forefront, have not been in vain. The French Revolution of 1789, and all its offspring of the nineteenth century, have not been in vain. The socialist revolutions of the twentieth century have not been in vain or without content. None of these revolutions has been totally ineffective for the creation of a better world. The world has never been the same.

The Latin American people believe that their future revolutions, too, will find another way to live—a better life, a Reign of God. They look for no paradise on earth, but they do expect the future Reign of God to come nearer. They believe that Spirit will be efficacious in history, promoting a concrete and temporal Reign, however incomplete. They do not believe that all of the activity of the Holy Spirit can be shut up in the confines of the church, or that there is nothing to be expected of the church but precisely the church. So they adopt the perspectives of old Joachim of Fiore, the spiritual Franciscans, and a whole Christian tradition that was sometimes an underground one. They glean from the Book of Revelation its outlook of partial realizations on this earth. No book is read with more passion than that "Apocalypse of John"—the book that sets down in black and white the current condition of the oppressed and expresses their hopes. This is also the book of the prophecies of the Spirit.

4. Dialectic of Church and World

The Christian church sprang from a reconciliation between Judaism and paganism by the power of the Holy Spirit (Eph. 2:14–22). The Spirit created a new society by kneading the leaven of Judaism into the legacy of all the nations of the earth. What was created then was neither a mixture nor a mere synthesis, but a genuinely new phenomenon—something in which Judaism and pagan civilizations could find themselves anew, elevated and perfected. Both poles shook off their limitations and all that divided them from each other, while losing nothing of the positive within them.

Some have understood the text of Ephesians as if the task of this reconciliation were already completed. Even in the Letter to the Romans, however, Paul proclaimed that the people of Israel would abide in separation until the end of the ages, in testimony to the incompletion of the work. The encounter between Judaism and paganism will always be a task to be performed anew, until the end of time—not only because Judaism abides, but because the other civilizations of the world, as well, represent ever more difficult challenges.

The church is the mediator of this work of reconciliation. It is the tool of the Holy Spirit, and the primary sign of the concrete efficacy of that Spirit. However, the church itself lives in concrete history and suffers history's impacts and influences. Despite its assignment to the work of reconciliation, the church allows itself to be reduced to the status of an "instrument of the already." It is simply like Judaism. And then like paganism. And then like Judaism again. And so on. By calling, it ought to transcend both. But historically, it vacillates between both poles of corruption. In the second and third centuries the church reassumed many of the elements of Judaism, and seemed another synagogue. From Constantine onward, the church allowed itself to be integrated into the Roman Empire and tended toward paganism. Up until the end of the Middle Ages the tendency toward paganism prevailed; hence the calls to reform that resound throughout the christendom centuries. Since the great Protestant schism and the gradual secularization of Western society, the church has inclined once more toward Judaism, defending itself by taking the shape of a synagogue. It defends itself through its law, its separation from the pagans, its intransigence, its fidelity to the letter and to its traditions. Today, the problem of reconciliation is posed once again. Vatican II took cognizance of the reality of a new pagan world to evangelize. Once again, then, the church is challenged to emerge from the protective walls of the synagogue. The Holy Spirit encourages this dialectic, showing Christians the signs of the times. Nowadays the prime challenge is the pagan world and evangelization. The stronger voice will have to be that of Paul, not James, of Corinth, not Jerusalem.

III. THE SPIRIT AND THE CHURCH

1. The Church is Born of the Holy Spirit

A constant thesis of Latin American ecclesiology has been that the church is "born of the poor" (Leonardo Boff, Gustavo Gutiérrez, Jon Sobrino, Ronaldo Muñoz, and so on). This thesis is an expression of the doctrine of the creation of the church by the Holy Spirit. The church was not born directly of the human obedience of the disciples to the instructions of Christ. Jesus did not found the church in the way that individuals found human institutions. He left everything very indeterminate. Although the church is the "continuator of Christ," the concrete, practical manner of its imitation of Christ does not proceed from a simple meditation of the teachings of Jesus. The role of the Spirit is far more radical than that of simply offering help. The sheer distance, in the books of the Christian scriptures, between Jesus and the church of Corinth testifies to the radical role of the Holy Spirit. It would be impossible to have "deduced" the church of Corinth directly from the teachings of Jesus. Indeed, a number of thinkers have called Paul, rather than Jesus, the creator of Christianity. Actually, it was the Holy Spirit who created the church, making use of Paul's services and creating a new expression of the will of Jesus. This creation of Christianity by the Spirit occurs in each succeeding age of church history. Vatican II acknowledged that we were on the threshold of a new era. Thus, the Holy Spirit is engaged in a new creation of the church.

The Holy Spirit causes the church to spring up in communities scattered throughout the world. The church is born not of a center, through a process of decentralization from that center, but is born of the periphery. It springs up in various places in the world simultaneously, or at least without apparent order. Subsequently, the various groups that have thus come into being seek out an appropriate manner of establishing contact with one another. While preaching is surely necessary in order to call forth a new community, that preaching is done discreetly and humbly by believers who undertake journeys from already established Christian communities to communities that have not as yet heard the Good News. This is church today, as well. Communities have arisen, in no predictable order, in various places in Latin America. They continue to spring up, without planning. These communities do not seek isolation. On the contrary, they seek closeness to all other Christian communities. They place themselves under the legitimate authority of the bishops and the pope. But they are born neither by the will of the bishop nor by the initiative of the pope.

The mystery of the church is bound up with its birth of the Spirit. The birth of the church is not the spontaneous effect of sociological forces, although these forces do have an influence on its concrete history. The church is born, in mysterious ways, of the Spirit, who finds created persons to be instruments of this birth.

The work of the Spirit is communion, within the communities and among the communities. Ecclesial communion must be more than a mere interior disposition. In the Christian scriptures, it necessarily includes material relations of an exchange of goods according to each one's needs. Where are these material relations to be found? They are present in the concrete reality of the communities of the poor, as well as in the service of those who, born rich, have stripped themselves of their wealth and become like the poor. Medellín's call for a poor church is a precondition of church communion.

The presence of the Spirit at the root of the church takes on an ethical orientation in communion and an esthetic orientation in prayer and festival. The Spirit is the source of the church's joy. In prayer, the products of the Spirit are joy, gratitude, and praise of the divine Parent. Although the creation of a new liturgy in Latin America is still lacking a great deal, it is an ongoing concern. In the meantime, the old forms of popular prayer are acquiring a new vitality.

2. The Spirit and the Marks of the Church

The Spirit is the driving force of unity in the church (1 Cor. 12:13, Eph. 4:5). In Latin America oneness among the communities is sought spontaneously. Unity with the bishops and the pope is taken for granted. No one calls it into question, despite the great diffidence manifested so often by bishops or the Roman Curia when it comes to the base communities. Many observers have the impression that the hierarchy is still obsessed with heresy and schism. For such a hierarchy, all laity are suspected of wishing to destroy the church and its unity. Therefore the hierarchy redoubles its application of human means in order to impose unity through uniformity: theological, liturgical, and canonical uniformity. In Latin America this approach to unity is interpreted as a lack of faith in the Holy Spirit. Will the Spirit be so feeble as to have need of so many purely human resources, after the fashion of political societies, indeed of the dictatorships of this world?

Will it not be an insult to the Holy Spirit that certain bishops, contrary to the will of their national episcopates, contrary to the desires of their clergy and their people, currently withdraw from their fellow Christians, simply because certain persons are more faithful executors of all the desires of the Holy See? Will it not be an insult to the Holy Spirit to engage in a general practice of informing against others as the predominant means of communication between the Holy See and the local churches? Will it not be an insult to the Holy Spirit to regard certain church matters as "classified information," with the result that the Christian people can know nothing of financial management in the church, nominations to higher offices and their motivation, or the reasons for the promulgation of certain local canons? Will it not be an insult to the Holy Spirit to engage in a practice of censorship that employs methods so reminiscent of the dictatorships that stink in the nostrils of Latin America? Will it not be an insult to the Holy Spirit to dispense with an authentic judicial system, in which the judge and the accuser are not the same person?

For the church born of the people, neither heresies nor schisms are problems of great urgency at the present. What is urgent is the evangelization of the poor, who have been abandoned by the clerical church for so many centuries. The poor place their trust in the power of the Spirit to maintain unity through dialogue, patience, and perseverance.

Ever since the first Pentecost the Spirit has seen to a church willing to be open to its neighbors. From the beginning Catholicism in Latin America has been crippled by the will of the Conquistadores and their successors. Officially, the colonization has sought moral legitimation through an appeal to the conversion of the Indians as its motive. The slavery of the Africans has been defended on the grounds of the boons of evangelization. In both cases, however, Christianity has been imposed by force. To our very day, a genuine evangelization of natives and blacks, apart from exceptional cases in widely scattered localities, has never left the drawing boards. The Christianity proposed to them is a Western culture that they are helpless to resist. A gospel in Western trappings is imposed upon them, and it is very difficult for them to distinguish between what is Christian and what is Western. The Holy Spirit is without a doubt on the point of raising up a native church and a black church, with all the necessary autonomy, in communion with the white church.

The church of the poor is inventing a new model of holiness. On a continent scarred by gigantic social and personal sins, where life counts for nothing, where murder always goes unpunished when it is committed by the powerful, where injustices reach incredible levels of oppression, where corruption is the very principle of public life, the emergence of such peaceable, such patient communities of solidarity constitutes an ongoing miracle. The word of the gospel stirs up miracles of holiness. This holiness culminates in thousands upon thousands of martyrs giving up their lives with calm and dignity: community advisers, leaders of popular associations, humble collaborators of the communities. Tens of thousands have earned the name of martyr. Here are witnesses of the Spirit indeed.

The apostolicity that proceeds from the Spirit is irreducible to the formal and juridical elements so frequently proclaimed in an apologetical ecclesiology coming down to us from the end of the Middle Ages. Authentic apostolicity consists in fidelity to the witness of the apostles as we find it in the Christian scriptures. The essential element of apostolicity is a return to the message of the apostles, delivered in a time when the church was poor, politically powerless, and without cultural prestige. Apostolicity is a spiritual phenomenon, then, and not merely a sociological one.

3. The Spirit and the Offices of the Church

The church is spiritual in its evangelization. By the Spirit, the church becomes a servant of the word of God. It submits to the written word of the Bible. By the enlightenment of the Spirit, the church discovers the current meaning and application of the written words of the Bible. The office of evangelization is not reserved to a few ministers. It belongs to the whole community and all of its members, within the common mission of the community. The Spirit awakens and feeds the "evangelizing potential of the poor," as Puebla calls it. The Spirit bursts the barriers of culture, and the wall of separation between the intellectual and the laborer. The Spirit enables the poor to discover the concrete scope of the biblical word.

In the Spirit, the church celebrates the event of liberation. "Christ our Pasch" is experienced in millions of particular Easters. Christ's Easter becomes today's Easter in the phenomena of the death and resurrection of the peoples. Christ relives his Easter amid the practice of liberation. The poor celebrate their sufferings and victories in the sufferings and victories of Christ. Thus they rescue the liturgy from the formalism that has infected it for so many centuries, or from the magical distortions so common among the poor (and the less poor). The sacraments are authentically spiritual when they produce a bonding between Christ and the lives of actual persons. The poor live their lives as an ongoing Easter. They are willing to recognize Christ in those lives.

The church also has the office of service through the various charisms. The rebirth of community life produces an abundance of services. The charisms are reappearing. The church is opening itself to the needs of the whole people. The service of human rights, of human dignity, of justice to workers, of the protection of life, is acquiring new meanings. In the church of the poor, service is no longer an expression of the paternalism of the privileged toward their victims. It is an expression of the solidarity of the poor.

4. The Holy Spirit and the Ministries of Authority

For centuries, indeed since Constantine, the ministries in the church have largely been understood by the analogy of the rungs in the ladder of civil authority. The office of bishop has been conceptualized as analogous to that of the governor of a province or city of the Roman Empire. Since Vatican II Latin America has begun to see departures from this model. Spiritual authority cannot run parallel to civil or military authority. There is a spiritual manner of exercising authority: "Since Vatican II and the Medellín Conference, a great change can be noted in Latin America in the way that authority is exercised within the Church. Greater emphasis has been put on its character as service and sacrament and on the dimension of collegial concern" (Puebla Final Document, no. 260).

Puebla insists that Paul's recommendation be applied to the bishops: "not to 'stifle the Spirit' or 'despise prophecy' (1 Thess. 5:19–20)" (Puebla Final Document, no. 249).

Indeed, a new model of episcopal action has appeared on the Latin American scene. The "Medellín generation" launched a phenomenon that is, at least in some degree and in particular countries, irreversible. The model to which we refer has found its ideal expression in the bishop-martyrs: Geraldo Valencia Cano of Buenaventura in Colombia, Enrique Angelelli of La Rioja in Argentina, and Oscar Romero of San Salvador. Together with them, the framers of Medellín make up a group deserving of the title the Holy Fathers of Latin America.

In the base church communities, many laity exercise genuine authority. Spontaneous and charismatic at first, this authority has gradually come to be recognized by the hierarchy itself, although it has not yet been authenticated by the universal laws of the Latin Church.

Many religious women and men have seen themselves challenged by the changes in the church. Frequently, these missioners had introduced in Latin America, mechanically, the same institutions they maintained in their native lands. In the light of the new church of the poor, they have been led to review their whole pastoral or spiritual involvement. They too have discovered the world of the poor. In the light of the poverty of the poor, they have questioned their vow of poverty. In the light of the slavery of the poor they have questioned the meaning of their vow of obedience. In the light of the misery and abandonment of the poor they have questioned themselves on the meaning of their vow of chastity.

The Spirit transforms all structures. It even manages to prick the tranquility of centuries-old customs and formalisms sacralized by time. The Spirit renews all forms of authority.

IV. THE NEW SPIRITUALITY IN LATIN AMERICA

1. A Spirituality of Liberation

The basic trait of the new spirituality of liberation is its spirituality *of* the laity *for* the laity. This spirituality is not the watered-down spirituality of a religious order or congregation. It springs not from the special experience of a specially gifted founder, but from the simultaneous practice of thousands of committed Christians, living in widely separated regions of our continent but in similar concrete conditions.

These Christians' basic spiritual experience is that of an integral liberation. They have felt in their own flesh domination and alienation in all its dimensions: political oppression, threats, prison, torture (sometimes to the death), the exploitation of their labor, subjection to official lies and to the brain-washing perpetrated by the media in the service of the dominators. They had assimilated the domination and made it their own, like the vast majority of the poor of Latin America. They had been convinced of the justice of injustice. But in the renewal of the church, their personhood has been gradually delivered from all of the bonds of slavery: political, economic, cultural, and all others. They have experienced this liberation as an action of the Holy Spirit within them. They know that the road is narrow and dangerous. Liberation costs a terrible price, but they are ready to pay that price.

Liberation engenders no pride, selfishness, individualism, or spirit of libertinage, as modernity has. To serve one another Latin American Christians have renounced any individual advantages that may be available to them in a consumer society. They seek to share in the common lot of their poor brothers and sisters. Their gradual liberation engenders service to the community and solidarity.

The spirituality of liberation is not taken from books, nor does it bring a great deal of literary expression itself. The poor live their spirituality; they do not write about it. Some day, perhaps, someone may be able to write about it as well. But it is living it that counts.

2. The Prayer of the Poor

By contrast, any spirituality is expressed in the language of prayer. The poor in Latin America have not lost contact with their traditional religion or the old popular expressions of Christianity. Often enough, these traditional expressions of popular piety have been deflected by the dominators and placed in the service of domination. But often enough as well, it is possible to restore to the poor the riches of their past. Traditional formulas can take on liberative meanings. Popular piety can be delivered from its distortions.

Further, in the popular communities the poor are learning to express themselves "on their own." They acquire freedom of speech even in their religious celebrations. In other times they were silenced, and silence was their sole participation. Now they learn to pray spontaneously—to transform their life and their death into prayer. As Paul recommends, they live in thanksgiving. Joy is their dominant theme. In the midst of their torments and misery, their fears and the threats made against them, they attain to gladness in a fashion altogether unfamiliar to the high and mighty. They live in joy because they live in deep, sincere friendship with one another. As one *campesino* put it, the wealth of the poor is friendship.

The basic theme of the new spirituality is the oldest Christian theme of all. It is the theme of the gospels themselves: the following of Jesus in his humanity—the imitation of the works of Jesus over the course of his earthly mission. There is no attempt to copy these works literally. The grace of the Spirit enables Latin American Christians to discover today's equivalents of the actions of Jesus. The Spirit shows them the hidden correspondences. And, lo, the life of Jesus revives, in the hidden, heroic life of the church of the poor.

—Translated by Robert R. Barr

9

Mary

IVONE GEBARA
MARÍA CLARA BINGEMER

I. ASSUMPTIONS

When we think about the mystery of Mary and mariology from the viewpoint of liberation theology, we make certain anthropological and hermeneutic assumptions. We base our new thinking about traditional mariology on them and use them as guidelines.

1. Anthropological Assumptions

Liberation theology sees and thinks about Mary within a *human-centered anthropology*. It does not consider only men to be the history-makers, image of the divinity and mediator of the relationship between God and humanity. All humanity, men and women, are regarded as the center of history and revealers of the divine. This anthropology takes into account women's historical activity for the Kingdom, and thus does justice to Mary, to women, in fact, to humanity created in the image and likeness of God.

It is also a *single anthropology*, not dualist, which affirms the existence of a single human history. It does not set up two competing histories, one divine and one human. Its starting point is human history, the scene of conflicts, joys, and sorrows of generations of different peoples. A Marian theology with a single anthropology returns to the realism of human experience marked by historical differences and shares profoundly in the mystery of the incarnation. The Word becomes flesh in human flesh, flesh of men and women, historical flesh marked by space and time, life and death, joy and sorrow, building and destroying, in short, by all the conflict inherent in being human in history.

Moreover, it is a *realist anthropology*, which combines objectivity and subjectivity. It does not claim to be purely objective and idealist, but takes on board the multiplicity of interpretations, hypotheses, and theories about different events. A realist anthropology sustains mariology in its attempt to respond to the changeable reality of human existence. The eternal is always historical. This viewpoint enables us to see the figure of Mary in a constantly new way. We cannot make her into an eternal model, or way of being; this historical figure of Mary must always enter into dialogue with the time, space, culture, problems, and actual people who relate to her. It is life today that gives life to Mary's life yesterday.

It is also a *multidimensional anthropology*, no longer one-dimensional. It looks at different human aspects in terms of their development, which is affected by countless different factors. A human being is not primarily a definition or essence, but a history marked by space and time. A human being is not initially good and then depraved, or initially perverse and saved later; the human is this complex reality, full of division and conflict, whose nature is both limited and unlimited. Its multidimensional anthropology gives Marian theology a human-divine foundation, which enables it to observe with justice and profound respect the human phenomenon—maker of history, created, loved and saved by God. It also allows these different aspects to appear in relation to Mary without one necessarily excluding the other. Each aspect is a profile, an expression, a word about human aspiration toward the divine, which dwells in human nature and structures it. Mary is the divine in the feminine expression of the human, a key expression of what we call wholly human.

Finally, it is a *feminist anthropology*, whose meaning is linked to the historical moment in which we are living, a time when women have become conscious of their oppression for millennia and their conniving submission over the centuries to these oppressive social structures. In general terms, a feminist anthropology means humanity's other side, the female side, recalling vital realities from which women have been alienated. A mariology with a liberation perspective does not try to bring out Mary's qualities as a woman, qualities which have been idealized and projected by different needs and cultures. It tries to take a fresh look at Mary from the viewpoint of our own time and its needs, and in particular, this special moment for humanity of the awakening of women's historical consciousness.

2. Hermeneutic Assumptions

For the hermeneutic used by liberation theology to speak about Mary we need to distinguish certain points:

1. After having been someone who lived in history, Mary has become someone who lives in God. Those who live in God have projected onto them the situation of those who live in history, a situation of limitation and at the same time unlimited desire. Everything in the life of those who live in history that mars the harmony, perfection, health, integrity, security, fulfillment, happiness, love, and values belonging to this desire for the unlimited, is what is sought and asked for in those who live in God. In Latin America the relationship of those who live in history with those who live in God helps them to overcome the deep sense of abandonment and dismay felt by the continent's poor and oppressed majorities. The cry for God and for those who live in God—Mary preeminently among the poor and believing people of Latin America—is a cry for help, whatever form this may take. This is what Latin American spirituality and, in particular, its Marian spirituality are made of. Mary is the hope, the mother, the protector, the one who does not forsake her children. So for a Latin American Marian theology, analysis of biblical texts and tra-

dition is not enough. It is fundamentally important to grasp the type of human experience to which devotion to Mary corresponds. In the Latin American continent this experience is essentially the experience of the poor discovering themselves as subjects of history—history makers—and organizing for liberation.

2. A Marian theology from the viewpoint of Latin America today must also have a different and special way of reading the biblical texts. The written text must always make the reader wonder and ask about what was not written, what was lost, and what was left out on purpose. A written text is always selective. The scriptural texts that speak about Mary are very few, but from these texts and different popular traditions, each historical epoch constructs an image of Mary and her past and present historical activity. Hence we cannot say that the only truth about Mary's life is in the little that we are told by the Christian scriptural texts. What is not said is also important.

3. The idea of the Kingdom of God is essential for the hermeneutics of a Marian theology concerned with liberation. To understand this idea we must go beyond the person of Jesus. It affects his whole movement, in which men and women actively share. So we read the facts about Mary in terms of the different images which the Kingdom of God assumes in scripture, tradition, and traditions. The facts about Mary make present the signs of God's Kingdom; they are particular actions that manifest the presence of salvation in human history. Mary speaks of God and the Kingdom, of divinity in a woman's life; she speaks of God's Son, who is born of the people and of a woman; she speaks of the many children engendered by the Spirit of God who are not born of the flesh or man's desire, but of God. A Marian theology from the viewpoint of the Kingdom will also enable us to see Mary's passion for the poor, her passion for God's justice. This theology enables us to recover through her the force of the Spirit acting on women in all eras. It is the recovery of the "dangerous memory" or "subversive memory," capable of changing things, because it not only keeps alive the hopes and struggles of women in the past, but gives birth and growth to a universal solidarity among the women of past, present, and future. In this light Mary is not only the sweet and charming mother of Jesus; she is a working woman, working for the harvest of the Kingdom, an active member of the movement of the poor, just as Jesus of Nazareth was. So this is the end for the old limited view of Mary as subject to her Son, as women were subject to men. It opens up a broader horizon in which Mary becomes one of those who see a new light shining from Nazareth, the symbol of the edge of the world.

II. MARY IN SCRIPTURE

A scriptural narrative may center upon a particular character, but it is really referring to a collective, a people. Thus the Hebrew scriptures' female figures who appear before Mary—Miriam, Anna, Ruth, Judith, Esther, and others—are at the same time images of women and images of a people. Through their actions God's power is revealed saving God's people. These female figures also represent this people's resistance. We do not deny that each individual has a mission, especially some with special gifts. But in our time we need to rediscover the collective dimension of human actions in the web of history past and present, the collective making of history.

This is how we read scripture in Latin America for our understanding of Mary's place and role today. We are not dealing only with the individual person Miriam of Nazareth, but with a woman who is the image of a faithful people, God's particular dwelling place. The statement "God became flesh in Jesus" must be completed by another with the same theological status: "God is born of a woman." The Christian scriptures try to show that with Mary and with Jesus a new time begins in the history of humanity. There is a sort of qualitative leap, the awareness of the presence of God in human flesh. God dwells on human earth and is discovered and loved in human flesh.

Although Mary is born into a patriarchal context, in which a woman is a thing, man's property at all levels, she is a figure standing between the two Testaments. She shares in and savors the new liberating experience of her Son's movement, which offers equal discipleship to men and women. Together with the other women at the church's beginnings, she is the bearer of a new hope and a new way of being a woman. She is the legitimate representative of the people of Israel, the symbol of faithful Sion. Equally she is the bearer of the new Israel, the new people, the new covenant God makes with humanity. In this women are no longer passive and subject to men, no longer inferior beings, but active subjects. They stand side by side with men and assume with them, shoulder to shoulder, many of the tasks inherent in the proclamation of the Good News.

In its few texts relating to Mary the Christian scriptures illustrate these perspectives.

Paul: In Galatians 4:1–7 Paul says that "in the fullness of time God sent his Son born of a woman." Here the figure of the woman who gives birth to the Son of God in the fullness of time means the convergence between eschatology and history, anthropology and theology. Henceforth there is no room for androcentrism or dualism of any kind. Any anthropological or theological reductionism gives way to the confession of faith that the Word became flesh in human flesh, flesh of men and women. It also says that the Kingdom has come, the fullness of time is now, the new creation has become reality because God has sent the Son, born of a woman. In the light of this mystery the Kingdom happens in the community of men and women, whose struggles and sufferings, sorrows and joys, constantly blossom with the inexhaustible freshness of love.

Matthew: This gospel looks at the story of Jesus as the fulfillment of Yahweh's promises to his chosen people. Upon the woman comes the Spirit of God as in the creation text (Gen 1:2). So Mary gives birth "without Joseph knowing her." Joseph is the synthesis of the ancient people, the primitive Jewish tradition which recognizes the Messiah in spite of doubts and difficulties. The woman is the symbol of the faithful people from whom the Messiah is born, and Joseph the ancient people called to a new wedding to begin love anew. Matthew's Mary is the symbol of virgin hope, a woman pregnant with life, the light-filled face of the people, God's faithfulness constantly reemerging from the ruins of destruction.

Mark: Mary's motherhood is a historical reference, a fact identifying the carpenter miracle-worker, who knows the Law and the prophets and defends the people, who is accepted by some and rejected by others. Mary, Jesus' mother, shares in this environment which opens and closes horizons, welcomes and rejects Jesus.

Mary stands with the humanity that "almost" rejects him; she is involved in the group of those who think "he is mad." But she is also pointed out as the one who has overcome the biological level of her relationship with Jesus and is among those who do God's will (cf. Mark 3:35).

Luke: This is the gospel with the most references to Mary. The annunciation to Mary (Luke 1:26–38) is in line with the many manifestations of God's faithfulness to his people (Sara, Abraham, Samson's mother). Mary (representing the people) is the new ark of the covenant, God's dwelling place, the place where God lives, the place where God can be met and loved. Luke uses the experiences and theological expressions of the Jews and gives them new meaning in terms of the great novelty experienced by Jesus' followers. Mary's visit to Elizabeth (Luke 1:40–45) is the encounter of the old with the new. Mary is now "blessed among women." The one who recognises and proclaims this is Elizabeth, an old Jewish woman from whom the last of the prophets of the old Law is to be born. Mary's song, the *Magnificat* (Luke 1:46–55), is a war song, a song of God's combat in human history, God's struggle to bring about a world of equal relationships, respect for every person, in whom the divinity dwells. The image of the pregnant woman who can give birth to the new is the image of God, who through the power of the Spirit brings about the birth of men and women dedicated to justice, living out their relationship with God in a loving relationship with their fellow human beings. Mary's song is the program for God's Kingdom, and also Jesus' program proclaimed in the synagogue at Nazareth (Luke 4:16–21). Mary's delivery (Luke 2:7) has a collective meaning. All men and women are involved in it as it goes beyond the limits of human biology and physiology. It is God's birth into humanity. In the two final texts that mention Mary (Luke 2:34–35 and Luke 2:48–49) Simeon's prophecy extends Mary's scope to all time. Those who struggle for God's Kingdom suffer hostility in this world. A sword continually pierces the heart of the poor and those who struggle for God's justice, those who put God's matters first and are possessed by a passion for liberation of their fellows.

Acts of the Apostles: This book shows us Mary present at the roots of the primitive Christian community, persevering in prayer and united with her Son's disciples. Present as the mother, the sister, the friend, the disciple, and teacher of a movement organized by her son Jesus, a movement whose historical roots lie in the proclamation of the presence of the Kingdom among the poor, those deprived of all recognition by the established powers.

John: The fourth gospel presents Mary on two occasions: the first is the wedding at Cana (John 2:1–11), when Jesus, at her intercession, works the first of his signs, changing water into wine. Mary's faith conceives and gives birth to the new Messianic community; it inaugurates the new people's time. This is the community of the Kingdom, where poor and despised Cana of Galilee becomes the place where God's glory is revealed. The second episode is at the foot of the cross, when Jesus is dying. Jesus entrusts his beloved disciple to her as her son. In the line of great female maternal figures of the Hebrew scriptures (Deborah, the mother of the Maccabees, and others) Mary stands as the mother of the new community of men and women who have become followers of Jesus because they believe in God's glory manifested in him. John's gospel sets Mary at the center of Jesus Christ's salvation event. She is the symbol of the people who welcome the message of the Kingdom and the fullness of Messianic times.

Revelation: In chapter 12 of Revelation a woman appears clothed with the sun and crowned with stars. She is in labor and fighting the dragon. Her vocation is victory, to be the bride of the lamb, the new Jerusalem where all who keep God's commandments and bear witness to Jesus will finally be united. The persecuted and martyred people of God bear the pledge of Jesus' victory. Mary is identified as this woman in Revelation 12, the figure of the people's humble and laborious faith, the suffering people who believe in the crucified savior without losing hope. She is the figure of a church persecuted by the world, by the forces of the anti-Kingdom and the powerful and oppressors of all kinds who, like the dragon in Revelation, want to "devour" the children and descendants of the woman, devour the project of the Kingdom, all that is life and liberty for the people, all that is the mature fruit of the woman's fertile womb. The new people of God, of whom Mary is the symbol and figure, is the "sign" that appears in heaven and on earth that to the woman Eve's descendants the grace and the power to triumph over the serpent has been given through the woman Mary's descendants. From her flesh the Spirit formed God's incarnation. She is the woman—people of God, from whose womb salvation has sprung, the community of those who "keep God's commandments and bear witness to Jesus."

III. RE-READING THE MARIAN DOGMAS

In Latin America today we need to rethink the church's dogmas—and in this case the Marian dogmas—in the light of the anthropological and hermeneutic assumptions we outlined above for liberation theology. We must rethink them in terms of the key theme guiding the Latin American church since the conferences at Medellín and Puebla: the option for the poor.

1. The Mystery of the Theotokos, Mother of God

Unlike other dogmas, whose biblical roots are questioned and which constitute genuine ecumenical problems, Mary's divine motherhood has deep and solid support in scripture. The Christian scriptures give Mary the title Mother more times than anything else (twenty-five times). For the gospel narratives, Mary is above all Jesus' mother. At the center of the mystery of the incarnation, a mystery which is salvation for the whole human race, the Christian scriptures set a man and a woman, Jesus and Mary. God takes on man's flesh through the flesh of a woman. The Council of Ephesus (431) expressly declares Mary to be *Theotokos*, Mother of God. Mary's divine motherhood is stated in the conciliar declaration as the key for interpreting the mystery of the incarnation. It explains the union of the two natures of God's Word and shows how it is possible. He who is begotten eternally by the Father is born of a woman according to the flesh, that is, he has united human nature to himself, hypostatically. After Ephesus the divine Mother becomes a unique title of honor and glory for her who is the mother of the incarnate word.

Recognizing Mary as Mother of God means professing that Jesus the carpenter of Nazareth, the Crucified, the son of Mary, according to human generation, is Son of God and himself God. The anthropological vision underlying this statement is a single whole. Every woman is the mother not only of the body but the whole person of her child. The mystery of Jesus, the Son of God's incarnation in Mary of Nazareth, teaches us that the human person is not split into an imperfect material body and a great transcendent spirit. On the contrary, only in the weakness, poverty, and limitations of human flesh can we experience and worship the Spirit's ineffable greatness. It also means proclaiming the Kingdom's arrival: "Now it is among us." God took on human history from within, himself living through its struggles and successes, defeats and victories, insecurities and joys. Mary is the figure and symbol of the people who believe in and experience this arrival of God, who now belong to the human race. She whose flesh formed the flesh of God's Son is also the symbol and prototype of the new community, where men and women love one another and celebrate the mystery of life, which has been revealed in its fullness. This also reveals all the greatness of the mystery of woman—a mystery of openness, source of protection and life. Mary is mother of all the living, the woman where the mystery of the source and origin of life reaches its maximum density. Thus she reveals a new and unexplored side of the mystery of God, who became incarnate in her womb; he himself is like a woman who gives birth, who suckles the child of his womb, and does not forget it (cf. Isa. 66:13; 42:14; 49:15). Finally, the *Theotokos* means we must recognize that this same woman, whom we call mother and our Lady, is the poor and obscure woman of Nazareth, mother of the subversive carpenter who was condemned to death, Jesus. We must look behind the glorious titles and the luxurious images with which traditional piety represents her to the no less real and theological title of Handmaid of Yahweh. This is an inspiration for the church, whose role in Latin America is to serve the poor, for whom Jesus' incarnation in Mary carries the Good News of liberation.

2. Virginity

Mary is a true daughter of Judaism, and Judaism does not think of virginity as having particular value. It is equivalent to sterility, to non-procreation; it attracts contempt and implies death because survival is in children. Mary's virginity cannot therefore be regarded as making a moralist or idealizing point. The biblical texts mean that the Son conceived in Mary is a divine being. The chain of human genealogy undergoes a radical break to give way to the Spirit, who invades history with a creative breath and makes life spring where it would be naturally impossible. Jesus, the new Israel who springs from Mary's womb, is the seed of the new people formed by the Spirit. Mary is also the figure and symbol of this people. The church's tradition has taken this indication to proclaim Mary's perpetual virginity throughout the history of the early centuries and finally at the Lateran Council (649).

Mary's virginity throws light on the anthropological question of what a human being is. The human creature is like unexplored virgin land, where anything can happen. And everything that happens should lead this human creature to the point

Mary reached: forming God in her womb. Mary's virginity, fertilized by the Spirit, corresponds to the vocation of every human being to be an open and available temple and dwelling place. The importance of Mary's virgin body lies in being a metaphor for human inability to achieve its own salvation without God's grace. Mary's virginity is a sign of total surrender to the God of life. It totally abandons the death-dealing idols and is a sign to all men and women who want to tread the path Jesus trod and live the historico-eschatological reality of God's Kingdom. Mary's virginity also shows the specific vocation of women as bearers of fullness of life, unlimited open space, a latent potentiality which grows ever greater the deeper its self-surrender. The dogma of Mary's virginity declares women to be an affirmative space where the Spirit of the Most High can alight and make its home. It also shows God's omnipotent glory, which is manifest in that which is poor, powerless, and despised in the world's eyes. Virginity, despised in Israel, is the place of the *shekinah*, the dwelling place of Yahweh's glory. God's preference for the poor becomes clear and explicit when God becomes incarnate in the womb of a virgin. Like her motherhood, Mary's virginity belongs to the service of Yahweh's poor who say, "Behold the handmaid of the Lord, do to me according to your word" (Luke 1:38).

3. The Immaculate Conception

This dogma, proclaimed in 1854 by Pius IX, does not have such explicit biblical roots as the previous ones. Our reference is the text of Genesis 3:15 (also called the *proto-evangelium*), in which the woman and her descendants appear as mortal enemies of the serpent, whom she finally destroys by crushing its head. As well as other less important references to the Ark of the Covenant, the Holy City, and others, there is the angel's greeting in Luke's gospel, which declares Mary to be "full of grace" (Luke 1:28) and Elizabeth's greeting, which declares her to be "blessed among women" (Luke 1:42). So Mary appears as God's most excellent miracle, creation that has reached its fulfillment, the blessed one who is full of grace. Christians expressed this feeling in their devotion before the church's magisterium officially recognized it as a dogma of faith.

By her immaculate conception Mary is the personified synthesis of the ancient Zion-Jerusalem. She is the exemplary beginning of the process of renewal and purification of the whole people, so that they can live God's covenant more fully. Belonging wholly to God, Mary is already the prototype of that which the people is called to be. The immaculate conception is thus a utopia that gives strength to the project and sustains the people's hope in their God (cf. Puebla Final Document, no. 298). It is the pledge that Jesus' utopia—the Kingdom of God—can be realized on this poor earth. But it is not just Mary's soul which is preserved from sin. Her whole person is penetrated and animated by grace, by God's life. Her body is the dwelling place of the holy God. Her immaculate conception proclaims to the people, whose figure she is, that the Spirit has been poured out upon all flesh and the lost paradise has been regained. Woman's body, which Genesis denounces as the cause of original sin, laying upon the whole female sex a defect and a burden difficult to bear, is rehabilitated through the gospel and the magisterium of the church.

This body, animated by the divine Spirit, is proclaimed blessed. In it God has worked the fullness of his wonders. Finally, we should not forget that the Immaculate Conception venerated on altars is the poor Mary of Nazareth, handmaid of the Lord, a woman of the people, insignificant in the social structure of her time.

The blessed Mary is the confirmation of God's preference for the most humble, little, and oppressed. Thus the so-called Marian privilege is really the privilege of the poor. The grace with which Mary is full is the inheritance of the whole people. Mary, the poor one of Israel, upon whom the gaze of the Most High rests with favor, is a model and a stimulus for the church to become increasingly the church of the poor.

4. The Assumption

The most recent of the Marian dogmas is the assumption, defined and solemnly proclaimed by Pius XII on November 1, 1950, in the Apostolic Constitution *Munificentissimus Deus*. The dogma's foundations are biblical texts, but read by the eyes of the church's tradition. The road traveled to the proclamation of the dogma is a road of faith, which has had to deal with obscure and challenging elements, scarce and contradictory objective data, relying on the people's religious feeling and what this has to say about their beloved Mary's final destiny.

The dogma of the assumption proclaims Mary to have been assumed into heaven "body and soul." The subject of the assumption is Mary's whole person. Mary is not a soul provisionally wrapped in a body, but a person, a body animated by the divine breath, penetrated by God's grace in every nook and cranny. Her bodily nature is fully assumed by God and carried into glory. Her assumption is not the reanimation of a corpse or the exaltation of a soul separated from its body, but the total fulfillment in God's absoluteness of the whole woman Mary of Nazareth. It also tells us something about the final eschatological destiny to which we are called. We are not a soul imprisoned in a body, and our body for its part is not an impediment to our fulfillment as human beings united to God. What we believe and hope for is already the case with Mary. Mary, glorified in heaven in body and soul, is also the image and the beginning of the church of the future, an eschatological sign of hope and comfort for the people of God marching toward its final home. This people, already redeemed and full of hope, but still in pilgrimage along the road of history, sees in Mary the real possibility of the Lord's Day arriving. With the assumption of Mary as the figure and symbol of the new people of God, the church is already, even in the midst of ambiguity and sin, the community of salvation, the faithful people it is called to be.

Mary's assumption also restores and reintegrates women's bodies, humiliated by the Jewish and Christian patriarchal prejudices, into the very heart of the mystery of God. Through Mary, women have the dignity of their condition recognized and assured by the creator of these same bodies. The masculine and the feminine in Jesus and Mary respectively are raised and assumed into heaven, finally to share in the glory of the Trinity.

Mary's assumption is closely connected to the resurrection of Jesus. Both events are concerned with the same mystery: the triumph of God's justice over human injustice, the victory of grace over sin. Just as proclaiming Jesus' resurrection means continuing to announce his passion, which goes on happening in the crucified and those who receive no justice in this world, so, by analogy, believing in Mary's assumption means proclaiming that this woman, who gave birth in a stable among animals, whose heart was pierced by a sword of sorrow, who suffered poverty, humiliation, persecution and her Son's violent death, who stood beside him at the foot of the cross, the mother of the condemned man, was exalted. Just as the Crucified One is the Risen Christ, so the Sorrowful Mother is the Mother assumed into heaven, the Glorious Mother. The assumption is the glorious culmination of the mystery of God's preference for what is poor, small, and unprotected in this world; there God's presence and glory can shine. The Father's same word confirms Jesus in the resurrection and Mary in the assumption. By doing this he indicates the road to follow, with Mary's example. Mary's assumption is sign of eschatological hope for the church, the people of God. It confirms its place among the poor, the outcast, all who are on the margins of society.

IV. HISTORY OF DEVOTION TO MARY IN LATIN AMERICA

In the history of Latin America there has always been devotion to and a cult of Mary. The first generation of the conquest was marked by much religious violence and destruction of the indigenous culture in the name of Christian purity and truth. The Conquistadores believed that the indigenous gods were evil and would certainly lead them to hell. As heaven was more important than earth, everything was permissible so that people did not lose the happiness of heaven after this fleeting life. For the Conquistadores Mary was always at their side against the Indians, whom they regarded as infidels. Theirs was a holy war, and so the Virgin protected them in the hard task of bringing the Indians to the faith.

With the second generation after the conquest the cult of Mary began to be integrated into Spanish-American and Portuguese-American customs. After the elimination of millions of infidels and the victory of the Conquistadores over the natives, there began a process of accommodation by the Conquistadores of the newly dominant religious culture. The integration of the cult of Mary did not take place immediately and without incident. The gospel preachers of the time strove to replace the native mother goddess by Mary, to prevent, they said, the continuation of idolatry. Despite this, we later find a syncretistic integration of the great indigenous divinities—and later of the black divinities—with Christianity. One example of this integration is the sanctuary in Mount Tepeyac in Mexico, a place of pilgrimage to the goddess Tonantzin-Cihuacoatl and later to Our Lady of Guadalupe.

During the nineteenth-century wars of independence from Spain and Portugal Mary played just as important a part as in the colonization period. The leaders of independence struggles in the Latin American countries believed that their devotion to the Virgin was one of the most important weapons they had in their fight for autonomy. In Portuguese America this happened on a lesser scale, but devotion to the Virgin was very popular from the time of the founding of the colony, where hermitages, oratories, and chapels were built in her honor. Mary was also the protector of many liberation movements, like that of the slaves.

Devotions to Mary multiplied in the eighteenth, nineteenth, and beginning of the twentieth centuries, with the growing influx of European religious congregations, who brought with them their homegrown devotions to the Virgin. Mary was the great companion and mother of many popular struggles in Latin America. Many peasant movements in Brazil, Bolivia, and Peru were stimulated by the people's love of the Virgin fighting with them for liberation. Another significant example is the devotion to the Purisima in Nicaragua during the period of the Sandinista struggle against Somoza. In El Salvador this same love for Mary led Oscar Romero to say: "The true homage a Christian can pay the Virgin is to strive with her to make God's life incarnate in the vicissitudes of our fleeting history."

Of all the devotions to the Virgin Mary in Latin America, the only one that can be said to result from an apparition held to be supernatural is the Virgin of Guadalupe. In other places on the continent devotion to the Virgin centers around an image, either found or sculpted by the natives or brought by the missionaries themselves. So Guadalupe has a special place in Latin American mariology. Fundamentally, its meaning is that the Virgin maternally adopts the "natives" of Mexico and with them the whole Latin American people. The apparition of the woman later called the Indita (little Indian woman) or Morenita (little dark woman) to the Indian Juan Diego has important historical implications. It demands absolute respect for the *other*; we must welcome this otherness and allow its right to be so. In this apparition the "divinity" of the white ones takes on the indigenous, or rather the indigenous takes this divinity as its own in order to assert its right to life in the face of white power. In her apparition the Virgin Mary speaks the same language as the Indian. She speaks his language, the language of his people, and not the colonists' language. The divinity appears to be taking sides with the weak, with the one to whom it is speaking and revealing itself. In order to raise the indigenous and give him power, the divinity speaks his language. The Indian understands her and feels absolutely certain of her protection. The apparition becomes an ally of the Indian, collectively, as the representative of an oppressed culture. The mission given to the Indian by the Virgin is to build her a temple. The initiative for this building comes from her, but the work of building it is done by the Indian. In this indigenous popular tradition it is the woman Mary who sends him out on a mission; in the Christian scriptures it is Jesus who sends. The Virgin does not have the same problems as the white oppressor. She loves the Indian and adopts him as her son. This gives him strength to fight for his own cause against the established church authorities. The carrying out of the Virgin's request means the affirmation of the identity of a people beginning a new moment in history. The apparition of the Virgin of Guadalupe and the growing devotion to her plays an important part in the restoring to an exploited people a religious identity that will help in the construction of a new national identity.

Our Lady of the Immaculate Conception, patron of Brazil, turned black in the waters of a river. She was welcomed by the poor and protected slave men and women and presided over black groups. When they "met" her in the waters of the River Paraiba, the fisherman Joo Alves and his two companions, who had not caught anything for a long while, suddenly caught an enormous haul of fish. The enslaved blacks of Brazil read the signs of Mary—among others she freed a slave chained to the door of her sanctuary—to indicate her disapproval of slavery in Brazil. Henceforth the black Virgin, who appears to the poor, has become a part of the inalienable heritage of the oppressed and marginalized black people of Brazil.

Many other faces and many other devotions signify the presence of Mary in the Latin American continent. However, we note these two because they relate to two sectors of the Latin American people who are particularly oppressed and discriminated against: the Indians and the blacks. For centuries both have been struggling and crying out for justice and for their place and their right to be acknowledged. The presence of Mary as an ally in their struggles is a significant factor for Marian liberation theology.

V. MARY AND THE ECCLESIAL BASE COMMUNITIES

It is not possible today in Latin America to speak of the church of the poor, of organization and the liberation struggle, without mentioning the ecclesial base communities. They are a new way of being a church, which has arisen among the people through God's Spirit. When we speak of the ecclesial base communities we turn to Mary again, this woman who carried in her womb and gave birth to the Liberator of the poor. She is the figure of the church and also of this church born among the poor.

The ecclesial base communities are a practical way of carrying out the church's mission. Their roots lie in God's word, in history, and in the new and original forms taking shape in their ordinary daily life. The base communities are made up of poor and suffering people who meet to reflect and celebrate their life and struggles in the light of God's word. This is why they are Good News. Mary was and is an actual person who carried out a project among the poor. With Jesus and Joseph she makes up a decent simple family struggling to live by the daily bread earned with difficulty. They are faithful followers of the line of Israelites who are "the poor of Yahweh." In her poverty and insignificance God plants in her the seed of liberation for a whole people.

The communities are a prophetic church happening in the midst of conflict. They worry the powerful, they are attacked and insulted by many, others want to manipulate them. Amid this web of conflicts the ecclesial base communities are trying to make their way and discover how to direct their faithfulness to the God of life. Conflict also underlay Mary's whole experience, through her "different" pregnancy up to her firm and faithful stance at the foot of the cross of her son, condemned as a subversive. At the heart of the dialectical tension between anguish and hope, love and sorrow, Mary and the people in the ecclesial base communities raise their prophetic cry of denunciation against injustices and proclaim the liberation that has already taken place for those who hope in God.

The ecclesial base communities have Mary very much in mind in their daily life and struggles. As well as a heavenly mother, holy and merciful, they see her as an earthly sister, a companion on the journey, mother of the oppressed, mother of the despised. She is the protagonist and the model for a new spirituality which has arisen from the well of life, the suffering and joys of the Latin American people. If Mary is—according to the Council—a figure of the church, we can surely say that in Latin America she is becoming more and more the figure of this church of the poor, happening in a special way in the base communities.

In her song the *Magnificat*, the people in the ecclesial base communities hear Mary's constant yes to God and God's plan, and at the same time her no to injustice and the state of affairs with which it is not possible to come to terms, no to the sin of indifference to the sufferings which make victims of others. Mary, the perfect figure and expression of the faithful people, the handmaid of the Lord, is also a prophetic woman who takes on God's word and the people's aspirations, who speaks and lives the denunciation of sin and the proclamation of the covenant.

So the church of the poor taking shape today in the ecclesial base communities needs to reflect more upon the person and mystery of Mary within the context of its oppression, struggle, resistance, and victory. Reflecting and working out a new theological discourse about Mary helps this church to take a look at itself, its identity and mission. It means confronting the person and figure of Mary, examining and discerning the truth of her yes and the timely daringness of her no. It means testing its witness and role as prophet, evangelist, and also martyr. It means evaluating itself in its commitment to announcing the Good News to the poor and outcast and denouncing everything that prevents this Good News becoming reality.

The document *Marialis cultus* vigorously asserts that Mary of Nazareth was "something quite other than a passively obedient woman to an alienating religiosity. She was the woman who had no doubt about proclaiming that God is the vindicator of the humble and oppressed and puts down the mighty from their seats" (no. 37). And Pope John Paul II states:

> The God of the covenant sung by the Virgin of Nazareth in the lifting up of her spirit is both the one who puts down the mighty from their seats and exalts the humble, he fills the hungry with good things and sends the rich empty away. . . . Therefore the Church is aware—and in our time this awareness is reinforced in a very particular way—that not only can these two elements of the message contained in the *Magnificat* not be separated, but we must also carefully safeguard the importance that "the poor" and the "option for the poor" have in the word of the living God. These are themes and problems organically related with the Christian meaning of freedom and liberation (*Redemptoris Mater* no. 37, par. 3, 4, and 5).

The church must look to her, mother and model, to understand in its wholeness the meaning of its mission. With her in mind the church must strive always to be converted every day to become a better servant of the Lord, the handmaid to whom he does great things.

—Translated by Dinah Livingstone

10

Ecclesiology in the Theology of Liberation

ALVARO QUIROZ MAGAÑA

Augustine's observation to the effect that theology has meaning primarily because it contributes to the fortification, purification, and invigoration of the faith, becomes particularly applicable today in the case of ecclesiology. No one today harbors the slightest doubt of the need for a serene, discerning, rigorous, and committed reflection, solidly based and pastorally oriented, on the church; that is, on what is and should be the church of Jesus today. What ought to be the manner of realization of the essence and mission of the church is not obvious and cannot simply be taken for granted in the present historical circumstances.

I. AN INESCAPABLE THEOLOGICAL TASK

This need for a reflection on the church has been very vividly experienced by the Christian consciousness of Latin America. We see it in the sheer number of ecclesiological works produced in recent decades. Many of these have been written with an eye to a particular pastoral situation which, in turn, supplies the raw material for the development of more complete and comprehensive syntheses.

There is nothing strange in this abundant ecclesiological production; for Latin America the current epoch has been one of great ecclesial vitality. We have the impulse of Vatican Council II. We have the challenge, confronted by Medellín, of effecting an ecclesial *aggiornamento* in lands of pillage and inequality, lands of misery, oppression, and injustice. We have the exodus of priests, laity, and religious to the periphery, out to where the poor live. We have the surprising resurgence of the church amid and from among these same poor, who burst upon the historical scene denouncing their unjust suffering and demanding justice and emancipation. We have the conflicts and tensions that arise within a society that resists change, and in a church the majority of whose members are more accustomed to preserving the status quo than to proposing social transformation. We have the dogged determination of Puebla not to give up, not to forget the poor, not to shut itself off from the grace of making its option for them. We have so much vitality in the church. All of this—truly the gift and power of the Spirit—lived in the midst of the humble and joyful, persevering and sanctified, crucified and suffering effort of men and women, groups and communities, has been the foundation, and is the substance, of this ecclesiological reflection.

This emerging, progressive ecclesial vitality stimulated the need as early as the 1970s, and with a growing urgency, to rethink the church. The classic ecclesiologies, which tended to be deductive, ahistorical, clerical, and hierarchical, were deemed insufficient for giving an account of faith and ecclesial life in this situation, amid the waxing, developing Christian praxis. It became essential to narrate the believing life anew, to allow the light of the gospel to shine upon it, to impel it toward a further pledge and commitment.

II. A NEW ECCLESIOLOGY FOR A NEW HISTORICAL SITUATION

In this context, an ecclesiological reflection of a liberative tenor has been taking shape within the vigorous current of Christian thought that is the theology of liberation. It is an ecclesiological reflection that presents itself first and foremost as "second word" (the first word is praxis), as critical reflection in the light of the gospel on life and on ecclesial Christian practice. It is a theological reflection that faces the question of the meaning of the church from the starting point of believers' growing commitment to the liberation of our peoples, from the liberative practices emerging in the midst of the poor.

1. A "New Praxis"

When we speak of a "new praxis," one demanding new kinds of theological reflection, we find it necessary to say something about the new and the old in the church of the Lord. There has been a great deal of reflection these last decades on the possibility and reality of change in the church. On the one hand, there has been a sense of the need to assert the indefectibility of this church, which is the Lord's, and which receives from him in ongoing fashion nourishment, origin, and life. On the other hand, it has been considered urgent to emphasize the fact that this very life, this very nourishment require that the church, at once holy and in need of purification (*Lumen Gentium*, no. 8), be constantly renewed, reshaped in every age in conformity with the demands of its being and mission. In this sense, new praxis is the same as renewal in fidelity. New praxis is response to a word that constantly summons us to emerge, to take the road, to go on a pilgrimage to a new land, to take up the cross and follow Jesus.

But a mere acceptance in principle that ecclesial change may be legitimate does not make it easy to identify and characterize that change. At any given moment the "new element" to be introduced is seen to be novel. Then it is gradually seen to be something belonging to all ages, a substantial datum of the church's fidelity. However, this does not cancel the novelty. The One who makes all things new is present and alive in the church, and communicates within it that novelty which, when all is said and done, is fidelity to what is most authentic, profound, and proper to that church. Thus, it is part and parcel of ecclesial commitment and responsibility to welcome, drive forward, and direct the element of the new that is being stirred up by the Spirit in the church of Latin America.

Latin American liberation ecclesiology does not pretend, then, that this is the first time the church has been renewed, or even the first time that the church has approached the poor. Indeed, this very ecclesiology has taken on the responsibility of demonstrating that, deep down, the church has always been faithful to the option for the poor (Eduardo Hoornaert, Clodovis Boff). Rather, what is meant is that for the first time in history, since this is what our epoch requires, the church has addressed the challenge of identifying with the poor and of walking with them along the road to liberation, to sociohistorical transformation. And this is seen as a privileged way of bringing into history the liberation of the gospel of Jesus.

On what does the novelty of this praxis rest? What is the basis and justification of this nascent ecclesiology? We are confronted here with a praxis that has come to be shaped by an emerging awareness that the current social situation is unjust and inhumane, that it cannot be willed by God—and likewise by an awareness that liberation is attainable, indeed part and parcel of God's salvific plan. It is a committed praxis, which seeks to overcome, with lucidity, all forms (so often dissimulated and concealed) of slavery, exploitation, institutionalized violence, and socioeconomic marginalization. It is a praxis that consists and can be summed up in the ecclesial option for the poor and their liberation.

In the same fashion this new praxis consists in the poor themselves bursting upon the historical and ecclesial scene. Our eyes have been opened; we cannot continue to overlook the suffering and unjust oppression of the poor who surround us. We went to them to bring them the gospel of liberation, and we discovered that we were being evangelized by them. We came to understand that we could not evangelize without a concrete involvement in the liberation of the poor, and we realized that the poor were the most important agent of this evangelizing liberation—these poor who, with their awareness, their words, and their actions, were proclaiming the gospel in a new way in our lands.

2. New Ecclesial Praxis, New Understanding of Reality

The theses of developmentalism have failed. Instead of diminishing, "under-development" or socioeconomic marginalization has grown tragically and enormously, compounded by political oppression and repression. This has obliged Latin Americans to formulate new conceptualizations of the reality of our peoples. Thus it has come to be understood that the situation in question is largely to be explained in terms of dependency; structural inequality; systematic exploitation; and the economic, political, and military interests of the mighty. Likewise, it has come to be seen that no change truly worthy of the name is possible without profound economic, political, and social transformation—a change in the social system itself. This, now formulated in terms of social theory, had previously become living reality in the concrete political practice of those who had already involved themselves in the process of transformation for justice.

Christians were not the pioneers here. Often others assumed the first, most difficult commitments. Providentially, however, Christians were soon incorporated into this dynamic, this practice of historical liberation. They committed themselves to it and gradually began to reflect on the situation of the church and the demands of the mission of that church in today's Latin America. Does the church have a concrete responsibility regarding the oppression of the poor in Latin America? Is part of the mission of the church to undertake a serious evangelical involvement in the historical liberation of our peoples? Does it pertain to the vital reality of the church to make a contribution to the formation of a historical agent capable of carrying forward this project of liberation?

All of these questions entered Latin American Christian consciousness, amidst a great ecclesial vitality. The church in Latin America had rediscovered the prophetic dimensions of the proclamation of the gospel, which remembered that persecution and martyrdom can result from following Jesus, and which found in communities of the poor, gathered around the word of God and living in a new way the kernel of the evangelical message, the very birth of the church by the power of the Spirit. Thus began one of the most important chapters in the history of the church of Latin America, and consequently of the history of the ecclesiology of liberation.

III. STAGES OF LIBERATION ECCLESIOLOGY

The history of liberation ecclesiology lies in the future, in two senses. First, there is a road to be taken. There must be growth, development, and advancement in commitment, reflection, and discernment. There are discoveries to be exploited, a pilgrimage in need of direction. One must persevere. Second, there must continue to be reflection on this life in the light of the gospel. Better theological syntheses must be constructed of what is most worthwhile in this reflection—a reflection to be carried out especially by the people of the poor and by those who are near them in a very special way. These must employ the charism they have received in gathering and restoring to the people the wealth aroused by the Spirit of God by way of that same charism.

Nevertheless, it is already possible to identify certain stages in liberation ecclesiology—stages that by no means constitute discrete, static, disconnected compartments adequately functioning on their own. In each of these stages, obviously, we shall encounter, however differently, the main components shaping the present historical and ecclesial era in Latin America. In each of them we shall observe the entry of the church into the world of the poor, and the irruption of the poor into the church and history. In each stage, we shall also observe an escalation in the quality of questioning—always in dependence upon the advance of life—a particular pace and tone in each step of this ecclesiology.

Pastoral Concerns: Approach to Life, to Reality

In a first stage, we might cite the ecclesiological reflections that have occurred as challenges to forms of pastoral ministry and church life that were no longer felt to correspond either to the reality of the times or to the requirements of change that were making themselves felt in our lands. Ecclesiological reflections were uncovering a certain "ecclesial malaise" in various groups of Christians, expressed in letters, communiqués, requests, proposals, and pastoral letters. Ecclesiology was registering the emergence of a "new awareness of the church of Latin America"

(Ronaldo Muñoz). More critical and analytical reflections, undertaken by theologians involved in this pilgrimage, were yielding the first elements of the theology of liberation. This first stage in Latin American ecclesiology is remarkable for the beginnings of a fertile interaction between church life, theological reflection, and episcopal magisterium. Conflicts between the magisterium of certain bishops and the propositions of certain theologians had not yet appeared. Later there would be talk of a "parallel magisterium."

Such reflections called attention to the inadequacy of a pastoral praxis that failed to take account of historical realities understood in the light of more critical analyses. A need was recognized for an understanding of the church in theological forms and models that would permit evolution, change, and adaptation (Juan Luis Segundo, Gustavo Gutiérrez, and others). It came to be seen that the battle for social justice, social commitment, and the transformation of the inhumane conditions of the concrete life of the majority of the inhabitants of Latin America ought to occupy the center of Christian life and the proclamation of the gospel.

Beginnings of Liberation Theology: Place of Reflection on the Church

The first extensive presentations of the theology of liberation (Gustavo Gutiérrez, Hugo Assmann, Juan Luis Segundo, Leonardo Boff, and so on) assigned a central place to ecclesiological reflection. These presentations reached the widest audiences, those of decisive importance in the shaping of this vigorous theological current in the contemporary church. They were not ecclesiologies themselves; far from it. They were works whose central reference, in the course of their advocacy of a new way of doing theology, was the central content of the evangelical proclamation. Their fundamental questions went back to basics. What is salvation? What does it mean to proclaim God as Father in a world of injustice and inhumanity? In what do the authentic life and message of Jesus of Nazareth consist? And so on. Of course, as they raised such radical questions, these works could scarcely avoid touching on their ecclesiological implications. Accordingly, they spoke, with prophetic vigor and unusual pastoral repercussions, of a decentralized church, a church in the service of the world and in solidarity with the poor and their cause, a church with a prophetic vocation, a church no longer able to use its much-vaunted uniformity as a palliative for historical division and antagonism among human beings, or its worship as a pretext for evasion or for the legitimation or dissimulation of reality.

Even the christological works that followed (Leonardo Boff, Jon Sobrino, and others) had decisive repercussions when the moment arrived for a reflection on a church that claims to be, seeks to be, and must be, a church that follows Jesus, a servant of the Reign of God, a sacrament of salvation in concrete history.

Reflection on "Models" of the Church

Liberation ecclesiology pointed out the insufficiency of the earlier models—christendom and neo-christendom—to respond to the new situation. The dual-level theologies, and the others that fail to account for the unity of history as authentic salvation history, must give place to theologies that speak more realistically of salvation in history and demonstrate the unity of the human and Christian calling (Gutiérrez, Ignacio Ellacuría, Leonardo Boff). Of course, this had repercussions on a view of the church; on the understanding of its fundamental being; on the way in which its biblical images ought to be understood, especially that of the people of God so dear to the heart of Vatican II; on the way in which the "notes" of the church, and the services and structures of that church, ought to be understood and projected. This was ecclesiology's "incarnational" way of accepting the invitation of Vatican II to make the church a church of communion.

All this made it necessary to examine at greater depth the various models of church. The clerical models had to be identified for what they were; more participatory models, which would enflesh an ecclesiology of communion already proclaimed at Vatican II, were proposed. Thus it was useful to characterize the various models, the various ways of being church, that had prevailed in history. These models represented concrete manners of incarnating the ecclesial calling, but not the only such manners. As models, they had their good points, but their limitations as well, and none could pretend to an exclusive validity for our own age.

On one hand, the models in question referred to the internal structure of the church (vertical model, participatory model). On the other, they had to do with its relationship with its broader surroundings, with its place in society as a whole, with its interconnections with the various sectors and classes of society (christendom, neo-christendom, *mysterium salutis*, church of the poor, and so on). This reflection on and discussion of ecclesial models rendered Christian consciousness more flexible, thus permitting the quest for a new model, a model shaped from the starting point of the poor, in the option for them, in the life rising up among them. This new model would respond to concrete situations of oppression and to the steps already beginning to be taken in the direction of liberation. The important thing, it was emphasized, was to find a model of church that would imply an interconnection, adequate for today, of the key categories of church, Reign of God, and world (Leonardo Boff), a model that would incarnate for present history the response of fidelity to the call of the gospel.

A Reflection at Once Convergent and Differentiated

It might be objected that, in the ecclesiological reflection of Latin American liberation theology, various necessarily united aspects of one and the same reality have come in for uneven emphasis. While sharing the same perspective, some ecclesiological works have attended more to the life of the church as community of faith and life, while others have emphasized the life of the church in its quality of concrete signification in and to the world.

Thus, some have set themselves the task of showing the Christian legitimacy of a new emerging model. They have sought to reinforce the thrust of a church reborn among the poor and making itself a charismatic community of faith and service—becoming a space for participation on the part of the poor, and remodeling its services and forms of authority. Others have insisted especially on the phenomenon of a people of the poor bursting upon the scene of a history built until now behind their backs and on their backs—an irruption that is a denunciation of death and proclamation of life, the presence of the God of life in a new experience of church and evangelization. Here it is that they have located the rebirth of the church.

Both tendencies or focuses have emphasized the potential for renewal with which this ecclesial rebirth is endowed. In these communities, poor and believing, weak and committed, praying and caught in the most unfavorable material conditions, the Father of Jesus, by the divine Spirit, is renewing the church of God.

Let us repeat: it is a matter of different emphases, not of mutually exclusive approaches. Indeed, if we examine the overall work of the various theologians respectively, we find what they regard as the two aspects of church: the ecclesial *ad intra* and *ad extra*. But this difference of emphasis is enriching for theology and for the life of the community. It calls attention to the reciprocity of a way of being church that, the more churchly it is, the more capable it becomes of plunging evangelically into the history of the poor and thus being a leaven of renewal for the church at large.

Finally, let us observe that these emphases also have their explanation in the various concrete ecclesial contexts in which liberation ecclesiology is produced—the various paths taken by a people whose constant suffering and trust in the Father of Jesus is reminiscent of the figure of Job, a people who, time and again over the course of their pilgrimage, drink from the well of their own spirituality (Gustavo Gutiérrez).

The Critical Accompaniment of the Church among the People

Beyond a doubt, in gathering up the experiences of the Christian community and handing it back as critical enlightenment and new impulse, this ecclesiological reflection has meant something precious to the pilgrimage of a church reborn with and among the poor—the church of a people, nevertheless, who pursue their course to liberation amidst an ever more evident and prolonged captivity.

Now, it is precisely in this last sense that liberation ecclesiology cannot be a finished whole, a closed system. It is an ongoing task, challenged at every moment by the novelty of history. What does it mean to be church in the midst of the emergence of the people? What is it to be church amidst repression and this obvious historical backsliding? What is it to be church amidst revolutionary struggles? What is it to be church amidst historical transformation, with the powerful seeking to apply a brake to the advance of the poor? And so on. All of these questions, which are anything but theoretical, constitute anguishing problems posed by reality itself. They must be addressed by ecclesiology on this continent of hope, as it has been called. It is indeed the continent where a believing community feels called to resist and to hope, even when there would no longer appear to be room to do so, a continent where successes are only seeds of future hope. In this sense, then, we must continue to speak of current liberation ecclesiology as an ongoing critical accompaniment of the pilgrimage of a people answering the call of the gospel of liberation.

IV. FUNDAMENTAL THEMES OF THE ECCLESIOLOGY OF LIBERATION

It is not easy to order the fundamental thematics of liberation ecclesiology. On the one hand, that theology has reformulated the central themes of classic ecclesiology and of the ecclesiology that stems from Vatican II. On the other, it has taken new paths in its search for a way to express, rather tentatively as yet, the effervescence of life engendered by the Spirit of God in the midst of the poor. Numerous ecclesiological compositions identify the notes of this new church. It will be useful, however, to present the main contributions of these various works.

1. The Church: Sacrament of Historical Liberation

Characteristic of Latin American life and ecclesial consciousness, and of Latin American critical reflection on the church, is the emphasis on the "mission of the church" in the face of the urgent need of salvation represented by, first, our all but universal misery and oppression, and second, by our longings and struggles for liberation. What we have, then, is an eminently practical consciousness, which keeps before its eyes the question of how to be and how to create church in the face of concrete challenges of this kind. Accordingly, when that consciousness reflects on the church as sacrament of salvation, it underscores the decentralization that this requires. The church is for the world. It exists because there is and must be salvation, and so it asks itself of what salvation it is the sacrament. It is the sacrament not of an individualistic salvation concerned with afterlife and existing outside of history, but rather of a salvation for the individual and for the collectivity. Such a salvation, while greater than history, is nevertheless realized in history itself. It is a salvation that, in today's Latin America, must be realized in the form of liberation—must be mediated in the economic, political, and social realities of human existence. Finally, it is a salvation that will be the rising up of the massacred and the eradication of institutionalized violence; a salvation consisting in real, concrete change, in a real community of sisters and brothers, reflected in the very structures of our social life. This is where eschatological salvation will have its starting point.

This is where the church of Latin America is coming to experience its mystery. Here, in the presence of the God of Jesus, this church is coming to discover that it will be a sacrament of salvation to the extent that it becomes a church of the poor and oppressed. This is meant not only in the sense that it makes an option for them, lives for them, and is persecuted for their sake (which would be no small matter), but mainly in the sense that it arises from them, from their believing response, and that thus they come to be the authentic and first subject of ecclesial life and structure.

2. The Church: Sign and Servant of the Reign of God

This understanding that the church is a sacrament of salvation has been deepened, in Latin American ecclesiological awareness, by a reflection on the church as sign and servant of the Reign of God. Appealing to Jesus' preaching and history as the foundation of the church, the church discovers itself to be the seed of the Reign, an entity in the service of the Reign. This service will necessarily be performed in the following and discipleship of Jesus—in the adoption of his Messianic practice and his cause. This is its response to the gift of the Reign of God, which it approaches in all awareness of its gratuity—a gift received, as well, where there is no actual church, but where there is an option for the human being, service rendered to the poor, a pilgrimage to a new, more just society of brothers and sisters. Shoulder to shoulder with those who, without professing the Lord, nevertheless do his will, the Latin American church understands that it must also labor in the construction of the anticipation of the Reign of God, the construction of its mediations.

Jesus centered his life on the proclamation of the Reign of God as gratuitous and salvific proximity. It was to be a Reign that, in conformity with the traditions of his people, would come as justice for the poor, eradication of sin, and actual transformation. Jesus himself was concretely at the side of the poor and oppressed, and he proclaimed them the special addressees of the Reign of God—not because they were better, surely, but because this is God's way of exercising sovereignty. He also preached the Reign as something future, while nevertheless corresponding to its approach by positing effective liberative acts even in the present. For the sake of the Reign—which necessarily comes in conflict with the selfishness and unjust power that oppresses the weak and thereby contradicts the spirit of God's family—he was sentenced and crucified. For his faithful obedience to death, he received in his resurrection not only the endorsement of his path and mission, but the definitive irruption, however inchoate, of the Reign he had proclaimed.

There can be no other authentic route for the church, then, than the following of Jesus in the service of the Reign. The ongoing conversion of the church, its words and its deeds, its internal structuring and its manner of presence in society, must be good news—an evangelization opposed to sin and effectively presenting the imminence of the Reign of God. In a historical reality like that of Latin America, then, the church must unequivocally embrace the service to the Reign that is to be performed by the church of the poor. After all, the latter are not only the priority addressees, but the actual vessels, as well, of evangelization, in their liberative practice as well as in their believing proclamation of its salvific, gratuitous meaning.

3. The Church: People of God

One of the biblical categories dearest to the heart of Latin American liberation ecclesiology is that of the people of God. In the wealth of this key biblical image, the theology that reflects from the underside of history, at the side of an oppressed, believing people, has found enlightenment and prophetic strength, a demanding calling and an attitude of thanksgiving, the opportunity to live in the following of Jesus amidst persistent captivity, and an implacable thrust toward liberation.

The expressions, "church among the people," "church of the poor," and "church of the people," are attempts to express the wealth of revelation in terms of a renewed ecclesial experience. They are expressions that have been and must continue to be submitted again and again to analysis and critique, so they may be consistent with the intention that has generated them; that is, the intent to give an account of an ecclesial renewal, arising from and transpiring among the poor. We speak of an ecclesial renewal that is calling, hope, and gladness for the entire church.

In keeping with Vatican II, liberation ecclesiology has underlined the fact that the church, the people of God, is not only structure and organization, but also, and principally, event. The church is the convocation of the people by God, and it is the people's response to God. Liberation ecclesiology has insisted on the primacy of Christian existence in the community over organization and functional differentiation within the same. It has understood and formulated with unusual clarity that the church that "recognizes in the poor and suffering the image of its poor and suffering founder" (*Lumen Gentium*, no. 8) must, in Latin America, be shaped as a church of the poor and oppressed, as a church of the people, if it is actually to be the people of God. Along these same lines, the ecclesiology of liberation has adopted the formula that the building of a church of communion must overcome the vertical, authoritarian, and closed structuring of a pyramidal, hierarchical model of church that fails to adapt to the basic content of the biblical category of people of God.

In order to begin to elucidate this theological category—people of God—liberation ecclesiology has developed a reflection along three intimately related lines. First, it seeks to explain what is meant by *people* in Latin America. This will be a necessary reference for a more concrete understanding of the church as people of God. It has identified the people as a people especially of the poor—those who answer the call of faith from out of their poverty—as well as of those who make an option for the poor, entering into solidarity with their suffering and their pathways of emancipation.

Second, liberation ecclesiology seeks in the biblical revelation concerning the old and new people of God elements that might shed light on the meaning of the church in its concrete configuration in Latin America today. Here it deals with a people summoned by the gospel of liberation and called in ongoing fashion to emerge from captivity and oppression to a life in the freedom and justice of the Reign of God, a people called to fidelity and ongoing conversion in the spirit of the Beatitudes: an authentic, persevering following of Jesus in this concrete history of ours.

Finally, on the basis of what has gone before, ecclesiological reflection plumbs the depths of the intense, concrete experience in Latin American lands of the birth of the church of a people poor and oppressed from out of their faith and their response to the Lord, from out of the experience of his mercy and his salvific tenderness. There the reflection discovers aspects of meaning and ecclesial vocation that have significance for the entire church. Thus, it finds that in a special way the base church communities are the locus of the gospel call to the poor and lowly. They, as communities of a crucified people, are the servant of Yahweh, called to establish justice and right, to uproot sin from the world precisely by taking it upon themselves.

In the privileged experience that the base church communities have begun to have is the vital root of this theological construction. It is here that the believing community experiences and formulates itself as people of God met together, as people of God called to emerge from oppression, as pilgrim people who, in conversion and faithfulness, are to become in truth a people. It is here that an oppressed, believing people has begun to take shape as agent of its own history—church history and overall history, sociopolitical history and spiritual history. It is here that an oppressed, believing people feels and knows that it is a people on the way to eschatological realization.

Particularly revealing, in this experience, has been the fact that the communities in question live in a renewed manner the communitarian dimension that typifies the people of God. This same experience is decisive in the accomplishment of the vocation of a scattered people to become a people assembled. The masses, which are not yet a people, find in these communities the indispensable impulse to raise their consciousness, "have their say," hear the word, respond to that word, and gradually become truly people of God.

When we speak of a church of the poor, then, we mean to testify to the rebirth of the people of God that is taking place on the outskirts of our cities, in rural areas, in native regions, in the places of socioeconomic marginalization and helplessness. The expression *church of the poor* connotes a church in which laity and religious, priests and bishops, have experienced a new call and have sought to respond with fidelity in service and solidarity with the poor; a church in which the gospel is announced in solidarity with the exploited classes; a church gathered by the proclamation of the gospel of liberation at the heart of the actual struggles for liberation; a church that is a congregation of all who, accepting Christ, receive the proclamation of his Reign and so serve to make that Reign a living reality.

A very special aspect of this acceptance and this service is solidarity with the poor. The solidarity in question is a concrete charity. It is solidarity with the individual and collective neighbor, solidarity with those near and far, solidarity with the compatriot and with the refugee, solidarity with the peoples who journey toward concrete, historical liberation.

The reason Puebla rejects the expression *popular church* is that it seems to indicate an alternative church to another, nonpopular, alienated church (Puebla Final Document, no. 263). Thus, with an insistence overlooked in certain ecclesiastical sectors, liberation ecclesiology emphasizes that, in Latin America, becoming the church of the poor is experienced not as the construction of an alternative church, but as the realization of a vocation. A church born of the people as church of the poor is the church of Jesus itself, a church of fidelity, of humble conversion and response to the call of the Lord who becomes living word in the oppressed, believing neighbor. It must be emphasized that this vocation of the church is the same vocation it has always had. After all, in all ages the purpose of the church has been to serve the Reign of God in the following of Jesus by the power of his Spirit. The new element today is that this purpose must be made concrete in the particular historical conditions of Latin America.

In this journey of a people of God, of the communities that in their lowliness are an authentic grace for the church of Latin America, liberation ecclesiology has also had a new experience and understanding of Mary—Mother of God and Mother of the poor—and of her role in Jesus' deed of liberation, of her place in the life of the believing community. It sees Mary as prototype of the church. She becomes once more the simple woman, the woman of the people, the mother of Jesus the carpenter's son, in solidarity with her folk and with the hopes of her people, handmaid of that Lord who topples the mighty from their thrones and exalts the humble, who fills the poor with good things and sends the rich empty away.

In this woman, who is blessed because she accepts and performs the will of God and maintains her fidelity to the last, her son's cross, in this nurturing mother of the nascent church gathered in the faith of the Risen One, liberation ecclesiology has found strength for the endorsement of Latin American women—doubly oppressed, as poor and as women. It has found the thrust to acknowledge and foster their participation in the management of the church, their role in the journey of a poor people who now burst upon history. In Mary, ecclesiology finds the creativity it needs to pursue the needed evangelization of popular religion.

4. Unity and Conflict in the Church

Inevitably and from the outset liberation ecclesiology has had to be concerned with the key theme of the unity of the church. In addressing this concern it has emphasized that the most serious breaches of this unity are those that reflect the objective division of society into counterpoised social classes. Here, our ecclesiology insists that the question of church unity cannot be dealt with apart from the sacramental reality of the church and its essential reference to the world. After all, the most profound truth of the unity of the church consists in the communion of believers with God and with one another, in the sharing of the trinitarian love that constitutes the concrete basis of all Christian relationships. The church, then, in our historical conditions, receives the gift of its unity and makes that gift real to the extent that it serves the process of the unification of the world. And in a world radically divided, the unifying function of the church community will be actualized in the struggle with injustice as the cause of division, and in the upbuilding of justice as the incarnation of concrete community.

By way of consequence—although on occasion it has been rather a point of departure—this approach to church unity seriously criticizes any ideological manipulation of church unity that promoting genuine unity, conceals and even legitimizes the historical divisions under which the poor of this continent are suffering.

Hand in hand with this reflection on unity, another is in progress: one concerning conflict in the church. The great ecclesial vitality to which we have been referring has been accompanied by significant tension in our church. Not all accept change in the same fashion, especially a sociohistorical change orientated toward a genuine participation and communion of our peoples. Not all accept the way in which the church must be committed here. This produces tension and conflict in the church.

The key to managing these tensions has been subordination to the Reign of God. Structures, norms, and institutional realities must be submitted to the norm of the Reign, and not vice versa. One must acknowledge one's own sin in this conflict-ridden situation; one must understand that it is not easy for the church to adopt this novel, liberative will of God, in the consciousness of which the new ecclesiology has been constructed. A spirituality of conflict, which is not plunged into panic by it but which is capable of discerning the will of God within it, which honestly seeks to transcend conflict in the direction of the Reign of God, and which is capable of undogged perseverance and deathless hope—all of this is the gift of the Spirit. It is a reproduction of the equally conflict-ridden experience of the first Christian communities, that is, their gradual discovery of God's will for the church in circumstances altogether novel and unforeseeable.

In this same area, the church of Latin America, and consequently the ecclesiology of liberation, inquires into the problem of ecclesial pluralism. How is the church to be *one*, faithful to the call of the Lord in the poor and oppressed, and at the same time a pluralistic church, marching to different drummers and expressing its response and its fidelity in different ways?

This whole theology of church unity is an actual experience, in hope, in the poor communities, the base church communities, which are like a "blessing from the Father who fills his church with new life" (Puebla Final Document, no. 96). These communities of true communion gradually are built up in a workaday reality. They are communities that make an effort to do honor to the name of God; communities in which the various charisms come to bear concretely on the building of a single church; communities that are not always heard within the church itself; communities that see their prophetic vigor and concrete commitment rejected by fear and power. Yet these communities not only maintain communion with the church universal but strive to promote it. Tirelessly they announce that the one gospel we must live in the church is that of Jesus Christ, the gospel of him who was crucified by the mighty of his time and raised up by the Father as savior for all women and men. They know and experience their weakness in complete surrender to the Father's mercy, and they know that their life and their opportunity to be seeds of the future in the church and in history rest in God.

5. New Services, Structures, and Ministries in the Church

Protesting concrete oppression and socioeconomic marginalization, and promoting actual participation on the part of Christians in the struggles and strivings of liberation, the Latin American church has felt the need for authority and ministry to be exercised in a different way. In the pastoral practice of the church of Latin America, and in the promising experience of the base church communities, a lively impulse of renewal has been at work. Initial successes have been realized in charismatic forms of ministry, service, and participation that are more in accord with the demands of the church's vocation today.

First, we see a growing, theologically sound participation on the part of laity—laity who are poor—in church administration. Everywhere we behold the appearance of new lay ministries. We witness greater autonomy of the laity as they participate as Christians in concrete struggles for liberation. There is an awareness that the praxis of liberation in actual ecclesial experience is a radical response to the Christian calling, and not the implementation of a charge received from the hierarchy. Nonetheless, this still calls for greater reflection and more practice before we arrive at a further clarification of the status of the laity in the church, a status that, on the other hand, must be on guard against an undue "clericalization" of the new lay ministries.

Second, there are new ways of exercising the priestly and episcopal ministry—more participatory ways, more democratic ways, ways that are more in the spirit of service and solidarity, ways more prophetic and more committed. Many pastors have carried their love to the limit, giving their lives for their brothers and sisters. This has not failed to have a clear impact on Christian awareness, which postulates that the service of Peter in the church universal be performed as that of a pope of the poor.

Before concluding this part of our reflection, we must cite the authentic transformation that is transpiring in the forms of religious life, as well—a life that has taken to the desert, to the outskirts, to the places of poverty whither none goes willingly or marches in triumph, to the frontier where the Spirit of God calls for the liberation of the people of God. There can be no doubt that the theological formulations that have inspired so many religious of both sexes in our time have to a large extent drawn upon the theology being developed from these new manners of practicing the following of Jesus and the service of the Reign of God.

V. ASPECTS OF CONFLICT AND POINTS OF DISPUTE

Discussion at the early stages, not only in the Latin American church but throughout the church, focused on the Christian legitimacy of liberation theology. An effort was made to show that the best liberation theology is a genuine contribution to the rediscovery of the Christian face of the church. It is a way of taking Vatican II seriously (Segundo). In this discussion, and in the indications of the pope and the bishops, a stimulus was found to avoid the dangerous extremes to which any theological reflection might be exposed. The same sources, however, provided a confirmation of the vocation of the church to become the faithful church of Jesus in the world of today.

Another important discussion, this time in the area of ecclesiology, centers on whether the church described in the ecclesiology of liberation is the authentic church of Jesus or an alternative church, a different church at the base or grassroots. As we have repeatedly stated throughout this chapter, the answer of the liberation church is that in Latin America becoming the church of the poor and being committed to the cause of their liberation is experienced not as an alternative, but as a calling of the entire church. Nor is this statement merely a piece of argumentation. Rather, it is witness borne in thanksgiving to the deed of the Spirit of God amid the people of God. It is also recognition of the church one and universal as both the source and the increasingly hearty welcomer of this same impulse.

Both discussions have a great deal more to do with the development of current events than with theoretical speculations—a great deal more to do with concrete solidarity with the cause of the poor and oppressed and their struggles for liberation than with dogmatic texts and definitions.

Precisely here is where a discussion has had to be sustained by the ecclesiology of liberation with other ecclesial sectors on the topic of the meaning of the option for the poor. Christian love cannot be divested of its radicality with adjectives that ignore God's partiality for the poor. Surely God wills that all persons attain salvation and come to the knowledge of the truth. But it is high time for an acknowledgment of the route that this universal salvific will has taken in the normative history of Jesus.

Once more in the area of liberation ecclesiology, an important investigation pursues the lines of an authentic integration of the political dimension into Christian and ecclesial life. What can be done so that we Christians, individually and in our communities, may responsibly assume the ineluctable political dimension of our faith? What aspects of this political dimension have a bearing especially on individuals? Which aspects concern Christian communities as such? What is the legitimate role, the role demanded by the gospel, of bishops, priests, and religious in their accompaniment of the poor? Here once more, the proposals that arise are in relation to the various concrete situations of our continent. Liberation ecclesiologists insist that concrete liberation is an intrinsic component of faith. Faith is more than an extrinsic motive for political praxis—as can be seen so clearly in the praxis of Jesus himself. Liberation ecclesiologists endorse a political participation on the part of the poor, a participation ever better, ever more lucid. We seek criteria for an adequate participation in this area on the part of priests and religious. We ascribe to politics a broader connotation than that of simple partisan militancy, especially in those countries in which any demand, any quest is considered in and of itself a confrontation with the power of the state.

What we are after, then, is a more adequate system of interconnection between the church reborn among the poor and the people's pilgrimage of liberation. What we promote is the creation of a subject characterized by solidarity and capable of seeing to it that history moves in the direction of the justice and communion of the Reign of God. In the face of such a challenge there are many different responses, but they all recognize the fact that praxis—experience subjected to reflection—will be able to contribute something more solid and reliable in this area.

VI. THE OUTLOOK FOR LIBERATION ECCLESIOLOGY

As we have indicated, one of the tasks that liberation ecclesiology has taken up is that of a committed, critical accompaniment of a people "on the way." In the execution of this task ecclesiology finds that the source of its progress is on the underside of history. It is not a matter of writing thicker and thicker books, with longer and longer indices. What is important is that the people live, that they have life in abundance, as the God of the Good News would have it. It is important that the pilgrimage of the people of God, the church reborn among the poor, is narrated with fidelity, criticized with authenticity, and thrust forward with vigor. Here, then, is a challenge to militant holiness, to full-time devotion to the people of the poor and to reflection with them. Here too is a challenge to theological dialogue and to teamwork—those characteristics so proper to the Latin American production of the theology of liberation.

Another of the tasks of the ecclesiology of liberation is to continue to demonstrate to the greater church the legitimacy of this way of being church. At issue, then, is not so much the legitimacy of a theoretical system as the legitimacy of a life that flows in novel, hope-filled channels, channels charged with pain and suffering, channels of conflict and cross, but channels, after all, of the precious grace that our divine Father has willed to give us in his beloved Child, Jesus. A greater openness on the part of the church in the difficult times of this winter of faith may be decisive if the people are to have life. The ecclesiology of liberation, with its solid, serious, and believing toil, its radical testimony rendered in communion (albeit at times in conflict as well), can be an important contribution to the maintenance, recovery, and enablement of that openness.

All of this takes place in the following and discipleship of the Crucified One, whom God has raised from the dead. God has given us in Jesus the true life that we ask for every day in the Our Father—that perpetual supplication Jesus bequeathed to us—when we ask for the Reign, for bread, for pardon, and for deliverance from every evil.

—Translated by Robert R. Barr

11

Sin

JOSÉ IGNACIO GONZÁLEZ FAUS

I. THE RICH WORLD AND THE LATIN AMERICAN WORLD

On the theme of sin the European and Latin American cultural situations look very different. So we need first to glance at these two situations.

In Europe there is endless talk about the "sin crisis"; sometimes there is even a denial that sin exists. There is no lack of data or cultural analyses of human experiences which seem to adopt such postures. Even though in Latin America there is the insistence that sin "brings death," in Europe the victims of this death may be ignored as not belonging to this world or are reduced—within it—to an easily hidden minority, or a minority unworthy of "democratic" consideration just because it is a minority.

However, in Latin America the vast majority are victims. Massive daily atrocities, oppression of human beings by others—or structural oppression—exist on such a huge scale that they are one of the most obvious factors in any assessment of the Latin American situation. This factor is so disproportionately great that when we perceive it we cannot help realizing that such atrocities cannot in any way be regarded as being caused by the limitations of a finite reality. They are gratuitous, unnecessary sufferings, caused by human responsibility and wrongdoing. They are not caused by the "unbearable lightness of being" so fashionable in Europe.

Hence, the danger in Latin America might perhaps be the overlocalizing of sin, thus *localizing it too partially*. The European danger lies in *blindness to responsibility* in the face of the shocking reality and the frightening depth of human guilt.

1. Human Beings Don't Just Sin—They Are Sinners

We must add that these cultural differences are not only to do with (economic and other) infrastructures. They are also linked to traditional superstructures, which in our case are theological ones.

To give an example, European theological tradition was very marked by the polemical insistence on works (resulting from arguments with Protestants), and also by the statement that humans are not radically corrupted beings (a statement also made in a polemical context against the so-called extreme Augustinians). So part of what is happening in the Catholic churches in the rich world can be explained by the fact that there is a price to pay for the onesidedness of those polemics.

The price of this onesidedness has been that, although the two above-mentioned statements were valid in themselves, they left the theological unconscious with the image of the human being as neutral in the face of good and evil, equidistant from both, not conditioned to decide for one or the other. (We might also inquire to what extent this latent image relates to the "sin crisis" characteristic of the First World. But for now we must leave aside questions of this sort.) In Europe the topic of sin is often tackled with this unconscious presupposition or image.

It was a Latin American (Uruguayan J. L. Segundo) who most clearly uncovered this latent image and brought it to consciousness. Instead of this "neutral" image (neither one thing nor the other), the Latin American trend has been to think of human beings in a more dialectical way (both the one and the other). Humans are beings infected by evil, almost identified with it; *at the same time* they are also beings enveloped in goodness and grace, called by it, and its seeds are sown in the deepest depths of their humanity. Both aspects belong to Latin American spirituality's most vivid experience.

2. Sin is Not a Matter of Weakness, But of Lying and Blindness

This theological difference has repercussions on a second point that is fundamental to the Latin American treatment of the theme of sin. We can illustrate this by another historical allusion.

In European ecclesiastical practice before the Council there was the impression that the fundamental example (the "first analogy") for speaking about sin was Paul's celebrated lament in Romans 7:14ff ("I do not do the good that I want but the evil that I do not want"). That is, the stress was on human experience of weakness and dividedness. Pre-conciliar preaching directed all the harshness of Paul's judgments toward this. Sermons harping on God's anger and human inexcusability amounted to a "pastoral tactic of fear." This probably also had something to do with the First World "sin crisis" we mentioned earlier.

To our surprise, the celebrated lament for human weakness in Romans 7 is situated in the chapters of the letter dealing with the justified person, who has "died to sin" and "lives in Christ Jesus" (cf., for example, Rom. 6:11). In these verses in Romans Paul does not mention God's anger at all. Indeed, he concludes with a surprising exclamation: "Thanks be to God through Jesus Christ! . . . There is now no condemnation for those who are in Christ Jesus" (Rom. 7:25–8:1).

On the other hand, Paul's judgment upon human sin and threat of God's anger are found, as we know, in the two first chapters of the letter. So it is here we must look if we want to find the fundamental analogy to speak about the theme of sin.

3. The Definition of Sin: Oppressing the Truth through Injustice

To sum up these two chapters, we can say that in them Paul vigorously unmasks the sin of pagans and Jews. Toward the end of chapter 3 he concludes that all are sinners and that in this respect the believer has no advantage over the Gentile.

It is important to note here that "Jews" and "pagans" do not simply designate two ancient peoples who no longer exist today. They refer to two ways of being human, or two components of every human being, personified in these peoples, but not confined to them. The proof of this lies in the fact that Romans 2: 14ff. calmly recognizes that there are good and honorable pagans, in spite of what has been said in chapter 1. This shows that chapter 1 was not talking about individuals—or groups of people—but about ways of being human. Likewise at the beginning of chapter 2, which speaks about the sin of the Jews, Paul is not speaking about the Jews as such but about "any man who sets himself up as judge," which shows that here too he is not talking about particular individuals but about ways of being human.

Of these two ways of being human, Paul says that God's anger is revealed toward the one (1:18) and that the others are inexcusable (2:1). Both these strictures affect each of the ways, because God's anger only threatens those who are inexcusable. Likewise, the definition of sin is the same in both cases, in spite of the difference that might occur in particular instances. So let us look at this latter fact a bit more closely.

The evil of the "pagan" way of being human lies in "oppressing truth through injustice" (1:18ff). The evil in the "Jewish" (or religious) way of being human lies in "judging the other while being the same as him" (2:1ff.). That is, the religious persons destroy the truth of their own equality with others through the injustice of one person condemning another. That is why Paul repeats throughout this chapter that only God is competent to condemn human beings. Pagans destroy the truth of their being as God's creatures and as the brothers and sisters of other human beings through the injustice of thinking of themselves as unique and like God and regarding their own wishes as the only moral norm.

The processes described by Paul are the following. "Pagans" commit "egolatry" of their own freedom; they oppress in this unjust "egolatry" the truth about the dignity and freedom of others. God's anger is revealed against them because they find they have become idolaters of things and, therefore, slaves to all the objects of their desire. The excuse mechanism generated by "pagans" to justify the divinization of their desires makes them become victim to them.

On the other hand, "Jews" make egoistical statements about their own morality and their own belief in God, thus using the good and even God as an excuse for setting themselves above others through the injustice of their pride in being superior. They too become inexcusable because by judging others they end up thinking of themselves as gods (like the pagans) and by raising themselves above others, they become subject to the same "dictatorship of desire" as the "pagans."

4. The Masking of Sin

"Jews" and "pagans" behave like this "without realizing." But they themselves are responsible for this unawareness, which makes it sinful, because it is the result of an impressive mechanism of excuses to blind and deceive themselves. For "pagans" the excuse is that God does not exist or is not concerned with what becomes of humans, or that the supreme norm of action is a presumed "rationality," which is not used as a means of criticizing the self and its desires but in the service of egoism. For "Jews" the excuse is that God is on their side because they say they are on God's side, or that God cannot fail to condemn the "pagans," and so on.

From this analysis of Pauline texts it follows that the first analogy for speaking about sin is not actions that we recognize as transgressions (*paraptomata*) for which we are sorry, suffer, or feel a sense of guilt. The sense of guilt acts a bit like a temperature in the sick organism; it is difficult to bear, but it implies a reaction against the disease by the healthy part of the organism. Real sin (Paul's *hamartia*) involves an *identification* with the sin by the one who commits it, which makes him or her become a liar (cf. John 8:44: Satan who is a liar and father of lies) or blinds his or her heart (cf. Mark 3:5). In this way sin is masked from human beings (or rather it is human beings who mask it from themselves) to the point where the sense of guilt becomes anesthetized. This, for example, is the sin of the Pharisees throughout the whole of the Fourth Gospel. Jesus comes to unmask this sin; if they recognized that they were blind they would no longer be guilty, but because they say they can see, their sin remains (cf. John 9:41).

Through this view of sin perhaps liberation theology, without realizing it, has acted in the same way as the Jesus of the Fourth Gospel did in confronting the religious power (or like Nathan the prophet before David); it has unmasked the sinful arrogance of the First World, which was camouflaging the truth with injustice to the point where "they became futile in their thinking and their senseless minds were darkened" (Rom. 1:21). In this context, as a very clear example, it is worth noting how often—in writings on spirituality!—Jon Sobrino has spoken about "keeping faith with the real" and paying attention to "the obvious" as surprising elements in any radical following of Jesus.

What we have to show now is that from this conception of sin as the masking of the truth by unjust egoism, derive the two other characteristics we must comment on as typical of liberation theology: the structural aspect of sin and the content of sin as damaging the human being.

II. STRUCTURAL SIN

One of the most characteristic contributions of Latin American theology to the theme of sin has been the notion of structural sin or structures of sin. One feels tempted to compare this notion with the traditional legend of the ancient Guarani people, about the search for a "land without evils." But here we must confine ourselves to the theological aspects of the subject.

For Cartesian individualism born together with the modern era in Europe, it has not been easy to understand this idea which, nevertheless, enables us to explain how personal evil is both active and masked at the same time. One person alone could not construct this whole system of excuses, which we saw in the previous section. Neither could a single individual reason place itself so effectively at the service of "pagan" covetousness if it were only acting individually and instantly. But where people live together they are never merely contiguous like a simple juxtaposition of stones. They are inserted into a world of mediations and institutions: family, marriage, profession, city, economy, culture, state, and so on.

Therefore the human community is always more than the sum of single human beings.

This is why the community and the structures governing life together in it can create, more easily than the individual, a series of situations making necessary (and therefore apparently reasonable) ways of behaving which favor individual greed, even though these harm the life and dignity of many others. Therefore evil, like the human being, is never just personal, although it is also personal. And therefore any personally sinful human being is both responsible and a victim.

In the space we have here we can only try to justify this notion of structural sin and show some of the consequences it entails.

1. Discussion and Justification of Structural Sin

By this insight Latin American theology has recovered another fundamental scriptural idea—the Johannine notion of the sin of the world. This notion is so central to the evangelist that sometimes he calls the sin of the world simply "the world," giving the world a negative significance it does not always have in his gospel. In these cases "the world" means a socioreligious order hostile to God or an oppressive system based on money or power for the few. This sin makes the world unable to grasp the truth: the truth that God is a Father and just (cf. John 17:25) and human beings are therefore God's children and brothers and sisters of one another. For this evangelist the sin of the world is the decisive antagonist of Jesus, who both unmasks it and dies as its victim. But then the evangelist sees this murderous death as the most radical demonstration of the sin of the world.

Liberation theology has recovered this Johannine notion, even though it may be said that it has formulated it almost exclusively in terms of economic structures (a logical procedure given the enormous cry for the most basic human necessities lacked by the great majority of Latin Americans). The recovery of this concept has met both with radical condemnation from some European theologians and the decisive support of Medellín and Puebla, as well as that of Pope John Paul II.

In fact, even in the introduction to its documents, Medellín spoke about oppressive structures which are the fruit of exploitation and injustice. It spoke of unjust situations in which the sins of unsolidarity are crystallized. Puebla teaches that sin, which it defines as a "rupturing force," prevents human growth in fellowship. Sin is not just something done by each individual but is also committed in these sinful structures, which are created by human beings (Puebla Final Document, no. 281). The teaching of both assemblies can be summarized in this simple circular phrase: *When human beings sin, they create structures of sin, which, in their turn, make human beings sin.*

But perhaps the best definition of structural sin, together with an intuitive perception of its novelty and profoundly Christian roots, is found in the following words of Oscar Romero's Second Pastoral Letter, written in 1977:

> The Church has denounced sin for centuries. It has certainly denounced the sin of the individual, and it has also denounced the sin which perverts relationships between human beings, particularly at the family level. But now it has again reminded

us of what has been fundamental from its beginning: of social sin, that is to say, the crystallization of individual egoisms in permanent structures which maintain this sin and exert its power over the great majorities.

This language was adopted by John Paul II when he visited the Puebla Assembly in Zapopán and spoke of "multiple structures of sin." More recently, in his encyclical on the social question, this language appears to have intensified. The pope asserts the legitimacy of the notion of structural sin. He also uses it to talk about the "theological reading of modern problems." Finally, in the conclusion he sums up by saying that liberation should overcome "sin and the structures of sin that produce it" (*Sollicitudo Rei Socialis*, nos. 36, 37, 46).

These teachings allow us at least to question the severe strictures by certain great theologians (Urs von Balthasar and J. Ratzinger, among others) against the language of structural sin. They accuse this language of denaturing what is most profound in sin—that it is the fruit of a personal and responsible freedom. These words cannot be applied to a structure. Therefore, according to these theologians, the concept of structural sin goes against Christian teaching on sin.

But it would not be theologically correct to limit ourselves to criticizing these attacks through an appeal to external authorities, even the authority of the church's magisterium. We must also point out in what way they are wrong. They forget the analogy of the Christian notion of sin. According to their argument, it would also not be Christian to speak of original sin, given that this cannot be defined as the fruit of a free and responsible decision by each person (or can only be explained thus in a completely mythological manner by supposing that the freedom of all human beings was already present in Adam's free will, as some post-Tridentine theologians say). If it is theologically legitimate to speak of original sin, it is also legitimate to speak of structural sin.

In the Christian notion of sin there are other features besides the fact that sin is the fruit of a personal and responsible freedom. Sin also means that which God rejects and cannot accept in any way. Therefore denying the notion of structural sin is equivalent to saying that the present situation of the world (and in particular the third-world countries) is not a situation that arouses God's rejection and anger. Accepting the notion of structural sin means we are saying that the relationship of all humanity with God has been degraded, precisely because of the degradation in the relationships of human beings to one another.

2. Consequences and Examples

It is necessary to stress that structural sin is the sin of the world and not only of a particular situation. Puebla speaks of it as a "permanent process" (Puebla Final Document, no. 281). It is structured in different circles according to the different cultural situations or economic relations. The center of each of these circles is always falsification or the oppression of some human beings by others.

Let us give some examples. The two ruling systems in our world are based upon a lie that is never stated but transmitted through the injustice of their socioeconomic relations. The false truth of capitalism is that a human being *is not worth anything*. The false truth of the communism existing at the moment is that a human being is *always an enemy*.

From these structural attitudes, personal forms of behavior necessarily follow, which are justified by the reasons inherent in the system. It is a well-known fact that during the great earthquake in Mexico City the owners of some firms were first concerned to get their machines out of the ruins, before the—still living—bodies of many of the buried women operators. This anecdote is not exclusive to a single country, especially not a "backward" country. The German journalist Günter Wallraff disguised himself as a Turkish immigrant and spent two years working in Germany in this disguise. The incredible stories he relates are far more inhuman than the Mexico story.

Facts like this seem incredible when we hear them as isolated anecdotes out of context. But they are completely rational within the logic of competition and profit maximization; the machine cannot be replaced without a considerable investment, whereas it is quite easy to replace the worker.

On the other hand, current socialist systems do not deny the value of human beings, but they do deny that human beings can be trusted. Because any human being may belong to another class, or may not have a correct consciousness of his or her own class (and so if left free will be an obstacle to the true interests of his or her class, which are only properly represented by the minority of Party members), Party members feel not just authorized but obliged to reserve to themselves all power of taking initiatives and making decisions—and denying this power to everyone else. This gives rise to a system as oppressive as the previous one.

One more smaller example, which is nevertheless worth quoting because it is very topical, is this. In my opinion the present culture of the North American masses (especially the culture "for export") is a system which exudes justifications and exaltations of violence—a violence which is indeed always masked as the defense of justice or freedom, even the defense of God (and sometimes simply boldfaced defense of one's own interests). It is impossible that a world which subliminally inhales these values, as a form of entertainment or relaxation, should not in the long term become inhumanly aggressive and violent.

All these examples show how difficult the struggle against structural sin is, because structural sin is not the sin of one single human system but of the whole human system. Fighting it and unmasking it can mean dying at its hands as Jesus did. Victory over it only happens gradually and slowly, and the human forms it takes are frequently forms of crucifixion.

III. SIN AS HUMAN DAMAGE

By the route outlined above and—above all—through the shocking experience of the suffering of so many innocent people, liberation theology has been able to identify the true meaning of the Christian notion of sin: human damage.

Perhaps this definition scandalizes scholastic theology, which has become accustomed to repeating mechanically that sin is only an "offense against God," managing by its routine traditionalism to confuse an offense against love with a mere offense "against the master." Therefore it is useful to remind ourselves that even in scripture the father of sin (Satan) is, even etymologically, the "enemy of man." This has an even stronger reading in the Fourth Gospel: Satan, "a liar and father of lies," is therefore "a murderer from the beginning" (John 8:44). Masking the truth is, as we have said, the way to kill or damage other human beings.

We cannot deny that here liberation theology appears also to be reacting to another theological tradition that immediately preceded it. This was an excessive stress on sin as a pure transgression of a law. This notion can have some legitimacy, but when it becomes exclusive it is enormously dangerous.

1. Sin and Transgression of the Law

Its legitimacy is rooted in the fact that if lying belongs, as we have said, to the essence of sin, human beings will always tend to deceive themselves with respect to what constitutes their true fulfillment and what damages it (as we saw happened to the "pagans" and "Jews" in our first section). In this sense Paul—in spite of his harsh attacks on the law—does not flinch when he then goes on to speak provocatively of the "law of Christ." But the conception of sin as a mere legal transgression is also subject to the following dangers:

1. The notion of law *through its very nature* never manages to overcome the impression of a certain arbitrariness. Here we may recall the blind alley that certain hoary old scholastic discussions got themselves into: Is something evil because God forbids it, or does God forbid it because it is evil? If we answer the second, then God is not free to be the ultimate lawmaker, because God is also subject to an external law and dependent on it. But if we answer the former, then God cannot help being an arbitrary God, because whether things are evil or no, the content of sin is often reduced to the unjustifiable pure whim of the lawmaker.

This sense of arbitrariness is reinforced by the abusive practice of the ecclesiastical power, which declared as mortal sins (that is, causes of a human being's *ultimate* failure!) certain practices connected with Sunday Mass, annual confession, and church tithes. This teaching contributed to the encouragement of the image of sin as an arbitrary or voluntary imposition rather than as real damage to the human being. This image is also the basis of the Western sin crisis.

The shocking experience of suffering and deprivation of the most basic conditions for humanity, affecting so many Latin Americans, has redeemed liberation theology from this one-sidedness into which first-world theology had fallen. If the capitalist who grows rich by paying miserable wages offends God by missing Mass on Sunday but not by letting his employees die of hunger, God becomes a sort of arbitrary little king, more like Herod than the Father of Jesus.

2. Law *in human experience* never manages to be free of all imperfection and injustice, especially toward those who are the most oppressed in any situation and have the least voice in it. Here we may quote the vigorous verses of Bishop Casaldáliga:

> . . . I want to subvert the law
> that turns the people into sheep
> and the Government a slaughterhouse.

He does not appear to be referring to a single law, because he also writes:

> Cursed be all laws
> drawn up by the few
> to defend fences and cattle
> and make the earth a slave
> and slaves of human beings.

Putting it more prosaically, with less lyrical imprecision, laws are bound to be *made* by the powerful, and therefore formulated to defend their *own* interests against the interests of the poor. The law is also *applied* by the powerful, and therefore even if it were perfect its application would always be (at least partially) unjust. The sabbath in Israel or the laws of the Indians in Latin America can be cited as typical examples of the enormous distance between their day-to-day application and what Jesus—in his polemic against the sabbath—calls "doing good to human beings" (cf. Matt. 3:4). Damage to human beings as the true compass point for any notion of sin is the only one that can overcome this degeneration and with it the degeneration of the consciousness of sin.

2. Sin and Offense against God

Finally, it is only through this fundamental compass point of human damage that we can recover the notion of sin as an offense against God. The church's magisterium has defended with clear insight that sin must also be defined in this way, in spite of apparent philosophical reasons against it. But the notion of an offense against God would have no meaning if we did not add something that was fundamental in primitive Christian theology (up to Thomas and his commentators): an offense against God is *human damage*.

Unfortunately, quite often both church practice and Western scholastic theology have been marked by an idea of sin as an immediate offense "against the gods," without any human intermediary. This is actually a pagan idea and comes from Greek mythology: Ixion, Prometheus, Sisyphus, and others. The first of these raped Juno. The second stole fire from the gods to give it to human beings. The third revealed to Aesop the place where Zeus was holding his kidnapped daughter. Their punishments are well-known in the corresponding myths. The important point to note here is that both Prometheus and Sisyphus offended the gods *for the sake of human beings*. The offense against the god was, in their case, good for human beings. Even when it rejected and demystified this conception of sin, Christian theology sometimes remained more imbued with it than it should have been. In my personal opinion (which I want to stress is not part of liberation theology) the claim of the past that the pope had power to impose things under the threat of a "grave offense against God"—even though this power is not used today—has been one of the greatest sins committed by the papal power and sometimes an offense against human beings, who were brothers and sisters of those popes and liberated by Jesus Christ from the curse of the law.

IV. CONCLUSION

Having said this we must recover the other element and add that this human damage lies precisely in the theologal dimension of sin. Let us describe this dimension in Jon Sobrino's words. He presents it as a *trinitarian* dimension. In every sin, precisely because there is an attack upon human beings—God's image recapitulated in Christ—there is a falsification of the trinitarian truth of God: God as God is and God who is the salvation of humanity. It so happens that human (historical, personal, and social) fulfillment comes about in a trinitarian form. Sobrino continues:

> Put negatively there is a sin against the Father when the mystery of being-referred-to-the-other in a saving way disappears in favor of one person's self affirmation. But sin also occurs when the Father is made exclusive and absolute. Then political monarchies appear and ecclesiastical paternalism, which confuse the Father's free plan with the imposition of an arbitrary will, the Father's absoluteness with despotism. They ignore the fact that God's mystery is expressed in Jesus and produces the liberty of the Spirit.
>
> There is sin against the Son when the scandalous actual historical reality of Jesus disappears in favor of pure transcendence or sentiment, as if Jesus were provisional and not God's definitive approach to human beings and of human beings to God. But there is also sin when the Son is made exclusive or absolute. Then we get voluntarist imitation, law without spirit, the closed sect instead of open fraternity. This ignores the joy of the Father's free giving and the Spirit's inventive imagination.
>
> There is sin against the Spirit when openness to historical novelty disappears as a manifestation of God. Acceptance of this openness brings life to history, instead of simply judging it from the outside from the standpoint of a truth that has become a deposit. This suffocates the ecstatic movement, which not only liberates us but makes us come out of ourselves. But there is also sin when the Spirit is made exclusive or absolute. Then we get anarchy, that disregards the actual reality of Jesus and rejects what is dangerous in his memory (Sobrino, "God," in *Concepos fundamentales de pastoral*, pp. 257–58).

Or in other words:

It is true that God is the term of "relegation" for human beings. But the power God has over human beings is none other than the human truth of the Word and the humanizing force of the Spirit—not a coercion alien or external to the human being. Thus the nature of humanity and the nature of an offense against God coincide.

It is also true that God has definitively approached human beings. But this approach does not cancel human history, making it merely a stage for a "test" of each human being or authorizing humans to escape it. God offers history to human beings as scope for their human creativity, so that they can transform it into the Kingdom of God: a space of freedom and justice, for giving and fellowship. Therefore an offense against God is through damage to human beings.

It is also true that God is inexhaustible newness for humanity; God is always greater than everything human and an affirmation of a supreme and unassailable freedom. But this newness has certain well-defined features in the new humanity of Jesus and the struggle for a new humanity for us. Therefore, lack of respect for the human or falsifying it is always an offense against God.

—*Translated by Dinah Livingstone*

12

Grace

JOSÉ COMBLIN

For purely practical reasons we shall divide this chapter into two parts: the grace of God from the point of view of being and the grace of God from the point of view of acting. Thus for purely didactic reasons we shall adopt the scholastic distinction between habitual and actual grace.

I. GRACE FROM THE POINT OF VIEW OF BEING

1. Visible or Invisible Grace? Material or Immaterial Grace?

Old scholastic theology firmly stressed that grace was invisible and could not be felt because of its "supernatural" character. Some scholastics defended the thesis that between a person gifted with supernatural grace and another deprived of this grace there would be no perceptible difference. According to this conception grace only affects the soul and would not penetrate into the human body; it is purely a modification of the soul. From our point of view grace is naturally nonmaterial and invisible in its origin: if God is invisible his gift of grace, his love for humanity, is also invisible; or rather, it is invisible in God, its source. However, if God's gift is received by a material bodily human being, it must in some way also be bodily and material. If grace does not produce material and bodily modifications, it does not exist for the human being, it does not penetrate human life, it remains alien to humanity. Therefore grace is material and bodily in the sense that it brings about modifications in the material and bodily human being. A human being does not have a pure spirit, which could remain separate from the body. It is not possible to imagine that something could penetrate a human soul without also penetrating the body. This bodily effect can be looked at from three points of view.

1. The human being is his or her relation to the material world, the cosmos. Human beings relate to the material world primarily through work. Therefore God's grace brings about a change in that work, the work regime, relationships, and experience. Communion with God is inscribed into the work regime, because God relates to human beings through matter, God's grace enters into conflict with slav-

ery, with forms of servitude, with capitalism, and with all regimes of alienation and exploitation at work. The sign of God's presence is the actual conflict itself with such work regimes.

2. The human being is also his or her relationship with fellow human beings. This means the relationship between man and woman and the relationship between brothers and sisters, community, primary or secondary groups, tribe, nation, race, the whole of humanity. These relationships are inscribed in customs, institutions, commitments, alliances, different forms of communion, conflicts, reconciliation. God's grace is thus a new relationship in all these dimensions, from the relationship between the sexes to the relationship between races and nations.

Relationships among human beings are also bodily ones—family relations of course, but other relationships are all conditioned by geography and set within the different situations of bodies on earth. They are set in villages and towns, houses and roads, natural regions and frontiers, continents and seas, mountains and rivers, climates and in the process of material production. God's grace is set geographically. We may think it was more present in ancient villages than in our present megalopolises with their shanty towns and cardboard cities. It was more present in the Paraguayan "reductions"—Indian settlements set up by Christian missionaries—than on the Conquistadores' great estates. It was more present in the indigenous villages themselves than in the Potosi mines.

3. God's grace has effects on the actual individual human body. Jesus' presence was a source of health for the sick, the blind, the deaf, and the dumb. There is a continuity throughout Christian tradition: grace restores health. It is true that in recent centuries the bourgeois churches have discredited the healing of the sick as a pastoral practice, but it has been always carried on in the popular churches. It has always belonged to popular Christianity. It is not healing by magic, the automatic application of a formula of words, signs, or remedies. But it does have beneficial effects upon the body's health.

A grace of God that only affected the human soul would not have any value for ordinary people. Grace must have visible and palpable effects, evident in the human body. This bodily effect is not something alien to the natural body. On the contrary, it is the body's health, a healthy way of living together for human beings, and health at work. The effect of grace is not something "over and above" the human body but within the natural mortal body. God has approached the human body and made it worthy of his intervention. Grace does not create another body but gives health to the body we have.

It is quite certain that what always constituted Christianity's great attraction for ordinary people was God's compassion for the human bodily state. Christianity was not a religion of notions and ideas, a religion for philosophers or intellectuals. It offered remedies for human ills, sufferings caused by sickness, social battles and disagreements, exploitation and alienation at work. God entered into the life of the human body.

Grace does not confer actual immortality; it does not eliminate all physical and moral evils, either individual or social. It does not eliminate them but it does alleviate them and make living in this world more tolerable, more human.

2. Grace as the Presence of the Future

The Christian message is Good News, that is, openness to a future, an open history. It offers humanity a future. This is not just a promise of a future life, especially not just a future life in another world after death. Ordinary people abandoned Christianity when they were given to understand that all the church had to offer them was heaven after death. This message is of no interest. It is of interest only to the privileged in this life, because it enables them to reject the just demands of those who are unjustly oppressed in order to preserve their privileges.

In Christianity the future becomes present. The life of heaven is of interest in so far as it offers a goal and a content for this life here on earth. Eternal life is of interest if it sets up a norm and a pointer to a better life here on earth. Jesus never separated his proclamation of the Good News from the present. What he proclaims, he demonstrates and creates in the present. In fact, in the Christian scriptures promises for the future mean the coming of a present reality. Grace is the presence now of humanity's future, of creation's final success. Jesus does not offer a present emptiness for the sake of future fulfillment. The future fulfillment is already a present fulfillment, limited only by the limitations of the present human condition.

A New World

The Christian scriptures announce the coming of a new creation. This has already begun. The Word of God, which was present at the creation, is acting again. It is remaking creation, restoring it. This means that human beings cannot be separated from the earth and the material world; their transformation is part of a transformation of the world, even though human beings are the culmination and heart of this new creation. Grace is the beginning of the new creation, as it can be experienced at the present stage of evolution. The Spirit is renewing the face of the earth. Grace is this renewal, necessarily linked to the renewal of humanity.

A New Humanity

Paul proclaims the coming of a new human being. The new human being is virtually the whole of humanity. It is Christ and it is humanity restored in the Risen Christ. It is the new humanity of the Risen Jesus, which penetrates human beings, and also groups, bodies of people, and human relationships at all levels.

The new humanity is the Kingdom of God spoken about in the synoptic gospels. God conquers the Kingdom, God battles to restore the Kingdom in creation. God reigns to the extent that justice and true peace are restored.

God's Kingdom is the reconquest of humanity. It is a struggle against alienation, corruption, and death. It is the resurrection of humanity in its perfection. The Kingdom of God is humanity restored to its dignity and true worth.

The Kingdom of God is among the poor and oppressed. It is the struggle for the release of the oppressed and the exaltation of the poor. God's Kingdom has been proclaimed by the Beatitudes, which are the heralds of the Kingdom. There, amid the poor and oppressed, God begins to reign once more.

The new humanity is also called the new people of God. Among the poor and oppressed a new people of God is arising. Among the poor and oppressed a new people is arising with all the attributes of the people of God. From a scattered multitude God creates a people. From the weakness of the poor God creates a power that challenges the powerful of the earth.

In this people of God there is a new covenant between God and humanity. In the festival of eating and drinking the eucharist, the new people celebrates its new covenant with God. Grace is the experience of this covenant in the life of the new people, in their common struggles, hopes, sufferings, and victories. Through the covenant God is committed to the poor and oppressed. God's faithfulness is the grace which lays the foundation of all rights and the dignity of the new people.

The Community

The new people is embodied in particular communities, in which particular people live their lives in their multiple day-to-day relationships. The community makes present all God's gifts and is the particular way in which grace becomes actual among the poor and oppressed. In the community the risen body of Jesus becomes present. Christ's body is experienced in the small communities. In the eucharistic communion the bodies of those present form a continuity: they all share the same bread and are united in the same loaf of bread and the same cup of wine. The Holy Spirit is in the community. The community is the time of the Spirit. In the multiplicity of its interwoven activities the diversity of the gifts of the Spirit are manifest. These gifts are the grace of God.

Christian life is lived, nourished, educated, expressed, and created communally. There is no individual grace isolated from other graces. God's graces in individuals are connected and form one single grace. God does not open to one person alone but to each person with his or her community and to each community within the community of communities that forms the people of God.

The Person

The communitarian character of grace does not take away its personal value, because the community is an exchange and communion of persons. The grace of God is the restoration of personality, the firmest guarantee of the human person, what permits it to exist in the fullness of personality, because the person is the correlative of the community, rather than being in contradiction with it. God's grace is directed toward every person within his or her community, which is precisely what enables a person to become a person. The human being is not a person to the extent that he or she shuns others, but to the extent that he or she communicates with them. The measure of personality is also the measure of community. It is true that grace is a dialogue between God and the human person, but this dialogue is not a closed dialogue—"God and my soul"—but a dialogue in which many other persons are present, with whom each person communicates, and who give him or her the actual content of their personality.

In the Bible grace is called life or eternal life. This life becomes present now. It is both the life of the person and the life of the community. It is the life of the people in the life of all the communities.

Grace is also justice and holiness. It is the moral perfection of the human being. It is the human being restored to fullness, although within the limits of the development of the individual, community, and culture to which the community belongs.

Finally, grace is freedom. Freedom is both a gift and a vocation. It is the supreme gift because it is the gift that makes a human being the image of God. God's grace is very far from absorbing the human being into God. Far from making the human being disappear into a divine pseudo-totality, grace restores freedom; it establishes the human being as a personal subject distinct from God, independent of God, autonomous, capable of taking up a position, even against God who has given him or her this freedom.

Freedom exists in a conditional and limited way in this world. However, it is not just an illusion. It can be born and grow. It does not have to exist. It requires work and conquest, a struggle against many obstacles and adversaries. Nevertheless, it can exist, and it is what constitutes both the person and the community.

Freedom does not remain on a purely metaphysical level. It is experienced at many levels in daily life. Freedom is experienced in the formation of individual autonomy within the bosom of the family and the community. It is experienced in the formation of the couple and the procreation of children. It is experienced at work, in the relationship between classes, and in struggles for human rights, both for individuals and the community. Freedom is not just given; freedom must be conquered or it does not exist.

3. The Traditional Attributes of Grace

The Gratuitousness of Grace

The traditional authors liked to stress the fact that grace was extrinsic. Within a mystique of obedience which was almost servile, appropriate to the mentality of the sixteenth and seventeenth centuries, centuries of despotism and absolute monarchies, they liked to stress human beings' total dependence and what amounted to God's arbitrariness. They insisted, as if it were a virtue, upon total passivity in the hands of an absolute despot—God. In this context grace was an almost arbitrary gift, like the gifts kings gave at whim to their favorites. These pure gifts were received with the highest gratitude and the most exaggerated expressions of servility. Can grace be this gratification of an absolute monarch, whose pleasure is everything?

People today dislike begging and groveling. They would not want to receive alms from God, particularly alms called grace. They see this as against human dignity. Even more, people today dislike a gift which constitutes an obligation. Because then it would be a gift that all are obliged to receive. What does a compulsory *grace* mean? Is there any point in keeping the vocabulary of "grace" if we then add that those who do not accept the gift will be severely punished?

This is why it is important to stress that God's grace comes to us through the work of the Holy Spirit, as an energy, a force, an internal movement which, far from doing violence to individuals, awakens them and sets them in motion. God takes the initiative, just as in creation. But this is not a gift which cancels human freedom, which pushes human beings along a road contrary to their own value judgment. The gratuitousness of grace cannot be the foundation of a spirituality which annuls the human, as happened in the past, particularly in the sixteenth and seventeenth centuries. This was a phenomenon of the times related to a culture which is now clearly superannuated and has almost disappeared. In the religious works of that period there is a language we find intolerable today. Of course God is God and the creature is creature. But God did not create human beings in order to humiliate them by reminding them continually that they are only creatures and God alone is God. This would be attributing to God those absolute kings' mentality—kings who felt the need to be told over and over again that they were the absolute sovereigns, who lacked personal security. We may suppose that God does not suffer from an insecurity complex! Through creation and through grace, God intends human beings to exist and to be able to share in the divine freedom and autonomy.

Divinization

Greek theology made the concept of divinization the center of its soteriology. Historians can show the connection between this theology and the religious and philosophical context of the Byzantine Empire. There is an immense cultural heritage in this concept. Peoples who have not inherited this idea do not find it easy to understand what divinization means.

At any rate, one thing that divinization cannot mean is the raising of the human being above the human condition to a different level, imagined as a higher condition than the human one. Divinization cannot mean that human beings leave the human condition behind, and in particular, it cannot mean that they leave their bodily condition in order to enter a purely spiritual or nonmaterial pseudo-condition. So it is not a question of minimizing the bodily condition or bodily activities. The divinization of humanity can only mean access to human fulfillment. It can only be justified as greater humanization.

At present there is the fear that through divinization human beings might lose their identity, dissolve into a pseudo-divinity, as if they were taking on a divine pseudo-condition. People today suspect that this soteriology of divinization expressed a certain contempt for the body, which did in fact exist in a particular oriental monastic tradition. For the poor, a spirituality that rejects the body and exalts the purely spiritual is a constant trial, it is a legitimization of the condition imposed on them by the oppressors.

Divinization can be understood only in the sense that humanity has been introduced into the dialogue of the divine person. Their actions make them one with Christ. Their actions are inspired by the Holy Spirit and are therefore acts of dialogue with the Father. Human beings have been admitted to the consortium of divine persons. However human, bodily, and material their actions are, they are worthy of God and constitute valid responses to the Father's word.

Forgiveness of Sins

The West has lived with guilt for centuries. Preachers and priests have made denunciation of sins the core of their message. Sin was seen as essentially the product of human malice. For the preacher this was an opportunity to denounce human malice, make people feel guilty, and humiliate them. Human sin was the church's joy; it provided it with its public and kept human beings tied hand and foot to the good will of their pastors. Sin enabled the church to blame people.

Today we are more aware that some of the blame for human actions comes from human poverty. Sin is often the consequence of this state of wretchedness. Some human beings are more deserving of compassion than blame. Although sin is committed by human beings, it is committed collectively and anonymously; it comes from established structures rather than the personal malice of individuals. This does not exclude the possibility of individual malice, but what is due to it bears no comparison with the enormous mass of evils proceeding from structures of domination and exploitation, in which human beings are more often manipulated than manipulators. Sin is the expression of an immense human passivity, a lack of freedom.

Consequently, sin does not so much need forgiveness that cancels it or removes the punishment, but rather liberation. If human beings are victims of a sin that is stronger than their individual will, they need to be liberated from their sin. In this sense grace is not an absolution, which cancels the sin and all the penalties laid down for the sin. Grace and forgiveness are instead the actual liberation movement through which people liberate themselves from the structures that crush them and take away their freedom. Grace, then, is liberation from sin and the achievement of freedom.

Sin oppresses a human being, first internally by fears or anguish that paralyze action. Individuals can know they are sinning, want not to sin, yet lack the strength to do what they want to do. Liberation conquers sin within the person themselves, making them capable of making decisions personally and acting freely.

Sin also oppresses human beings from the outside, through external pressures. The strongest of these come from education, the family, the immediate environment, the school environment, the group, and the closed world of everyday life.

Sin also comes from the pressures of economic and political forces, domination by wealth or weapons. Human beings can enter into complicity with the sin that comes from outside. They both commit the sin and suffer from it. Grace frees from sin; it is liberation. This liberation is both emancipation from the force that comes from sinful structures and the capacity to resist the temptation to sin, which is personal.

This aspect of sin's domination over human beings does not mean that it is not also an offense against God and that forgiveness for the offense is not also part of the remission of sins. Nevertheless, we cannot separate this aspect from the other.

II. GRACE FROM THE POINT OF VIEW OF ACTING

Grace renews the human being and human action. Action cannot be separated from being. In fact, we have no words to name a "being" that is not also an "acting." God's grace enters into human being-acting. Human beings exist in their action and inseparably are their action, as is the case with all living things. Nevertheless, the limits of our language oblige us to separate conceptually and verbally what is in reality united.

1. God's Action and Human Action

God's action and human action are inseparable. God's action is expressed through human action. God's action—grace—does not destroy or suppress or diminish or replace anything in human action. A human action directed by God's action has no less initiative, no less spontaneity, no less creativity, no less autonomy than human action in general. On the contrary, the presence of God's grace makes human action more fully human, with more initiative, more spontaneity, more autonomy, than if grace were not present.

We cannot see human action animated by grace as an experienced passivity. Just as there was monophysitism in certain deformations of ancient christology, there was also a certain anthropological monophysitism of grace, which persisted through Christian history. In a certain monastic or mystical tradition God's grace takes the place of human will and makes the human being a mere instrument that lets itself be used. Passivity, if this is the adequate word, usually refers to a purely abstract and metaphysical level, without any contact with human psychology and behavior. But grace acts like creation. Just as creation makes human beings the doers of their own actions, so too, and even more so, does grace make human beings the doers of their own actions, more autonomous, freer, more fully human than without grace.

The Father acts by means of the Holy Spirit and according to the way of the Spirit. The Spirit gently penetrates human beings and accompanies them. There is no question of forcing. The Spirit gives energy and dynamism, restores human beings to the fullness of their powers. The Spirit sets up a long restoration process for human action, following all the stages marked by obstacles, slowness, and human rhythms. An individual life is a history analogous to the history of communities and peoples. The Spirit adapts to the slowness of history. The Spirit does not make great leaps; there are strong moments and weak moments. There are eras which appear to be dead and other times when history speeds up. God does not do violence to history. The way in which God accompanies the development of history means that the presence of grace cannot be precisely pinpointed. There are no phenomena of which it can be said: here is the pure grace of God. The Spirit acts in the continuum of human action.

2. Individual and Social Grace

If sin is both personal and social, never purely personal, never purely social, so is grace. The human being acts socially. Even prophets who anticipate and appear to cry in the wilderness need at least a small audience to listen to them. Without an audience they would not be prophets. There is an initial nucleus, the beginning of the people the prophet wishes to enlighten. The grace animating the prophet acts at the same time in the nucleus of the audience. The prophet's grace would be ineffective if it were not linked to the grace of the group that receives the prophecy. In reality, both constitute a single action.

The same thing happens in all manifestations of divine grace. A single grace envelops the family, the community, the group of believers, the Christian people, the whole church. Its effects are correlative. There is a single action, which acts at a multiplicity of application points, all connected. The same grace can act with varying intensity at its different application points. The important thing is to be aware of the solidarity of actions by human beings. A purely solitary act would have no meaning and would be impossible. Nobody invents anything. All share in inspirations, suggestions, examples, invitations from others. Even the most solitary monks are within a monastic tradition of hermits and act together with the tradition in which they live.

This solidarity and continuity of God's grace is symbolized by the sacraments, which are community acts in which the community shows in communal signs that it is receiving the grace of the Holy Spirit.

3. Grace and the History of the Poor

God's grace enters human history. But it does not identify with the history of empires or civilizations. The dominant history is made by the great, the strongest, the conquerors in the competition among peoples and human groups. Grace does not intervene in the conquests of the great or in their efforts to hold on to their empires. In former times, even in the Hebrew scriptures, it was held that God gave victory in battle, that God was with the conqueror. We know this is a lie.

It was explained to the inhabitants of the Americas that God had granted victory to the invaders and had delivered their kingdom in this world to the king of Spain or Portugal. The indigenous people believed them and accepted their conquerors' religion through fear. Nevertheless, we believe they were wrong. It is not true that God is the author of conquests and empires. If a deity of the conquerors, God would not have allowed the Son to be crucified and conquered by his enemies. The cross shows us that God enters human history, but not on the side he is usually believed to. The Father enters history on the side of the oppressed and the poor. He is the God of the liberation of the poor. Thus God's grace is the force that awakens, animates, and maintains the struggle of the oppressed, who are victims of injustice and evil.

Grace is the liberation movement itself, or rather, the soul of this movement. It is not identified with everything that happens in such movements, of course. Nevertheless, it is present according to the way of the Holy Spirit at the root of the liberation of the poor.

Grace produces a history, not the one that is written, but the one that is experienced in the hidden part of the world. It produces a parallel history of those who suffer in the midst of the triumphs of the conquerors and the persecuted. Grace is present in the hidden history of the poor. It produces resistance, faith, hope. It produces in all peoples something similar to the history of the poor of Israel, as it is recorded in the Bible.

This liberation history of the poor also has its victories and is not pure patience. It has its moments of glory. It keeps the memory of its past glories. These victories are the winning of poor people's rights, the overthrow of systems of domination. Although the poor never get total justice in this world, neither can we say that they are always suffering in the same way. Some systems are more intolerable than others. It is not true that because complete justice is never achieved, it is not worth struggling for justice, as if all struggles were ineffectual. God's grace is not ineffectual. It does not remain on the purely spiritual level, remote from this earthly history. Its effects are perceptible even if they do not bring about in this world what is reserved for the end of time. Grace does not destroy determinisms, inertia, the weight of the past and of structures. Nevertheless, it introduces a new element, a force which revives the hope of the oppressed. If there were no perceptible effects, grace would be nothing but a stimulus to resignation. People today are very much aware of everything that might become a paralyzing force in human life. A grace that produced only resignation could not be from the God of life.

God's grace accompanies the development of history. The needs of the oppressed change with the times. There are times of adversity and pure patience; there are times of organization and protest; there are times of insurrection and initiative. There are times when the dominators are at the height of their power; at other times they are divided and then there is scope for the weaker to break in. Grace will have different effects according to the situation. Things that give opportunities to the poor are mistakes, rivalries, and the irrational behavior of the great. By and large, empires and all forms of domination destroy themselves. Action by the poor depends upon the signs of the times. God's grace also follows the signs of the times. The Spirit sends the signs and the power to act in accordance with what they are indicating. The Hebrew scriptures show how God withdraws grace from the powerful, and how their empires destroy themselves by their own lack of vitality or by rivalry among themselves. Amid the battles of the giants, the little people seek their way. This is why the books of the Bible are still relevant today. If the Bible is the history of the poor, it is also the history of God's grace. To read the Hebrew scriptures is to read the history of God's grace in paradigmatic form. What is written there is relevant to all periods.

4. God's Grace and the Challenges of History

By and large human beings make their own circumstances. God's grace also consists in setting human beings in situations which oblige them to go beyond themselves, to overcome their limitations and increase their forces. An external circumstance is the beginning of a conversion, a new road. Human beings who live in a state of protection or overprotection cannot produce miraculous results. God's grace consists in taking their protection away from them, along with their security and peace of mind and body. God's grace may consist in taking away one person's wealth, another person's power, another person's health, another person's family. In such a situation the human being is called to accomplish much more than the usual, to produce more vigorous effects.

God's grace can set before a human being the challenge of persecution and martyrdom. Then we see that the important thing is not how long that person has lived but the density and value of these years. Jesus only lived for thirty-three years, but his years are worth more than others' who lived for seventy or eighty. For many, God's grace has meant prison, concentration camp, exile, giving up their wealth, work, career, social position, even though God's grace is not always recognized in these challenges.

—Translated by Dinah Livingstone

13

Sacraments

VICTOR CODINA

I. A NEW HORIZON FOR UNDERSTANDING THE SACRAMENTS

The theology of liberation does not profess a sacramentology "parallel" to the magisterium of the church. It accepts the common sacramental doctrine and praxis of the church, but like any theology it tries to systematize them according to an ultimate principle, to set priorities and to organize all the information in a coherent way, and in the case of the theology of liberation, a way that responds to the cry of the poor and believing people.

What characterizes a new theology is not the new subjects it raises, but its new theological horizon; everything is seen differently because the mental paradigm or the cognitive framework is changed. The same is true of the theology of liberation, which is not a "genitive" theology of revolution or violence, but rather a reflection on the whole Christian mystery from the perspective of the liberation of the poor.

1. The Horizon of Traditional Sacramentology

During the first millennium the church celebrated the sacraments of faith without developing a systematic treatise on the sacraments, although it reflected unceasingly on Christian initiation, the eucharist, and penance. The church of the first millennium participated symbolically in the Christian mystery through its liturgy, without undue concern for defining or systematizing the different kinds of sacraments, or for structuring each one.

In the twelfth century the church began to elaborate the treatise *De sacramentis in genere*, which, enriched by the great scholastics, and fundamentally assumed by Trent and developed by the post-Tridentine and neoscholastic theologians, would remain prevalent until Vatican II.

Describing the outlines of traditional sacramentology, we might say that during these centuries what prevailed was not so much the symbolic dimension of the sacraments, typical of the patristic era, but its instrumental dimension: the sacraments are effective instruments of grace. Although the significative aspect of the sacraments did not disappear altogether ("effective signs of grace"), the accent was placed on their effectiveness, on their causality ex opere operato, which did not depend on the holiness of the minister but on the merits of the passion of Christ. For the validity of the sacrament it was necessary and sufficient that the minister have "the intention of doing what the church does." This objective effectiveness of the sacraments would be emphasized in the anti-Protestant polemic to make the point that the sacraments are not simple pedagogical aids for the faith of the subject. Although the condition of the subject who "receives" the sacrament (opus operantis) was always considered important, these conditions seemed to be reduced to "not putting an impediment" to the grace offered in the sacrament. The doctrine of the number of the seven sacraments, which had a markedly symbolic origin, was interpreted more and more arithmetically and less symbolically. The introduction of Aristotelianism into medieval theology offered very precise intellectual tools for the study of the sacraments (matter and form, substance and accidents, causality), but it led to the reification of sacramentality at the level of objective and impersonal realities. The sacraments always maintained their reference to Jesus, author of the sacraments, through his power of "excellency," and never ceased to be considered a "memorial of the passion." Some authors, like Thomas Aquinas, developed a sacramental anthropology, following the evolution of the great moments of personal and social life. Thomas himself related the sacraments to the liturgical worship of the church. But in reality, traditional sacramentology never developed the personal, let alone the ecclesial dimensions of the sacraments. The sacraments were seen as instruments of the humanity of Jesus, distributing to each person the grace that Christ obtained for us with his passion.

It was only a step from there to considering the sacraments as "channels of grace." The richness of early scholasticism was slowly lost, and the sacraments were increasingly turned into sacred objects that, regulated by ritual laws, produced sanctifying grace. The faith of the subject, the liturgical and ecclesial dimension, the very connection of the sacraments with the Paschal mystery, were slowly relegated to the shadows.

This sacramentology, typical of the church in medieval Christianity, incapable of reformulating itself in response to the criticism of the Reformation and later of the modern age, fell victim to the triumphalism, juridicism, and clericalism that characterized the church before Vatican II. Throughout these centuries the sacraments not only were instruments of grace, but also brought together and shaped "Christian society," and have served to sacralize unjust situations.

The cultural horizon of classical sacramentology is that of the objective, the natural, the static; the sacraments belong to the world of things, although they are "sacred things," in which the faithful participate when they receive the sacraments "administered" by the priests. The underlying theological horizon is that of juridicist positivism, in the framework of an Anselmian christology, without either ecclesiology or pneumatology.

All this should not be interpreted as unfaithfulness to its origins on the part of the church. The church, guided by the Spirit, continued to live and celebrate the sacraments of the faith and to defend their value. But through the centuries its reflective systematization of the sacraments, although full of insights and nuances, has lost much of the theological richness of the patristic and early scholastic periods. That is why Vatican II sought to renew sacramentology by invoking a "return to the origins."

2. *The Sacramental Horizon of the Theology of Vatican II*

The sacramental theology that emerged around Vatican II represented a change not only of content but of cultural and theological paradigm. Its horizon is that of *Modernity*: the predominance of the anthropological over the cosmic, of the subject over the object, of the evolutional over the static, of reason, consciousness and freedom over the individual, of the "I" over the "we." At a strictly theological level, we can say that it placed the sacraments in the ecclesial context, and specifically within a church that is wholly proto-sacrament, a universal sacrament of salvation. The seven sacraments are the essential moments of the ecclesial proto-sacrament, the clearest manifestations of the victorious and eschatological grace of Jesus in the church, expressions of the primordial sacrament. In each sacrament there is a personal encounter with the resurrected Kyrios. Ecumenical dialogue with the Reformation has helped to rediscover the dimensions of the word and of the faith, while conversation with the Eastern Church has led to new respect for the symbolic, iconic, and pneumatic dimensions.

This sacramental vision has recovered much of the early patristic and medieval tradition that was lost in the second millennium and has enabled the church to relate the sacramental world to the challenges of Modernity. The importance of the subject has been recognized and the individual's faith appears as an essential constitutive moment of the sacrament, which is "sacrament of the faith." The liturgy recovers its communal and celebrative character, in which the word occupies a decisive place. The epiclesis or invocation of the Spirit is recognized as a constitutive sacramental element, thus overcoming the unfortunate impression of cosmic automatism from the earlier period. The eucharist has returned to its central place in the church, and the other sacraments take their place around it. Once more "the church makes eucharist and the eucharist makes the church." The constitutions *Lumen gentium* and *Sacrosanctum concilium*, at the theoretical level, and at the practical level the reform of the sacramental rituals, have brought these rich ecclesial perspectives to the sacraments. The sacraments are once more becoming the essential symbolic and celebrative moments of the church as proto-sacrament.

Nevertheless, this sacramental horizon, with all its undeniable richness, still raises questions in the Third World and especially in Latin America.

The church's belated acceptance of the horizon of Modernity (the first Enlightenment) cannot conceal the ambiguous elements in which Modernity is rooted: its connection with the dominant sectors of the modern world (bourgeois, precapitalists, capitalists, neocapitalists), which are largely responsible for the dependency of the Third World; its enlightened rationalism, which not only leads to increased elitism but degenerates into privatistic individualism, into the technocracy of "instrumental reason," and into the idolatry of earthly goods; in short, a crass individualism that leads to materialistic consumerism and to the ecological destruction of the planet itself.

In the sacramental context the modern ecclesiological horizon entails the risk of degenerating into an elitist and ahistorical liturgy, into sacraments well prepared and well celebrated by the minority sector of society, into an encounter with the Resurrected One which neglects to follow the historical Jesus, into a progressivist and somewhat naive optimism which forgets about sin, suffering, and death in the world, into an aesthetic symbolism that does not include the poor person as privileged image of Jesus (Matt. 25), into celebrations that conceal the reality of cruel inequality with liturgical rites, into an excessive concern for the freedom of a few, without considering the lack of freedom of the great majorities, into drawing-room communitarianism rather than real solidarity with the people, into disrespect or at least ignorance toward popular religion and its sacramentals. This situation has led even first-world theologians to seek new and liberating ways for the sacraments.

When the theology of liberation seeks a new sacramental horizon, it does not do so out of intellectual zeal, but from a sincere desire to respond to unresolved questions which, thanks to Vatican II, can now be raised again. In this sense the new sacramental horizon of the theology of liberation—like the theology of liberation itself—is the fruit of Vatican II, although it goes beyond the Council. In the last analysis, was not John XXIII himself the first to speak of the church of the poor as the image of the conciliar church?

3. The New Sacramental Horizon of the Theology of Liberation: The Kingdom of God

The theology of liberation has made the Kingdom of God the central object of its reflection, the ultimate principle around which it articulates the content of the Christian faith and the paradigm which best responds to the reality of Latin America, to the cry of the mostly poor, mostly Christian people of this region.[1]

The key concept of the Kingdom of God permits the theology of liberation to unite transcendence with history, overcoming all dualism; it makes it possible to historicize salvation, specifically as the liberation of the poor; it serves as a prophetic denunciation of the anti-Kingdom that is present in our history; thanks to this last principle it can respond to the hopes of the poor majorities and thus orient the praxis of historical transformation to God's plan: the Kingdom.

This structural principle of the theology of liberation corresponds to a new theological horizon, a change of trajectory, a new paradigm, a new matrix. For this reason the theology of liberation is not a "regional" theology but a new way of doing theology, though always provisionally, as anything historical must be done. There is an "epistemological break" from other ways of doing theology, and it is not simply a "postmodern" way. There is a change of social subject; it is done from below, from the viewpoint of the poor. This is one of the things that create conflict in the church and in society, but also one of the things that arouse hope in the popular sectors.

This does not mean that the slate of earlier theologies is wiped clean, or that the basic elements of faith and theological tradition are not incorporated. But it is done within a new global horizon, from a new formal perspective: everything seems new.

Philosophically and culturally, this new paradigm moves in the dialectical relationship between the objective and the subjective, in the overlapping relationship between humanity and its world. It accentuates the social, the structural, the historical, and the liberative. Its dialogue is not only with the first Enlightenment, but with what has been called the second Enlightenment; not only with reason, but also with the praxis of social transformation.

This new horizon, which becomes specific in the Kingdom of God, has already served to structure different theological themes:

- God is the God of the Kingdom, the Abba of Jesus;
- Christ is the eschatological mediator of the Kingdom, but the Kingdom is still an unfinished task in history and requires successive historical mediations;
- the church is sacrament of the Kingdom and must continually undergo conversion to the Kingdom, if it seeks to be church of the poor and historical sacrament of liberation;
- spirituality is liberation with Spirit, following Jesus in the historical building of the Kingdom.

The affirmation that the Kingdom of God is the horizon of sacramentology in the theology of liberation is a logical step forward in this theological systematization, the practical corollary of which is to make the sacraments liberative, especially for the poor.

As we shall see, the horizon of the Kingdom of God, far from denying the valid aspects of the traditional and modern sacramentology, incorporates them in a new synthesis. The Kingdom of God incorporates both christological and ecclesiological affirmations, but it insists on certain presuppositions which are in fact new: the starting point is the cry of the poor. But there is something more: it is the new theological reflection on the mystery-sacrament that will intrinsically lead us to the sacramental horizon of the Kingdom of God.

4. The Kingdom of God as Primordial Mystery-Sacrament

All authors agree that both the etymological and the theological grounding of the sacraments must be oriented to the mystery, the biblical mysterion, which Tertullian translated as sacramentum in applying it to Christian worship.

In its biblical origins the mystery does not exclusively denote the cognitive dimension of a secret, and even less the cultic dimension of our sacraments. The essence of the mystery is the merciful plan of God, God's will for salvation, which is realized in this world.

Thus Daniel, in revealing to Nebuchadnezzar the mystery of his dream of that majestic statue with feet of clay, speaks of "a kingdom that shall never be destroyed, nor shall its kingdom be left to another people. It shall crush all these kingdoms and bring them to an end, and it shall stand forever" (Dan. 2:44–45, *NRSV*; cf. verses 18, 27–30, 45–47).

This mystery that Paul and the Pauline writings identified with Christ and saw specifically in the opening to the Gentiles (Rom. 16:25–27; 1 Cor. 2:6–10; 2 Thess. 2:7; Col. 1:27; Eph. 1:22, 2:11–22, 3:10–21; 1 Tim. 3:9, 16) would have its eschatological fulfillment at the end of time (Rev. 1:20, 10:7, 17:5).

This mystery is specifically the Kingdom of God, as it appears in the only passages of the Synoptics which refer to the mystery: Mark 4:11; Matthew 13:11; and Luke 8:10.

Thus it is necessary to unite the notion of mystery with that of the Kingdom of God; the primordial mystery is this salvific plan of God, revealed in successive stages, centered in Christ and consummated in the new earth and the new heaven. This Kingdom-Reign of God, announced by the prophets (of which Israel is an instrument), comes near to us in Christ (Mark 1:15). But the realization of it is extended and realized in the time of the church, so that God may be all in all (1 Cor. 15:28). This is the primordial mystery of the faith, the original sacrament.

To put it differently, placing sacramentality in the horizon of the Kingdom of God, as the theology of liberation tries to do, is not only a change from ecclesial tradition, but a return to the biblical and earliest historical origins of the mystery-sacrament. It reassumes the personalistic, christological, and ecclesiological horizon in the broader horizon of the Kingdom of God, of which Christ is the only eschatological mediator and the church is its visible ferment in history. This means that the seven sacraments must be interpreted in the light of the Kingdom of God, and therefore their meaning, their effectiveness, their validity, their very ecclesiality, must always be considered in reference to the Kingdom of God. If from the first millennium sacramentality referred only to the sacramental rites that seemed to be its only expression, and if since Vatican II it refers primarily to the church, the perspective of liberation theology places it in the Kingdom, which roots it in the earliest tradition of the patristic church.

Now let us draw a conclusion from this first affirmation. The Kingdom overflows the church. It is not merely intra-ecclesial; it is realized in history, in the world, in secularity, in the sociopolitical, economic, and cultural spheres, in the structures and conditions of life of the peoples. The sacraments must be oriented to this Kingdom. The cry of the poor comes into ecclesial sacramentality thanks to this horizon of the Kingdom. The cry of the oppressed can legitimately resonate in the liturgy without offending either esthetics or pastoral theology, because the mission of the sacraments is to dignify and prophetically celebrate this Kingdom, which as we shall see, has to do with the liberation of the poor. To ask the soldiers at a eucharist to stop the repression, as Archbishop Romero ordered "in the name of God" on the eve of his assassination (March 22, 1980), is not an injection of politics into the liturgy, but a clear prophetic orientation of sacramentality to the Kingdom of God. The Church Fathers did the same thing in the fourth century.

II. THE SACRAMENTS AS PROPHETIC SYMBOLS OF THE KINGDOM

Let us now apply to the sacraments the new sacramental horizon of the Kingdom of God, which we have been proposing and discovering.

1. The Sacraments of the Kingdom in History: The Poor

In human history, inside and outside the church, we find situations of sin that produce victims. These victims of the anti-Kingdom are the poor. They are sacraments of the Kingdom sub contrario, precisely to the extent that the privation of life, the sin of the world, and the negation of the Kingdom are manifest in them. Their cry is a cry for the Kingdom; it is a protest against the whole society.

Theologically, their cry is a sign of the times (GS, 4, 11, 44), the greatest sign of the times in today's world.

Paradoxically, in the light of a theology of the cross and of the Crucified One, Christ is made present in the poor. And responding to the cry of the poor becomes an ineluctable condition for entrance to the Kingdom (Matt. 25:31–45).

For this reason, by analogy but truly, the poor can be called sacraments of the Kingdom; they are a living prophecy of the Kingdom insofar as they denounce the anti-Kingdom, in anticipation of the eschatological judgment of God and proclamation of the mysterious presence of the Crucified One in them. Thus, C. Boff writes:

> The sacrament of the poor shows us the God they want and not God helping them; here God is challenge, not consolation; questioning, not justification. In effect, faced with the poor, human beings are called to love, service, solidarity, and justice. So receiving this sacrament is bitter to the taste. Yet it remains the *only "sacrament" absolutely necessary* for salvation. The ritual sacraments allow of exceptions, and many; this allows of none. It is also the *absolutely universal "sacrament"* of salvation. The way to God goes necessarily, for everyone without exception, through human beings—human beings in need, whether their need is of bread or the word.[2]

When we affirm that the church is sacrament of salvation or sacrament of the Kingdom, we mean that, among other things, in the church this analogical and anonymous sacrament of the poor becomes visible and explicit by reference to Jesus; and vice versa, that ecclesial sacramentality cannot be understood either in theological theory or in pastoral practice apart from the poor, who constitute the eschatological test of all sacramentality. This sacramentality must always be a response to the cry of the poor and must be oriented to their integral liberation. In the light of faith the acts, sometimes heroic acts, of many non-Christians who struggle and die for the liberation of their people, become profoundly meaningful because, without knowing it, they are anticipating the realization of the Kingdom of God. And the Spirit is with them.

Pedro Casaldáliga, the Brazilian bishop, poet, and prophet, has expressed it with his typical lucidity:

> The Spirit
> has decided
> to administer
> the eighth sacrament:
> the voice of the People![3]

2. The Sacraments of the Church: Prophetic Symbols of the Kingdom

The sacraments of the church are those prophetic symbols of the Kingdom that the church celebrates liturgically and that orient Christian existence not only to the church but to the Kingdom of God, of which the church itself is a sacrament. Let us make these affirmations explicit.

The Sacraments Are Prophetic Symbols of the Kingdom

The sacraments are those symbolic acts of the church that are oriented to the realization of the Kingdom of God, in continuity with the salvific actions of Yahweh in the Old Testament and of Jesus in the New. They are particularly intense and transparent moments of the Kingdom of God in the church, Paschal steps on the way from death to life, moments of pentecostal effusion in which the presence of the Kingdom of God is manifested as gift and as task. They are the privileged times (*kairos*) in the life of the individual and the community, in which the symbol is opened to its deepest meaning, transfigured into the eschatological grace of the Kingdom.

As prophetic symbols:

1. *They announce* the Good News of the Kingdom of God, especially for those who always receive bad news. It is a proclamation of life, forgiveness, hope, and communion, linked to Jesus and his word, and his life, death, and resurrection. In this sense the sacraments are a memorial of Jesus, *signum rememorativum* in the Thomist tradition (III q. 60 a. 3).

2. *They denounce* the sin of the world, the anti-Kingdom present in history and in persons, the root of death. In this sense a sacramental celebration can hardly be liberating if it does not in some way begin with the situation of personal and social sin. By demonstrating what the Kingdom is (signum demonstrativum), the sacraments denounce what is contrary to the Kingdom. For this reason the sacraments have a strong critical burden, for they question the prevailing system; they are a subversive memory of Jesus. The eucharistic symbol of shared bread denounces the accumulation of goods by a few and the hunger of the world, as contrary to the Kingdom.

3. *They transform and demand the transformation* of personal and historical reality, and in this way they are an eschatological sign of the Kingdom of God, which is already present (*signum prognosticum*). The effectiveness of the sacraments springs from their very existence as *prophetic signs*; it is the effectiveness of prophecy in actu, of actions that realize what they symbolize prophetically. It is the effectiveness—feared by some, celebrated by others—of the prophetic acts of the prophets and of Jesus. In the sacraments the Kingdom is already present. Their effectiveness is not only *ecclesial* (establishing a link to the church) but *basileic* (on the order of the Kingdom or basileia). They are gift and task, opus operatum and opus operantis, they demand personal and social conversion; they move toward the transformation of the society in the direction of the Kingdom of God. For this reason the sacraments must be made effective in history; they impel the faithful to follow Jesus. This explains how the sacraments can be defined as "community celebrations of the following of Jesus in the important moments in the life of the person."[4] And the test of any sacramental celebration must always be the liberation of the poor, according to Matthew 25:31–45.

In terms of classical sacramentology, the sacramentum tantum is the prophetic symbol, the *res et sacramentum* is the ecclesial dimension, firstfruit of the sacrament, and the res tantum is the realization of the Kingdom.

But it is all grace and gift of the Spirit in the church, which itself is sacrament of the Kingdom.

Celebrated in the Church

The subject of the sacraments is the ecclesial community, itself a sacramental symbol of the Kingdom of God. The church not only teaches the gospel, not only exhorts the faithful to fulfill the gospel, but celebrates prayerfully, through symbols, the mystery of the Kingdom, which is embryonically [nuclearmente] realized in the death and resurrection of Jesus, but which must go on being realized in the history of persons and peoples.

The symbolic acts of the church are not empty, for the church itself is animated by the same Spirit who acted through the prophets and guided the work of Jesus. It is the community of Jesus and the Spirit that announces the Kingdom, denounces the anti-Kingdom and anticipates the Kingdom symbolically in its sacraments. The difference between these ecclesiological affirmations and the typical affirmations of postconciliar sacramentology is that in this perspective the sacraments not only accentuate their ecclesial linkage, but orient the church toward the Kingdom and invite it as a community to be converted to the Kingdom of God. In this way both the demand of commitment and the gratuitousness of the sacraments appear more clearly: it is God's Kingdom, and we must give thanks for its nearness in Christ, but it has not yet reached its fullness; we must go on building it, if only partially, because it always overflows and transcends our efforts. The epiclesis or invocation of the Spirit, typical of church tradition, especially in the oriental church, takes on a new meaning: the Spirit transforms not only the symbolic gifts, not only the community, but the whole of reality, transfiguring it into the Kingdom. The invocation "thy Spirit come" is equivalent to "thy kingdom come," and in both cases it is an eschatological and also christological prayer of the church: it is the "come, Lord Jesus" of the early church (Rev. 22:20). In this supplication the church sums up not only its liturgical prayer but the cry of the people for the Kingdom and the liberation it brings. The sacraments as prophetic symbols are the church's liturgical prayer, the place where the cry of the people becomes the cry of Christ and his church to the Father, where the cry of the poor is condensed in the cry of the Crucified One and in the groaning of creation begging for liberation (Rom. 8:22ff.).

Finally, let us say that the festive dimension of these celebrations is increasingly emphasized by the praxis of the basic ecclesial communities and the popular sectors of the church. The people rejoice and celebrate, with a sense of gratuitousness. And through these celebrations they express their faith, as St. Thomas pointed out in discussing the faith of the least cultured sectors, who know and live the mysteries of faith in the liturgical celebrations of the church ("*de quibus ecclesia festa facit*": *De Ver* q. 14, a. 11).

III. OUTLINE OF A LIBERATING SACRAMENTOLOGY

1. The Sacraments of the Poor: Sacramentals

Classical sacramentology distinguishes between the seven sacraments and the sacramentals. The sacramentology of liberation, in contrast, considers the sacramentals as sacraments of marginalization and of the poor; therefore, they should be considered in speaking of the sacraments. They comprise the sacramental practice that is most widespread and deeply rooted in the people, and they differ from one circumstance and place to another. Some are linked to the defining moments of life (birth, death, the passage from childhood to youth, from youth to maturity), to places (sanctuaries), to festive times (Christmas, Holy Week), to the agricultural cycle (planting, harvest), to special moments (inauguration of a house, a trip, illness, work). A whole range of symbols are mixed together: images, processions, candles, pilgrimages, blessings, flowers, meals, water rites. They are often led by lay people themselves; at other times they require a qualified presence of the ministers of the church. These sacramentals, typical of popular religion, can degenerate into magic, passivity, or excess. But in their basic form they are prophetic symbols of the Kingdom, which the poor and powerless long for. They are a symbolic expression of desire, of faith, of piety, of trust in the God of life. Through them is expressed the evangelizing potential of the poor. They must not be rejected. Nor should we fear to include them in the sacramental environment, since the early tradition of the church was not too disdainful to identify as sacraments such realities as footwashing, the consecration of virgins, the blessing of objects, funeral rites, and others.

A double theological task is required: to tie in these sacramentals with the sacraments of the church and with other sacramental moments of the Christian life.

2. The New Prophetic Symbols

Along with the classical sacraments, the theology of liberation is beginning to reflect on the new flowering of prophetic symbols in the Latin American church, brought about by a strong eruption of the Spirit. These are sacramental acts in Christian life, which enrich liturgical sacramentality and lead it to new configurations of Christian praxis. The new lay ministries of men and women, the emergence of the basic ecclesial communities, the new presence of women in the church and in theology, the new ways of living the episcopal and priestly ministry in service to the poor, the new forms of insertion of religious life, the transmission of the faith through families that are sometimes torn apart . . . these are prophetic and symbolic forms of the Kingdom and responses to the cry of the poor.

Certainly martyrdom is the clearest prophetic symbol of this new liberating sacramentality. The long list of martyrs in Latin America is a bloody testimony to the power of the Spirit, who inspires these living symbols of the Kingdom. They are a living prophecy of the God of life in a world of death, a denunciation of injustice, and an anticipation of the utopia of the Kingdom. All this is a way of following Jesus in defense of justice on the basis of the baptismal faith. The very fact that many have died at the hands of the governments and citizens who call themselves Christian shows the inadequacy of ecclesiality as a criterion for the evangelical discernment of sacramentality. One must look to the Kingdom, to following Jesus, for the evangelical discernment of sacramentality. Who can doubt that the life and death of Archbishop Romero are a prophetic symbol of the Kingdom? The simple people have understood it and visit his tomb to ask or thank him for favors.

The sacramentality of the church is not only ritual, but extends to the whole of Christian praxis. Medellín clearly affirms the Kingdom orientation of all Christian liturgy.

3. The Seven Sacraments

The seven sacraments of the church are the maximum symbolic expression of all these levels and types of sacramentality. They are the places and moments of clear ecclesial reference for human sacramentality, the sacramentals, and the new prophetic symbols. If classical theology tried to justify them by linking them to the institutional acts of the historical Jesus, and modern sacramentality has considered them as the constitutive moments of the church as proto-sacrament, the theology of liberation places them in the context of the Kingdom: they are privileged steps on the way from death to life, and they orient our life to the service of the Kingdom in the key moments of our existence. They are prophetic symbols of the Kingdom with respect to liberation from all that oppresses the person and society. Rather than drawing a priori deductions, the theology of liberation tries to show that the sacraments of the church are oriented to the Kingdom and reveal the great contents of the Kingdom: mercy, life, justice, liberation, gratuitousness, solidarity, hope, community. The number of the seven sacraments goes beyond arithmetic importance and enters into the symbolic, into the fullness of the Kingdom.

In an experimental way, let us dissect the aspects of liberation and of Kingdom orientation in each sacrament, respecting the traditional hierarchy among them: the principal sacraments (baptism and eucharist), and the secondary sacraments (all the rest).[5] It is not a matter of structuring a complete sacramentology, but only of specifying in the seven sacraments the sacramental horizon of the Kingdom of God, as it is emphasized in the theology of liberation.

The Principal Sacraments

i. Baptism. This sacrament, the most popular and widely celebrated even among the poorest people, has been considered for centuries almost exclusively in its individual dimension (erasing the original sin that impedes salvation). The general application of child baptism and the reduction of the symbolic meaning of water to that of washing contributed to this individualization, which is not false but diminishes the richness of the sacrament. The sacramentology of Vatican II has rediscovered the ecclesial dimension of baptism (LG, 9–10), and modern sacramental theology (for example, K. Rahner) has made incorporation into the church not merely one effect but the first effect of baptism, from which the others are derived. The theology of liberation considers baptism not only as incorporation into the church, but as eschatological orientation and initiation into the Kingdom of God, of which the church is a sacrament.

The biblical stories themselves reinforce this perspective. The baptism of John, a prophetic and popular rite especially for the marginal sectors of Judaism and of society, is oriented to the eschatological Kingdom of God, which is coming now (Matt. 3:2), and for which the people must prepare with radical conversion (Luke

3:1–20). John's baptism of Jesus implies the beginning of his evangelizing activities oriented to the Kingdom (Mark 1:15). But this baptism of Jesus in the Jordan would be existentially realized in his death (Luke 12:50, Mark 10:38–39), and in his descent into hell (Matt. 12:40, Luke 11:30), whence he would rise in triumph over death and sin (Rev. 1:18).

Water symbolizes the passage from death to life, from life marked by sin (personal, historical, and social) to life that begins to anticipate the utopia of the Kingdom. Thus the first baptisms of the Jerusalem community at Pentecost not only added new believers to the church (Acts 2:41) but led to a life of fellowship and solidarity (Acts 2:42–47) that anticipated the utopia of the Kingdom. The early history of this sacrament itself presupposes great seriousness in personal conversion and in orientation to the values of the Kingdom as they were incarnated in Jesus. The catechumenate, with its requirement not only of biblical formation but of conversion, expressed that baptism requires a clear orientation to the Kingdom. Baptismal grace is the gift of the Spirit that forgives sins and gives strength to follow in life the way of the Kingdom initiated by Jesus. It is the Spirit itself, sent by Jesus to announce the Good News to the poor and the liberation of captives (Luke 4:16–21), who impels the Christian to make the Kingdom of God present in history and to struggle against the structures of sin. This eschatological orientation to the Kingdom may have been lost over the years, giving way to an excessive ecclesiocentrism.

The [practice] of baptism in Latin America is not centered on the baptism of children but on the struggle against the structures of sin; in any case, the problem is the baptism of the rich. On the other hand, given the high rate of infant mortality today, it would be unconscionable to postpone baptism. The many popular rites centered on birth and baptism may be reinterpreted as sacramental forms, which in connection with baptism, orient the child to the Kingdom, to life, and to solidarity. The [practice] of baptism must interpret historically the generic concepts of sin and grace, death and life, and encourage the search for utopian alternatives to the prevailing structures of sin. All this is done in the church and with the church, but in openness to the Kingdom and liberation.[6]

ii. Eucharist. This sacrament has been studied since the Reformation from an apologetic, anti-Protestant perspective. The classical treatises on the eucharist have been about real presence, sacrifice, and sacramental communion. Vatican II has given the eucharist a communitarian orientation (*Sacrosanctum Concilium,* no. 10; *Presbyterorum Ordinis*, no. 6), rediscovering the ecclesiality of the eucharist as it was in the first millennium; as the aphorism describes it, "eucharist makes the church, the church makes eucharist" (H. de Lubac). The theology of liberation, far from denying this, deepens it. The primary eucharistic symbol is the fellowship of sharing one meal and cup. In the Bible it is the image of the banquet that best expresses the utopia of the Kingdom. In the gospels, meals and banquets symbolize the Kingdom in the parables (Matt. 8:11, 22:1–4, 25:1–13); in the miracles (the multiplication of the loaves for hungry people, Mark 6:34–44, Mark 8:1–10); and in the symbolic actions of Jesus when he ate with sinners and marginalized people (Mark 2:16, Luke 15:2, Matt. 11:19). The meals of the Resurrected One (Luke 24:13–35, Luke 24:41–43, John 21:12–13) also symbolize the newness of the

Kingdom of life inaugurated by the resurrection. At the center of these meals is the Last Supper of Jesus, where in an atmosphere of farewell and in a clear reference to the table of the Kingdom (Matt. 26:29, Mark 14:25, Luke 22:15–18, 1 Cor. 11:26), the Lord gave us his body and his blood as the food of the Kingdom. In the eucharist we not only commune with Jesus, but with his Kingdom project; we not only edify the church but anticipate the banquet of the Kingdom. Thus the eucharist is inseparable from the fellowship of love and service, as John testifies in transmitting to us the symbolic act of footwashing (John 13). For this very reason a eucharist without real sharing, as occurred in Corinth, "is not the Lord's supper (1 Cor. 11:20–21). The patristic tradition corroborates this dimension of the eucharist, which is not only ecclesial but social: the offerings of the faithful for the poor; the presence of the slaves and the exhortation for their manumission; the preaching of the Fathers on justice and the defense of the poor; the liturgical excommunication of public sinners, who must be reconciled with the church in order to be readmitted to eucharistic communion.[7]

The eucharist cannot forget the Paschal context of the Lord's supper, the Jewish passover, the feast of the liberation from Egypt, and especially the Paschal act of Jesus, murdered for preaching the Kingdom and for denouncing the anti-Kingdom. The gift of the Resurrected One must become the seed for a new earth and a new heaven, not only liturgically but historically (GS, 38–39). The eucharist is not simply a celebration of small historical victories, but a token of the final and full realization of the Kingdom of God. Thus it is not only a subversive memorial (J. B. Metz), but a source of hope and the beginning of transfiguration. The bread and wine are transformed into bread and wine of the Kingdom, the beginning of the final utopia. And Jesus, eschatological mediator of the Kingdom, is made present with his transforming power. The epiclesis is not limited to the transformation of the gifts or of the community, but of all history into the body of the Lord.

The theology of liberation has reflected on the eucharists of the first missionaries and bishops of Latin America, on the eucharists of the basic ecclesial communities, and on the eucharists of Archbishop Romero.[8] Once again, the *lex orandi* illuminates the *lex credendi*.

The Other Sacraments

The other sacraments, or secondary sacraments in the patristic formulation, are derived from or ordered by the first two. Let us reflect briefly on each of these, from the horizon of the Kingdom of God.

i. Confirmation. Originally a part of Christian initiation, it was separated from baptism for pastoral and historical reasons. Its theology was gradually unlinked from its baptismal roots and from the initiating perspective. Modern theology restored confirmation to its roots of initiation and emphasized its ecclesial and pneumatic dimensions (LG, 11). The theology of liberation emphasizes that the pentecostal and missionary aspect of this sacrament is oriented to the Kingdom. From the time of the Old Testament, anointment has symbolized the gift of the Spirit in the sense of righteousness and justice for the poor and weak (Ps. 72:1). What the kings of Israel could not bring about would be fulfilled by the Messiah, anointed by the Spirit, to establish righteousness and justice (Isa. 7, 9:6, 11:6, 61; Luke 4). Jesus, the Christ, was anointed by the Spirit in baptism for his Messianic mission; he passed through the world doing good and liberating those who were oppressed by the devil (Acts 10:38).

The gift of the Spirit, communicated by confirmation through the symbolism of anointment, possesses a prophetic and eschatological orientation to the Kingdom, to justice and liberation. It reminds the baptized one and the church that their mission is the world and the Kingdom. To reduce confirmation to a renewal of baptism or an affirmation of the Spirit, without referring to the historical Jesus and his commitment to the Kingdom, is to distort the meaning of this sacrament.

ii. Penance. This actualizes the power of baptism for sins committed after baptism. Its early ecclesial orientation, forgotten in the centuries when penance was privatized, and administered for a fee, has been renewed by the theology of Vatican II. The first effect of penance (*res et sacramentum*) is once again ecclesial reconciliation. What the theology of liberation emphasizes is that neither sin nor reconciliation is purely intra-ecclesial. Sin wounds the ecclesial body, but it possesses a dynamic of death that affects society and history: structures of sin. Sin kills the life of personal and ecclesial grace, and it also kills the brother or sister. Archbishop Romero's definition of sin is paradigmatic: "Sin is what killed the Son of God and what kills the children of God." It follows that conversion must be not only personal but also social, historical, and structural. Reconciliation with the church must be oriented to undoing the consequences of personal and social sin, to "taking away the sin of the world," following the way of Jesus (John 1:29). In penance the church prophetically announces God's mercy, denounces the sin of the world and initiates its transformation by communicating the Spirit of Jesus (John 20:19–23) for the forgiveness of sins. The dynamic of this Spirit leads to liberation from all slavery (Rom. 8:19–27). This sheds light on the many penitential rites of popular religion. It also shows the ambiguity of certain practices of communal penance, which soothe the economically powerful sectors with a collective absolution that requires no profound change of personal life. In contrast, this new horizon of the Kingdom must from time to time encourage the church as a community to seek the forgiveness of God and the world for its collective sins in the past (the colonial period) and in the present (its alliance with the powerful). As servant of Yahweh the church must bear the sin of the world, intercede for sinners, and anticipate liberation.

iii. Marriage. Few sacraments have suffered as much distortion as that of marriage. In the best of cases it is lived as a sacrament of the family or of an often very closed sort of personal love. Modern theology has struggled to transpose marriage into an ecclesial key, as symbol of the love of Christ for his church in line with Ephesians 5:32–33, "a domestic church" (LG, 11), but without great pastoral success.

Before the theology of liberation takes up this sacrament, we believe it must clarify a series of prior problems. The maturity (human, affective, sexual, Christian) of a couple requires minimal social, economic, and cultural conditions not present amid the prevalence of poverty, unemployment, the promiscuity of inhuman living quarters, and so on. Before reflecting on the sublimeness of Christian sacramental marriage we must reflect on the poor person's body as an object of continual exploitation, on sexuality, and on the condition of poor women, who are doubly exploited in Latin America by machismo and the culture of consumerism. We must also study the types of couples and marriage rites that prevail in Indian and Afro-American cultures. Only then can we elaborate a theology of marriage, which should be open not only to the ecclesial dimension, but to the eschatology of the Kingdom, symbolized in the union of Adam and Eve (Gen. 2:22), which prefigures not only the union of Christ with his church, but that of God with humanity. To the new Adam (1 Cor. 15:45) we must also unite the new humanity, the new Jerusalem, "prepared as a bride adorned for her husband" (Rev. 21:2). But meanwhile the bride is with child, crying out in her pangs of birth, in anguish for delivery (Rev. 12:2).

Christian marriage must proclaim the power of the generous love of God; it must denounce selfishness and begin to anticipate, not only in the family but also in society, the new humanity, new human and social relationships, which are described in symbolic and utopian terms in the paradise of Genesis. In this way marriage will be a sacrament of the church and of the definitive Kingdom of God, biblically expressed in the nuptial banquet and the wedding of the Lamb. Only the grace of the Lord is capable of carrying out this miracle, symbolized in the new wine at Cana (John 2:1–12). This eschatological dimension will also allow us to focus evangelically on a series of moral issues in marriage, for example, divorce.

iv. Ministry. For centuries the priestly order has been defined almost exclusively in relation to the sacraments: the priest is the man of the sacraments, the other Christ, who consecrates and who forgives sins. Modern theology transposes the ministry into an ecclesial key: the priest as man of the word and of the community, the one who presides over it "in the person of Christ and in the name of the church." The theology of liberation, by placing the priest in the horizon of the Kingdom, rediscovers other aspects.[9] As always, the theology of liberation does not begin with an a priori idea but with the situation of poverty and injustice in Latin America. What is the primary evangelizing service, the salvific approach of God to a poor people? What was the priesthood of Jesus? His whole life was a mediation, but this mediation was done through mercy (Mark 6:34, Matt. 9:36, Luke 7:13, Matt. 14:14, Mark 1:41, Matt. 20:34); in the letter to the Hebrews the high priesthood of Jesus consists in sympathizing with our weakness (Heb. 4:15), in being merciful (Heb. 2:17). Mercy is the constitutive element in the priesthood of Jesus, which led him to the cross and resurrection. This is the constitutive element of the Christian priesthood of the faithful and of the priestly ministry. The priest is not only the man of the sacraments, of the word and community, but above all the man of mercy to the poor and sinners. This does not devalue the liturgical element but orients the priesthood to the Kingdom, just as John did not devalue the eucharist by speaking of the fellowship of service, symbolized and recommended in the act of footwashing (John 13). In the sacrament of priestly orders this function of mercy takes on an ecclesial and official charge, and the grace of the Spirit for this pastoral function. Evangelization, sacraments, practice, and so on, should all be oriented to this horizon. The figures of the great bishops and missionaries of the first evangelization of Latin America and the figures of the modern bishops martyred for defending the rights of the poor people give this reflection a historical and theological grounding. That, in turn, sheds light on other subjects such as the new lay ministries, women and ministry, new priestly lifestyles, and more.

v. Anointing of the Sick. This is not only the sacrament of the dying but of the sick. That does not detract from its eschatological orientation to the Kingdom, still keeping in mind its ecclesial dimension (James 5:13–15). It is a prophetic way of announcing the salvation of Jesus, of denouncing the present sickness and death as consequences of sin, and of anticipating the wholeness of the Kingdom by the transformation of weakness into strength, of sin into grace, and even of sickness into health. It is the sacrament that speaks of eschatological wholeness and of the abundant life of the Kingdom of God.

This sacrament should not be limited to the liturgical anointing of the sick or to caring for the aged, but should include general concern for health and for removing the causes of so many curable diseases and so many premature deaths. Moreover, the ceremonial richness of popular religion with regard to sickness and death should not be unlinked from this sacrament, because anointing is a liturgical prayer for life in all its wholeness. It is an act of faith and hope in the God of life. In the last analysis the anointing of the sick is part of the early apostolic mission of announcing the Kingdom of God (Mark 6:12–13, Luke 9:3, Matt. 10:7–8).

IV. A FINAL POINT

Let us conclude with these brief observations:

1. Its approach to reality will always be the unalterable point of departure for liberating theological and sacramental reflection. We must walk "with one ear tuned to the gospel and the other to the people" (Bishop Enrique Angelelli). The cry of the people is still a privileged theological locus for sacramental theology and must be incorporated into ecclesial liturgy.

2. Sacramental theology will be strengthened to the degree that the church's option for the poor is made real, that the basic ecclesial communities grow in number and maturity, that popular religion is evangelically embraced, and that reflection on sacramental praxis is broadened (including theology done by women). But some of the traits that shape a new vision of sacramentality centered on the Kingdom, on liberation, and on the poor, are already appearing. The ultimate aspiration is not simply to possess a coherent theological synthesis that can compete with those elaborated in the First World, but principally, to make the sacraments liberating symbols for the people.

3. All systematization entails risks; the new sacramentology of the theology of liberation also does. If in its sacramentology the theology of liberation unlinks the Kingdom from the church, and the church from Jesus, the sacraments deteriorate into purely sociopolitical or humanistic symbols. If the sacraments are reduced to celebrating the historical liberations already achieved and pedagogically encouraging ethical commitment in the future, sacramentality loses its christological, ecclesial, and pneumatic identity and deteriorates into a simple method of conscientization. Sacramentality must always maintain its gratuitousness, its sense of feast and symbol. In order to avoid these risks we must continually return to ecclesial praxis, to scripture, to the gospel, to the historical Jesus, who in his sym-

bolic acts, especially in baptism and the supper, prophetically united trust in the Father, solidarity with the people, and faithfulness to the Kingdom. The Kingdom of God is always a gift of the Spirit, and so too are its prophetic symbols. The sign of the coming of the Kingdom of God is the exorcism of all evils, and this is only done by the finger of God, that is, with the Spirit (Luke 11:20).

—*Translated by Margaret D. Wilde*

NOTES

1. See Juan Luis Segundo, "Revelation, Faith, Signs of the Times," chapter 15 in *Mysterium Liberationis*.
2. C. Boff and J. Pixley, *The Bible, the Church, and the Poor*, trans. Paul Burns (Maryknoll, N.Y.: Orbis Books, 1989), p. 114.
3. P. Casaldáliga, *Cantares de la entera libertad* (Managua, 1984), p. 73.
4. J. Sobrino, *Introducción a los sacramentos* (Mexico, 1979), p. 29.
5. Y. Congar, "The Idea of Major or Principal Sacraments," *Concilium* 31 (1968), pp. 24–37.
6. V. Codina, "¿Es licito bautizar a los ricos?," *Selecciones de Teología* 57 (1975); "Dimensión social del bautismo," in *Fe y justicia* (Salamanca, 1981), pp. 99–133.
7. J. M. Castillo, "Donde no hay justicia no hay eucaristía," in *Fe y justicia*, pp. 135–71.
8. E. Dussel, "The Bread of Celebration, Communitarian Sign of Justice," *Concilium* 72 (1982), pp. 236–49.
9. J. Sobrino, "Hacia una determinación de la realidad sacerdotal," *Revista Latinoamericana de Teología* 1 (1984), pp. 47–81.

14

Spirituality and the Following of Jesus

JON SOBRINO

The subject of spirituality has come in for unaccustomed interest in our times, and not only among those who devote themselves to "the things of the spirit," nor even only within the churches, but also, and especially—even when the word *spirituality* is not mentioned—in the world. Current history, with its crises and its questionings, its opportunities and its demands for the building of a human and humane future, challenges human beings and humanity as such. The challenge may go unheard; it may be manipulated or even perverted. But for perceptive persons, the questions mightily resound once more: What are you, and what ought you to be? What do you hope for, and what might you hope for? What are you doing, and what should you be doing? What are you celebrating, and what could you be celebrating? From out of the midst of history itself, the call has sounded: Answer for the truth of history truthfully. Shape that history; do not be dominated by it or merely slip and slide passively through it.

I. THE IMPORTANCE OF "LIVING WITH SPIRIT"

The task—the perennial, inescapable task—of responding to these questions, to this call, becomes all the more urgent in moments of crisis and "unhinging"—when the old hinges are no longer up to bearing the weight of the new edifice. The creation of new hinges for history to turn on, and turn well—a history in which men and women can live, or live again, as human beings—surely presupposes many elements, both of theory and of praxis. But integrating and living all of them adequately is a matter of spirit. It is this "being-human-with-spirit"—which responds to the elements of crisis and promise residing in concrete reality, unifying the various elements of a response to that reality in such a way that the latter may be definitively a reality more of promise than of crisis—that we call spirituality.

In the churches, too, the emphatic question of spirituality arises. This is primarily due to the fact that the churches participate—knowingly or not—in the current history of humanity. More specifically, it is due to the fact that the churches themselves have been the scene of an unhinging under the impact of the novelty, the enormous element of the new, introduced by Vatican II and Medellín. There is no use denying that new doctrinal, theological, pastoral, and liturgical elements today accompany those bequeathed to us by tradition. Nor can it be denied that the living experience of faith today occurs in a context in which the world itself has irrupted into the life of the churches—the world with its progress, surely, but also, and especially, with its concrete reality of terrifying injustice, with the unconcealable cries of the suffering, hope-filled poor. Just as undeniably, the urgent new synthesis of these and so many other things—in theory, and far more so, in practice—presents its difficulties, and a variety of attempts are under way to create it. In some persons and groups, a taste for the new predominates, and they bend their efforts to integrate the old into the new. In other persons and groups, a fear of the new provokes a longing for the old.

The traditional mosaic of the church, with all its pieces and colors, has shaken apart and now must be fitted back together again. In the face of such an arduous and demanding task, with the dangers it might entail, one could of course make an option for a simple reconstruction, with an appeal to doctrinal security and calling on the hierarchy to take a firm stance administratively. Surely doctrine and administration continue to be necessary and important. But of themselves alone they will not be enough to rebuild the edifice. On the other hand, absolutely necessary and urgent though Christian praxis surely is, neither will it be enough, of itself alone, to re-create the whole edifice. Thus, Johannes B. Metz speaks of a "mysticism and politics of discipleship"; and Ignacio Ellacuría called for "the contemplative in action for justice." Whatever terms we may want to use to describe this new situation and challenge, the important thing is the emphasis on something called spirit rather than only on theory and praxis—or, of course, only on doctrine and administration.

Finally—for these and other, more specific, reasons—theology, too, has taken a serious interest in spirituality. First, it was noticed that a doctrinal, purely explanatory and deductive theology was no longer adequate to the twin explosions of concrete reality and faith—since the first explosion was driving believers back to something predoctrinal, something more comprehensive. This is how the most alert theologians saw things. Hans Urs von Balthasar and Karl Rahner had been urging for years that the wall between theology and spirituality be torn down. A purely doctrinal theology, then, had become irrelevant. And a distribution of the identity and relevance of theology among, on one hand, the doctrinal dogmatic treatises or tractates, and on the other, those of Christian praxis and spirituality, had not solved the problem either. After all, the problem does not reside in the formal organization of the content of theology, but in theology's across-the-board attitude—the spirit with which theology is done, and the spirit communicated by the theology that is done.

In a like context, the in-depth renewal of theology has consisted primarily not so much in an emphasis on new or forgotten content, but in an effort to address and focus on content that by its nature engenders spirit, and that ought to be addressed and communicated with a particular spirit. For example, in my opinion the key discovery of modern theology is this: the objective reality of the Reign of God, and its corresponding subjective reality—hope and praxis—have become an increasingly important focus for many theologies, and indeed for liberation theology, the central content. But the reason why these become central in theology is not that we know something important that Jesus proclaimed. The reason why this Reign and its corresponding hope and praxis suddenly belong to the core of Christian theology is precisely that the objective member of the pair launches a rocket of hope and calls for a practice. Without that, there is no grasping the meaning of the Reign of God. The hermeneutic problem is not reducible to the opportunity to understand a text. The hermeneutic problem is also a problem of spirituality—of what is the spirit that moves us to read a text, that enables us to interpret it, and that permits us to communicate its spirit for today. A theological treatment of the subject of the Reign of God, then, both requires and renders possible the doing of theology with a specific attitude. This hope-charged praxic attitude, this attitude of hoping and acting "with spirit," is what has set theology on the road to becoming spiritual through and through—to being shot through with spirituality—rather than relegating the latter to one of the tractates (usually, of course, regarded as secondary).

In Latin America the theology of liberation has been very attentive to spirituality, and the performance of its task has been steeped in a particular spirit from the very start. But it is not by some voluntary decision on the part of liberation theologians that this has been the case. Rather, it is because this theology wishes to take account of, and constitute a response to, concrete, historical church reality, with its real cries and real hopes. The very fact that liberation theology is an account of something concrete, formulated for the purpose of turning that concrete reality into something really new, demonstrates that a particular spirit has been present in the very execution of its task. And it is because the theological task has been executed with spirit, we think, that this theology has made spirituality something central. As Gustavo Gutiérrez said, with liberation theology still in its infancy: "A vital, comprehensive, and synthetic attitude is needed—one that will inform our life part and parcel. A spirituality." The important thing, again, is to remember the reason for this fact. The reason is that, from its first beginnings, the theology of liberation has sought to be a creative synthesis of what it means to be human and to be Christian in the real world of today, specifically in the world of the hoping, suffering poor, whose sudden appearance on the scene has been what has unhinged the old world and its theology, while at the same time giving the new synthesis its bearings and thrust.

From this outlook I should like in this chapter, to address spirituality as it is developing in Latin America. Rather than speaking of spirituality in the abstract, however, I should like to work from a point of departure in the concrete spirit that actually becomes present in human beings and animates their thoughts, feelings, and actions. After all, while it may be difficult to define spirituality, the presence of human beings is both evident and instructive. Let me begin, then, with the proposition that spiritual persons are persons who live with spirit—those who, in Christian terms, "are filled with the Spirit of Christ, and this in a living, observable manner because the strength and life of that Spirit invests their whole person and their whole action" (Ignacio Ellacuría).

It is not easy to discover a single methodological route to the treatment of the subject of spirituality. The various dimensions of "life with spirit" intermingle. We should now like to offer two kinds of reflections. The first turns on the basic spirituality of every human being, which we call the fundamental, objectively theological dimension. This reflection will be of a more comprehensive kind, then, but we think it necessary to entertain it if we hope to be able to restore spirituality to its original place, or to comprehend Christian spirituality not as something added to the human, but as a deepening of the human—such as occurred in the *homo verus*, Jesus. The second approach that we shall use will be an explicitation of the Christian element of spirituality, with its christologic and pneumatologic dimension, which we shall address simultaneously. Here, it will be a matter simply of answering these questions: What is the spirit required in order to live in a Christian manner? What is the spirit that produces the Christian life?

II. THE FUNDAMENTAL, OBJECTIVELY THEOLOGICAL DIMENSION OF SPIRITUALITY

Every human being has a spiritual life. Like it or not, know it or not, each of us is confronted with reality and endowed with the ability to react to that reality with ultimacy. The expression *spiritual life* is tautological, then. Every human being lives his or her life with spirit. It is another matter, of course, with what spirit a person lives. But at all events, he or she lives with spirit.

It seems to us important to recall this tautology, since, whatever spirituality may be, it does not directly intend a relationship with some manner of purely spiritual, invisible, immaterial realities, as if only in that case the spiritual life would begin to have meaning, and as if some human beings were spiritual and others were not. The spiritual life is not something "regional," and still less does it stand in opposition to another, "material" kind of life. Surely immaterial realities exist: first and foremost, we have the mystery of God. But this does not mean that the spiritual element of life consists in a direct relationship with the nonmaterial by way of nonmaterial or less material activities that would be, or would be intended to be, only spiritual. Indeed, this would actually prevent the revelation of God, by which God has actually become present in definitive attachment to the material element of Jesus' flesh, as well as to the material element of concrete history and of history's special offspring, the poor.

No, spirituality is the spirit with which we confront the real. It is the spirit with which we confront the concrete history in which we live, with all its complexity. Thus it will be possible to speak of what spirit is adequate and what is not; but each, the adequate spirit and the inadequate one, will have its reference to the real with a view to facing that real and deciding what to do with it. Let us now present what, in our opinion, is the adequate spirit with which that concrete reality ought to be confronted. It will be the basis of all spirituality, including the Christian, as well as the basis of the spiritualities (in the plural) that have been handed down to us by Christian tradition.

1. Honesty with the Real: Respecting the Truth of Concrete Reality

First of all, it is an act of spirit—and spirit is necessary in order to perform it—to be *honest with the real*. Intellectually, this means grasping the truth of concrete reality; practically, it means responding to the demand made by that reality. More precisely, it means—and this is why this honesty is not so very much in evidence—coming to a grasp of truth and actually making a response to reality. This is accomplished not only by way of overcoming ignorance and indifference, but in confrontation with our innate tendency to subordinate truth and to evade reality.

To grasp and accept truth is to allow reality to be, in the first place, that which it is, and not subject it to a violence calculated to adjust it to our own tastes and interests. To this purpose a spirit of honesty is required. In every human being the temptation is innate, and very often succumbed to, to imprison truth by means of injustice (see Rom. 1:18). The fact of the matter, however, is that the problem of truth is posed not only in terms of ignorance in the face of reality—when we start out with nothing to get to something, try to move from a not knowing to a knowing—but also in terms of our tendency to conceal the truth by means of a lie. In John, let us remember, the Evil One is a liar (cf. John 8:44).

This mighty proclivity to the lie is an expression of human sinfulness. We should like to suppress the truth. To overcome this proclivity, we have need of spirit. Sin is that which puts persons to death, but precisely therefore, it simultaneously seeks to hide itself—to pass itself off as something it is not. And so every scandal comes clad in its own concealment.

Honesty with the real, then, is a matter of great activity and requires spirit. If this basic honesty with the real is not exercised, the consequences for the human being are catastrophic. As Paul says, the heart is darkened (subjectively) and concrete realities are no longer creatures, sacraments of God (as they are objectively), but manipulated things. Indeed, from the root of this basic dishonesty follow all the sinful fruits catalogued by Paul, and God's wrath, instead of God's grace, spills out over the heads of those who are not honest with the real.

What dialectical theology (especially in Karl Barth) has asserted of human cognition and the possibility (and actuality) that it be used against God in one's own behalf will of course apply to a cognition of concrete reality. There is a way of knowing the real whose purpose is to defend the knower from the real. The right way to know is to know for the purpose of defending the real and its objective interests.

This is what we mean when we speak of honesty with the real. In polemical terms we mean overcoming the temptation to oppress truth. Positively speaking, we mean keeping our eyes open to the sight of reality—having the pure heart that enables one to see God, as the Beatitudes say.

2. Honesty with the Real: The Reaction of Mercy

Honesty with the real primarily means responding to the demand of concrete reality itself. To put it in still more general language, it means that, when the truth of reality is not imprisoned through injustice, that truth itself gives rise to an unconditional yes to life, and an unconditional no to death. Concrete reality cries no to its own negation—to the absence, lack, and annihilation of life. In biblical terminology this no is no to Cain the fratricide, no to the oppression in Egypt, and the prophets' no to those who sell the just for a pair of sandals. No theology or theodicy can subsequently silence or relativize this primary no uttered by reality.

To put it in a positive way, this ethical practice of honesty is mercy or pity in confrontation with reality. Mercy, here, or compassion, is not reducible to an affective movement of the emotions, although this may accompany it. Mercy denotes a reaction in the face of the suffering of another, which one has interiorized and which has become one and the same thing with oneself, with a view to saving that other. Mercy is the primary and ultimate, the first and the last, of human reactions. It is that in terms of which all dimensions of the human being acquire meaning and without which nothing else attains to human status. In this mercy, the human being is perfected, becomes whole, as Luke teaches in the parable of the Good Samaritan. The gospels use it to typify Jesus himself, who so often acts after being "moved with compassion." The Bible actually uses it to typify God, whose bowels grow so tender that the divine Father welcomes and embraces the prodigal. Mercy, then, is the correct manner of responding to concrete reality—as well as the ultimate and decisive manner thereof, as we learn from the parable of the Last Judgment. Everything—absolutely everything—turns on the exercise of mercy. On it depends not only transcendent salvation, but our living here and now, in concrete history, as saved human beings.

To be sure, this mercy will have to be exercised in a variety of ways, depending on the nature of the wound suffered by the victim lying in the ditch. Thus it must take various forms: emergency relief, assistance and support, reconciliation, and so on. In the presence of entire crucified peoples, as in Latin America, mercy must take the form of structural justice, which is having mercy on the masses.

What we are concerned to emphasize here, however, is the primary and ultimate nature of mercy as the primordial act of spirit. We have said that mercy is first and last; we mean that it is exercised for no other reason than that someone else is suffering, and that we have internalized that suffering. This, indeed, is how mercy and pity are presented in the gospel. The Good Samaritan is presented as an example of someone who fulfills the greatest of the commandments; yet, in the parable, the Samaritan appears not as a person acting in order to fulfill a commandment, but as a person "moved to pity" (Luke 10:33). The father in the parable, like our heavenly Father, reconciles the prodigal with himself personally, but the reason he goes out every day to look for him and offer him the embrace of welcome is not that he is trying to find some tactic that will get the child to return the parent the honor that is the latter's due. It is because he is moved to pity. It is the same with God and us.

Here we notice that mercy is, as we said, first and last. All other things whatsoever—personal risks, doubt, the rights of the institution—must be subordinated to mercy. No other interests, not even legitimate ones, may be appealed to in order to ignore mercy or relegate it to secondary status.

This primordial mercy constantly makes its reappearance in concrete history at key moments to recall to us its quality as fundamental and ultimate—as that beyond which it is impossible to go. It is related of Jesus that, after having healed the person with the withered hand in the synagogue, he asked: "Is it permitted to do a good deed on the sabbath—or an evil one? To preserve life—or destroy it?" (Mark 3:4). Bartolomé de las Casas said: "A live Indian is better that a baptized corpse." Archbishop Romero said: "Nothing is more important for the church than life, especially the life of the poor, who are God's favorites . . . We must defend the minimum which is all the maximum gift of God: life." What all of these quotations have in common, in their different accents, is the primary and ultimate character of mercy. One cannot go beyond it, or argue with anyone in its favor, or avoid any risk it may require. In the solemn words of Micah, God says to each and every human being:

You have been told, O man, what is good,
and what the Lord requires of you:
Only to do right and to love goodness (Mic. 6:8).

Here is no anthropological argument, or even a religious one, in favor of mercy, as if mercy and compassion were being identified for the first time as a demand on the part of God. The great question, the invitation and demand for mercy, is concrete reality itself. When we respond with mercy, we are being honest with reality.

3. Fidelity to the Real

Honesty with the real must not only be exercised in our time, but it must be maintained all down through history, in whatever history proposes as a thing to be endured, or as something new, or as perilous or blessed surprise. Thus, honesty with the real becomes fidelity to the real. History has its span—an intuition that the Catholic tradition has always maintained—and the span of history ever introduces novelties, obscurities, and risks. History must needs be traversed—"walked with," as Micah puts it, "humbly," and not imagining that a first act of honesty, or the original direction of our route, will automatically carry us to our destination.

Historically, this is evident. To maintain that first honesty with the real is difficult and costly. We need spirit to maintain our honesty regardless of where it leads.

Concrete reality frequently clouds over, even after the first honest choice, and may become temptation. It is the cumulative experience of history, down to our very day, that when the truth about reality is maintained, when the lie that would imprison that truth is unmasked, when reactions of love, in all its forms—and certainly in the form of justice—are seen, they are not welcome; the one who seeks to foster life is expected to give of his or her own life, or even to give up that life. The honest denunciation of sin becomes having to take on the burden of sin, with all its consequences. In addition to attacks from without, one experiences the intrinsic difficulty of finding light—of changing course precisely in order to be honest with one's fundamental intuition in seeking to bestow life. This is when fidelity is demanded, amidst darkness, as with Abraham's fidelity; amidst petition and supplication, as with the high priest Jesus, of the Letter to the Hebrews. To be honest is to come to be honest by passing through the crucible of having failed to be so. One arrives at fullness through history, with all its vicissitudes, as did that high priest.

At the same time, however, it is also a fact that, rising up out of concrete reality itself is a hope that cannot be silenced, and that there exists a hope-charged current of humanity, which is endlessly fascinating. In Pauline language, it is as if creation were suffering birthpangs and crying to be delivered. In concrete reality itself, then, there is something of promise and of unsilenced hope. This is the experience of centuries. Reality itself, in spite of its long history of failure and misery, posits ever and again the hope of fullness. Always there arises a new Exodus, a new return from Exile, a deliverance from captivity—although none of these, surely, is ever definitive. And this hope, with which reality itself trembles, finds spokespersons all down through history. There was a Moses to proclaim a land of promise, then an Isaiah who once again announced a new heaven and a new earth, and then a Jesus of Nazareth who once again proclaimed the Reign of God, and then an Archbishop Romero who once again announced liberation. This recurrence of hope is part of concrete reality, too, and to it, as well, one must be faithful, especially when so many other concrete historical experiences counsel skepticism, cynicism, or resignation.

Fidelity to the real, then, includes hope—a hope made possible by reality itself. But this hope is an active one, and not only an expectant one. It helps concrete reality to come to be what it seeks to be. And that is love. Love and hope—in that order—are two sides of the same coin: the conviction, put in practice, that reality has possibilities. Love and hope mean helping to bring to light the better, the more humane, presently gestating in the womb of reality. Hope and love are each other's sustenance. That the world may have life can only be hoped for in the act of giving that world life; in the activity of giving life, hope grows that life is possible. This fidelity to the real, then, is not an exigency arbitrarily imposed, or even the observance of the most exalted of the commandments. It is the most finished and perfect harmony with reality.

4. Allowing Ourselves To Be Led by the Real

As we have said, hope is nourished by reality, and love is facilitated by reality. This means that concrete reality is an opportunity, not just a difficulty. It means that reality is also Good News, not merely demand. This reality is transformed into the "heavy burden become light," as Karl Rahner says of the gospel; the more you carry it, the more it carries you.

This means that concrete reality is also steeped in grace; reality itself offers us a direction and a strength to traverse, and make, history in that direction. This is the case because in concrete reality is an accumulated goodness, as well, which moves us. There is a hope-filled, honest, loving current there, which becomes a powerful invitation to us, and once we have entered it, we allow ourselves to be carried along by it. Just as there is an original sin that becomes a structural dimension of reality, so also there is an original grace, which becomes a gracious structure of reality. That structural grace is more original, surely, in the logic of Christian faith than original sin, although the fruits of the latter appear to be quantitatively greater than those of the former.

To accept that grace emerging from concrete reality, to allow ourselves to be permeated with this grace, to place our wager on it, is also an act of spirit. To accept that grace is to plunge headlong into reality and allow ourselves to be borne up on the "more" with which reality is pregnant and which is offered to us freely, again and again, despite all. To accept the grace emerging from reality is to allow ourselves to be borne forward by a future of goodness—a utopia—which, while it has never existed and never will, nevertheless gives us food for the future and supplies us with the strength to keep on searching for it and building it.

In more personal language, to allow ourselves to be supported and carried along by reality means allowing ourselves to be helped and supported by the "cloud of witnesses" (Heb. 12:1), those who have generated the best of human and Christian traditions, who invite us to graft ourselves onto these traditions and build on them.

Tradition is that which has been handed over to us; in other words, what has been given us, and that too is grace. Reality, then, not only makes demands, but offers opportunities as well. This gracious structure of reality calls for a response with the spirit of gratuity and gratitude. And because concrete reality has this structure of grace, therefore it, too, is worthy of celebration.

5. Fundamental Theologal Spirituality

Honesty with the real, fidelity to the real, and allowing ourselves to be carried forward by the real, are acts of spirit that, in one form or another, by action or omission, every human being performs. Thus we have called them, all three taken together, fundamental spirituality, because they concern every human being, and every Christian is a human being. We also call them "theologal," because—although we have not yet mentioned God in connection with them, with the divine call and demands, with God's invitations and grace—the mystery of God does indeed become present *in* concrete reality. Transcendence becomes present *in* history. In this wise, in responding to reality, explicitly or implicitly we have the experience of God in history.

If we call it experience, it is because this contact with the transcendent in history is personal, as well. It is an individual experience (and analogously, a collective or group experience). The exigency and grace of reality are addressed to concrete persons, who have names, beings who are called—whether or not they interpret it in this way—by name to react to reality in this way. The believer will feel called by name by a God who also has a name. The nonbeliever will not attempt to give a name to reality's call, but will be unable to escape being called by name.

Indubitably, merely to have described—precisely as we have done, and not otherwise—a fundamental spirituality presupposes a particular view of God. The God in terms of which we have given our description is the God of Jesus. In the conclusion of this chapter, we shall make this explicit, and in Christian terms. What we have sought to emphasize thus far is only that the spirituality that we shall later call Christian, or the spiritualities that have proliferated throughout history, or the spirituality of liberation, are but concrete manners of realizing this fundamental human spirituality without which the others would be vain and empty.

III. CHRISTIAN SPIRITUALITY: THE FOLLOWING OF JESUS IN THE OPTION FOR THE POOR

What we have said so far will call for an option for or against a fundamental spirituality. But even if that fundamental spirituality is accepted as we have described it, it will become concrete in various forms. Christian spirituality is no more and no less than a living of the fundamental spirituality that we have described, precisely in the concrete manner of Jesus and according to the spirit of Jesus. This is the following of Jesus.

The following of Jesus has two dimensions, which are interrelated: the christological dimension, and the pneumatological dimension, that is, the concretion of Jesus as *norma normans*, and the Spirit that renders Jesus present in history.

The following *of Jesus* is what Jesus himself offered to and required of certain of his own, and what very quickly after the resurrection came to be understood by Christians as the essence of the Christian life. Paul raised it to an intrinsically theological category with the declaration that God's plan is for us to become daughters and sons in the Son. The christological dogmas of the church, if taken seriously and reread adequately, lead to the same conclusion. In Jesus, God has been revealed, and the human being has been revealed. Jesus was not merely *vere homo*, truly a human being; he was precisely *homo verus*—the true, authentic, genuine human being. What dogma is really saying here, then, is that to be truly a human being is to be what Jesus is. To live with spirit, to react correctly to concrete reality, is to re-create, throughout history, the fundamental structure of the life of Jesus.

This has been grasped very well by great Christians all through history, especially in ages of crisis, and of church and historical renewal. Francis of Assisi simply wished to be like Jesus. Ignatius Loyola constantly besought of Jesus an interior knowledge of Christ in order to love him and follow him. Dietrich Bonhoeffer pointed out that Jesus' first and last words to Peter were "Follow me." On the morning of the day he was assassinated (March 24, 1980), Archbishop Romero wrote to Bishop Pedro Casaldáliga that they could be "happy to be running the same risks as Jesus by identifying with the causes of the dispossessed."

The following of Jesus, then, is a constant in the history of the Christians who have lived with spirit. However, it adopts a particular guise in this or that particular era. This is what actually happens, and this is what ought to happen. Jesus should be followed, continued, updated in history—not imitated. The Spirit always adapts Jesus to a given time and place; at the same time, the Spirit can only refer a follower back to Jesus, can only actualize Jesus, and nothing else whatsoever. The dialectic is a familiar one: the Spirit, says Jesus, will introduce his disciples into all truth, all through history, and will even see to it that Jesus' followers do greater things than Jesus himself has done. And so Jesus says that it is a good thing that he is going away. On the other hand, the Spirit can only refer us to Jesus himself, who becomes present ever and again, throughout history.

This new actualization of Jesus in function of the context of a given time and place does actually occur. It focuses on a given new historical reality in which the activity of the Spirit is seen anew. For example, Medellín proclaimed the presence all around us of a longing for liberation from all servitude to be a sign of the Spirit. While not exhausted therein, the Spirit has its correlative in this emergence of Jesus' presence with each new, concrete, historical situation, as the latter comes along in its new focus. So it is that, in Latin America, the novelty of the Spirit is objectively manifested in the "irruption of the poor" on the social scene—their seeming sudden materialization as if from nowhere. From a point of departure in this novelty, the Christian "rereads" again, the *homo verus* who is Jesus—thereby rediscovering him once more as he really was, rediscovering him as the gospels present him. From the subjective standpoint, the fundamental act of the Spirit today, we believe, is the option for the poor.

While Christian spirituality today is as it always has been, the following of Jesus, it is not a "following of Jesus" by way of mechanically reproducing this or that aspect of his historical life. The authentic following of Jesus today occurs by reproducing the whole of that life in terms of the option for the poor. This can be real because that option is not only regional or pastoral, but comprehensive, all-embracing, as well. It is an option involving the totality of the human being in his or her confrontation with reality. In terms of what we are able to know, it means grasping and understanding the whole of reality, God and human beings alike, from a starting point in the poor. In terms of what we can hope for, that option means sharing and allowing ourselves to be led by the hope of the poor. In terms of what we have before us as a task, it means destroying the anti-Reign that victimizes the poor and building a Reign in which the world can be hearth and home to the poor. In terms of what is offered to us to celebrate, it means rejoicing with one another in the life, the hope, the creativity, and the love of the poor.

Jesus and the option for the poor can be set in a relationship. They *must* be set in relationship in our concrete history today as well as with our regard turned toward the past. An affinity between Jesus and poverty is abundantly evident throughout the Christian scriptures. In fact, that Jesus himself is the historical sacrament of God's option for the poor, and that he himself implements that option in his concrete life, appear altogether clearly. From the standpoint of the transcendent, we may say that Jesus is the maximal historicization or concretization of God's option for the poor. The gospels present his incarnation in a consciously slanted manner. They present it as a movement toward what is lowly, as an incarnation in the direction of the poor, the least, the oppressed. Indeed, the metaphor of impoverishment is used to express this abasement, this descent. And although we say metaphor, the question is why this particular form of incarnation was selected and no other. From a historical viewpoint, there can be no doubt that Jesus' life, mission, fate, and even resurrection would lack its internal logic without an essential relationship between Jesus and the poor of this world, or without his option for them.

What we mean by this is that the following of Jesus and the option for the poor, comprising the current formulation of Christian spirituality, have their own affinity. The new element manifested by the Spirit is the everlastingly old. According to this new-and-old element, and from this standpoint, let us now examine the structure of the life of Jesus that any Christian spirituality must reproduce as it acquires form and shape in our present age. We must see the successes and the problems of the currency enjoyed by this particular Christian spirituality. The structure to be reproduced can and must be examined in terms of the essential elements of Jesus' life. The actual reproduction of that structure today, when all is said and done, can only be recounted. It would be a contradiction in terms to speak of the Spirit without recounting what kind of life that Spirit produces—how that Spirit manifests itself in the spirit of human beings. In all consistency, then, we shall not speak only of a pneumatology of spirituality, but we shall narrate the acts of spirit that the Spirit requires and produces.

1. Incarnation: The Holiness of Poverty

The first element of the structure of the life of Jesus is the incarnation. Jesus was born a human being, of course, but not just any human being, any more than any of the rest of us. He came to the human state in a specific manner. He became flesh, in the weakness of flesh, of course, but not just any flesh. Altogether obviously, the gospels present him as a person of the poor, surrounded by the poor, and serving the poor. His initial, programmatic message has meaning only when seen within the scriptural tradition of God's option for the poor of this world, for the orphans and the widows, for the outcast and despised. Jesus' view of this world and his basic judgment of it is guided by how things are going with the poor. His hope is a hope of the poor and for the poor. Thus, Jesus comes before us as the human being united with the hopeful current of history, the current of so many who have come before him and who are to come after him, the current whose protagonist is the people of the poor.

Jesus' incarnation in poverty is basic for a spirituality of today. Systematically, that incarnation means making an option for the poor. Descriptively, it means that the poor are, as Puebla says, the locus of, or setting for, conversion and evangelization. They are the locus of conversion because their own situation is the clearest question about what we are and what we ought to be. Here, then, is the most universal setting for God's question: "What have you done with your brother?" (cf. Gen. 4:9), and thereby of the question of our fellow human beings precisely as our brothers and sisters.

The poor are the locus of evangelization by virtue of their positive values: their simplicity, their openness, their sense of community, their hope of life, and their love and commitment, to cite Puebla's list. Thus they become gospel, Good News, gift, and grace received unexpectedly and without desert.

The poor, then, are the locus of spiritual experience—encounter with God. They are an ethical demand, but they are more than that. Incarnation means descent and encounter, primordial decision to come to be within the authentic reality of this world; it also means allowing oneself to be found by the God who is hidden but present in that reality.

Hence it is that Gustavo Gutiérrez's words are more than rhetoric: the poor "drink from their own wells." The poor, and the world of poverty, are like some huge well filled with water—the symbol of life—for the poor have filled it with their life, their suffering, their tears, their hope, and their commitment. All of this water now becomes water for others. We can drink of it. It is a grace offered us. Indeed, we must drink from it. It is the basic option.

Incarnation, then, is costly descent, gladsome discovery, and decision ever to drink of that well of water in the lowlands of history. In this consists the holiness of poverty; it means a sharing in the history of that concrete reality in which the God who is holy, ever distant, and beyond us, becomes the God who is near, hidden but present, in the poor.

2. Mission: The Holiness of Love

The second element in the structure of Jesus' life is mission. Mission is an activity performed for the purpose of changing reality. The mission of Jesus' life materializes against a background of the Reign of God as God's will for the world, for history, and—within history—for each and every human being. Through his option for the poor, Jesus proclaims the Reign to the poor of this world and inaugurates it with signs (miracles, exorcisms, his welcome extended to sinners and to all who have been deprived of their dignity). Those signs are only signs; they do not change the structure of reality. But they point in the direction of the Reign, and they kindle a hope that the Reign is possible.

Besides working these signs, Jesus applies his teaching to society. He does so in a denunciation and unmasking of the negative, rather than in positive theoretical elaborations. He denounces and unmasks all structurally oppressive power—religious, economic, intellectual, and political. And, he proclaims a different society, one that will be delivered from those oppressive powers.

Words, signs, and praxis, then, are the concrete form that Jesus' mission takes. They all spring from the mercy of which we have spoken, and they find their adequate expression in any suffering whatever from which persons are to be freed. Thereby they enunciate, by making it concrete, the fundamental principle of the Christian life: love. Even had Jesus not declared this the greatest of the commandments, his life as mission would elevate it to the basic principle of the Christian life.

It is having a mission that gives meaning to Jesus' life. In fact, it is not Jesus who has the mission—although he begins with it in its broad traits; rather, it is Jesus' mission that constantly shapes his life—his outward life, of course, but also his interior life, his life in the presence of God.

Living with spirit, then, is action—a doing from love and with love. Doing is not everything, as we shall presently see. There is gift and grace, too. But without loving action, without at least a readiness to posit signs and foster a praxis, any spirituality is open to suspicion.

Mission continues to be central today, for any spirituality. It is mission that maintains the supremacy of love in the Christian life, and specifically, in Latin America, has concentrated the mission of the church in the liberation of the poor—understanding liberation in its most comprehensive expression. Upon this mission the theology of liberation has been erected.

Liberation, toil, and struggle for liberation, justice—this, before all else, is love, and great love. It means bringing Jesus' mission to the here and now on an oppressed continent out of love and with love. Without a practice of liberation, spirituality in Latin America today would have no meaning.

We shall delve no further here into this familiar concept, as it is addressed in other chapters in the present work. We should like, however, by way of an excursus, to examine two points that call for specific treatment: (1) the spirit needed in order to bring about liberation and to heal its negative by-products, and (2) the relationship between liberation and grace.

3. The Need for Spirit in the Practice of Liberation

The fact that there is a practice of and a struggle for liberation is itself a great testimonial to spirituality, as it is a great act of spirit. Indeed, that practice and struggle are the basic act, since it constitutes the introduction of Jesus' mission into the here and now, the actualization of a life lived with love and a struggle motivated by love. Generally speaking, this is what we discovered in Latin America in the

1970s: that there could be no spiritual life without real life. We came to see that faith and justice, God and this oppressed world, Jesus and the poor, must be brought together—that, with historical and Christian urgency, a practice of liberation was needed. This being said, however, we also observed and saw that the practice of liberation would need to be imbued with spirit, and with a specific spirit, and this was the lesson of the 1980s that so many Christians—theologians among them—accepted with all their heart. Combining the two insights, we came to know how good and necessary liberation is in order that there be spirit, and how good and necessary it is for there to be spirit in the practice of liberation.

The practice of liberation is right and necessary. It is good, and it is Christian. But, like any human practice, it is not only open to the finest opportunities, it is also threatened by limitations, temptations, even sinfulness. The practice of liberation does not mechanically solve all human and Christian problems. It helps prayer, for example, or the living of the religious life, or life in the base communities, or growth in faith and hope. But these things also need a specific cultivation of their own. Thus, while the practice of liberation furnishes a correct and necessary channel—the most correct and necessary channel in a situation of oppression—still the channel is not everything.

Furthermore, the most perceptive of those who have devoted themselves to the practice of liberation have grasped that, of its very nature, this practice, like any human thing—even prayer, for example, although that is often forgotten—also has a tendency to engender negative by-products, and that these side effects sometimes actually materialize. In the writings of Archbishop Romero—defender to the last of the practice of liberation—liberation generates the following temptations.

1. Diverse groups dedicated to the struggle for liberation may come into conflict with one another, to the detriment of unity and effectiveness.

2. The popular element may be gradually displaced: the popular masses may come to be replaced by organizations, the organizations by their officers or leaders, and the officers and leaders by the most outstanding among them, with the attendant danger of isolation from the concrete needs and sufferings of the people.

3. A dogmatism may crop up in the analysis (observation and interpretation) of the facts; now the facts will only seem to confirm set positions, which will no longer be subjected to verification by the yardstick of reality.

4. Some specific mechanism of liberation practice (social, political, or armed) may become absolutized, with the consequent reduction of reality to one of its parts, as if from the fullness of one of those parts the perfection of all of the others would automatically flow.

5. A false sense of ethical superiority may blind one individual or group to the contributions of other individuals or groups by the mere fact that the latter are not doing what the former are doing.

6. In some instances religion is manipulated—beyond its legitimate use in terms of the convergence of liberation and the gospel—and this may do violence to popular piety, the concrete religiousness of the peoples; furthermore, it may deprive these peoples of their important religious motivation for self-liberation.

7. Power is ambivalent. It has an innate tendency to be used for self-assertion instead of for service—especially in the case of armed power (where it might be-

come legitimate, or at any rate historically inevitable), so that violence is transformed into a mystique.

8. Weariness or disenchantment may occasion the desertion of the practice of liberation because of the price to be paid and the risks to be run, and because liberation is so long in coming.

All of this shows us why liberation must be practiced with a particular spirit: in order to heal the negative by-products, maintain the correct direction, persevere in the practice of liberation, and enhance that practice exponentially. Therefore we speak of *liberation with spirit*. Whatever the spirit—besides the fundamental spirit of love—that will enhance the love of the practice of liberation and heal it of its most specific temptations, we present it here programmatically, from a starting point in those who exemplify the spirit of the Beatitudes.

The *single-hearted* (Matt. 5:8—literally, the pure of heart) are those who see God and therefore see human beings. They remain ever open to the truth, accepting that truth whatever it may be, without attempting to dominate or manipulate it, without deceiving themselves about themselves or about the processes of liberation, and without falling into the temptation to transform the truth into propaganda. This purity of heart shows profound chastity of knowledge and will, whereby they refuse to impose their own ideas or to promote their own interests in liberation.

The *merciful* are those who take up the task because their hearts have been moved to compassion by the incredible suffering of the poor. This "original mercy" imbues their prophetical labors and makes their struggle a struggle waged for love. But it also requires of them that, in the practice of liberation, they continue to keep before their eyes, from first to last, the pain of the poor, which must never be reduced to the concept of a simple social price to be paid for progress. It requires of them that, in the strategies and tactics of liberation, in their alliances and divisions, they take very close account of what all of that is likely to produce in terms of an increase or lessening of the pain of the poor. Structurally, pity or mercy is the manner in which they express the presence, right from the start and all through the liberation process, of a great love for the people of the poor.

Peacemakers are those who have not made the battle itself their ultimate goal, "gotten used to" it, placed their whole trust in it, or transformed it into a mystique. Positively, they are those who, even in time of struggle and conflict—so inevitable in liberation—seek to humanize their conflicts, bringing all other means, as well, to bear on ending them, and through thick and thin, fostering the reconciliation to come with signs of reconciliation in the present.

Those who can *forgive* are unwilling to close off the future from their adversary or their enemy. They toil for reconciliation in its personal form and in structural forms—by dialogue, by negotiation—and they posit signs of the same, since without it no triumph is lasting and no society humane.

The *poor in spirit*, finally, believe that in weakness there is strength. They strive for the utopia of poverty or at least of a shared austerity. They live in and as community, overcoming any elitism—and isolation—of the personal or group ego. They are the wellspring of spirit.

What we are trying to say in all of this is that the practice of liberation is itself an act of spirit, and the most radical of all such acts, because it is an act of love.

Thus, the practice of liberation is the indispensable channel of spirituality. It furnishes the material from which so many other acts of spirit can spring. But it needs spirit in its own turn, in order to maintain itself and not degenerate.

4. Practice of Liberation and Gratuity

Liberation is practice. It is a doing, a living, a desire to spend one's life for the life of the poor. This is what is required by concrete reality, and the gospel is supremely demanding when it comes to the practice of love, mercy, and justice. Just as emphatically, however, that gospel says that practice is not everything. Or rather, practice must be shot through with something else if it is to become Christian practice. That something else is gratuity and generosity: the willingness to give without receiving in return. In words of dire warning, we are told: "When you have done all you have been commanded to do, say, 'We are useless servants. We have done no more than our duty' " (Luke 17:10). In words of invitation, we hear: "God loved us first. Love one another" (cf. 1 John 4:19,7).

This generosity is perhaps the most difficult reality to conceptualize and put in words. But something can be said about it and its importance for liberation practice in the presence of a "graced" human being, who has had such a powerful experience of the divine gratuity. In terms of a need for healing on the part of the practice of liberation, while admitting that that practice calls for great enthusiasm, we must also say that generosity and gratuity forbid hubris—a feeling of ethical superiority—or anything like a personality cult. Generosity recalls that all have their limitation and sin. In the words of Ignacio González Faus, "One must fight a revolution as someone forgiven." Positively speaking, the experience of gratuity entails gratitude to something greater than oneself, and the response of the one who has been forgiven and "graced" multiplies spirit and practice exponentially. After all, from gratitude springs the generosity of commitment—although a convert's enthusiasm has its dangers—freedom of spirit, and the joy of having found the pearl of great price. The experience of gratuity engenders creativity.

The dimension of generosity in spirituality—the spirit of gratuity and its correlative of gratitude—is essential to Christian faith, and accordingly, to any Christian spirituality, including that of liberation. At the center of our faith is the fact that God has loved us first, and that a response to that love, a love for our brothers and sisters, has its life from, and is imbued with the power of, being loved by God. As Gustavo Gutiérrez says: we are "loved in order to love, set free in order to set free." Generosity is not only salvation for oneself, but liberation from oneself. And this enables the practice of liberation.

To give in grateful response to having received moves us to give anew and tremendously enhances our giving. This can only be observed. But to cite a single instance, the grace Archbishop Romero received not only converted him, it swelled his generosity to astonishing extremes; not only did he carry his people on his shoulders, but his people carried him as well. "With this people," he said, "it costs nothing to be a good shepherd."

To sum up what we have said in this section: the essential dimension of spirituality is mission—an activity that, today, has to be liberation, since this is the form that love for the masses will necessarily take. That love is healing if, as with Jesus' own mission, it is accompanied by the spirit of the Beatitudes and by grace. Then we see the holiness of love, and we see that, besides, this holiness is most fruitful for liberation. It bears concrete fruit, and we observe this in Latin America, where there are so many saints of liberation. Ignacio Ellacuría used to say: "Holiness is the ultimate weapon of the church of the poor."

5. The Cross: Political Holiness

Jesus was faithful to his incarnation and mission, and that led him to persecution and the cross. Neither of these was sought by Jesus; neither can supply spirituality with its foundation. But they are prerequisites. After all, spirituality presupposes utter fidelity to the real, and in the real world the Reign of God is not proclaimed and inaugurated on a clean slate. The Reign of God is proclaimed and inaugurated in the presence of, and in opposition to, the anti-Reign. The anti-Reign inevitably produces persecution and death, because the God of life—the God of Jesus—and the gods of death are locked in mortal combat. They do battle, just as do their intermediaries.

Christian spirituality, then, is not a spirituality of the cross or of suffering. It is a spirituality of honest, consistent, and faithful love—a wide-awake love that knows the necessary risks it is taking. Christian spirituality is the spirituality of a crucified love. This is not because of some secret design on the part of God, or because God requires or relishes human suffering. It is because incarnation occurs in a reality shot through with an anti-Reign that is determined to throw every possible obstacle in the way of the proclaimers and initiators of the Reign.

This is what we find exemplified in the cross of Jesus. There is an anti-Reign, and it has to be fought. This must be done from outside the anti-Reign, yes, but ultimately the anti-Reign can only be uprooted from within itself. From without, sin must be denounced and combated. But from within, one must take on the burden of sin and thus share in the annihilation exerted by sin upon the victims of this world.

If anything is clear in Latin America today, it is that we must take on the sin of the world. We must be open to the possibility of the cross. This possibility is very real. Since Vatican II Latin America has mounted many assaults on the anti-Reign; therefore there have been, overwhelmingly, more persecution and more martyrs on that continent.

A number of important things must be said of these martyrs. In the first place, today's Latin American martyrs appear concretely more like Jesus than did the martyrs of the past. We are not comparing the subjective holiness of the martyrs, all down through history. We only mean that, in our own times, a kind of martyrdom occurs for the same reasons as Jesus' martyrdom occurred. The Latin American martyrs are martyrs not for anything directly ecclesial. They are martyrs for the cause of humanity. They are martyrs of the poor. While Thomas à Becket, for example, was murdered at the altar for defending the legitimate interests and freedom of the church, Archbishop Romero was murdered at the altar for defending the interests of the poor, not those of the church as such. The new martyrs, then, are martyrs of the Reign of God, martyrs of humanity.

In the second place, martyrdom in Latin America is the fullest, most integral expression of the incarnation that takes place in concrete Latin American reality. In the chilling words of Archbishop Romero: "I rejoice, my brothers, that priests have been murdered in our country. It would be a sad thing if, when so many Salvadorans are being murdered, no priests would be murdered. They show that the church has taken flesh in poverty." The martyrs, those active followers of Jesus, also become concrete, eloquent symbols of a far more secular, more massive, and more cruel martyrdom: the crucifixion of entire peoples.

In the third place, the martyrs show that it is possible—because it actually happens—to have a convergence between actual Latin American reality and actual Christian reality. They show that, the deeper you are immersed in the one, the deeper you are immersed in the other, and that is no small benefit that they bequeath to us.

Finally, martyrdom is the most integral form of a holiness today that we shall call political holiness. We call it political, because martyrdom here today is offered in the name of society, the city, the *polis*. Some, those who fight for the anti-Reign, kill others; they kill those who fight for the Reign. That Reign has a concrete social shape. Because they have proclaimed the Reign and attacked the anti-Reign—not only because they have exercised mercy toward individuals or small groups—the best of human beings and Christians are murdered. If anything shows that the martyrs' love has been political, it is—just as in the case of Jesus—their martyrdom. And if there is any doubt that Christian love needs to be political, the martyrs, those witnesses par excellence of faith, are there to remind us.

We call it holiness because martyrdom is the most remarkable exercise of faith, hope, and charity. Martyrdom makes concrete the specifically Christian. To put it somewhat scandalously (and Christianity is charged with the scandalous): Is it really more blessed to give than to receive? Do those who lose their lives really save their lives? Does salvation really come from a person who has been crucified? Is it true that we ought to leap for joy on the day we are persecuted? At stake in the answer to these scandalous questions is the essence of our faith. In faith, we accept the tragedy of history: that in order to give life, one must give of one's own life. But martyrdom also says, and says it straight out, with no beating about the bush, that the essence of Christianity is what it has always been said to be: love. There is no greater love than this, that one lay down one's life for one's friends.

The spirituality of martyrdom, then, is nothing other than love for a world of victims. This is the basic thing. Then comes the need for a spirit of courage to keep faithful to the end, and then the credibility that engenders martyrdom in others.

Actual martyrdom presupposes and generates a specific spirituality in the survivors. First of all, the martyrs are not forgotten. "Woe to the peoples who forget their martyrs!" says Pedro Casaldáliga. Next is gratitude for their having shown the "greatest love." Finally comes the invitation to be grafted onto the tradition that the martyrs have created with their love and their blood. The martyrs—beginning with Jesus of Nazareth—engender a powerful, Paschal tradition. That is where we should be heading. We must build on that tradition if we are to keep moving forward in history.

6. Resurrection: The Holiness of Joy

It is said of Jesus that justice was done him, and that he was raised by the Father. For once, at least, the executioner has not triumphed over the victim. The action of human beings in putting the just and the innocent to death is answered by the action of God in restoring them to life in fullness. Jesus lives in fullness and pours that fullness out on the rest of human beings. He is the Lord of history.

Where spirituality is concerned—unless we have only been spouting words—this means that even here and now, in history itself, we can and should live as persons raised to life. Spirituality must take on the dimension of resurrection, too.

Resurrection has nothing in common with sterile attempts to live in concrete history the "immateriality" of Jesus' presence in history today, or with an effort to associate oneself with Jesus' presence today through some kind of act of "intention." The history of the church is a fine demonstration of all this. For a long time the religious life was presented as a state of perfection because the vows of religion were thought to place the members of religious orders and congregations, structurally, in a less material state. The dangers are obvious. In the name of immateriality, the flesh of this world is left to its misery.

If resurrection is life in its fullness, it can only be love in its fullness. How can one live in fullness in this life? The answer is simple: by repeating the following of Jesus in the spirit of Jesus on this earth. The one who lives in this way lives even now as someone raised to life amid the very conditions of history.

However, resurrection also has the dimension of triumph—the triumph of life over death—and the question becomes how that dimension can be reflected in the spirituality of Jesus' followers. The reflection, in history, of the triumphal element in resurrection consists, it seems to us, in hope that does not die, in freedom versus slavery, and in the joy that conquers sadness.

The hope that does not die is founded in the conviction that love does not die and that its fruits abide. It is founded in the conviction that the executioner will not triumph over the victim, that the deepest stratum of reality is good and positive, and that therefore we must keep calling, "*Abba* Father."

Freedom in the following of Jesus is not only, or even basically, the freedom of a laissez-faire liberalism jealous of its own rights (when they are its rights), or the freedom of an estheticism that urges human beings to "become themselves" freely (when there is indeed beauty in such an enterprise). Freedom in the following of Jesus is the liberty of love. It is the freedom of those who detach themselves from all things in order to do good, the freedom of those who give their life freely, without anyone taking it from them. It is the freedom of Paul to become a slave to all. It is the freedom of Jesus, whose life no one takes from him, but he lays it down himself.

Joy in the following of Jesus, finally, is having found the pearl of great price, the hidden pearl that banishes sorrow. As Gustavo Gutiérrez explains, in the words of a *campesino*: the opposite of joy is not suffering—and the poor have plenty of that—but sadness. And the *campesino* added: The poor suffer, yes; but they do not sorrow. To live with joy, to be glad to be alive, is to live with ultimate meaning—with the ability to be grateful and to celebrate, the ability to be for others and be with others. This is why we can pray with gladness, as Jesus did, when the "least ones," the outcast as well as his friends, sit around the same table.

In this fashion the element of resurrection in this very life, under the conditions of this temporal existence, becomes present. Resurrection is the presence of transcendence in the element of fullness and plenitude to be had under concrete historical conditions.

We do have to add that in Latin America, that continent of death, paradoxically, this life-in-fullness has been facilitated and offered to all precisely by the poor of this world. The crucified—who are precisely those on the point of resurrection—engender and enable that hope, that freedom, and that joy. They make them contagious.

IV. AN OBJECTIVELY THEOLOGICAL CHRISTIAN SPIRITUALITY

Having analyzed the spirituality of the following of Jesus in concrete history today, let us return, by way of conclusion, to the objectively theological dimension of spirituality—but this time, the objectively theological dimension of a specifically Christian spirituality. In other words, let us apply the foregoing analysis to our actual experience of God, the encounter with the God of Jesus.

Following implies moving along a path. Christologically, we are called to follow Jesus through history. Theologically, we are called to journey with the God of history—to walk with our God, as Micah says. On the basis of our faith, that walking with God, with all of the humility of which Micah speaks, leads to the ultimate, definitive encounter with God, that discovery of God that will occur when "God will be all in all" (cf. 1 Cor. 15:28). But what is there of encounter with God even now, in concrete history? Or more precisely, what is there even now, of allowing oneself to be found by God?

Concrete, mystical, contemplative, and ascetic spiritualities describe the experience of this encounter with God in various ways. In order to learn what is central in that encounter, however, we turn to Jesus. This is our methodology as Christians. We seek to conform all subsequent Christian spirituality, even the loftiest mysticism, to the norm that was Jesus' experience of God, and not the other way around.

When Jesus places himself before God, on the one hand he calls God his Father and experiences God as such—as the One who is absolutely near, bounteous, and tenderly loving. In that Father Jesus' heart rests at last, and this fills him with gladness. Jesus rejoices in his Father; he is glad that God is good, and that it is good that there is a God. To find himself with God is for Jesus to allow himself to be found by the God who is good, the God in whom he can repose, and in whom he can ever place his trust.

On the other hand, when Jesus places himself before this Father of his, he finds that Father to be God indeed—ultimate, ineffable, unmanipulable Mystery, whom one must in some sense leave alone, let be God. Hence Jesus' active, total availability to God—his absolute obedience. Thus, Jesus reposes in the Father, but the Father does not allow him repose. Once more in complete trust, Jesus lets God be God.

This, we think, is how the encounter with God has occurred throughout history: in a persevering openness to and acceptance of the dialectic of the Father-God. In more systematic language, we might say that the encounter with God is given in "affinity" and in "otherness." It is given in affinity inasmuch as it kindles, in one's own self, time, and place, that trust in God that leads us to become—in the concrete, historically—like God, who is good. Be good as your heavenly Father is good (cf. Matt. 5:48, 19:17). It is given even in affinity with the element of mystery in God, in our actualization of utopia, as we allow ourselves to be borne up, borne along, by its attraction to a future that will be more God's future, in peace, justice, reconciliation, and in our attempt to do two things at once that resist being done together: peace and justice, truth and forgiveness, and the like.

The encounter with God is also given in otherness. It occurs in our effort ever to maintain our openness to the divine mystery, to the element of the new and even of the scandalous in God, as we strive to grasp a crucified God. Yes, God is surely mystery.

In the words of Gustavo Gutiérrez, "God is to be contemplated, and God is to be practiced." We encounter God in bringing the divine goodness to a concrete realization, which is a practice, and in letting God be God, which is contemplation. We encounter God in responding to a God of complete otherness and in corresponding to God by rendering the divine reality itself real in our history. To put it in still another way, I encounter God when I am a "contemplative inaction," as St. Ignatius puts it. In activity, we correspond to the God of goodness and bounty, and the objectively theological presupposition of this activity is the goodness of God. In contemplation we seek the face of God: we seek and find the divine will, as St. Ignatius so often urged us to do, under the premise of that quality of the substance of God that God is mystery and therefore is that which is to be sought and found.

This trust and obedience, brought to realization in the face of the mystery of God, is what the Bible calls faith. Experience of God, encounter with God, is nothing other than faith; conversely, faith is experience of God and encounter with God. Hence it is that a synthesis of the theologal dimension of a theologal spirituality is lived today in the form of mercy toward human beings (our correspondence to the Father who is good) and as fidelity (our constant response to God's mystery).

Finding God, logically enough, always occurs in the human being whom God has found: "Before they call, I will answer" (Isa. 65:24), and God is the Father who goes forth upon the highway day after day, walking it as the father of the prodigal—in the hope that his child will come. This experience of gratuity—God's own supreme generosity—is central and specific to the Christian experience of God. That experience, by definition, can neither be programmed nor conceptualized before it occurs. But it occurs. Along with God's demand comes the divine self-offering and its acceptance: "You have seduced me, Yahweh, and I have allowed myself to be seduced" (Jer. 20:7). It is the dimension of Good News in the experience of God that permeates all things Christian, Good News in the form of the Good that is both unexpected and undeserved: God, who comes forth to meet us. Here is the God who "first loved us" (1 John 4:19).

The encounter with God, as trust, availability, and gratitude, occurs especially in the concrete life of the believer—in his or her actual faith, hope, and charity. But it must also be posited in word. The human constitution of the believer requires this, as does the content of the experience itself. Faith and availability must surely be put into words. But especially, gratitude must find such expression. Thankfulness cannot remain silent indefinitely.

The expression in words of a reality that has been personally experienced is what we may call prayer. Prayer is not distinct from real life, let alone divorced from it. Prayer and life overlap. Prayer is the meaning of a vital, living experience, issuing in condensed expression. To pray is to say, with Jesus, in utter availability and readiness: "Father, . . . not my will but yours be done" (Luke 22:42). To pray is to say, with Jesus, in trust and confidence: "Father, into your hands, I commend my spirit (Luke 23:46). To pray is to say, with Jesus, in gladness and gratitude: "Father, . . . to you I offer praise: for . . . you have revealed [this] to the merest children" (Matt. 11:25; par. Luke 10:21). For our own part, we shall have to add the prayer of the prodigal: "Father, I have sinned against heaven and against you" (cf. Luke 15:21).

The experience of God—the personal encounter with God in history and its verbalization in prayer—has a strictly individual dimension and a strictly communitarian dimension. The believer who follows Jesus, who lives in history, who makes history and suffers it, finds himself or herself confronted with truth, life, cross, and hope. All of this is placed by the individual in reference to the mystery of God. But this mystery comes forth to meet the individual, as well, giving him or her a concrete, nontransferable name. The God who is mystery calls Abraham by his name and asks him to leave his house and go to the place that God will show him. He calls Jeremiah by his name and sends him to prophesy. He calls Mary by her name and proclaims to her the Good News that, through her, God will be "God with us." In giving us names, God enters into a personal relationship with us. Therefore human beings, as well, have dared to give a name to God. Here is the personal element of the encounter with God. As something personal, a name connotes solitude and loneliness before God at some times, plenitude and fullness at others. But the important thing is that this personal encounter occur. Archbishop Romero loved to recall this eternal truth. Shortly before his assassination, in a famous homily in which he railed against atrocities and defended an oppressed people, he also spoke of the best he had to offer: "Oh, dear brothers and sisters, that someone would tell me that the fruit of this homily would be that every one of us should encounter God, and live the glory of God's majesty and our littleness! No human being knows himself or herself until that being encounters God."

But this experience is not an individualistic one. An essential element of the encounter with God is to have it within a people of God, a community. The personal experience of God must be open to the experience other human beings have of God. It must be open to giving of one's own experience of God and to receiving it from others. It may be said that God is the God of a people, and that the experience of God must be had by a whole people. In more systematic language it must be said that there is no concrete personal experience of God that would exhaust the mystery of God, and that amid the concrete personal experiences of God on the part of the whole people, one may approach asymptotically the encounter with God in plenitude. To the divine, or theologal dimension of spirituality then, belongs its "popularity," its openness to give to others and receive from others. No one ought to be so timorous as to think he or she has nothing to offer to others out of his or her own faith, and no one must be so presumptuous as to think he or she has nothing to receive for his or her own faith from that of others.

This is something that has become more and more evident in recent history. The old division—the language used until very recently—between the faith of an "enlightened" believer and the faith of the "man on the street," if presented as a hard and fast division, is scarcely a Christian one. To be sure, the faith of each of these persons, with their respective manners of encountering God, has its specificities. But the enlightened should offer the best of their faith to the more common person, and receive the best of the latter's faith in return—and vice versa. We see it constantly today: believers of all climes and milieus, with different personal histories and manners of faith, are coming to believe and to encounter God precisely in one another's company. *Campesinos* and intellectuals, Latin Americans and first-world groups, women and men, are leading each other in their respective faith experiences. This is the most splendid, most familiar, level of solidarity: the encounter with God as community, as a people internally differentiated, yes, but as a people from start to finish, within which each member, in his or her faith, leads and carries along, while being led and carried by, all of the others.

In conclusion, let us observe that the encounter with God has a place of its own. To determine that place is not, when all is said and done, something that can be done strictly beforehand, precisely because it is a matter of finding, or rather being found by, God. And no one can dictate to God where God must come forth to meet someone. But in terms of faith, two things can be said, if they are stated in dialectical unity: "It is not a philosophical truth, but it is indeed a Christian truth, that the one who seeks God has already found God" (Karl Rahner); and "It is a matter not of seeking God, but of finding God in the place where God has promised to be: in the poor of this world" (Porfirio Miranda).

The former proposition means something important, even if it is basically tautologically. God never abandons an honest person. (Indeed, God makes a self-bestowal even on the ungrateful.) And God is at work in this very honesty. The encounter with God employs manifold mediations, and history bears witness to the fact. But the second statement is no tautology. It is revelation. The locus par excellence, the privileged place of the encounter with God, and the most appropriate in the current concrete reality of this world, as well as in terms of the consciousness that this world has now generated, is the world of the poor. This is what Matthew 25 sanctions and declares. God is in the weak, in the poor, in the helpless. God is hidden there, but God is there. More radically, in the current Latin American situation God is present in crucified peoples, in countless women and men impoverished beyond imagining, in the imprisoned, in the tortured, in the "disappeared," in the murdered. In them, to borrow a phrase from St. Ignatius's contemplations on Jesus' passion, "the divinity hides itself." But, however hidden, God is there.

A contemplation of God in those crucified peoples is not what one might have expected to be invited to undertake. And yet, this is precisely where God is to be contemplated. Or at least, this is where one must begin to contemplate God. To practice God before these crucified peoples is to take them down from their crosses.

Not every encounter with the poor of this world is mechanically and automatically an encounter with God, but there can be no encounter with the God of Jesus without an encounter with the poor and the crucified of this world. Thus, as we have heard so often in Latin America, the encounter with the poor is a spiritual experience, an experience of God. In these terms the proclamation of Micah acquires its historical logic. As we stand before the poor, as we stand before the crucified peoples, the demand becomes utterly clear: to practice justice and to love with tenderness. In this fashion one walks with God in history, humbly. What Jesus adds to this demand is that this humble walking is a genuine walking with God and toward God. To follow Jesus is to walk toward God, and to walk with God, in history. It is to that walk that God invites us. And that walk is spirituality.

—Translated by Robert R. Barr

15

The Crucified People

IGNACIO ELLACURÍA

If we are to understand what the people of God is, it is very important that we open our eyes to the reality around us, the reality of the world in which the church has existed for almost two thousand years, since Jesus announced the approach of the Reign of God. This reality is simply the existence of a vast portion of humankind, which is literally and actually crucified by natural oppressions and especially by historical and personal oppressions. This reality prompts in the Christian spirit inescapable questions: What does the fact that most of humankind is oppressed mean for salvation history and in salvation history? Can we regard suffering humankind as saved in history when it continues to bear the sins of the world? Can we regard it as savior of the world precisely because it bears the sins of the world? What is its relationship with the church as sacrament of salvation? Is this suffering humankind something essential when it comes time to reflect on what the people of God is and what the church is?

Posing these questions indicates the historic gravity and theological relevance of the issue. Many christological and ecclesiological topics are wrapped up in this question; in fact, we could say that we find here the whole of christology and ecclesiology in their character as historic soteriology. How is the salvation of humankind achieved starting from Jesus? Who continues in history this essential function, this saving mission that the Father entrusted to the Son? The answer to these questions can give historic flesh to the people of God, and thus avoid dehistoricizing this basic concept, and also avoid spiritualizing or ideologizing it falsely. Historic soteriology provides an essential perspective in this regard.

Historic soteriology here means something referring to salvation, as it is presented in revelation. But the accent falls on its historic character and that in a double sense: as the achievement of salvation in the one and only human history and as humankind's active participation in that salvation, and specifically the participation of oppressed humankind. Which historically oppressed humankind it is that preeminently continues the saving work of Jesus, and the extent to which it does so, is something to be uncovered throughout this chapter. That task is one of the things required of historic soteriology and clarifies what such a soteriology must be. To begin with, it must be a soteriology whose essential reference point is the saving work of Jesus, but it must likewise be a soteriology that actualizes in history this saving work and does so as the continuation and following of Jesus and his work.

The analysis will be carried out from only one angle: the passion and death which unify the figure of Jesus with that of oppressed humankind. There are other angles but this one is essential and merits study by itself. At this point all life flows together and from it the future of history opens outward.

I. THE PASSION OF JESUS AS SEEN FROM THE CRUCIFIED PEOPLE; THE CRUCIFIXION OF THE PEOPLE AS SEEN FROM THE DEATH OF JESUS

Here we have something required by theological method as understood in Latin American theology: any situation in history should be considered from the angle of its corresponding key in revelation, but the focus on revelation should derive from the history to which it is addressed—although not any moment in history is equally valid for providing a proper focus. The first aspect seems obvious from the angle of Christian faith, even though it conceals a problem: that of finding the proper key in order not to take as the key for one situation one proper to another. The second aspect, which has a circular relationship with the previous one, is not so obvious, especially if we mean that the situation enriches and makes present the fullness of revelation, and if we mean that revelation cannot bear its fullness and its authenticity in any situation whatsoever.

In this instance we confront two crucial poles with regard to both revelation and situation. Treating them together clarifies a basic problem: the historicity of the passion of Jesus and the saving character of the crucifixion of the people. In other words, both the saving character of the salvation of Jesus and the saving character of the history of crucified humankind are clarified, once it is accepted that salvation is present in Jesus and this salvation must be worked out within humankind. Both the passion of Jesus and the crucifixion of the people are thereby enriched, and that means an enrichment of Jesus and of the people. However, that approach faces a very serious problem: making sense of the seeming failure involved in the crucifixion of a people after the definitive proclamation of salvation. Involved here is not only the failure of history, but also the direction and meaning in history for the vast majority of humankind, and even more important, the historic task of saving it.

Hence, the focus here is primarily soteriological. The accent will fall not on what Jesus and the people are, but on what they represent for the salvation of humankind. Of course we cannot separate what are called the ontological from the soteriological aspects, but we can accent one side or the other. Here the accent will be on the soteriological aspects, keeping in mind that the aim is not to reduce the being and mission of Jesus nor the being and mission of the people to the dimension of soteriology in history, although neither being nor mission in either case is properly illuminated if soteriological reflection is left aside.

If this warning is important for avoiding one-sided reflections on Jesus, which are so only if they are absolutized, it is also important for avoiding confusion about the historic task that falls to the oppressed people in their struggles in history. This task does not come down to simply that which shines out when it is likened to the passion and death of Jesus. Neither Jesus nor the crucified people, as they will be considered here, are the only salvation of history, although the salvation of history cannot reach fulfillment without both of them, even with respect to salvation in history. The former is clear and acknowledged, as long as the structural complexity of human history is taken into account; the latter is clear for believers, at least with regard to the first term, but it must be proven to nonbelievers. This should be done in such a way that their contribution to salvation is the historic verification of Christian salvation; at the same time, it should not be turned into a sweetening and mystification that would hinder the political organization of the people and their effective contribution to liberation in history.

To propose salvation on the basis of the crucifixion of Jesus and the people assumes the same scandal and madness, especially if we wish to give to salvation a content that can be verified in the reality of history, where *verifiable* does not mean *exhaustible*.

Today from a Christian standpoint it is not scandalous to say that life comes from the death of Jesus in history, even though it was indeed a scandal for those who witnessed that death and had to proclaim it. Nevertheless, we must recover that scandal and madness if we do not want to vitiate the history-making truth of the passion of Jesus. We must do that in three dimensions: with regard to Jesus himself, who only gradually was able to comprehend the true path toward proclaiming and bringing about the Reign of God; with regard to those who persecuted him to death, because they could not accept that salvation involved particular positions in history; and finally, with regard to scandal in the church, which leads the church to avoid passing through the passion when it proclaims the resurrection.

It is indeed scandalous to hold the needy and the oppressed as the salvation of the world in history. It is scandalous for many believers who no longer think they see anything striking in the proclamation that the death of Jesus brought life to the world, but who cannot accept in theory, and much less in practice, that today this life-giving death goes by way of the oppressed part of humankind. It is likewise scandalous to those who seek the liberation of humankind in history. It is easy to regard the oppressed and needy as those who are to be saved and liberated, but it is not easy to see them as saviors and liberators.

Whether or not it is a scandal to hold that the passion and crucifixion of Jesus and of the people are central for human salvation, it is clear that precisely because of its implausibility as salvation, the passion of Jesus casts light on the implausibility of the people's crucifixion as salvation, while this latter hinders a naive or ideologized reading of the former.

On the one hand, the resurrection of Jesus and its effects in history are hope and future for those who remain in the time of passion. Certainly Jesus maintained hope in the definitive victory of God's Reign, to which he devoted his life and for which he died. Behind Luke 22:16–18 (and its parallel, Mark 14:25), despite the touching up done by the early community, we can reconstruct a double prophecy of the death of Jesus: after his death, Jesus will again celebrate the passover and will organize a banquet in the Reign of God, which of necessity must arrive. His death will not prevent the salvation to come and he himself will not remain imprisoned by death forever. Hence, as Schürmann says, the inbreaking of the Reign and Jesus' sudden death are not to be separated. Jesus' death is inseparately connected to the eschatological and historic coming of the Reign, and for that purpose the resurrection means not only a verification or consolation, but the assurance that this work must continue and that he remains alive to continue it.

This hope of Jesus was not of such a nature that the passion ceased being so, even to his anguished cry of abandonment on the cross. His struggle for the Reign, and his certainty that the Reign of God would triumph definitively, did not prevent him from "seeing" the connection between his personal days of tears, between the momentary failure of the coming of the Kingdom, and the glory of final victory. That is why he is an example for those who look more like the wretched of the earth than like its saviors. In being condemned personally, Jesus had to learn the road to definitive salvation—a salvation, let us repeat once more, that was essentially a matter of the coming of God's Reign and not a personal resurrection separate from what had been his earthly preaching of the Reign.

On the other hand, the ongoing passion of the people and paralleling it the historic reign of sin—as opposing the Reign of God—do not permit a reading of the death and resurrection of Jesus removed from history. The fundamental flaw in such a reading would lie in uprooting the history of the Reign of God so as to relegate it to a stage beyond history, so that it would no longer make sense to continue within history the life and mission of Jesus, who announced the Reign. That would be a betrayal of Jesus' life and death, which was entirely devoted not to himself but to the Reign. Moreover, identifying the Reign with the resurrection of Jesus would leave unfulfilled Jesus' message which predicted persecutions and death for those who were to continue his work. When Paul speaks of what is still wanting in the passion of Christ, he is rejecting a resurrection that ignores what is happening on earth. It is precisely the reign of sin that continues to crucify most of humankind and that obliges us to make real in history the death of Jesus as the actualized passover of the Reign of God.

II. THEOLOGICAL IMPORTANCE OF THE CROSS IN SALVATION HISTORY

An ascetic and moralizing focus on the Christian cross has nullified the importance of the cross in history and led to a rejection of everything that has to do with it. Such a rejection is fully justified if it is not simply a matter of the immature outburst of people being liberated from their emotional fantasies. The renewal of the mystery of the cross has little to do with gratuitous repression, which places the cross where one wants it and not in its real site, as though what Jesus had sought for himself was death on the cross and not the proclamation of the Reign.

Even more dangerous is the effort to evade the history of the cross in those theologies of creation and resurrection that at most make of the cross an incident or an isolated mystery that mystically projects its efficacy over human relationships with God.

A "naturalistic" view of creation, as faith inspired as it might regard itself, is ignorant of the novelty of the Christian God revealed in salvation history. It even ignores the fact that Israel did not come to the idea of the creator God through rational reflection on the course of nature, but through theological reflection on what had happened to the chosen people. Von Rad has shown clearly that it is in the political struggles of the Exodus that Israel becomes aware that Yahweh is its savior and redeemer, that this salvation has been conceived as the creation and launching of a people, and that faith in God who creates the world is a subsequent discovery that occurs when the historic experience of the people of Israel in the failure of the Exile gradually points it toward a universalizing consciousness, which demands a universal God, creator of all humans. Hence a faith apart from history, a faith apart from historic events, whether in the life of Jesus or in the life of humankind, is not a Christian faith. It would be at best a somewhat corrected version of theism.

Neither is a position that takes its support exclusively from the faith experience of the Risen One and ignores the historic roots of the resurrection. That temptation is an ancient one, and most probably came up even in the early communities, forcing them to emphasize very soon the continuity of the Risen One with the Crucified One. Otherwise, people live with the false assumption that the struggle against sin and death is over with the triumph of the resurrection. The Reign of God again would be reduced to something in the future, which either does not require human effort (because it is imminent), or reduces the Reign to the resurrection of the dead (because it is a long way off). If the life of the Risen One victorious over death is the future of salvation for Christians and for a new humankind, as Pannenberg points out, the life of the Risen One is the same life as that of Jesus of Nazareth, who was crucified for us, so that the immortal life of the Risen One is the future of salvation only insofar as we abandon ourselves to obedience to the Crucified One, who can overcome sin.

Hence, to connect creation and resurrection is false from a Christian viewpoint, whatever the understanding of the original "image and likeness," the historic process of death and resurrection. Every process in history is a creation of the future and not merely a renewal of the past. The fallen human is not restored, but rather the new human is built up; that new human is built up in the resurrection of one who has struggled from death against sin. To put it another way, eschatological hope is expressed equally as Reign of God and as resurrection of the dead, which for Pannenberg—who is not exactly a liberation theologian—means that the Reign of God is not possible as a community of human beings in perfect peace and total justice, without a radical change of the natural conditions that are present in human life, a change that is called the resurrection of the dead. He also says that the individual destiny and the political destiny of human beings go hand in hand.

Thus, the resurrection points back toward the crucifixion: the Crucified One rises, and rises because he was crucified; since his life was taken away for proclaiming the Reign, he receives a new life as fulfillment of the Reign of God. Thus, the resurrection points back toward the passion, and the passion points toward Jesus' life as proclaimer of the Reign. As is well-known, that is the sequence followed in putting the gospels together. The need to historicize the experience of the Risen One leads to a reflection on the passion story, which occupies a disproportionately large space in the gospel accounts, and which, in turn, requires historical justification in the narration of the life of Jesus. In any case, the gospels as a whole seek to give theological weight to two facts that are part of a single reality: the fact of Jesus' failure in the scandal of his death, and the fact of the persecution that the early communities soon undergo.

Hence, this is not an expiatory masochism of a spiritualizing sort, but the discovery of something real in history. It is not a matter of grief and mortification, but of making a break and a commitment. Jesus' death makes it clear why really proclaiming salvation runs up against the resistance of the world, and why the Reign of God does combat with the reign of sin. That is made manifest both in the death of the prophet, the one sent by God, and in the ravaging and death of humankind at the hands of those who make themselves gods, lording it over humankind. If a spiritualizing approach to the passion leads to an evasion of that commitment to history that leads to persecution and death, a historic commitment to the crucified people makes it necessary to examine the theological meaning of this death, and thus, to go back to the redeeming passion of Jesus. Reflecting historically on the death of Jesus helps us to reflect theologically on the death of the oppressed people, and the latter points back toward the former.

III. THE DEATH OF JESUS AND THE CRUCIFIXION OF THE PEOPLE ARE REALITIES OF HISTORY AND THE RESULT OF ACTIONS IN HISTORY

1. Historic Necessity of Jesus' Death

We may admit that the death of Jesus and the crucifixion of the people are necessary, but only if we speak of a necessity in history and not a merely natural necessity. It is precisely their nature as historic necessity that clarifies the deep reality of what happens in history, at the same time as it opens the way toward transforming history. That would not be the case if we were dealing with a merely natural necessity.

The scriptures themselves point out this necessity when they try to justify the passion of Jesus, and they even formulate it as a kind of principle: "Did not the Messiah have to undergo all this so as to enter into his glory?" (Luke 24:36). But this "having to" undergo "so as to" reach fulfillment is a historical "having to." It is historic not because the prophets had announced it, but because the prophets prefigured the events in what happened to them. Through what happened to the prophets, this necessity is grounded in the opposition between the proclamation of the Reign and the fact that sin is obviously a reality in history. The resistance of the oppressive powers and the struggle for liberation in history brought them persecution and death, but this resistance and struggle were simply the consequence in history of a life in response to God's word. That long experience, explicitly recalled by Jesus, leads to the conclusion that in our historic world arriving at the glory of God requires passing through persecution and death. The reason could not be clearer: If the Reign of God and the reign of sin are two opposed realities, and human beings of flesh and blood are the standard bearers of both, then those who wield the power of oppressive domination cannot but exercise it against those who have only the power of their word and their life, offered for the salvation of many.

Hence, this is not the biological image of a seed dying in order to bear fruit, nor of a dialectical law that demands undergoing death in order to reach new life. Of course, there are scripture texts that speak of the need for the seed to die; these texts point toward the necessity and the dialectical movement of this necessity, but they do not make it "natural." Making it natural would entail both eliminating the responsibility of those who kill prophets and those who crucify humankind, thereby veiling the aspect of sin in historic evil; it would also imply that the new life could emerge without the activity of human beings, who would not need to be converted internally or to rebel against what is outside. It is true that biological images of the Reign sometimes emphasize how the growth is God's affair, but we cannot, thereby, conclude that human beings should cease caring for the field of history.

Necessity in history, on the other hand, forces us to emphasize the determining causes of what happens. Theologically speaking, the fundamental cause is expressed countless times to scripture: passing from death to glory is necessary only given the fact of sin, a sin that takes possession of the human heart, but especially a sin in history that collectively rules over the world and over peoples. There is, in Moingt's phrase, a "theological and collective sin," and it is to that sin that the proclamation of the death of Christ for our sins refers, not directly to our individual and ethical sins; it is a "collective reality," grounding and making possible individual sins. It is this theological and collective sin that destroys history and hinders the future that God wanted for history; this collective sin is what causes death to reign over the world, and hence, we must be freed from our collective work of death in order to form once more the people of God. It is Moingt himself who goes so far as to say that redemption is simultaneously "the political liberation of the people and their conversion to God."

This historic necessity differs in its relationship to death and to glory: it is necessary to go through death to reach glory, but glory need not follow death. There is one attitude for struggling against death and another for receiving life. In both cases, there is something external to the individual human being. The evil of the world, the sin of the world, is not simply the sum of particular individual actions, nor are these foreign to this sin that dominates them; likewise, the forgiveness and transformation of the world are things that human beings initially receive so as to then offer their own contribution. The external aspect is different in the case of evil and of good, of sin and grace; sin is the work of human beings, and grace is God's work, although it is something that operates within and through human beings, and thus, there is no question of passivity. Although God gives the growth, the effort of human beings is not excluded but in fact is required, especially for destroying the objective embodiment of sin, and then for building up the objective embodiment of grace. Otherwise, necessity would not have any historic character but would be purely natural, and the human being would be either the absolute negation of God or a mere executor of presumably divine designs.

The "necessary" character of Jesus' death is seen only after the fact. Neither his disciples nor he himself saw in the beginning and not through reflection on scripture, that the proclamation and victory of the Reign had to go by way of death. When it happened, the surprised minds of the believers found in God's designs, manifested in the words and deeds of the scriptures—Moses and the prophets—the signs of the divine will that made death "necessary."

This "necessity" is not based on notions of expiation and sacrifice. In fact, when the Servant of Yahweh in Deutero-Isaiah is used to explain the meaning of the death of Jesus, the thread of discourse is not "sin—offense-victim-expiation-forgiveness." This framework, which may have some validity for particular mindsets and which expresses some valid points, may turn into an evasion of what must be done in history in order to eliminate the sin of the world. In times when consciences were oppressed or felt oppressed by a Christianity centered on the idea of sin, of guilt, and of eternal condemnation, it was utterly necessary that there be a framework of forgiveness, in which a God offended forgave sin and wiped out condemnation. But even with its valid points this framework does not emphasize either the collective embodiment of sin or human activity—destroying injustice and building love—which are "necessary" in history. A new theology of sin must move beyond the expiatorial frameworks but should not permit the existence of sin itself to be forgotten. To forget it would, among other things, leave the field open to the forces of oppression, which are overwhelmingly dominant in our world, and it would also neglect the area of personal conversion.

2. *Implications*

Emphasizing the historic character of the death of Jesus is fundamental for Christology and for a history-engaged soteriology, which as such would take on a new meaning.

The historic character of the death of Jesus entails, to begin with, that his death took place for historic reasons. New christologies are increasingly emphasizing this point. Jesus dies—is killed as both the four gospels and Acts so insist—because of the historic life he led, a life of deeds and words that those who represented and held the reins of the religious, socioeconomic and political situation could not tolerate. That he was regarded as a blasphemer, one who was destroying the traditional religious order, one who upset the social structure, a political agitator, and so forth, is simply to recognize from quite distinct angles that the activity, word, and very person of Jesus in the proclamation of the Reign were so assertive and so against the established order and basic institutions that they had to be punished by death. Dehistoricizing this radical reality leads to mystical approaches to the problem, not by way of deepening but by way of escape. We cannot simply settle the matter of the "died for our sins" by means of the expiatory victim, thereby leaving the direction of history untouched.

It likewise implies that Jesus followed a particular direction in history not because it would lead to death or because he was seeking a redemptive death, but rather because that was what truly proclaiming the Reign of God demanded. Whether the emphasis be on the soteriological character of Jesus' death, as in Paul, or on the soteriological character of the resurrection, as in Luke, it cannot be forgotten that the historic Jesus sought for himself neither death nor resurrection but the proclamation of the Reign of God to the point of death, and that brought resurrection. Jesus saw that his action was leading to a mortal showdown with those who could take his life, and it is utterly inconceivable that he did not realize that he was probably going to die, and even soon, and realize why this was so. Indeed, he was aware earlier and better of the saving value—in a broad sense—of his person and his life than of the saving value of his death. He does not begin by focusing his activity on waiting for death but on the proclamation of the Reign; even when he sees death as a real possibility, he does not hesitate in that proclamation or shrink back from his conflict with power. Putting all the saving value on his death cannot be reconciled with his life and his demands of his disciples; it cannot be said that there is in him a gradual shift from life to death as the center of his message, since ever in the many texts about following him being difficult and contradictory, the accent is on the continuity of life with death and not on the break of death with regard to the way of salvation that his life represents.

Salvation, therefore, cannot be made exclusively a matter of the mystical fruits of the death of Jesus, separating it from his real and verifiable behavior. It is not merely a passive and obedient acceptance of a natural fate, let alone a fate imposed by the Father. It is, at least in a first level, an action that leads to life by way of death, in such a way that in the case of Jesus what is salvific cannot be separated from what is historic. Consequently, Jesus' death is not the end of the meaning of his life, but the end of that pattern that must be repeated and followed in new lives with the hope of resurrection and thereby the seal of exaltation. Jesus' death is the final meaning of his life only because the death toward which his life led him shows what was likewise the historic meaning and the theological meaning of his life. It is, thus, his life that provides the ultimate meaning of his death, and only as a consequence does his death, which has received its initial meaning from his life, give meaning to his life. Therefore, his followers should not focus primarily on death as sacrifice, but on the life of Jesus, which will only really be his life if it leads to the same consequences as his life did.

Historic soteriology is a matter of seeking where and how the saving action of Jesus was carried out in order to pursue it in history. Of course, in one sense, the life and death of Jesus is over and done, since what took place in them is not simply a mere fact whose value is the same as that of any other death that might take place in the same circumstances, but was, indeed, the definitive presence of God among human beings. But his life and this death continue on earth and not just in heaven; the uniqueness of Jesus is not in his standing apart from humankind, but in the definitive character of his person and in the saving all-presence that is his. All the insistence on his role as head to a body, and on the sending of his Spirit, through whom his work is to be continued, point toward this historic current of his earthly life. The continuity is not purely mystical and sacramental, just as his activity on earth was not purely mystical and sacramental. In other words, worship, including the celebration of the eucharist, is not the whole of the presence and continuity of Jesus; there must be a continuation in history that carries out what he carried out in his life and as he carried it out. We should acknowledge a trans-historic dimension in Jesus' activity, as we should acknowledge it in his personal biography, but this trans-historic dimension will only be real if it is indeed trans-historic, that is, if it goes through history. Hence, we must ask who continues to carry out in history what his life and death was about.

3. The Crucified People, Principle of Universal Salvation

We can approach the question by taking into account that there is a crucified people, whose crucifixion is the product of actions in history. Establishing that may not be enough to prove that this crucified people is the continuation in history of the life and death of Jesus. But before delving into other aspects which prove that such is the case, it is well to take the same starting point as that of the saving value of the death and life of Jesus.

What is meant by crucified people here is that collective body, which as the majority of humankind owes its situation of crucifixion to the way society is organized and maintained by a minority that exercises its dominion through a series of factors, which taken together and given their concrete impact within history, must be regarded as sin. This is not a purely individual way of looking at every person who suffers even due to unjust actions by others or because such a person is immolated in the struggle against the prevailing injustice. Although looking collectively at the crucified people does not exclude an individual perspective, the latter is subsumed in the former, since that is its historic context. Nor is the viewpoint here one of looking at purely natural misfortunes, although natural evils play a role, albeit derivatively, insofar as they take place in a particular order within history.

Not only is it not foreign to scripture to regard a collective body as subject of salvation, but that is in fact its primordial thrust. For example, as J. Jeremias points out, an individual can only become a servant of Yahweh insofar as he or she is a member of the people of Israel, since salvation is offered primarily to the people and within the people. The communal experience that the root of individual sins is in a presence of a supra-individual sin and that each one's life is shaped by the life of the people in which he or she lives, makes it connatural to experience that both salvation and perdition are played out primarily in this collective dimension. The modern concern to highlight the individual side of human existence will be faithful to reality only if it does not ignore its social dimension. That is not the case in the individualistic and idealistic frenzied individualism and idealism that is so characteristic of Western culture, or at least of its elites. All the selfishness and social irresponsibility borne by this notion is but the reverse proof of how false this exaggeration is. There is no need to deny the collective and structural dimension in order to give scope to the full development of the person.

From a theological standpoint, this assertion is not arbitrary, and it is even less so in terms of the real situation. It is something obvious in historical experience now viewed from the standpoint of soteriology. One who is concerned as a believer for the sin and salvation of the world cannot but realize that in history humanity is crucified in this concrete form of the crucified people; by the same token one who reflects as a believer on the mangled reality of this crucified people must inquire what there is of sin and need for salvation here. In view of this situation, which is so extensive and so serious, considering the particular cases of those who do not belong to the crucified people becomes quite a secondary matter, although we should here repeat that the universalist and structural approach by no means has to do away with the individualistic and psychological approach, but simply provides it with a framework rooted in reality. What Christian faith adds after it is really clear that there is a crucified people is the suspicion that, besides being the main object of the effort of salvation, it might also in its very crucified situation be the principle of salvation for the whole world.

This is not the place to determine the extent and the nature of the ongoing oppression of the bulk of humankind today or to carry out a detailed study of its causes.

Although it is one of the fundamental realities that should serve as a starting point for theological reflection, and although it has been scandalously ignored by those who theorize from the geographical world of the oppressors, it is so obvious and widespread that it needs no explanation. What it does need is to be lived experientially.

Now although there are undeniably "natural" elements in the present situation of injustice that defines our world, there is also undeniably a side that derives from actions in history. Just as in the case of Jesus, we cannot speak of a purely natural necessity, so the oppression of the crucified people derives from a necessity in history: the necessity that many suffer so a few may enjoy, that many be dispossessed so that a few may possess. Moreover, the repression of the people's vanguards follows the same pattern as the case of Jesus, although with different meanings.

This general formulation should be made in historic terms. It does not happen everywhere in the same way or for the same reasons, since the general pattern of the oppression of humans by humans takes on very different forms both collectively and individually. In our universal situation today, oppression has some overall characteristics in history that cannot be ignored, and those who do not take a stand on the side of liberation are culpable, whether actively or passively.

Thus, within this collective and overall framework more specific analysis must be carried out. While maintaining the universal pattern of people crucifying others in order to live themselves, the subsystems of crucifixion that exist in both groups, oppressors and oppressed, should also be examined. As has often been pointed out, in a number of ways among the oppressed themselves, some put themselves at the service of the oppressors or give free rein to their impulses to dominate. This serious problem forces us to get beyond simplistic formulas with regard to both the causes of oppression and to its forms, so as not to fall into a Manichean division of the world, which would situate all good in the world on one side and all evil on the other. It is precisely a structural way of looking at the problem that enables us to avoid the error of seeing as good all the individuals on one side and as evil those on the other side, thus leaving aside the problem of personal transformation. Flight from one's own death in a continual looking out for oneself and not acknowledging that we gain life when we surrender it to others, is no doubt a temptation that is permanent and inherent in the human being, one that structures and history modulate but do not abolish.

The focus on the death of Jesus and the crucifixion of the people, the fact that they refer back and forth to each other, makes both take on a new light. The crucifixion of the people avoids the danger of mystifying the death of Jesus, and the death of Jesus avoids the danger of extolling salvifically the mere fact of the crucifixion of the people, as though the brute fact of being crucified of itself were to bring about resurrection and life. We must shed light on this crucifixion out of what Jesus was in order to see the salvific scope and the Christian nature of this salvation. To that end we must examine the principles of life that are intermingled with the principles of death; although the presence of sin and death is overwhelming in human history, the presence of grace and of life is also very prominent and palpable. We must not lose sight of either aspect. Indeed, salvation can only be understood as a victory of life over death, a victory already announced in the resurrection of Jesus, but one that must be won in a process of following his steps.

IV. JESUS' DEATH AND THE PEOPLE'S CRUCIFIXION IN TERMS OF THE SERVANT OF YAHWEH

One of the approaches on which the primitive Christian community fastened in order to understand Jesus' death, and give it its adequate value, was the figure of the Servant of Yahweh as described in Second Isaiah. This entitles us to appeal once more to the Suffering Servant in order to see what, in one of its aspects, the death of Jesus was, and especially what, in one of its aspects, the crucifixion of the people is.

Thus, this section will have three parts. In the first, we shall list some of the characteristics of the Servant as proposed in Second Isaiah. In the second part, we shall align these characteristics with the concrete reality of Jesus' life and death. Finally, in the third part of this section, we shall draw up a corresponding list of what are or ought to be the characteristics of the oppressed people if they are to be the extension of Jesus' redemptive work. The first two parts will be orientated toward the third: thus, even if we do not manage to show that the oppressed people are the historical extension of the crucifixion, and of the Crucified one, at all events we shall have indicated the route to be followed if that people is to conform its death with that of Christ—keeping account, meanwhile, of the distinction between the two realities, and of the different functions incumbent upon each.

1. Characteristics of the Servant of Yahweh

We shall make our analysis of the afflicted servant of Yahweh from the outlook of the crucified people. Any reading is done from a situation—more than from a pre-understanding, which is in some sort determined by the situation. Those who claim to be able to do a neutral reading of a text of scripture commit a twofold error. First, they commit an epistemological error: they attempt to do a nonconditioned reading, which is impossible. And they commit a theological error: they neglect the richest locus of any reading, which will always be the principal addressee of the text in question. This addressee is different at each historical moment, and the hypothesis with which we are working is that at this particular moment of ours the addressee of the Songs of the Servant is the crucified people—a hypothesis that will be confirmed if indeed the text sheds light on what the crucified people are, and if, conversely, the text is enriched, and endowed with currency, by the reality that is this historical addressee. This is not the place for a discussion of the epistemological and theological justification of this methodological procedure—which does not exclude the most careful utilization of exegetical analyses, but only subordinates them. Suffice it to have enunciated this procedure in order not to go astray in our analysis of the text at hand.

Our analysis will prescind from whether the "servant" is a collective or individual personage, a king or a prophet, and so on. None of this is relevant for our purpose, since what we formally intend here is to see what the text says to the oppressed people—what the text declares to this historical addressee. What we propose, of course, is not an exhaustive treatment, but an indication of the basic lines of the text in question.

The theology of the Servant proposes that the encounter with Yahweh occurs in history, and that that encounter thus becomes the locus both of Yahweh's intimate presence with the people, and of the people's response and responsibility (Joachim Jeremias). The unity prevailing between what occurs in history and what God seeks to manifest and communicate to human beings is, in the text of Second Isaiah, indissoluble. We need only recall the references we find in that text to the humiliation of Babylon, or to the triumph of Cyrus, in order to have overwhelming proof of this. This is the context in which the four Songs of the Suffering Servant must be read.

The First Song (Isa. 42:1–7) speaks of the election of the Servant. He is a chosen one, a favorite of Yahweh: upon him God has placed his spirit. The finality of this election is explicitly proclaimed: "He shall bring forth justice to the nations." Indeed, not content with this quite explicit formulation, the sacred writer emphasizes and amplifies it:

> A bruised reed he shall not break,
> and a smoldering wick he shall not quench,
> Until he establishes justice on the earth;
> the coastlands will wait for his teaching.

In question, accordingly, is an objective implantation of right—especially, of justice in the real, concrete sense of justice to be done to an oppressed people. It is a matter of creating laws in which justice, rather than the interests of the mighty, has the preeminence (although account is also kept of the need for an interiorization of the love of justice). That is, what is at stake is the appearance on the scene of a new human being, who would actually live, and experience, right and justice. Likewise, there is a universal gaze upon the nations and the "coastland"—that is, a purely Judaic ambit is transcended. Finally, all of this will be God's response to that which peoples deprived of justice and right await, what they hope for—a response to be implanted by the Servant, who will never waver or be shaken in his mission.

The election, the choice, is God's. Political as the Servant's mission may appear in its first stage (there is no talk of restoring worship, converting sinners, or the like, but only of the implantation of right), this is what is wanted by that God who "created the heavens and stretched them out," by the God who consolidated the earth. After all, it is that God who has chosen the Servant in order to cause justice to be, in order to do justice:

> I, the Lord, have called you for the victory of justice,
> I have grasped you by the hand;
> I formed you, and set you
> as a covenant of the people,
> a light for the nations. (NAB 2:6)

And the Song repeats, with explanation, what it is to do justice:

> To open the eyes of the blind,
> to bring out prisoners from confinement,
> and from the dungeon, those who live in darkness. (42:7)

And thus says the Lord, for "Lord" is his name: that is, this is how his being for created persons is expressed, in this is his proclamation of a future in contrast to what has been occurring.

The Second Song underscores the nature of this election by God. God has chosen someone whom the mighty despise, who seemingly lacks the strength to have justice reign over the world, and who, nevertheless, has God's backing and support:

> Yet my reward is with the Lord,
> my recompense is with my God . . .
> Thus says the Lord,
> the redeemer and the Holy One of Israel,
> To the one despised, whom the nations abhor,
> the slave of rulers;
> When kings see you, they shall stand up,
> and princes shall prostrate themselves
> Because of the Lord who is faithful,
> the Holy One of Israel who has chosen you. (49:4, 7)

The purpose of the election is the building of a new land and a new people: "To restore the land and allot the desolate heritages" (49:8). The people will emerge from their state of poverty, oppression, and darkness into a new state of abundance, liberty, and light. And the reason for God's intervention through his servant is clear:

> For the Lord comforts his people
> and shows mercy to his afflicted. (49:13)

This notion, that God is on the side of the oppressed, and against the oppressor, is fundamental in the text, and refers to an entire people, and not merely to particular individuals:

> I will make your oppressors eat their own flesh,
> and they shall be drunk with their own blood
> as with the juice of the grape.
> All humankind shall know
> that I, the Lord, am your savior,
> your redeemer, the Mighty One of Jacob. (49:26)

The Third Song takes a new step, setting in relief the potential importance of suffering in the people's march toward liberation. The long experience of being crushed can lead to a shattered confidence, of course, but the Lord means to support that suffering, and put an end to it, giving victory to someone seemingly confounded and routed:

The Lord God is my help,
therefore I am not disgraced [*do not feel the outrages];
I have set my face like flint,
knowing that I shall not be put to shame. (50:7)

A great hope arises, a hope bearing on the future of the afflicted and persecuted. The suffering of these is not in vain. God stands behind them. And this is a hope which they shall touch with their hands, and which will transform their lives altogether:

Those whom the Lord has ransomed will return
and enter Zion singing,
crowned with everlasting joy;
They will meet with joy and gladness,
sorrow and mourning will flee. (51:11)

But it is the Fourth Song that most explicitly and extensively develops the theme of the Servant's passion and glory. Here the rhetorical figure of contraposition is employed, strikingly, in order to focus the Servant's real situation, and concrete capacity for salvation:

See, my servant shall prosper,
he shall be raised high and greatly exalted.
Even as many were amazed at him—
so marred was his look beyond that of man,
and his appearance beyond that of mortals—
So shall he startle many nations,
because of him kings shall stand speechless;
For those who have not been told shall see,
those who have not heard shall ponder it. (52:13–15)

It is here that the description of the persecution of the Servant in his mission of "implanting right" acquires characteristics very similar to those that the oppressed people suffer today:

He grew up like a sapling before him,
like a shoot from the parched earth;
There was in him no stately bearing to make us look at him,
nor appearance that would attract us to him.
He was spurned and avoided by men,
a man of suffering, accustomed to infirmity,
One of those from whom men hide their faces,
spurned, and we held him in no esteem.

Yet it was our infirmities that he bore,
our sufferings that he endured,

While we thought of him as stricken,
as one smitten by God and afflicted.

But he was pierced for our offenses,
crushed for our sins;
Upon him was the chastisement that makes us whole,
by his stripes we were healed.
We had all gone astray like sheep,
each following his own way;
But the Lord laid upon him
the guilt of us all.

Though he was harshly treated, he submitted
and opened not his mouth . . .
Oppressed and condemned, he was taken away,
and who would have thought any more of his destiny?

When he was cut off from the land of the living,
and smitten for the sin of his people,
A grave was assigned him among the wicked
and a burial place with evildoers,
Though he had done no wrong
nor spoken any falsehood.

If he gives his life as an offering for sin,
he shall see his descendants in a long life,
and the will of the Lord shall be accomplished through him.
Because of his affliction
he shall see the light in fullness of days.
Through his suffering my servant shall justify many
and their guilt he shall bear.
Therefore I will give him his portion among the great,
and he shall divide the spoils with the mighty,
Because he surrendered himself to death
and was counted among the wicked;
And he shall take away the sins of many,
and win pardon for their offenses. (53:2–12)

This text, which is fundamental for any salvation theology, any soteriology, admits of various readings, since it can elucidate different problems. In the problem at hand, it is impossible to ignore the applicability of the description in the text to what is occurring today among the crucified people. A reading that has become traditional sees a prefiguration of Jesus' passion here. But this is no reason why we should shut our eyes to the element of concrete description—all "scriptural accommodation" notwithstanding—of what is today a vast majority of humanity. From this outlook, we may underscore certain historicotheological moments in this impressive Song.

In the first place, the personage we contemplate is a figure shattered by the concrete, historical intervention of human beings. We have a person of sorrows here, someone accustomed to suffering, who is carried off to death in helplessness and injustice. Scorned and contemned by all, he is someone in whom there is no visible merit.

In the second place, not only is this figure not regarded as a potential savior of the world, but, quite the contrary, he is regarded as someone who might have leprosy, someone sentenced to death, someone wounded by God, someone brought low, and humiliated.

In the third place, he appears as a sinner—as the fruit of sin and as filled with sins. Accordingly, he was given burial with the wicked, and with evildoers. He has been reckoned among sinners, because he took upon himself the burden of the sin of so many.

In the fourth place, the believer's view of things is a different view. The Servant's state is not due to his own sins. He suffers sin without having committed it. He has been pierced for our rebellions and crushed for our crimes—wounded for the sins of the people. He has taken on sins that he has not committed: thus, he is in his desperate situation because of the sins of others. Antecedently to his dying for sins, it is sins who have carried him off to death. It is sins that kill him.

In the fifth place, the Servant accepts this lot, this destiny. He accepts the fact that it is the weight of sins that is bearing him off to death, although he has not committed them. By reason of the sins of others, for the sins of others, he accepts his own death. The Servant will justify so many, because he has taken their crimes on himself. Our punishment has fallen on him, and his scars have healed us. His death, far from being meaningless and ineffective, removes, provisionally, the sins that had been afflicting the world. His death is expiation, and intercession for sins.

In the sixth place, the Servant himself, crushed in his sacrificed life and in the failure of death, triumphs. Not only will others see themselves justified, but he will see his offspring and will live long years. He will see light, and be satiated with knowledge.

In the seventh place, it is the Lord himself who adopts this condition. God takes our crimes on himself. Indeed, we read that the Lord actually wished to crush the Servant with suffering, and deliver his life over in expiation for sin, although afterwards he will reward him, and give him complete recompense. This is very strong language. But it admits of the interpretation that God accepts as having been wished by himself, as salutary, the sacrifice of someone who has concretely died for reason of the sins of human beings. Only in a difficult act of faith is the sacred writer able to discover, in the Songs of the Servant, that which seems to the eyes of history to be the complete opposite. Precisely because he sees someone burdened with sins that he has not committed, and crushed by their consequences, the singer of these songs makes bold, by virtue of the very injustice of the situation, to ascribe all of this to God: God must necessarily attribute a fully salvific value to this act of absolute concrete injustice. And the attribution can be made because the Servant himself accepts his destiny to save, by his own suffering, those who are actually the causes of it.

Finally, the comprehensive orientation of this Fourth Song, together with that of the three that have preceded—their prophetic sense of a proclamation of the future, and their ambit of universality—prevent a univocal determination of the Servant's historical concretion. The Suffering Servant of Yahweh will be anyone who discharges the mission described in the Songs—and, par excellence, will be the one discharging it in more comprehensive fashion. Or better, the Suffering Servant of Yahweh will be anyone unjustly crucified for the sins of human beings, because all of the crucified form a single unit, one sole reality, even though this reality has a head and members with different functions in the unity of expiation.

For all the accentuation of the traits of suffering and seeming failure, the hope of triumph emerges paramount. And it is a hope, let us not forget, that must have a public, concrete character, and a relationship with the implantation of right and justice. No "substitutive" elements it may have militate against its historical reality and effectiveness.

2. Life and Death of Jesus, and the Servant of Yahweh

Before any Christian interpretation of the Suffering Servant had come to be, this figure had already been set in relationship with that of the Messiah. One line of theological reflection saw that the triumph of the Messiah would come only after a passage through pain and suffering, and this precisely because of the existence of sin. It is impossible to ignore the fact that Second Isaiah itself, which so strongly emphasizes Yahweh's love for the people, places harsh reproaches in the mouth of God when it comes to that people's wicked behavior. The mystery of sin and evil continues to make its way toward integration into a more complete interpretation of God's activity in history.

The New Testament does not teem with explicit references to the Servant of Yahweh. The title, *pais Theou*, appears only once in Matthew (12:15) and four times in Acts (3:13–26, 4:27–30). However, the theology of the Suffering Servant of Yahweh, along lines of suffering and oblation for sins, is of prime importance in the New Testament for the attempt undertaken there to present a theological explanation of the historical fact of Jesus' death. The almost complete disappearance of the term may be attributed to the fact that the Hellenistic communities very soon began to prefer the title, "Son of God," to that of "servant of God," which they less readily assimilated. For Joachim Jeremias, the christological interpretation of the Servant of Yahweh of Second Isaiah belongs to the earliest Christian communities, and corresponds to the Palestinian, pre-Hellenistic stage. Cullmann maintains that the christology of the Servant is probably the oldest christology of all.

However, it is not the common opinion of exegetes that Jesus himself was aware of being the Servant of Yahweh spoken of in Second Isaiah. We need not enter into this discussion here, since our concern is to emphasize that the primitive community justifiably saw the theological background of the Suffering Servant in the historical events of the life of Jesus, so that, without being explicitly aware of it, Jesus will have carried out the Servant's mission. It might be objected that the concrete events narrated in the gospels are only the historical flesh placed by the primitive communities on the framework of their theological thought concerning the Servant, in order to historicize that thought. But even in that case—which does not seem, across the board, to represent an acceptable explanation—we would be satisfied with this acknowledgment of the need for a historicization of salvation and of the manner of salvation. If, on the other hand, Jesus himself was aware that he was the full realization of the Suffering Servant of Yahweh, obviously he did not have this consciousness from the beginning of his life, or even from the commencement of his public life; from which we must again conclude that only his real, concrete life of proclamation of the Reign and of opposition to the enemies of the Reign led him to an acceptance, in faith and hope, of the salvific destiny of the Servant: in both Jesus and the Servant, the struggle with sin came before death for and by sin.

On the face of it, it is difficult to admit that Jesus publicly and solemnly manifested the notion that his death was to have a salvific scope (Schürmann). Jesus' preaching and behavior are not orientated toward his future death, and do not depend upon it (Marxsen). A more difficult question is whether he did communicate the salvific meaning of his death to his closest disciples, at least on the eve of his passion, if not indeed when they were sent on the mission of announcing the Reign. In order to answer this question, we should of course have had to be present at the Last Supper. We cannot enter in depth into this question here, but we can rely on exegetes' intermediate positions, between Jeremias' literal positivism and Bultmann's historical skepticism. Schürmann, after a lengthy exegetical analysis, concludes as follows. The deeds of offering of someone who is going to die and who proclaims eschatological salvation are best explained in a soteriological perspective. In these deeds of the Servant performed by Jesus, eschatological salvation becomes comprehensible in the symbolic activity of someone willing to give the gift of self to the very hilt, to very death as a culmination of all of that person's life, which in turn has ever been a pro-existence—that is, it has always been a life defined by its total commitment to others. An acknowledgement, after the Resurrection, of the salvific value of Jesus' death was possible only on the basis of Jesus' pro-existent attitude, as solemnly expressed in the actions of the Last Supper and as reconsidered in the light of the scriptures, especially in the light of the Suffering Servant. It came to be seen that Jesus' death was necessary, that it was conformable to the scriptures, that it had a salvific value for those who had followed him and that that value could be extended to the sins of the many.

Running counter to a full self-understanding, in terms of his death, on the part of Jesus himself, however, is his cry on the cross as reported by Matthew (27:26) and Mark (15:35), which seems to indicate an absolute abandonment by God, and consequently a failing in Jesus' faith and hope. The difficulty presented by this text is so grave that the other evangelists substitute words of trust (Luke 23:46–47) or consummation (John 19:30). Indeed, since it is possible to see, in Jesus' words of abandonment, the first words of Psalm 22, which ends with words of hope similar to those of the Song of the Servant, we cannot be certain that the tenor and sense of the words placed on Jesus' lips by Matthew and Mark is one of dereliction by God. For Xavier Léon-Dufour, Jesus intended to express his state of dereliction, his condition of abandonment, that is death, a death which in and of itself is separation from the living God. However, the experience of abandonment is simultaneously proclaimed and denied in a dialogue expressing the presence of the one who seems absent—a dialogue that abides uninterrupted, even though God seems to have disappeared. Jesus calls Yahweh not "Father," but—the only time he does so in the Synoptics—"God." All of this arouses the suspicion that the "Why have you forsaken me" remains without immediate response, which will only appear after his death, and which the evangelists posit in the voice of the centurion: "Clearly this man was the Son of God!" (Mark 15:39).

Consequently, although Jesus would not have had an explicit awareness of the complete meaning of his death, he would have had the firm hope that his life and death were the immediate announcement of the Reign—in other words, that the definitive coming of the Reign was through his life and his death, between which a continuity must be accepted, so that his death was but the culmination of his life, the definitive moment of his total surrender and commitment to the proclamation and the realization of the Reign. And all of this to the point that the sacrificial and expiatory meaning of the sufferings of the Suffering Servant would be more clear than that of Jesus' death. Only later would that death come to be understood as that of the universal victim of the sins of the world.

Obviously, the crucified people is not explicitly conscious of being the Suffering Servant of Yahweh, but as in the case of Jesus, that is not a reason to deny that it is.

Nor would the fact that Jesus is the Suffering Servant be such a reason, since the crucified people would be his continuation in history, and thus, we would not be talking of "another" servant. Hence, it would be sufficient to show that the crucified people combines some essential conditions of the Suffering Servant to show that the people constitute the most adequate site for the embodiment of the Servant, even if that is not true in all its fullness.

If it is acknowledged that Jesus' passion is to be continued in history, it should also be acknowledged that in order to be historical that continuity can take on different shapes. Leaving aside individual figures, that is, the need for Jesus to continue in each of his followers, the continuation in history by the people should also take on different shapes. In other words, we cannot say once and for all who constitutes the collective subject that most fully carries forward Jesus' redeeming work. It can be said that it will always be the crucified people of God, but as corrected as it is, that statement leaves undefined who that people of God is, and it cannot be understood simply as the official church even as the persecuted church. Not everything called church is simply the crucified people or the Suffering Servant of Yahweh, although correctly understood this crucified people may be regarded as the most vital part of the church, precisely because it continues the passion and death of Jesus.

This historicity does not mean that we cannot come to an approximation of the present-day figure of the Servant. It might vary in different historic situations, and it might represent the Servant's fundamental traits under different aspects, but it would not thereby cease to have certain basic characteristics. The most basic is that it be accepted as the Servant by God; that acceptance, however, cannot be established except through its "likeness" to what happened to the Jesus who was crucified in history. Therefore, it will have to be crucified for the sins of the world, it will have to have become what the worldly have cast out, and its appearance will not be human precisely because it has been dehumanized; it will have to have a high degree of universality, since it will have to be a figure that redeems the whole world; it will have to suffer this utter dehumanization, not for its sins but because it bears the sins of others; it will have to be cast out and despised precisely as savior of the world, in such a way that this world does not accept it as its savior, but on the contrary judges it as the most complete expression of what must be avoided and even condemned; and finally, there must be a connection between its passion and the working out of the Reign of God.

On the other hand, this historic figure of the Servant is not to be identified with any particular organization of the crucified people whose express purpose is to achieve political power. Of course, the salvation promised to the historic mission of the Servant of Yahweh must be embodied in history, and such historic embodiment must be achieved through an organizing process that if it is to be fully liberating, must be intimately connected with the crucified people. But the aspect through which the crucified people—and not a purely undifferentiated people—brings salvation to the world, continuing the work of Jesus, is not the same as that by which it effects this salvation in historic and political terms. In other words, the crucified people transcends any embodiment in history that may take place for the sake of its salvation in history, and this transcending is due to the fact that it is the continuation in history of a Jesus who did not carry out his struggle for the Reign through political power. The fact that it transcends, however, does not mean that it can be isolated from any embodiment in history, for the Reign of God entails the achievement of a political order, wherein human beings live in covenant in response to God's covenant.

The crucified people thus remains somewhat imprecise insofar as it is not identified, at least formally, with a specific group in history—at least in all the specific features of a group in history. Nevertheless, it is precise enough so as *not to be confused* with what cannot represent the historic role of the Suffering Servant of Yahweh. To mention some examples with two sides: the First World is not in this line and the Third World is; the rich and oppressive classes are not and the oppressed classes are; those who serve oppression are not, no matter what they undergo in that service, and those who struggle for justice and liberation are. The Third World, the oppressed classes, and those who struggle for justice, *insofar* as they are Third World, oppressed class and people who struggle for justice, are in the line of the Suffering Servant, even though not everything they do is necessarily done in the line of the Servant. Indeed, as was noted at the beginning of this chapter, these three levels must by necessity develop—although we cannot here go into studying the ways this takes place—into some embodiments that are strictly political and others that are not formally political, though they are engaged in history.

This likening of the crucified people to the Servant of Yahweh is anything but gratuitous. If we can see common basic features in both, there is moreover the fact that Jesus identified himself with those who suffer—or that was the view of the early Christian community. That is, of course, true of those who suffer for his name or for the Reign, but it is also true of those who suffer unaware that their suffering is connected to the name of Jesus and the proclamation of his Reign. This identification is expressed most precisely in Matthew 25:31–46, and indeed, that passage appears just before a new announcement of his passion (Matthew 26:1–2).

The passage has a "pact structure," says Pikaza, in its two-part statement (I am your God, who is in the little ones, and you will be my people if you love the little ones); the pact takes place through justice among human beings. It is the judgment of the Reign, the universal and definitive judgment, that brings to light God's truth among human beings; this truth is in the identification of the Son of Man, become King, with the hungry, the thirsty, wayfarers, the naked, the sick, and prisoners. The Son of Man is he who suffers with the little ones; and it is this Son of Man, precisely as incarnate in the crucified people, who will become judge. In its very existence the crucified people is already judge, although it does not formulate any theological judgment, and this judgment is salvation, insofar as it unveils the sin of the world by standing up to it; insofar as it makes possible redoing what has been done badly; insofar as it proposes a new demand as the unavoidable route for reaching salvation. This is, lest we forget, a universal judgment in which sentence is passed on the whole course of history. Pikaza notes that Matthew 25:36–41 entails a dialectical vision of the Jesus of history; he has been poor and yet it is he who helps the poor. Seen from the Pasch, Jesus appears as the Son of Man, who suffers in the wretched of the earth, yet is likewise also the Lord, who comes to their aid.

Thus the crucified people has a twofold thrust: it is the victim of the sin of the world, and it is also bearer of the world's salvation. But this second aspect is not what we are developing here in terms of the Pauline "died for our sins and rose for our justification." This present chapter, halting at the crucifixion, presents only the first stage. A stage focused on the resurrection of the people should indicate how the one crucified for the sins of the world can by rising contribute to the world's salvation. Salvation does not come through the mere fact of crucifixion and death; only a people that lives because it has risen from the Death inflicted on it can save the world.

The world of oppression is not willing to tolerate this. As happened with Jesus, it is determined to reject the cornerstone for the building of history; it is determined to build history out of power and domination, that is, out of the continual denial of the vast majority of oppressed humankind. The stone that the builders rejected became the cornerstone, stumbling-block, and rock of scandal. That rock was Jesus, but it is also the people that is his people, because it suffers the same fate in history. Those who once "were now people" are now "people of God"; those who were "viewed without pity" are now "viewed with mercy." In this people are the living stones that will be built into the new house, where the new priesthood will dwell and will offer the new victims to God through the mediation of Jesus Christ (cf. 1 Pet. 2:4–10).

—Translated by Phillip Berryman
and Robert R. Barr

16

Hope, Utopia, Resurrection

JOÃO BATISTA LIBÂNIO

I. TWO PARADOXICAL FACTS

Two paradoxical facts intrigue and challenge the theologian. One concerns the societies of abundance, both those within the geographical frontiers of the rich countries and those that exist within the poor countries. To some extent both share the same modern world, which is undergoing a profound change in its fundamental values. The other fact concerns the poor sectors that also exist in the rich countries and constitute the great majority of people in the Third World. We are concerned here in particular with the Christian areas of Latin America.

1. End of Utopia and Hope: There is No Resurrection

The End of Utopia is not just the title of a work by Marcuse; it also expresses the modern spiritual climate. The death of utopia, the end of hope does not arise from a desperate situation, scepticism, darkening horizons. What it expresses is euphoria. There is no longer any room for utopia or hope, because the era has come to an end in which the objective conditions were lacking to make viable social and historical realities. "Any new way of life on earth, any transformation of the technical and natural context is a real possibility which has its own place in the historical world."[1] The only limits upon human enterprise are scientific laws of biology.

Research into the values held in nine rich European countries shows an anti-utopian mentality, precisely because Europeans "feel happy." Three-quarters of Europeans say they are happy, and one-fifth feel very happy. Only one in every hundred does not admit to being happy.[2] This happiness comes from family, profession, and financial satisfaction and is thought of on the strictly personal level.

Marxism has also declared the death of utopia, as it thinks of socialism as the definitive step from utopia to science. Now we no longer need to hope, as we can trace the future scientifically.[3]

The death of utopia and hope is the end of the long march of individualism in the West. From an individual born in-relation-with-God, the product of Christian teaching, and the value of the individual in opposition to the world belonging to the Hellenistic schools, we have progressed to the modern individual who turns this upside down and becomes the individual-in-the-world, without God.[4] Absolutely autonomous and self-sufficient, such individuals no longer need utopias or hope and can reach fulfillment within history with the resources they have acquired. In particular among these resources are unlimited planning powers with the help of computers and information science.

The death of utopia and hope shows a clear opposition in the West to the Christian resurrection as a victory over death. According to Ph. Murray's fascinating thesis, the nineteenth century, not simply as a chronological period but as a spirit, mentality, attitude, and style of knowledge, is characterized by implacable conflict with and obsessive rejection of the fundamental Christian dogma of the resurrection of the dead, in favor of history as the only eternity possible for humanity: a place in the final procession of the dead in the irreversible entropy of nature and humanity.[5]

2. Rise of Utopia and Hope: Faith in the Resurrection

In 1968 the Latin American bishops met at Medellín and proclaimed a "new historical epoch for our Continent, longing for total emancipation, liberation from all forms of slavery, personal growth, and collective integration" (Medellín, 4). *Liberation* became the word that galvanized the energies and longings of the whole Latin American continent. It is the great utopia. And given that it arose and grew in Christian Territory, it became closely linked with eschatological Christian hope. In the last analysis it implies faith in the resurrection, so that utopia, hope, and faith in the resurrection are an intimately connected trilogy.

Puebla takes up this utopia again with increased vigor. The theme of liberation permeates the whole document. It appears above all as the cry of the people. At Medellín it was a rumble, but now "it is clear, growing, impetuous and at times threatening"—a cry that is raised by millions of exploited people who are in a situation of "extreme poverty" (Puebla, 88–90). The origin of this utopia is a profoundly significant event in Latin America:

> Those who are absent from history are becoming present in it. The poor are passing to center stage in society and in the Latin American church. As they do so, they provoke fear and hostility among the oppressors and arouse hope among the dispossessed.[6]

This utopia and hope gives rise to the "birth of a new historical awareness" of liberation.[7] It is the "greater utopia" or "greatest utopia" of the people expressed as a general desire ("Oh, that all would gather, as God commands!") passing through historical hope ("The day when the people hold power in their hands") to end up with eschatological hope ("but this will only happen in heaven").[8]

The particular nurturing grounds for this utopia are the ecclesial base communities. They are not just "hope for the church" (EN, 58), but places that generate hope. In them people sing of utopia and hope, as we find graphically illustrated in this very common song in the communities:

I want to sing a new song, joyful
with my people celebrate the dawn.
My liberated people!
The struggle has not been in vain!
Pilgrim through a world unequal
Exploited by the greed of capital
By the plantation owner's power made landless
Not knowing where to go I'm homeless . . .
With hope I stick together with the rest
I know God never forgets the oppressed who cry
And Jesus sided with the poor and dispossessed.
The prophets keep on denouncing the evil-doers
because the earth belongs to us as family.
There should be share and share alike at table
Kindness makes the whole world lovable
and its bright stars light my way.
In rivers of justice, common labor,
Rice fields will flower . . .
And we will harvest liberty!

II. UTOPIA AND THE HOPE OF THE POOR IN LATIN AMERICA

The terms *utopia* and *hope* have a variety of meanings. So we need to define them in order to avoid misunderstanding. We start here by distinguishing between *utopia* and *hope* and giving precise definitions.

1. Preliminary Considerations

The term *utopia* was invented by the English Christian humanist Thomas More (1561), who used it as the title of his political novel. The term's possible twofold etymology gives us its basic semantic elements. *Utopia* comes from *ouk-topos*, "no place." It refers to a "place which does not exist anywhere." It is imaginary, ideal, unreal, not here, nowhere in this world. But the term can also have the etymology *eu-topos*, "good place." This expresses the dimension of happiness, joy, space, fulfillment. It reveals our human capacity to anticipate through imagination things which can become reality. In this sense *utopia* means "the place where we are really at home; the place where we can feel comfortable."[9] It exists somewhere, and so it can become a model to copy. The reality we desire (*eu-topos*) is the counterweight to the unreal dimension (*ouk-topos*). Thus the term has an intentional ambiguity between the real and unreal.

Utopia expresses a human aspiration toward a truly just order, a social world that is wholly human, which corresponds fully to the dreams, needs, and deepest aspirations of human life. It is the image of a perfect society, which acts as a horizon and guideline for a real historical project or for the desire for an alternative project to the present situation.

Utopia has two fundamental structural elements: it is a criticism of the present situation and a proposal for what should exist. As a criticism it shows its character of rejection, denunciation, "subversion" of the existing order. Through its property of "having no place" it accuses this world of not having permitted it to exist. It points toward what should exist, the right to want, seek, and aspire to another reality. In this case utopia is anticipatory. It offers alternative models, and it announces the plausibility of a different world, something completely new, different, other.

The term *hope* is considered here in its theological, eschatological dimension. Whereas the term *utopia* stresses the horizontal, intra-historical, immanent, worldly dimension, hope points to the absolute future, the divine mystery, toward fulfillment, God's self-communication.

Hope is theological because it is directed toward God. It is eschatological because it refers to our final end, which is already present in our historical reality in sacramental form, as sign and mediation, but will be unveiled and fulfilled beyond death.

Utopia says no to the present and points toward a future within history. Hope says yes to the absolute future, already present, which comes to meet every human being but is always future in the sense that it is never totally achieved and known. It always keeps its character of being something to come, an unforeseeable surprise, wholly new. Hope reveals the structure of the real as movement toward this absolute future and not toward emptiness or nothing.[10]

2. Historical Considerations

Utopias are born at moments of crisis and transition.[11] So in times of change, as with the passage from feudalism to the birth of capitalism, we get the Renaissance utopias (More, Campanella, Bacon). The struggle of the rising bourgeoisie against feudal lords generated the liberal utopias (Harrington, Rousseau, Locke). Protest against the oppression of the working masses gave birth to the social utopias (Saint-Simon, Fourier, Owen, Blanc). The dehumanizing effects of technology, progress, and the functionalization of human relationships gave rise to the commune utopias (hippies). Utopias arise when the present becomes unbearable. They point toward a possible change in human history, the creation of a new, different world.

Hope, however, grows in much more difficult and hostile ground. Its true origin is an impossible situation in human terms, one we cannot overcome by relying on our present potential and human strength, but only on God's promises and power. It is an experience of God within our own human courage, our own unbreakable hope. The biblical model is Abraham (Rom. 4:18–22), who hoped against all hope.

The current situation in Latin America is favorable to the rise of utopias and nourishes theological hope. Utopia's particular field is the economic and political crisis rocking the continent. Economically speaking, the most obvious sign of the crisis is the gigantic foreign debt, which in purely financial terms and within the orthodoxy of the ruling international economic order is absolutely insoluble. Politically, the crisis is manifest either through the continuing existence of illegitimate authoritarian regimes or the precarious nature of democratic institutions for those who enjoy at least an apparent legality. They are institutions whose instability does not allow for profound changes without the enormous risk of reverting to dictatorship. In a word, capitalism's savage power is strangling people's lives so that they are turning toward an alternative reality.

But the brutal reality sometimes seems to block even utopian imagination, only leaving space for hope in God. And as these oppressed people are Christians, their faith drives them to act. The bridge between faith and liberating action is hope in God. So it is not surprising that the most dominant tone in the people's songs and prayers is that of the psalmist crying: "Be pleased O Lord, to deliver me! O Lord, make haste to help me! . . . Thou art my help and my deliverer; do not tarry, O my God!" (Ps. 40:14, 18).

3. Anthropological Foundation

Humans are *utopian beings*. This fundamental condition derives from the insuperable tension between our openness to the world as a whole and our particular situation in limited time and space. On the one hand, we face boundless horizons, regions and lands without limit. We are self-transcending spirit. We are imagination, desire, creativity. Our questioning never ceases. Our will is not satisfied with any particular good. We want good in itself, unconditional good. We are directed toward the future. We are dynamic, in movement. "Every human being lives primarily to the extent that he or she aspires to the future."[12] We are beings-tending-to-be-more. We live with a permanent calling to the future. Our being is a project.

At the same time we are situated in very particular conditions. We live on the Latin American continent full of contradictions—a dark tunnel for our aspirations; a closed horizon to our possibilities; a territory with limited scope. The economic situation strangles the people and makes them become an oppressed mass, whose plans and projects are determined and defined by outside forces. The political situation offers no future to the poor. The cultural situation forces them continually to assimilate important elements that are alien to their tradition.

This violent tension between what they essentially are and how they exist in their concrete situation, between their aspirations and what they really experience, impels Latin Americans toward liberating utopias.

Their very being consists of theological hope. They want to transcend themselves not just within history, in relation to the present and their particular situation. They want transcendence that goes beyond history. This is being-for-the-absolute-future, not just for the more limited earthly future. The absolute future comes in the form of grace. Grace enters history as a real possibility. So in each free, historical human action human beings confront the ultimate, definitive, absolute future. With this theological hope as part of their being, Latin Americans do not consider the terrible oppression and exploitation they suffer as mere historical facts, but as "structural sin." Hoping means fighting against this sin, the work of evil, sin committed by human free will, which crystallizes into structures that end up leading to future sins. It is not just a utopia of liberation but hope of total liberation, which begins in history but goes beyond it, sustained by God's grace.

As utopian beings, Latin American people confront the oppression under which they live and where they experience their own limitation and weakness and the temptation to pessimism, bitterness, and fatalism. Creating utopias means staying alive in a situation which speaks of death on all sides. Utopia helps them to humanize the inhuman work processes to which they are subjected.

This utopian impulse is not exempt from risk and temptations. People committed to a utopia of liberation feel they are makers of history, creators of meaning for a reality they wish were different. The risk lies in believing they are able to give history its *whole* meaning. They believe they can create the perfect society within historical human space and time, the city of absolute humanity. They suppose human beings are capable of designing and building a radical definitive project that would be absolute perfection. They want to create the absolute Kingdom on earth with the fragile material of history.[13]

This danger is less in Latin America, because Latin Americans are believers and therefore imbued with theological hope. The horizon of the absolute future has a double function in the way they see themselves. On the one hand, they are more easily aware that no situation is nonviable, however closed and terrible it may be, because they hope in the absolute Lord of history and the universe. On the other hand, the claim to build the perfect city on earth gives way to the hope that only God can conquer all their adversaries, especially sin and death, by giving the gift of resurrection and glorifying history.

Thus for Latin Americans, *being-hope* corrects the arrogant pretension of *being-utopian*. But being-utopian offers particular ways of embodying hope in history. This leads us into politics.

4. Scope of Politics

Two fundamental political tensions underlie utopia. In fact, the political utopias of recent centuries turn in practice around two conflicting axes. On the one hand, they may try to create a utopia of unlimited spontaneous freedom, but at the expense of and in painful conflict with justice and equality; on the other hand, the utopia of justice and equality may be constructed at the expense of freedom.

A second fundamental tension lies in the political direction given to utopia. Utopia may become an apologia for what already exists, by assuming a clear conservative color and projecting a perfected (utopian) future as a prolongation of the present. We find this in its most expressive form in A. Huxley's *Brave New World*, where even death is thought of as continuing this pleasant world in which all suffering, fear, and anguish are overcome by the chemical means of drugs.

This utopia can be turned by the exploited and oppressed into a protest against the present situation, against kowtowing to the ruling system. It becomes a factor for change, in opposition to the real present and in favor of the desired future. It shifts the weight of the present onto a different future of novelty and creativity.

In the political field utopia has been attacked by Marxist socialism, which calls it alienation. Its ideal character is seen as demobilizing and a source of frustration, as idealism lacking in realism. Thus Marxism presents itself as a scientific reading of reality, which is incompatible with utopia in its vagueness and lack of scientific rigor. Utopia is seen as an evasion of the present, leading to historical irresponsibility and castle-building in the air, instead of taking on struggle and conflict with a view to setting up a new society.

Another political attack comes from historical experience. Utopias which begin from below, with the exploited, end up in the hands of those who are on top and become ideology. So utopia is degraded into ideology. Historically we know the case of the utopia of freedom—absolute, liberal, spontaneous—which ended up producing mechanisms of oppression and highjacking this freedom to serve the ruling classes. Thus the utopia of freedom destroyed the possibility of freedom for the masses.

We saw how utopia tempted people to turn finite human history into infinite perfection, inviting hubris. When this dynamic operates politically, the most violent forms of totalitarianism arise. For when people rely only on immanent historical forces to build a perfect society of justice overcoming human limitations, they brook no opposition and silence every enemy. Only by extreme violence can they employ the human demiurge in empirical time to construct the definitive future. They do not accept the possibility of any other freedom that is not embarked on the same revolutionary adventure. Thus they attribute the divine quality of perfection to their historical construct and cannot tolerate objections, opposition, or dissent. Their effectiveness is based on their capacity for fanaticism. So utopia becomes closer to violence than to dispassionate reason. It becomes a secularized religion leading to totalitarianism, as we saw with Nazism and Stalinism.[14]

However, these dangers accompanying utopia do not take away its fundamental role as a driving historical force. It does not cease to be so because it may succumb to human pride and lead by its internal logic to totalitarianism. There are many human realities which if taken to their logical extreme end up generating contradictions. This does not mean they cease to be necessary. Their logic can be halted at a certain point. Utopia belongs to this kind of thinking that must not be taken to extremes. What stops utopia on its road to pride and totalitarianism is hope.

Thus utopia is relevant to our situation without incurring the dangers pointed out by K. Popper and others. For a people left on the margin of history, or rather, living on the "underside of history,"[15] it is an historical force for liberation. It rejects the defeatism and fatalism generated and nourished by the dominant ideology and is an anticipation of the future as a different, possible, longed for reality. It keeps alive the conviction that present reality can be changed, that it is not a natural order imposed by God but the result of interested human decisions. Utopia is a mysticism inspiring action for change. Utopia impels to action, opening new spaces, which previously appeared to be closed off.

When this utopia is animated and penetrated by Christian hope, its force becomes irresistible. At the same time this Christian hope offers it a critique which saves it from human pride with its absolute and totalitarian pretensions. The root of this hope lies in the revelation which entered history and reached its highest point in the mystery of the resurrection of Christ.

III. THE RESURRECTION, FOUNDATION OF THE THEOLOGICAL DIMENSION

1. Utopias in the Bible

Of course the term utopia, invented in the sixteenth century, cannot be biblical. Nevertheless, if by *utopia* we mean historical projects realized within this world, and by *hope* a theological attitude which maintains a direct relationship with God's presence acting in history and with the absolute future, we can say that the Bible contains utopias. Although its horizon is always one of hope, as it trusts in God for fulfillment, nevertheless at first this hope was thought of as preferably, if not exclusively, within history. So provisional models of how Israel should live, produced by prophets and constantly reinterpreted, should be interpreted as mediations of a final intervention by God at the end of time. Thus Israel's history knew a number of utopias. J. Pixley lists the utopia of a peasant society where "they shall sit every man under his vine and under his fig tree" (1 Kings 5:5, Mic. 4:4, Zech. 3:10) in a "land flowing with milk and honey" (Exod. 3:8,17; 13:5; 33:3, and elsewhere); the utopia of the beneficent king (Ps. 72:1–9, 12–14, 17; Ps. 101:1–8: Isa. 11:1–5); the utopia of a wise law and docile people (Jer. 31:31–34; Ezek. 36:24–32; Isa. 2:2–4); the priestly utopia of a land without blemish (Ezek. 40–48); the utopia of a communist society (Acts 4:32–35; 3:17–21); the utopia of holding spiritual goods in common until the Lord comes (1 Cor. 12:12–13; 7:21–24); the apocalytic utopia of blessedness (Rev. 6:9–11; 22:1–5).[16]

2. Centrality of Hope in the Hebrew Scriptures

The biblical revelation that begins with Abraham is presented as a promise.[17] This experience of promise and hope is projected backward, so that the first pages of Genesis, with their account of the first sin also contain promise and hope: "Her descendant shall bruise your head" (Gen. 3:15). From the ruins of the flood, the symbol of the rainbow arises as the promise of God's covenant with future generations. It is God's promise that such a catastrophe will never happen again (Gen. 9).

Israel lives by hope, in hope: hope of its progeny (Gen. 13:16), the nation (Gen. 12:2), the land (Gen. 12:7), of liberation from slavery (Exod. 3:7ff.), of a perpetual covenant with God (Exod. 19), of the new covenant (Jer. 31:31ff.). In its pilgrimage Israel experienced reality in tension with this promise. God's self-revelation to the people is always related to promising land, a future, a covenant. And the promises are so great and so far removed from the present reality and foreseeable outcome that they always remain promises. So the people's spiritual food is hope. Hope becomes even sharper when Israel finds itself in exile, captivity, or suffers defeat and persecution. It is a hope which the people perceive as hope in history—until with the resurrection of Christ it is finally seen as being beyond earthly history.

The ultimate basis of this hope was Yahweh's faithfulness—faithfulness which the people celebrated in their great liturgical celebrations and the reciting of their short creeds. Yahweh's past deeds were set before the people's eyes to keep hope in God alive in the present and the future.

Israel's experience of hope was not easy. The people were required to leave the land, undergo trials and temptations, not despair over defeats and national catastrophes. Incomplete fulfillment and new adversities always brought the people back to this hope. This was the horizon for a nomadic people. But hope continued even after they took possession of the land. So Yahweh's name should be interpreted in accordance with the dynamic of hope rather than ontologically. Not "He who is" (an ontological reading) but "He who will always be with his people."[18]

Therefore Israel's decision to trust in God, who calls them, is directed toward the future and nourished by hope. Hoping means believing in love, and Israel experienced God's love as a promise. Thus hope is a constitutive experience of the people's awareness of God, and scripture's message-theology is hope. In this Israel was an exception, as the neighboring peoples lived under the religious-mythical threat of a return to the initial chaos. Their religions promised protection against this reversion, whereas Yahweh pointed Israel to the future through anticipatory signs of the divine presence among God's people. In the last resort this future was God, who became present while also announcing a future presence. Abraham's example is paradigmatic. When God grants him the child of the promise (fulfillment), God orders him to sacrifice the child in order to make him hope again. Every conquest by Israel is an Isaac, given to them and demanded from them, so that they may hope for it again as a new gift by Yahweh. As this promise is never completely fulfilled, it becomes a source of earthly utopias for Israel and also a critical standard for them, always driving the people toward the future true Isaac: Jesus Christ.

3. Jesus Christ, Source of Utopias and Reason for Hope

Israel of the flesh wanted the promises to be fulfilled on earth. Israel of the Spirit glimpsed—and therefore hoped (in the theological sense)—that the fulfillment of the promise would surpass the limits of this age. In Jesus' time the term in which this hope was expressed was the Kingdom of God. But the utopian expectations of this hope were different: kingdom of the law perfectly fulfilled (Pharisees), kingdom of the pure and spiritual living in a community of saints (Essenes), national kingdom free from Roman rule (Zealots), kingdom of the cult and temple (priests). In his proclamation of the Kingdom Jesus did not go against any of these utopias, but he criticized the arrogance and absolute claims made for them by human interests. This cost him his life.

Nevertheless, his preaching has given rise to countless earthly utopias throughout history. Millenarianism has caught the imagination of many Christians, who dreamed of an earthly kingdom of happiness before the last judgment. In particular, they were inspired by the famous passage in Revelation 20:4–10. Political thinking in the Middle Ages was subject to the paradox that, on the one hand, they hoped for a descent from heaven to bring judgment and redemption, and on the other, they had faith in the Holy Roman Empire as an earthly promise and expression of paradise.[19] The Holy Roman Empire was considered as an ideal, as the place for the desired reconstruction. Thus the biblical notion of the reign of David was translated into the Carolingian rule: David was the model for the Frankish king, who was also a new Moses—*rex et sacerdos*—through his anointing. Jerusalem was transferred to Gaul. Christian Europe in the Middle Ages lived with this tension between hope in the future possible rebuilding of Israel as a holy community, and eschatological hope in the form of individual salvation.[20]

Jesus Christ preached the kingdom of God as an "eschatological reality" in the future (Luke 11:2; Matt. 6:10; Luke 10:9; Matt. 10:7; Mark 1:15) and in the present (Luke 11:20; Matt. 12:28).[21]

This Kingdom of God is God's power already acting in the present. It is the dynamic of God's sovereignty over humanity, history, and the cosmos. Its fulfillment will come only at the end of time, through definitive victory over its enemies—including death—and eternal dominion over all things and all people (1 Cor. 15:15, 24, 26, 28).

In this sense, God's Kingdom is not a utopia because its fulfillment will be the victory over sin and death. If historically it generated utopias with a purely earthly character, it nevertheless remains the critical standard for all utopias, including those of the church itself, which is its sacrament.

This reality is clarified theologically by the resurrection of Jesus. In this eschatological event Jesus' body, as a unique and personal center of decision as the representative of history and cosmos, achieves the definitive quality of life, which forever surpasses time and the confinement of space. With him, the cosmos and history become ripe for God's eternity.

The resurrection is not a terminus, it is not a *topia*, it is not to be found in any of the "utopias" which are simply the creations of human imagination, aspiration, and desire. The resurrection is the place, the *topia* of theological hope. Only through hope can we look toward the resurrection, since it is the work of God the Father's absolute freedom and love, by the power of the Spirit. The Son's humanity was snatched from the fragility of flesh to belong to the sphere of the "Spirit," as the "firstfruits of them that slept" (1 Cor. 15:20), "the firstborn of the dead" (Col. 1:18; Rev. 1:5), as the "precursor" (Acts 3:15; 5:31) of all of us.[22]

Each of us shares doubly in Jesus' resurrection; sacramentally, in germ, in earthly history, through faith, baptism, the eucharist, charity, through every free act welcoming Christ's victorious grace. When we die we will share in Christ's resurrection fully. In God's final Kingdom, which during our lives was a spur, present as a sign, history reaches it final stage that began to be manifest in Jesus' resurrection. With the resurrection all human hope, which during history nourished the struggle of the poor—so many moments of victory and disaster—reaches its fulfillment. History, which it fertilized, comes to fruition. The truth of all utopias appears; in comparison with this fulfillment they are infinitely limited: "No eye has seen, nor ear heard, nor the human heart conceived, what God has prepared for those who love him" (1 Cor. 2:9). In their turn, the utopias appear as mediations directed toward this moment of fulfillment, a response to genuine human aspirations. Deep within human longing lies God's call to communion with the Holy Trinity in the fullness of the resurrection.

Thus human utopias reveal their true nature as anonymous Christian hope, and hope is the goal of every true utopia. This hope becomes clear in the resurrection, when human beings, laden with history and cosmos, finally break through the limits of time into God. God's finality, which is already present in history whenever human freedom confronts the divine freedom through human, cosmic, historical actions, now through the resurrection attains the whole of human life, giving it the dimension of incorruptibility, glory, power, spirit (1 Cor. 15:42–44).

Through the resurrection of the dead, which is God's fundamental act of love, the eschatological significance of God's preference for the poor appears more clearly. Those who suffered so greatly in earthly history, who were familiar with weakness, humiliation, now share in the victory, power, and glory of God, who raised Jesus and who will raise these poor of the earth.

IV. CONCLUSION

Utopias are human creations that spring from human longing for a better life in the face of the hard sufferings of the present. It is above all the poor who dream of utopias, because the present is much harder for them. This human character of creating utopias as a spur to political activity, attempting to change things, would remain an enigma, lacking its true meaning, unless theological hope revealed its real origin and final destiny. Human beings were created by a Trinity that is community, the first and most perfect community. Therefore our whole lives are permeated by this deep aspiration toward living together in community.

Hope would also point toward a goal, a destiny which would remain a dark horizon. But Jesus' resurrection fully revealed humanity's utopian structure, its limits, and its anticipatory significance. The resurrection showed that hope in Yahweh does not lead to frustration but to life.

Jesus' resurrection is the prototype, precursor, and anticipation of all resurrections. In it the end of history has already happened. It also shows that only those who give their lives for their brothers and sisters rise again. Lastly, it is the ultimate key to all revelation.

The last word on history has already been said. No human power, no dictator, no ruling power will decide the final destiny of the poor. God's love raised Jesus and will raise all those he loves and who love him. And among these the poor have first place.

—*Translated by Dinah Livingstone*

NOTES

1. H. Marcuse, *El final de la utopía* (Barcelona, 1968), p. 10.
2. J. Stoetzel, *Les valeurs du temps présent: une enquêete européenne* (Paris, 1983), p. 174.
3. L. Silbermann and H. Fries, "Utopie und Hoffnung," in *Christlicher Glaube in moderner Gesellschaft* (Freiburg, 1982), p. 69.
4. L. Dumont, *Essays on Individualism* (Chicago, 1986).
5. Ph. Murray, *Le 19e sièle à travers les âges* (Paris, 1984).
6. G. Gutiérrez, *The Power of the Poor in History* (Maryknoll, N.Y., 1983), p. 76.
7. L. Boff, *Teologia do cativeiro e da libertaãao* (Petropolis, 1980), p. 13.
8. G. Pixley and C. Boff, *The Bible, the Church, and the Poor* (Maryknoll, N.Y.: 1986), p. 213.
9. K. Kerenyi, *Ursinn und Sinnwandel des Utopischen* (Zurich, 1964), p. 12.
10. K. Rahner, "Marist Utopia and the Christian Future of Man," in *Theological Investigations* VI (New York: Crossroad), pp. 59–68.
11. J. A. Gimbernat, "Utopia," in C. Floristan and J.J. Tamayo, eds., *Conceptos fundamentales de pastoral* (Madrid 1983), p. 1016.
12. E. Bloch, *The Principle of Hope* (Cambridge, Mass., 1986).
13. H. Cl. Vaz, *Escritos de filosofia* (São Paulo, 1986), p. 296.

14. K. Popper, *The Open Society and its Enemies* (London, 1945).

15. Gutiérrez, *The Power of the Poor in History*, pp. 169–221.

16. J. Pixley, "Las utopias principales de la Biblia," in R. Vidales and L. Rivera, eds., *La esperanza en el presente de América latina* (San José, 1983), pp. 313–30.

17. E. Brunner, *Offenbarung und Vernunft* (Zurich, 1981), p. 98.

18. J. C. Murray, *Das Gottes-problem: Gestem und Heute* (Freiburg-Basel-Vienna, 1965), pp. 15ff.

19. L. Silbermann-H. Fries, "Utopie und Hoffnung" (1982), p. 59.

20. Ibid., pp. 66ff.

21. H. Merklein, *Jesu Botschaft von der Gottesherrschaft* (Stuttgart, 1983), p. 24.

22. M. Gourges, *A vida futura segundo o Novo Testamento* (São Paulo, 1986), pp. 62ff.

Bibliography

[Eds. note: This bibliography includes works on Latin American liberation theology available in English.]

I. DOCUMENTS OF THE MAGISTERIUM

Second General Conference of Latin American Bishops, convened at Medellín, Colombia (August 24–September 6, 1968), Final Documents, *The Church in the Present-Day Transformation of Latin America in Light of the Council*, vol. 2, *Conclusions* (Washington, D.C.: U.S. Catholic Conference, 1970). Documents on "Justice," "Peace," "Family and Demography," "Poverty of the Church," appear in *The Gospel of Peace and Justice*, ed. Joseph Gremillion (Maryknoll, N.Y.: Orbis Books, 1976).

Third General Conference of Latin American Bishops, convened at Puebla, Mexico, January 1979, *Final Documents*, in *Puebla and Beyond*, eds. John Eagleson and Philip Scharper (Maryknoll, N.Y.: Orbis Books, 1979).

Fourth General Conference of Latin American Bishops, convened at Santo Domingo, Dominican Republic, October 1992, Conclusions, in *Santo Domingo and Beyond*, ed. Alfred T. Hennelly (Maryknoll, N.Y.: Orbis Books, 1993).

"Instruction on Certain Aspects of the 'Theology of Liberation,' " Congregation for the Doctrine of the Faith (August 6, 1984), in *Liberation Theology: A Documentary History*, ed. Alfred T. Hennelly (Maryknoll, N.Y.: Orbis Books, 1990), 393–414.

"Instruction on Christian Freedom and Liberation," Congregation for the Doctrine of the Faith (March 22, 1986), in *Liberation Theology: A Documentary History*, 461–97.

John Paul II, "Letter to Brazilian Episcopal Conference" (April 9, 1986), in *Liberation Theology: A Documentary History*, 498–506.

II. HISTORY, METHODOLOGY, AND DISTINCTIVE FEATURES OF THE THEOLOGY OF LIBERATION

Antoncich, Ricardo, *Christians in the Face of Injustice: A Latin American Reading of Catholic Social Teaching* (Maryknoll, N.Y.: Orbis Books, 1987).

Aquino, María Pilar, *Our Cry for Life: Feminist Theology from Latin America*, trans. Dinah Livingstone (Maryknoll, N.Y.: Orbis Books, 1993).

Araya, Victorio, *God of the Poor*, trans. Robert R. Barr (Maryknoll, N.Y.: Orbis Books, 1987).

Assmann, Hugo, *Theology for a Nomad Church*, trans. Paul Burns (Maryknoll, N.Y.: Orbis Books, 1976).

Berryman, Phillip, *Liberation Theology* (New York: Pantheon, 1987).

Boff, Clodovis, *Theology and Praxis: Epistemological Foundations*, trans. Robert R. Barr (Maryknoll, N.Y.: Orbis Books, 1987).

Boff, Leonardo and Clodovis Boff, *Introducing Liberation Theology*, trans. Paul Burns (Tunbridge Wells: Burns & Oates; Maryknoll, N.Y.: Orbis Books, 1987).

———. *Salvation and Liberation*, trans. Robert R. Barr (Maryknoll, N.Y.: Orbis Books, 1984).

———. *Faith on the Edge*, trans. Robert R. Barr (New York: Harper & Row, 1989; Maryknoll, N.Y.: Orbis Books, 1991).

———. *When Theology Listens to the Poor*, trans. Robert R. Barr (San Francisco: Harper & Row, 1988).

Brown, Robert McAfee, *Gustavo Gutiérrez: An Introduction to Liberation Theology* (Maryknoll, N.Y.: Orbis Books, 1990).

Croatto, J. Severino, *Biblical Hermeneutics*, trans. Robert R. Barr (Maryknoll, N.Y.: Orbis Books, 1987).

———. *Exodus: A Hermeneutics of Freedom* (Maryknoll, N.Y.: Orbis Books, 1981).

Dussel, Enrique, *Ethics and Community*, trans. Robert R. Barr (Maryknoll, N.Y.: Orbis Books; Tunbridge Wells: Burns & Oates, 1988).

———. *Ethics and the Theology of Liberation*, trans. Bernard F. McWilliams (Maryknoll, N.Y.: Orbis Books, 1978).

———. *A History of the Church in Latin America: Colonialism to Liberation* (Grand Rapids: Eerdmans, 1981).

———. *History and the Theology of Liberation*, trans. John Drury (Maryknoll, N.Y.: Orbis Books, 1976).

———. *Philosophy of Liberation*, trans. Aquilina Martinez and Christine Morkovsky (Maryknoll, N.Y.: Orbis Books, 1985).

———, ed. *The Church in Latin America: 1492–1992*, trans. Paul Burns (Tunbridge Wells: Burns & Oates; Maryknoll, N.Y.: Orbis Books, 1992).

Ellacuría, Ignacio, *Freedom Made Flesh: The Mission of Christ and His Church* (Maryknoll, N.Y.: Orbis Books, 1976).

Ellis, Marc and Otto Maduro, eds. *The Future of Liberation Theology: Essays in Honor of Gustavo Gutiérrez* (Maryknoll, N.Y.: Orbis Books, 1989).

Gibellini, Rosino, ed., *Frontiers of Theology in Latin America*, trans. John Drury (Maryknoll, N.Y.: Orbis Books, 1979).

Gutiérrez, Gustavo, *The Power of the Poor in History*, trans. Robert R. Barr (Maryknoll, N.Y.: Orbis Books, 1983).

———. *A Theology of Liberation*, trans. Sister Caridad Inda and John Eagleson (Maryknoll, N.Y.: Orbis Books, 1973; revised edition, 1988).

———. *The Truth Shall Make You Free: Confrontations*, trans. Matthew J. O'Connell (Maryknoll, N.Y.: Orbis Books, 1990).

Hennelly, Alfred T., ed. *Liberation Theology: A Documentary History* (Maryknoll, N.Y.: Orbis Books, 1990).

Hinkelammert, Franz, *The Ideological Weapons of Death: A Theological Critique of Capitalism*, trans. Phillip Berryman (Maryknoll, N.Y.: Orbis Books, 1986).

Maduro, Otto, *Religion and Social Conflicts* (Maryknoll, N.Y.: Orbis Books, 1982).

Mesters, Carlos, *Defenseless Flower: A New Reading of the Bible*, trans. Francis McDonagh (Maryknoll, N.Y.: Orbis Books, 1989).

McGovern, Arthur, *Liberation Theology and Its Critics: Toward an Assessment* (Maryknoll, N.Y.: Orbis Books, 1989).

Míguez Bonino, José, *Doing Theology in a Revolutionary Situation* (Philadelphia: Fortress Press, 1975).

———. *Toward a Christian Political Ethic* (Philadelphia: Fortress Press, 1983).

Miranda, José Porfirio, *Marx and the Bible*, trans. John Eagleson (Maryknoll, N.Y.: Orbis Books, 1974).

Moser, Antonio and Bernardino Leers, *Moral Theology: Dead Ends and Alternatives*, trans. Paul Burns (Tunbridge Wells: Burns & Oates; Maryknoll, N.Y.: Orbis Books, 1990).

Pixley, George, *On Exodus: A Liberation Perspective*, trans. Robert R. Barr (Maryknoll, N.Y.: Orbis Books, 1987).

———. *God's Kingdom* (Maryknoll, N.Y.: Orbis Books, 1981).

Segundo, Juan Luis, *Faith and Ideologies*, trans. John Drury (Maryknoll, N.Y.: Orbis Books, 1984).

———. *The Liberation of Dogma*, trans. Phillip Berryman (Maryknoll, N.Y.: Orbis Books, 1992).

———. *The Liberation of Theology*, trans. John Drury (Maryknoll, N.Y.: Orbis Books, 1976).

———. *Signs of the Times: Theological Reflections*, trans. Robert R. Barr (Maryknoll, N.Y.: Orbis Books, 1993).

———. *Theology and the Church* (San Francisco: Harper & Row, 1985).

Tamez, Elsa, *Against Machismo* (Interviews), trans. John Eagleson (Oak Park: Meyer Stone, 1989).

———. *The Bible of the Oppressed*, trans. Matthew J. O'Connell (Maryknoll, N.Y.: Orbis Books, 1982).

———, ed. *Through Her Eyes: Latin American Women Doing Theology* (Maryknoll, N.Y.: Orbis Books, 1989).

III. SYSTEMATIC CONTENTS OF THE THEOLOGY OF LIBERATION

The Liberating Design of God

Boff, Leonardo, *Jesus Christ Liberator*, trans. Patrick Hughes (Maryknoll, N.Y.: Orbis Books, 1978).

———. *Trinity and Society*, trans. Paul Burns (Tunbridge Wells: Burns & Oates; Maryknoll, N.Y.: Orbis Books, 1988).

———. *The Lord's Prayer: The Prayer of Integral Liberation*, trans. Theodore Morrow (Maryknoll, N.Y.: Orbis Books, 1983).

———. *The Maternal Face of God* (San Francisco: Harper & Row, 1987).

Bussman, Claus, *Who Do You Say? Jesus Christ in Latin American Theology* (Maryknoll, N.Y.: Orbis Books, 1985).

Cardenas, José Pallares, *A Poor Man Called Jesus* (Maryknoll, N.Y.: Orbis Books, 1982).

Comblin, José, *Jesus of Nazareth*, trans. Carl Kabat (Maryknoll, N.Y.: Orbis Books, 1976).

———. *Sent from the Father: Meditations on the Fourth Gospel*, trans. Carl Kabat (Maryknoll, N.Y.: Orbis Books, 1979).

———. *The Holy Spirit and Liberation*, trans. Paul Burns (Tunbridge Wells: Burns & Oates; Maryknoll, N.Y.: Orbis Books, 1989).
Echegary, Hugo, *The Practice of Jesus*, trans. Matthew J. O'Connell (Maryknoll, N.Y.: Orbis Books, 1984).
Gebara, Ivone and María Clara Bingemer, *Mary: Mother of God, Mother of the Poor*, trans. Phillip Berryman (Maryknoll, N.Y.: Orbis Books; Tunbridge Wells: Burns & Oates, 1989).
Gutiérrez, Gustavo, *The God of Life*, trans. Matthew J. O'Connell (Maryknoll, N.Y.: Orbis Books, 1991).
Mesters, Carlos, *God, Where Are You*? (Maryknoll, N.Y.: Orbis Books, 1977).
Míguez Bonino, José, ed., *Faces of Jesus in Latin America*, trans. Robert R. Barr (Maryknoll, N.Y.: Orbis Books, 1984).
Miranda, José Porfirio, *Being and the Messiah: The Message of St. John* (Maryknoll, N.Y.: Orbis Books, 1977).
Muñoz, Ronaldo, *The God of Christians*, trans. Paul Burns (Tunbridge Wells: Burns & Oates; Maryknoll, N.Y.: Orbis Books, 1990).
Richard, Pablo, et al, *The Idols of Death and the God of Life* (Maryknoll, N.Y., 1983).
Segundo, Juan Luis, *The Christ of the Ignatian Exercises*, trans. John Drury (Maryknoll, N.Y.: Orbis Books, 1987).
———. *An Evolutionary Approach to Jesus of Nazareth*, trans. John Drury (Maryknoll, N.Y.: Orbis Books, 1985).
———. *The Historical Jesus of the Synoptics*, trans. John Drury (Maryknoll, N.Y.: Orbis Books, 1986).
———. *The Humanist Christology of Paul*, trans. John Drury (Maryknoll, N.Y.: Orbis Books, 1986).
———. *Our Idea of God*, trans. John Drury (Maryknoll, N.Y.: Orbis Books, 1973).
Sobrino, Jon, *Christology at the Crossroads*, trans. John Drury (Maryknoll, N.Y.: Orbis Books, 1978).
———. *Jesus in Latin America* (Maryknoll, N.Y.: Orbis Books, 1987).
———. *Jesus the Liberator*, trans. Paul Burns and Francis McDonagh (Maryknoll, N.Y.: Orbis Books; Tunbridge Wells: Burns & Oates, 1993).

The Liberation of Creation

Boff, Leonardo, *Ecology & Liberation,* trans. John Cumming (Maryknoll, N.Y.: Orbis Books, 1995).
———. *Liberating Grace*, trans. John Drury (Maryknoll, N.Y.: Orbis Books, 1979).
———. *Saint Francis* (New York: Crossroad, 1985).
Comblin, José, *Retrieving the Human*, trans. Robert R. Barr (Maryknoll, N.Y.: Orbis Books; Tunbridge Wells: Burns & Oates, 1990).
Segundo, Juan Luis, *Evolution and Sin*, trans. John Drury (Maryknoll, N.Y.: Orbis Books, 1974).
———. *Grace and the Human Condition*, trans. John Drury (Maryknoll, N.Y.: Orbis Books, 1973).
Trigo, Pedro, *Creation and History*, trans. Robert R. Barr (Maryknoll, N.Y.: Orbis Books; Tunbridge Wells: Burns & Oates, 1991).

Church of the Poor, Sacrament of Liberation

Avila, Rafael, *Worship and Politics* (Maryknoll, N.Y.: Orbis Books, 1976).

Azevedo, Marcello, *Basic Ecclesial Communities in Brazil* (Washington, D.C.: Georgetown University Press, 1987).

Barreiro, Alvaro, *Basic Ecclesial Communities* (Maryknoll, N.Y.: Orbis Books, 1982).

Boff, Clodovis and Jorgé Pixley, *The Bible, the Church, and the Poor*, trans. Paul Burns (Tunbridge Wells: Burns & Oates; Maryknoll, N.Y.: Orbis Books, 1989).

Boff, Leonardo, *Church: Charism and Power* (New York: Crossroad, 1985).

———. *Ecclesiogenesis: The Base Communities Reinvent the Church*, trans. Robert R. Barr (Maryknoll, N.Y.: Orbis Books, 1986).

———. *New Evangelization: Good News to the Poor*, trans. Robert R. Barr (Maryknoll, N.Y.: Orbis Books; Tunbridge Wells: Burns & Oates, 1991).

———. *Sacraments of Life, Life of the Sacraments* (Washington, D.C.: Pastoral Press, 1987).

Comblin, José. *The Church and the National Security State* (Maryknoll, N.Y.: Orbis Books, 1979).

Fragoso, Antonio B., *Face of a Church*, trans. Robert R. Barr (Maryknoll, N.Y.: Orbis Books, 1987).

Gáldamez, Pablo, *Faith of a People*, trans. Robert R. Barr (Maryknoll, N.Y.: Orbis Books, 1986).

Hoornaert, Eduardo, *The Memory of the Christian People*, trans. Robert R. Barr (Maryknoll, N.Y.: Orbis Books; Tunbridge Wells: Burns & Oates, 1988).

Pastoral Team of Bambamarca, *Vamos Caminando: A Peruvian Catechism* (Maryknoll, N.Y.: Orbis Books, 1985).

Richard, Pablo, *Death of Christendom, Birth of the Church*, trans. Phillip Berryman (Maryknoll, N.Y.: Orbis Books, 1987).

Segundo, Juan Luis, *The Hidden Motives of Pastoral Action*, trans. John Drury (Maryknoll, N.Y.: Orbis Books, 1978).

———. *The Sacraments Today*, trans. John Drury (Maryknoll, N.Y.: Orbis Books, 1974).

Sobrino, Jon, *The True Church and the Poor*, trans. Matthew J. O'Connell (Maryknoll, N.Y.: Orbis Books, 1984).

Torres, Sergio and John Eagleson, eds. *The Challenge of Basic Christian Communities* (Maryknoll, N.Y.: Orbis Books, 1981).

Wright, Scott, *Promised Land: Death and Life in El Salvador* (Maryknoll, N.Y.: Orbis Books, 1994).

The Spirit of Liberation

Azevedo, Marcello, *The Consecrated Life*, trans. Guillermo Cook (Maryknoll, N.Y.: Orbis Books, 1995).

Alves, Rubem, *I Believe in the Resurrection* (Philadelphia: Fortress Press, 1986).

———. *A Theology of Human Hope* (New York: Corpus, 1971).

———. *Tomorrow's Child* (New York: Harper & Row, 1971).

Barbé, Dominique, *Grace and Power: Base Communities and Nonviolence in Brazil*, trans. John Pairman Brown (Maryknoll, N.Y.: Orbis Books, 1987).

———. *A Theology of Conflict: And Other Writings on Nonviolence*, trans. Robert R. Barr (Maryknoll, N.Y.: Orbis Books, 1989).

Boff, Clodovis, *Feet-on-the-Ground Theology: A Brazilian Journey*, trans. Phillip Berryman (Maryknoll, N.Y.: Orbis Books, 1987).

Boff, Leonardo, *God's Witnesses in the Heart of the World* (Chicago: Claret House, 1981).

———. *Passion of Christ, Passion of the World*, trans. Robert R. Barr (Maryknoll, N.Y.: Orbis Books, 1987).

———. *The Path to Hope: Fragments from a Theologian's Journey*, trans. Phillip Berryman (Maryknoll, N.Y.: Orbis Books, 1993).

———. *Way of the Cross, Way of Justice*, trans. John Drury (Maryknoll, N.Y.: Orbis Books, 1980).

Cardenal, Ernesto, *The Gospel of Solentiname*, trans. Donald Walsh (Maryknoll, N.Y.: Orbis Books, 1986).

Casaldáliga, Pedro, *In Pursuit of the Kingdom: Writings 1968–1988*, trans. Phillip Berryman (Maryknoll, N.Y.: Orbis Books, 1990).

Casaldáliga, Pedro, and José-María Vigil, *Political Holiness*, trans. Paul Burns and Francis McDonagh (Maryknoll, N.Y.: Orbis Books, 1994).

Comblin, José, *Cry of the Oppressed, Cry of Jesus*, trans. Robert R. Barr (Maryknoll, N.Y.: Orbis Books, 1988).

Cussianovich, Alejandro, *Religious Life and the Poor: Liberation Theology Perspectives* (Maryknoll, N.Y.: Orbis Books, 1979).

Galilea, Segundo, *The Beatitudes*, trans. Robert R. Barr (Maryknoll, N.Y.: Orbis Books, 1984).

———. *Following Jesus* (Maryknoll, N.Y.: Orbis Books, 1981).

———. *Spirituality of Hope*, trans. Terrence Cambias (Maryknoll, N.Y.: Orbis Books, 1989).

Gutiérrez, Gustavo, *On Job: God-Talk and the Suffering of the Innocent*, trans. Matthew J. O'Connell (Maryknoll, N.Y.: Orbis Books, 1987).

———. *Las Casas: In Search of the Poor of Jesus Christ*, trans. Robert R. Barr (Maryknoll, N.Y.: Orbis Books, 1993).

———. *We Drink from Our Own Wells*, trans. Matthew J. O'Connell (Maryknoll, N.Y.: Orbis Books, 1984).

Jaen, Nestor, *Toward a Spirituality of Liberation*, trans. Phillip Berryman (Chicago: Loyola University Press, 1991).

Libânio, J. B., *Spiritual Discernment and Politics: Guidelines for Religious Communities* (Maryknoll, N.Y.: Orbis Books, 1982).

Paoli, Arturo, *Gather Together in My Name: Reflections on Christianity and Community* (Maryknoll, N.Y.: Orbis Books, 1987).

Romero, Oscar, *Voice of the Voiceless*, trans. Donald Walsh (Maryknoll, N.Y.: Orbis Books, 1985).

Sobrino, Jon, *Archbishop Romero: Memories and Reflections*, trans. Robert R. Barr (Maryknoll, N.Y.: Orbis Books, 1990).

———, ed. *Companions of Jesus: The Jesuit Martyrs of El Salvador* (Maryknoll, N.Y.: Orbis Books, 1987).

———. *The Principle of Mercy* (Maryknoll, N.Y.: Orbis Books, 1995).

———. *Spirituality of Liberation*, trans. Robert R. Barr (Maryknoll, N.Y.: Orbis Books, 1988).

Sobrino, Jon and Juan Hernández Pico, *Theology of Christian Solidarity* (Maryknoll, N.Y.: Orbis Books, 1985).

Contributors

María Clara Bingemer is professor of systematic theology at the Pontifical Catholic University of Rio de Janeiro. She is co-author of *Mary: Mother of God, Mother of the Poor.*

Clodovis Boff, a Servite priest, was born in Concordia, Brazil in 1944. He received his doctorate in theology from the Catholic University of Louvain. He is professor at the Pontifical Catholic University of Rio de Janeiro, advisor to the Brazilian Conference of Religious, and a member of the National Pastoral Institute. His works include *Theology and Praxis* and *Feet-on-the-Ground Theology.*

Leonardo Boff was born in Concordia, Brazil in 1938. He received his doctorate in theology from the University of Munich. His books include *Jesus Christ Liberator, Ecclesiogenesis, Trinity and Society*, and *Ecology and Liberation.*

Carlos Bravo, a Jesuit, was born in Guadalajara, Mexico in 1938. He is director of the journal *Christus* and professor of New Testament in the Jesuit Theological Institute in Mexico City. His books include *Jésus, hombre en conflicto.*

Victor Codina, a Jesuit, was born in Barcelona, Spain in 1931. Since 1982 he has lived in Bolivia, where he is professor of theology at the Catholic University. He has published many books, including *De la modernidad a la solidaridad* and *Sacramentos de Iniciación.*

José Comblin was born in Brussels, Belgium in 1923. He has lived in Latin America since 1958, principally in Brazil, both teaching theology and doing pastoral work. His many books include *The Holy Spirit and Liberation, Retrieving the Human*, and *The Church and the National Security State.*

Ignacio Ellacuría, a Jesuit, was born in 1930 in Portugalate, Vizcaya in Spain. He was sent to El Salvador in 1949. He received his licentiates in the humanities and philosophy at the Catholic University of Quito (Ecuador), and his doctorate in philosophy from the University of Madrid. He was rector of the Central American University of San Salvador before his assassination by government troops in San Salvador on November 16, 1989, while work on this collection was in progress. His publications include *Freedom Made Flesh.*

Ivone Gebara was born in São Paolo, Brazil in 1944. She received her doctorate in philosophy in Paris and a licentiate in theology from the Pontifical Catholic University in São Paolo. She has taught theology at the Theological Institute in Recife. She is co-author of *Mary: Mother of God, Mother of the Poor.*

Gustavo Gutiérrez was born in Lima in 1928. He studied medicine, psychology, and theology in the Universities of Lima, Louvain, and the Gregoriana of Rome. He received a doctorate in theology from the University of Lyons. He is founder and director of the Instituto Bartolomé de las Casas. His works include *A Theology of Liberation; We Drink from Our Own Wells; The Truth Shall Make You Free; The God of Life; On Job: God-Talk and the Suffering of the Innocent*; and *Las Casas: In Search of the Poor of Jesus Christ.*

João Batista Libânio, a Jesuit, was born in Belo Horizonte, Brazil, and received his doctorate in theology from the Gregoriana in Rome. He is professor and director of the faculty of theology of the Society of Jesus in Brazil. His works include *Spiritual Discernment and Politics* and *Escatologia Cristã.*

Ronaldo Muñoz, a Sacred Heart priest, was born in 1933 in Santiago, Chile, and received his doctorate in theology at the University of Ratisbon in Germany. He is director of the journal *Pastoral Popular*. Since 1972 he has lived in a working-class barrio in Santiago. He is the author of *The God of Christians.*

Alvaro Quiroz Magaña, a Jesuit priest, was born in Guadalajara, Mexico in 1942. He studied philosophy and theology in Mexico and received his doctorate in theology from the University of Barcelona. He is professor of ecclesiology at the Theological Institute in Mexico City.

Jon Sobrino is a Jesuit priest. He was born in Barcelona, Spain in 1938, and has lived in El Salvador since 1957. He received his licentiate in philosophy and master's in engineering mechanics at St. Louis University and his doctorate in theology from Frankfurt. He is director of the Centro Monseñor Romero and professor of theology at the University of Central America in San Salvador. His many books include *Christology at the Crossroads, Jesus in Latin America, Jesus the Liberator*, and *The Principle of Mercy.*

Index

Abba, 70, 78-79, 100-102, 110-11, 129
Adam, 199
Angelelli, Enrique, Bishop, 231
Anthropology, 165-66, 283-84
Anti-Reign, 43, 52, 63, 129-30, 250; reality of, 64, 249
Aquinas, Thomas, St., 5, 11, 154, 217, 224
Arrupe, Pedro, 13
Augustine, St., 5, 178

Baptism, 79, 226-27
Base ecclesial communities, 36, 160, 162-63, 176-77, 187-88
Beatitudes, 28-29, 30-34
Bible, 16, 17-18, 167-68, 227-28, 285-88; freedom and, 149-50
Bingemer, María Clara, 165-77
Bloch, Ernst, 17
Boff, Clodovis, 1-21, 222
Boff, Leonardo, 46, 58-59, 75-89
Brave New World (Huxley), 284
Bravo, Carlos, 106-23
Bultmann, Rudolf, 39, 53, 59

Casaldáliga, Pedro, Bishop, 201-2, 222
Christopraxis, 132-33, 135-37
Church, 18-19, 30-37, 71, 158-63, 178-93; conflict in, 189-90, 191-92; fundamental themes of, 184-91; hierarchical conception of, 76, 160, 162; models of, 85-86, 182-83, 190-91; sacraments of, 222-24, 226-31; unity of, 160, 189-90
Codina, Victor, 216-32
Comblin, José, 146-64, 205-15
Congregation for the Doctrine of the Faith, 1, 3
Cross, 57, 249-50, 260-62
Cullman, Oscar, 60, 274

Daniel, 220
David, 287
Declaration on Religious Freedom (Vatican II), 149-50
Desde el Lugar del Pobre (L. Boff), 95
Dodd, C.H., 59

Ecclesiology. *See* Church
Elizabeth, 169
Ellacuría, Ignacio, 64, 71, 134, 143, 257-78; concept of poor, 144n10
End of Utopia (Marcuse), 279
Ephesus, Council of, 170
Eucharist, 218, 227-28
Evangelii Nuntiandi (Pope Paul VI), 16

Faith, 2-3, 6-7, 38, 88, 255; Christology and, 131-34; in Latin America, 106-7; light of, 15; sacraments and, 218; trinitarian, 75-77, 81
Florence, Council of, 85
Freedom, 139, 148-50, 209, 251

Gaudium et Spes (Vatican II), 155
Gebara, Ivone, 165-77
God, 11, 58, 90-105, 196, 205-15; experience of, 90-91, 241, 252-56; as Father, 70, 78-87, 97-102, 110-11, 118, 129; as Holy Spirit, 78-85, 87-88, 146-64; human personality and, 208-9; of life, 95-97, 153-54; mercy of, 97-99; of oppressed, 93-94, 95; sin and, 201-4; as Son, 78-79, 87,

106-23; Trinity, 75-89, 102-3. *See also* Reign of God
Grace, 205-15, 216-17; in action, 211-15; human community and, 207-9; nature of, 205-7; traditional attributes of, 209-11
Gratuity, 64, 65-66, 209-10, 248-49, 253
Gutiérrez, Gustavo, 22-37, 40, 144, 244, 248

Hermeneutics, 11, 15-19, 63, 166-67
Holy Spirit, 78-85, 87-88, 146-64; church and, 158-63; in history, 154-59
Hope, 63, 139, 239-40, 279-83, 286-87
Huxley, Aldous, 284

Ignatius, Loyola, St., 253
Incarnation, 171, 243-44
"Instruction on Certain Aspects of the Theology of Liberation" (Cardinal Ratzinger), 19
Irenaeus, St., 78
Isaiah, 62, 268-74

James, St., 32
Jeremias, Joachim, 55, 266
Jesus Christ, 79, 99-101, 106-45, 227, 241-45; anti-Reign and, 52; Christopraxis, 132-33, 135-37; death of, 53-54, 95-96, 118-21, 258-78; denunciations of, 51-52, 113-15, 118-19; divinity of, 70, 122, 127; following of, 131-35, 241-43, 252; God of, 52, 57, 91-92, 252-56; humanity of, 70, 91-92, 108-9, 122, 127-28; incarnation of, 170-71, 243-44; mercy of, 230, 238; miracles of, 49-51, 113; mission of, 244-45; Reign of God and, 34, 45-58, 70-72, 124-39, 259-60, 275-78, 287-89; Sermon on the Mount, 30-34, 98; Servant of Yahweh and, 268-78; titles of, 107, 122, 128-29, 137; Trinity revealed by, 78-80, 87; truth of, 140-41. *See also* Resurrection
Joachim of Fiore, 157-58
John, St., 79-80, 149-50, 169-70
John the Baptist, 110-11, 115
John XXIII, Pope, 30, 35
John Paul II, Pope, 5, 12, 25, 27, 199; on Trinity, 75; on Mary, 177
Joseph, St., 168

Kasper, Walter, 45, 46-47
Khan, Genghis, 76
Kingdom of God. *See* Reign of God

Laborem Exercens (Pope John Paul II), 12
Las Casas, Bartolomé de, 27
Latin America, 106-7, 146-49, 166-67, 174-76, 188-89; new spirituality in, 163-64, 178-81, 235; racism in, 23; sexism in, 24; suffering in, 94-97, 148, 194; trinitarian mystery in, 77-78; utopian impulse in, 283-84
Libânio, João Batista, 279-90
Liberation, 4, 93-94, 135, 146, 245-49; Jesus Christ and, 50, 122, 137-42; language and, 150-51, 163-64; new spirituality of, 163; from sin, 211; temptations of, 246-47
Liberation theology, 1-21, 40-49, 60, 65-69, 72-73; books of the Bible preferred by, 17-18; forms of, 8-9; Holy Spirit and, 146; literary works of, 95; methodology, 9-21; and modern revolutions, 157; as new theology, 182, 191, 219-20; poor as focus of, 142-44; resurrection in, 41-42; sin in, 198; traditional theology and, 18; Trinity, 84-88
Libertatis Conscientia (Congregation for the Doctrine of the Faith), 1, 3
Libertatis Nuntius (Congregation for the Doctrine of the Faith), 1, 3
Life, 66-68, 95-97, 153-54, 192-93
Luke, St., 28-31, 33-34, 79, 88, 148; and Mary, 169
Lumen Gentium (Vatican II), 35, 86, 187, 218

Marialis Cultus(Pope Paul VI), 177
Mark, St., 108, 168-69, 275-76
Martyrdom, 37, 96-97, 249-50
Marx, Karl, 13
Marxism, 13, 150, 279, 284

Mary, 88, 165-77, 188-89; Assumption of, 173-74; Immaculate Conception of, 172-73
Matthew, St., 27-34, 79, 168, 275
Medellín Conference, 22, 23, 26, 34, 35-36; on injustice, 198; "Medellín generation," 162; on peace, 143
Mediation, 11-21, 59-60, 125, 126; hermeneutic, 11, 15-19; practical, 11, 20-21; socioanalytic, 11-15
Mercy, 50-51, 97-99, 230, 237-39, 247
"Message of John Paul II to the Episcopate of Brazil," 1, 3, 5, 6
Micah, 72-73, 238-39, 252, 256
Miracles, 49-51, 113
Miranda, José Porfirio, 255
Mission del pueblo que sufre (Mesters), 95
Mission, 36, 82, 137-38, 244-45
Modalism, 81, 83
Moltmann, Jürgen, 39-40
Monoteismo como problema politico (Peterson), 76
More, Thomas, 281
Munificentissimus Deus (Pope Pius XII), 173
Muñoz, Ronaldo, 90-105
Murray, P., 280

Nicea, Council of, 81

Octogesima Adveniens (Pope Paul VI), 19
On Job: God-Talk and the Suffering of the Innocent (Gutiérrez), 95
Oppression, 11-14, 50, 93-94, 95, 266-67; of truth, 150, 195-96
Option for the poor, 22, 26-30, 36-37, 61-62, 241-52

Pannenberg, Wolfhart, 39, 47-48, 59, 261
Paul, St., 34, 148, 149, 159, 168; on the cross, 57; on primacy of the natural, 4; on the Reign of God, 220; on sin, 195-97; on truth, 62, 236-37
Paul VI, Pope, 16, 19
Peter, St., 79, 115, 139
Peterson, Erik, 76
Pius XII, Pope, 173
Pixley, Jorge, 286
Poor, 5, 22-37, 142-45, 244, 255-56; as addressees of the Reign, 54-58, 111-12; Bible of, 16; and Christian communities, 152-53, 183-84; church of, 30-37, 161, 186-89; as crucified people, 265-74, 276-78; Holy Spirit and, 156; interpretations of, 12-15, 24-25, 144n10; new presence of, 22-23; as people of God, 186-89; prayer of, 163-64; sacraments and, 221-22, 224-25. *See also* Option for the poor
Power of the Poor in History (Gutiérrez), 95
Praxis, 2, 10-11, 48-49, 64-66, 179-81; in Christology, 132-33, 135-37
Prayer, 163-64, 254
Puebla Conference, 22, 75, 162, 190, 198-99; on faces of oppression, 11-12; on Jesus Christ, 143; on the poor, 12, 23, 26, 27, 244; on utopia, 280

Quiroz Magaña, Alvaro, 178-93

Racism, 14, 23
Rad, Gerhard von, 260-61
Rahner, Karl, 5, 115, 132, 255
Ratzinger, Joseph, Cardinal, 19
Reality, 236-41; of anti-Reign, 64, 249; of Jesus Christ, 140-41
Redemptoris Mater (Pope John Paul II), 177
Reign of God, 34, 38-73, 101, 110-16, 124-39; addressees of, 54-58, 111-12; church and, 71, 185-86; comprehensive nature of, 69-73; current reassertion of, 59-61, 234-35; as eschaton, 40-43; in the gospel, 45-58; gratuity of, 64, 65-66; and Holy Spirit, 154; Jesus Christ and, 34, 45-58, 70-72, 124-39, 259-60, 275-78, 287-89; in liberation theology, 40-41, 42-49, 60, 65-69, 72-73; and new humanity, 207-8; praxis of, 64-66; premises of, 61-63; primacy of, 40-45; resurrection and, 39-40, 126, 261; sacraments and, 219-24; systematic concept of, 66-

69; of as utopia, 287-88. *See also* Anti-Reign
Resurrection, 41-42, 108, 121, 251-52, 279-80; as foundation of theological dimension, 285-89; Holy Spirit and, 151, 154; liberative aspects of, 139-40; Reign of God and, 39-40, 126, 261
Revelation, Book of, 17, 158, 170
Romero, Oscar A., 26, 53, 68, 134, 143; on eve of assassination, 221; experience of God, 254; generosity of, 248; martyrdom of, 250; on Mary, 175; as prophetic symbol, 225; on sin, 198-99, 229; on temptations of liberation, 246-47

Sacraments, 88-89, 216-32; principal, 226-28; as prophetic symbols of the Kingdom, 223; secondary, 228-31; traditional sacramentology, 216-17; and Vatican II, 218-19
Sacrosanctum Concilium (Vatican II), 218
Salvation, 46-48, 49-50, 185
Satan, 200-201
Schillebeeckx, Edward, 48, 50, 122n1
Schnackenburg, Rudolf, 54
Schweitzer, Albert, 59, 130
Segundo, Juan Luis, 53-54, 56, 61, 195
Sermon on the Mount, 30-34
Servant of Yahweh, 268-78
Sexism, 14, 22, 24, 166
Sin, 43, 93-94, 119-20, 194-204, 211; collective, 263-64, 266-67; as human damage, 200-202; St. Paul and, 195-97; structural, 197-200
Sobrino, Jon, 38-74, 124-45, 197, 203, 233-56; present-day discipleship, 123n2
Sollicitudo Rei Socialis (Pope John Paul II), 25, 27, 199
Spirituality, 71-72, 163-64, 178-81, 233-56
Subordinationism, 76, 81, 83

Theology for a Nomad Church (Assmann), 95
Theology of Liberation (Gutiérrez), 40, 95
Trinity, 75-89, 102-3, 203; in communion, 84-86; human reason and, 81-84; in liberation theology, 84-88; revelation of, 78-80; sacraments of, 88-89
Tritheism, 76, 81
Truth, 62, 150, 195-96, 236-37

Utopia, 68-69, 227-28, 279-90
Utopia (More), 281

Vatican Council II, 35, 36, 183, 186-87, 218-19; on Holy Spirit, 149-50, 155

Wallraff, Gunter, 200